Landmark Essays

Landmark Essays

on

Rhetoric and the Environment

Edited by Craig Waddell

LEA **Hermagoras Press**
An Imprint of Lawrence Erlbaum Associates, Publishers

Landmark Essays Volume Twelve

Cover design by Kathi Zamminer

Lawrence Erlbaum Associates, Inc., Publishers
10 Industrial Avenue
Mahwah, New Jersey 07430

Library of Congress Cataloging-in-Publication Data

Landmark essays on rhetoric and the environment / edited by
    Craig Waddell.
        p.   cm. — (Landmark essays : v. 12)
Includes bibliographical references and index.
ISBN 1-880393-28-X (pbk. : alk. paper)
  1. Environmentalism. 2. Environmental policy. 3. Rhetoric.
I. Waddell, Craig. II. Series.
GE195.L36   1997
363.7—dc21   97-5851
                                                        CIP

Books published by Lawrence Erlbaum Associates are printed on
acid-free paper, and their bindings are chosen for strength and dura-
bility.

Printed in the United States of America

10 9 8 7 6 5 4 3 2

About the Editor

Craig Waddell is Associated Professor and Director of Scientific and Technical Communication at Michigan Technological University. His work has focused on environmental rhetoric and has appeared in *Philosophy and Rhetoric; Science, Technology, & Human Values; Quarterly Journal of Speech; Social Epistemology; Technical Communication Quarterly;* and *Green Culture: Environmental Rhetoric in Contemporary America.*

Acknowledgments

I am grateful to numerous colleagues for recommending essays for this volume, but most especially to Jimmie Killingsworth, Jonathan Lange, Christine Oravec, and Tarla Rai Peterson for their early and sustained interest and support. I am also especially indebted to five graduate students who read and made recommendations on candidate essays: Helen Correll, Margaret Faler-Sweany, M. Rene Johnson, Bryan Sandoval, and Kathryn Wingard.

Table of Contents

Introduction

Introduction
by Craig Waddell

Classical rhetoric was fundamentally concerned with public deliberation about matters of policy. As Michael Halloran has pointed out, classical rhetoric "gave primary emphasis to public discourse . . . it was in essence a rhetoric of citizenship" (263). Aristotle argued that rhetoric concerned itself with "the things about which we make decisions, and into which therefore we inquire" (1357a25). Prominent today among those things about which we make decisions and into which we therefore inquire are matters of environmental policy. Nevertheless—as both Lange and Killingsworth and Palmer point out in their essays in this volume—a literature on rhetoric and the environment has only recently begun to emerge. The journal literature in this area has only about a twenty-year history, and book-length studies or anthologies (e.g., Short; Killingsworth & Palmer; Richardson, Sherman, & Gismondi; Myerson & Rydin; Herndl & Brown; Muir & Veenendall; Cantrill & Oravec) have only recently appeared. One additional measure of the newness of this subfield is that eight of the eleven essays included in this volume were first published since 1991.

The purpose of this volume is to collect together in one place some of the best essays yet published on rhetoric and the environmental. The collection should appeal to an interdisciplinary audience, including those interested in rhetoric (especially rhetoric of science and rhetoric and the environment), environmental studies, and modern American history/American studies. It should be appropriated for use in graduate or upper-division undergraduate courses in any of these areas as well as by scholars working in these areas.

Selection Procedures

Selecting landmarks in any field is a daunting and humbling task, and one that I tried to pursue with care. Having published in the field of rhetoric and the environment over a period of eight years and having served on the organizing committee for the 1995 biennial Conference on Communication and Our Environment, I was initially able to select half-a-dozen strong candidates for inclusion in this volume. I next contacted the authors of these essays (Oravec, Killingsworth & Palmer, Peterson, and Lange) and asked their recommendations for additional candidates. I also reviewed the lists of works cited in these initial essays for additional prospects.

My next step was to conduct a key-word search in ComIndex (a database of more than 22,400 articles from 55 key journals in communication) for such words as *environment, ecology,* and *conservation.* I also searched ComIndex for additional works by my initial list of authors. I eventually followed the same procedure on CommSearch 95, the Speech Communication Association's CD-ROM index of 22 journals in communication studies. I also polled subscribers to five relevant e-mail discussion lists (lists in science and technology studies, environmental history, environmental literature, environmental communication, and rhetoric) for their suggestions.

After screening the suggestions raised by these methods—and given LEA's constraints on the length of volumes in this series—I selected a preliminary list of 14 essays. I next polled for their suggestions those authors on this preliminary list whom I had not previously polled. I also searched ComIndex for additional works by the authors on this preliminary list. On the assumption that I might identify additional candidate essays among those articles citing one or more of the essays on this preliminary list, I searched the following on-line databases for citations to these articles: Arts & Humanities Search, Social SciSearch, and SciSearch.

After a preliminary screening of the essays identified by the above procedures, I asked five graduate students (Helen Correll, Margaret FalerSweany, M. Rene Johnson, Bryan Sandoval, and Kathryn Wingard) to read and evaluate 26 candidate essays. Since all of these students were focusing their graduate work on rhetoric and the environment, they were well positioned to assess these essays. Simultaneously, they served as an excellent test market for a key intended audience for this volume.

The reading group developed their own elaborate criteria for evaluating candidate essays. From among the fifteen essays they rated most highly, I selected eleven that both complement one another and present a diversity of authors, subject matter, methodologies, and theoretical approaches.

The Essays

With the exception of the first and last essays—which, as I explain below, can serve to frame the rest of the collection—I've arranged the essays chronologically, not by the date of original publication, but by the date of the events, texts, or developments they analyze. In this way, the volume can more easily complement (or be complemented by) such histories of the American environmental movement as those of Fox, Hays, and Shabecoff.

In the first essay, Robert Cox sets the stage for much, if not all, of what will follow by examining the persuasive force of appeals to the irreparable nature of a choice or action (e.g., "Extinction means forever."). Cox points out that the irreparable loss of something unique is made even more poignant when it is contrasted with the commonness or vulgarity of that for which it is being sacrificed, as when environmentalists charge that whales are being hunted to extinction in order to produce mink feed and cosmetics. Among the strategic implications of Cox's analysis are that "opponents of high-risk courses of action . . . have available a *locus* [i.e., a general category of argument] that is grounded in a fundamental presumption of society: the preservation of future choice."

Christine Oravec is the only author in this collection to examine events prior to the 1962 publication of Rachel Carson's *Silent Spring*. She examines the turn-of-the-century debate over whether to preserve Hetch Hetchy Valley as an integral part of Yosemite National Park or to construct a municipal dam, thus flooding the valley to provide a water supply for San Francisco. This debate proved a defining moment in the early history of the American environmental movement, one in which the distinction between *preservationist* and *conservationist* was defined. The preservationists, including John Muir, argued for preserving the valley for its aesthetic value. In so doing, they appealed to a generally defined *national* interest that —although consistent with nineteenth-century nationalism—was inconsistent with progressivism, which was rapidly becoming America's dominant social philosophy. Rather than appealing to vague national interests, conservationists such as Gifford Pinchot, who supported the dam, appealed to the utilitarian interests of an identifiable (and quantifiable) population: the 800,000 people of San Francisco. In doing so, they were able to ally themselves with the utilitarian values of progressivism. Furthermore, although conservationists were able to co-opt the preservationists' aesthetic appeal, when preservationists attempted to do the same with the conservationists' utilitarian appeal, the attempt worked against them. Oravec concludes that those who appeal to the public interest would be well advised to ensure that the image of the public they construct is consistent with that implicit in the prevailing social philosophy.

Taking a neo-Freudian approach, Jimmie Killingsworth and Jacqueline Palmer examine the charge by anti-environmentalists that environmental advocates—such as Rachel Carson, Paul Ehrlich, and Lois Gibbs—create environmental hysteria. They argue that this charge "represents an attempt by opponents in the environmental debate to defuse the threat [posed by environmental advocates] and maintain the stability of the social order." In order "to use the psychoanalytic model to display and examine the emotions at work in the environmental debate," Killingsworth and Palmer develop an extended analogy—though not a one-to-one correspondence—between the discourse of environmental crisis and the discourse of hysteria. They focus this discussion on the controversy surrounding the publication of Rachel Carson's *Silent Spring*. Both the success of and the controversy over this book were in part a consequence of Carson's apocalyptic rhetoric, a rhetoric reminiscent of that displayed by the neurotics whom Freud studied. This is not, however, to concede the point to the antienvironmentalists. Positivists of nineteenth-century medical science found no neurological cause for hysteria and, hence, accused hysterics of faking. Freud, on the other hand, accepted hysterics' symptoms as a sign of the intimate relationship between body and mind. Likewise, Killingsworth and Palmer see an intimate relationship between nature (the environment) and nature become conscious of itself (humankind). Hence, while they acknowledge the antienvironmentalists' charge of hysteria, they also rob it of its sting: If environmental advocates are "hysterical," they have good reason to be so. Furthermore, Killingsworth and Pàlmer point out that "the enemies of environmentalism have regularly devised apocalyptic narratives of their own." They conclude by pointing out that "there remains a trace of unresolved hysteria in the rhetoric of *Silent Spring* [in that it] makes no effort to rehabilitate or convert the other side." Killingsworth and Palmer acknowledge that such rhetoric serves a purpose (builds communities of support, etc.), but they regret that "it fails to meet the continuing need for dialogue, deliberation, and consensus-building."

In my own essay in this volume, I argue that the classical ideal of the polymath orator—which lies at the root of the Western tradition of a liberal education—is both more important today than ever before and more difficult to achieve. Nevertheless, just as humanists engaged in environmental deliberation would do well to inform themselves of the basics of environmental sciences, scientists engaged in environmental deliberation would do well to inform themselves about relevant humanistic disciplines, such as history, philosophy, and rhetoric. In this light, I examine Paul Ehrlich's rhetoric in his classic text *The Population Bomb*. Ehrlich himself claims that his appeals have failed—in the 22 years following the publication of *The Population Bomb,* the human population increased by 50 percent—but he attributes this failure to an evolutionary biology that has programmed humans to respond only to striking events, such as the charge of a lion. I look instead to his rhetoric. What I find is an explicit characterization of his audience as people who cannot be moved by "an appeal to beauty, or a plea to mercy" and would "compete for the privilege of shooting" the last California condor. Even if—as he claimed in a rejoinder (240)—Ehrlich intended this passage to shock people into action, the appeals throughout the book are consistently to a lower, rather than higher, common denominator. With an issue as sensitive and emotionally charged as population control, such appeals can foster, if not create, misogyny, zenophobia, and racism (in his 1978 update of *The Population Bomb*, Ehrlich acknowledges the problematic connection between racism and appeals for population control). Hence, I suggest that environmental advocates have two tasks. First, in appealing to those who *do* care about preserving natural beauty and wilderness, they should focus on ecocentric arguments in order to move such people from conviction to action. Second, in appealing to those who are moved primarily by homocentric or egocentric appeals, they should offer such appeals, but they should orchestrate or juxtapose these appeals with ecocentric appeals, thereby increasing the likelihood that such people will either adopt new values or interpret old values in new ways.

Drawing on earlier work by Farrell, Thomas Farrell and Thomas Goodnight distinguish technical from social reasoning: "Technical reasoning, interested in prediction and control, employs non-reflexive procedures in order to solve puzzles integral to specialized codes. By contrast, social reasoning focuses upon situation-dependent problems, employing self-criticism in order to inform choice and guide conduct toward a more perfect society." They offer a traditional definition of rhetoric: "and art preoccupied with the formation of public discourse . . . defining practical questions for prudential reason and conduct," and they suggest that recent studies in the rhetoric of science have collapsed the distinction between technical and social reasoning, thus, overextending the realm of rhetoric. In the modern era, technical reasoning has usurped the role of social reasoning, but it has proven itself inadequate to the task of informing public judgment. The worldviews of industry, ecology, and energy so construed the discourse thought competent to address questions of nuclear energy as to constrain public deliberation of this issue. In these worlviews, the public is perceived as inadequately prepared to attend to, let alone adjudicate, such complex technical questions: "because the practices of more specialized forms of inquiry have tended to fragment problems to fit each branch of expertise, there has been little need to consult general audiences . . . And the onoc-cstccmed art called rhetoric is abandoned altogether." In a technological crisis, such as that at Three Mile Island, diverse experts are drawn together to address the general public. In such situations, "a breakdown in consensus, a contest of specialized interests, and an intermittent search for social consensus" highlight the failure of technical reasoning to adequately inform public deliberation. Farrell and Goodnight contend that "even as technical reasoning encompasses an increasing array of social questions, its very logic precludes its practitioners from full responsibility" and it leaves the public "without impulse, knowledge of alternatives, or direction." They argue that "the failures of Three Mile Island suggest the extent to which the art of deliberative rhetoric is constrained by prevailing conceptions of the public." They propose, instead, "an ideal conception of the public as a knowledgeable and responsible collection of citizens, making prudential judgments." Although they contend that "the limits of technical communicative discourse are severe, recurrent, and perhaps irreparable," they suggest that "if the public is to be revitalized, then the language, the modes of decision-making, and procedures for establishing consensus must be discovered for both experts and generalists alike."

Brant Short examines the impact of Earth First!'s agitative rhetoric. Following the work of Haiman, McEdwards, Bailey, Cathcart, and Bowers & Ochs, Short argues that agitation and confrontation are forms of rhetoric and should not be disqualified from scholarly study as such because they are extra-discursive or nonrational. Instead, agitition and confrontation should be seen as persuasive strategies to which extreme elements in social movements are sometimes forced to resort due to inequities in the balance of power. These nondiscursive forms of persuasion both draw attention to an organization's or movement's rational appeals and serve as forms of rhetorical appeals themselves, challenging, as they do, the values of the prevailing political system. Short concludes that Earth First!'s agitative rhetoric has elicited a response both from within and outside the larger environmental movement and, among other things, has helped to make the more mainstream groups, such as the Sierra Club, seem reasonable.

The next two chapters both address the recent old-growth/spotted owl controversy in American's Pacific Northwest, and they illustrate the diverse approaches communication scholars can take to the same issue. In one of the two qualitative case studies included in this volume (the other being Peterson and Horton's),

Jonathan Lange concludes that in conducting their competing information campaigns, "advocates' and counter-advocates' rhetorical and communicative strategies *mirror and match* one another as disputants engage in a synchronous, spiral-like 'logic of interaction'." This approach leaves the disputants talking past one another and addressing "just about anyone *except* the other party." Lange identifies and describes five major and overlapping strategies of mirroring and matching. The first of these strategies is "frame and reframe" in which facts and explanations are framed in a way that is most favorable to a group's goals and then reframed by the opposition in order to put *their* position in the most favorable light. For example, while the timber industry wants to make jobs the primary issue, environmentalists argue that—due to automation, foreign competition, resource depletion, raw log exports, etc.—jobs will be lost whether the spotted owl is protected or not. The second strategy is "select high/select low" in which a group selects facts and studies that best emphasize its position and that are most damaging to the opposition. For example, while the timber industry cites a study indicating that 147,000 jobs could be lost in the effort to preserve spotted owl habitat, environmentalists cite a study indicating that only 12,000 jobs would be lost. The third strategy is "vilify/ennoble" in which each side tries to vilify the other and to ennoble its own cause. The fourth strategy is "simplify and dramatize" in which each side reduces complex issues to slogans that dramatize the controversy for mass consumption (e.g., "Save a Logger, Eat an Owl" vs. "Save an Owl, Educate a Logger"). The final strategy is "lobby and litigate"; as Lange notes, "both groups believe that the most serious theaters for the conflict are in the courts and in Washington, D. C."

Mark Moore also examines the old-growth/spotted owl controversy. Drawing on the work of Burke and McGee, Moore suggests that public argument in this controversy is "rooted in conflicting owl synedoches that conceptualize competing social realities": environmentalists present the spotted owl as an "indicator species" (hence, the part [owl] stands for the whole old-growth forest); and the timber industry presents the spotted owl as an economic scapegoat (hence, the part [owl] stands for the whole set of factors contributing to loss of jobs in the timber industry). Moore argues that these conflicting synecdoches and the competing realities they represent prevent resolution of the controversy by becoming issues in and of themselves and obscuring the larger issue of preserving the forest. As Moore says, "representational ideographs [e.g., synecdoches] can hold meaning for society at large, but they can also limit discourse to a part of the problem that does not resolve the conflict."

Tarla Rai Peterson and Cristi Choat Horton conduct the second qualitative case study in this volume. They provide a rhetorical analysis of in-depth interviews with 28 Texas ranchers in hopes of identifying common values to which ranchers, environmentalists, and governmental resource managers can appeal in their efforts to resolve those habitat-preservation disputes in which private-property rights might be compromised. The particular case in question is preserving the habitat of the endangered golden-cheeked warbler. Drawing on the work of Burke, Doty, Ivie, and others, Peterson and Horton abstract from their interviews the ranchers' dominant mythic theme or "mytheme": a widely shared and strongly held sense of stewardship. They further identify three key dimensions of this mytheme: common sense, independence, and a unique human-land connection. While acknowledging that not all ranchers share this mytheme, Peterson and Horton argue that steward-ship provides a common ground for dialogue among ranchers, environmentalists, and governmental resource managers. Rather than simply informing ranchers of land management policy after the fact, government agencies should appeal to the ranchers' sense of stewardship, draw upon their invaluable experience with the land, and include them in land-management planning.

Phil Brick's essay on the Wise Use movement was originally published in the October 1995 issue of *Environment*; it is unique in being the only essay included in this collection that was originally addressed to environmentalists rather than to communication scholars or philosophers. (Founded in 1958 by Barry Commoner and others, and with a current circulation of over 10,000, *Environment* is one of America's oldest and most distinguished environmental magazines.) In the follow-ing essay, Bruner and Oelschlaeger note that "in order for discourse to promote social change, it must achieve a hearing before a large audience." Brick, a political scientist, provides one example of adapting scholarly analysis of environmental discourse to make it more accessible to a larger audience. Although he avoids the technical vocabulary common to much rhetorical analysis, he provides an effective rhetorical analysis of the Wise Use movement and offers rhetorical advice for environmentalist who would respond to this movement. Brick describes three rhetorical tactics employed by the Wise Use movement. First, Wise Users depict environmentalists as "predisposed to big government solutions and intrusive regu-lations." As Brick points out, environmentalists often find themselves" in the uncomfortable position of defending federal regulations at a time when it is politically inexpedient to do so." The movement's second—and perhaps most powerful—rhetorical tactic is its focus on private property rights. If the federal government were required to purchase all lands needed to implement environ-mental legislation, it would be prohibitively expensive to implement such laws as the Endangered Species Act and the wetlands preservation provisions of the Clean Water Act. Hence, appealing to the Fifth Amendment, Wise Use advocates have defined legislation that restricts private property rights as a form of "taking," for which, they argue, property owners are entitled to compensation. The final rhetori-cal strategy Brick describes is framing "key environmental disputes in terms of 'jobs versus the environment.'" Brick concludes his analysis with rhetorical advice for environmentalists. First, "given the current climate of disillusionment with government, they will have to rely less on regulatory coercion and more on market-based programs and local initiatives." Second, "the environmental move-ment [should shift and] may already be shifting its focus toward membership in more local and regional groups. Many believe that these grassroots groups represent the future of U.S. environmentalism."

In the final essay in this volume—originally addressed to environmental ethicists—Michael Bruner and Max Oelschlaeger combine their expertise in, respectively, rhetoric and philosophy. The essay provides a good conclusion to this volume, first, because it raises the ancient and perennial question of the relationship between rhetoric and philosophy and, second, because it recommends putting theory into practice, a recommendation that might apply not only to environmental ethicists, but also to rhetoricians. (As Karl Marx said in his *Thesis on Feuerbach,* "The philosophers have only *interpreted* the world in various ways. The point, however, is to *change* it" [245]. An example from one contributor to this volume is Professor Cox's service as President of the Sierra Club.) Bruner and Oelschlaeger argue that although environmental ethics (or "ecophilosophy") has produced a substantial body of literature, it "has not to this date effected consequential social changes." They attribute this to two factors: first, to infighting among environmental ethicists and to the arcane nature of their discourse; and second, to environmental ethicists' indifference, even hostility, toward rhetoric. Anti-environmentalists, on the other hand, have shown an impressive command of rhetoric; they "have been effective in accomplishing their objectives at least in part because of their ability to articulate persuasive rationales through slogans, myths, and narratives." Such anti-environmental rhetoric, however, has obscured three fundamental issues: (1) "environmentalism is not categorically in opposition to the basic premises of a market society"; (2) "environmentalism has been mislabelled as a contest between people and nature"; and (3) "the *potential power* of environmentalism as a social movement has been co-opted" by marginal adjustments to economic activity. Bruner and Oelschlaeger go on to argue that "for philosophers who have taken the linguistic turn, the notions that philosophy is one thing and rhetoric something else . . . are not cogent." For ecophilosophy to help transform society, it must meet at least three criteria: (1) "its discourse must be cognitively plausible"; (2) "it must evoke sentiment"; and (3) "[it] must reach a majority of the people." In all of these respects, rhetoric is an invaluable resource. Among other things, critical rhetoric reveals how the discourse of power" contextualizes issues in ways which lead to narrowly defined debates over policy that inevitably lead to pre-established ends that are themselves never discussed"; architectionic rhetoric rejoins wisdom with eloquence and can help to create new, more inclusive communities; and persuasive rhetoric can break from traditional, linear models of persuasion and replace them with a more interactive view that "has the advantage of preserving freedom of choice and accountability."

Further Research

My review of the emerging literature on rhetoric and the environment suggests a number of areas in which further research seems desirable. I believe the field would benefit from more of the following (arranged in no particular order):

1. Empirical/qualitative case studies, such as those of Lange and Peterson & Choat.
2. Studies, such as Killingsworth & Palmer's, of environmental classics (e.g., of Aldo Leopold's *A Sand County Almanac*).
3. International and cross-cultural studies.
4. Studies, such as Oravec's, of the period prior to the publication of *Silent Spring*.

5. Studies, such as Short's, of the rhetoric of significant issues or movements within contemporary environmentalism (e.g., of ecofeminism, environmental justice, and global climate change).
6. Studies that examine visual/graphic aspects of environmental communication.
7. Studies, such as Brick's, that broaden the audience for rhetorical analyses of environmental discourse.
8. Studies that apply theory to practice and/or practice to theory in celebration of the *vita activa* (the active life) and what Brian Vickers calls "the Isocratean-Ciceronian celebration of the utility of rhetoric to society" (44).
9. Studies that further enchance the already transdisciplinary nature of rhetorical analyses of environmental discourse by drawing upon (among other fields) rhetoric, philosophy/ethics, history, political science, psychology, law, and environmental sciences.
10. Work that abstracts from diverse studies of environmental rhetoric a new rhetoric, a general theory of public deliberation in a democratic culture.

I hope that some readers of this volume will contribute to the next generation of scholarship in rhetoric and the environment and, in doing so, will consider undertaking studies such as those listed above.

Works Cited

Aristotle, (1854). *The rhetoric & the poetics*. Trans. W.R. Roberts. New York: Modern Library.

Cantrill, J. G. & Oravec, C. L. (Eds.). (1996). *The Symbolic earth: Discourse and our creation of the environment*. Lexington: University Press of Kentucky.

Ehrlich, P. (1994). Perils of a modern Cassandra: Some personal comments. *Social Epistemology, 8*, 239-240.

Fox, S. (1981). *The American conservation movement: John Muir and his legacy*. Madison: Madison: University of Wisconsin Press.

Halloran, S. M. (1982). Rhetoric and the American college curriculum: The decline of public discourse, *PRE/TEXT 3*, 245-269.

Hays, S. P. (1987). *Beauty, health, and permanence: Environmental politics in the United States, 1955-1985*. Cambridge: Cambridge University Press.

Herndl, C. G., & Brown, S. C. (Eds.) (1996). *Green culture: Environmental rhetoric in contemporary America*. Madison: University of Wisconsin Press.

Killingsworth, M. J. & Palmer, J. S. (1992). *Ecospeak: Rhetoric and environmental politics in America*. Carbondale: Southern Illinois University Press.

Marx, K. (1959). Thesis on Feuerbach. In L. S. Feuer (Ed.), *Marx & Engles: Basic writings on politics & philosophy* (pp. 243-245). Garden City: Anchor.

Muir, S. A., & Vennendall, T. L. (Eds.) (1996). *Earthtalk: Communicative empowerment for environmental action*. Westport: Praeger.

Myerson, G. & Rydin, Y. (1996). *The Language of environment: A new rhetoric*. London: University College London Press.

Richardson, M., Sherman, J., & Gismondi, M. *Winning back the words: Confronting experts in an environmental public hearing*. Toronto: Garamond Press. 1993.

Shabecoff, P. (1993). *A fierce green fire: The American environmental movement*. New York: Hill and Wang.

Short, B. (1989). *Ronald Reagan and the public lands: America's conservation debate, 1979-1984*. College Station: Texas A&M University Press.

Vickers, B. (1988). *In defense of rhetoric*. Oxford: Oxford University Press.

Credits

Cox, J. Robert. "The Die Is Cast: Topical and Ontological Dimensions of the *Locus* of the Irreparable." Reprinted from *Quarterly Journal of Speech* 68 (1982): 227-239. Copyright National Communication Association, 1982. Reprinted with permission.

Oravec, Christine. "Conservationism vs. Preservationism: The 'Public Interest' in the Hetch Hetchy Controversy." Reprinted from *Quarterly Journal of Speech* 70 (1984): 444-458. Copyright National Communication Association, 1984. Reprinted with permission.

Killingsworth, M. Jimmie and Jacqueline S. Palmer. "The Discourse of 'Environmentalist Hysteria'." Reprinted from *Quarterly Journal of Speech* 81 (1995): 1-19. Copyright National Communication Association, 1995. Reprinted with permission.

Waddell, Craig. "Perils of a Modern Cassandra: Rhetorical Aspects of Public Indifference to the Population Explosion." Reprinted from *Social Epistemology* 8 (1994): 221-237. Copyright Taylor & Francis, 1994. Reprinted with permission.

Farrell, Thomas B. and Thomas G. Goodnight. "Accidental Rhetoric: The Root Metaphors of Three Mile Island." Reprinted from *Communication Monographs* 48 (1981): 271-300. Copyright National Communication Association. Reprinted with permission.

Short, Brant. "Earth First! and the Rhetoric of Moral Confrontation." Reprinted from *Communication Studies* 42 (1991): 172-188. Copyright Central Speech Communication Association, 1991. Reprinted with permission.

Lange, Jonathan I. "The Logic of Competing Information Campaigns: Conflict over Old Growth and the Spotted Owl." Reprinted from *Communication Monographs* 60 (1993): 239-257. Copyright National Communication Association, 1993. Reprinted with permission.

Moore, Mark. "Constructing Irreconcilable Conflict: The Function of Synecdoche in the Spotted Owl Controversy." Reprinted from *Communication Monographs* 60 (1993): 258-274. Copyright National Communication Association, 1993. Reprinted with permission.

Peterson, Tarla Rai and Cristi Choat Horton. "Rooted in the Soil: How Understanding the Perspectives of Landowners Can Enhance the Management of Environmental Disputes." Reprinted from *Quarterly Journal of Speech* 81 (1995): 139-166. Copyright National Communication Association, 1995. Reprinted with permission.

Brick, Phil. "Determined Opposition: The Wise Use Movement Challenges Environmentalism." Reprinted from *Environment* 37.8 (October 1995): 17-20+. Copyright Helen Dwight Reid Educational Foundation, 1995. Reprinted with permission.

Bruner, Michael and Max Oelschlaeger. "Rhetoric, Environmentalism, and Enviromental Ethics." Reprinted from *Environmental Ethics* 16 (1994): 377-396. Copyright Michael Bruner and Max Oelschlaeger, 1994. Reprinted with permission.

The Die is Cast:
Topical and Ontological Dimensions
of the *Locus* of the Irreparable
by J. Robert Cox

*Whether the results of it be good or evil, the irreparable event is a source of terror
for man . . . .[1]*

THUCYDIDES reports that when the isle of Melos refused to surrender, Athenian envoys warned its magistrates: "Think over the matter . . . and reflect once and again that it is for your country that you are consulting, that you have not more than one, and that upon this one deliberation depends its prosperity or ruin." When the Melians still refused, the Athenians pressed their siege and subsequently put to death all adult males and sold the women and children of Melos for slaves.[2]

The argument by the Athenian envoys illustrates the use of a rhetorical commonplace derived from the irreparable nature of choice or action. Claims that a decision cannot be repeated or that its consequences may cause an irreplaceable loss are invoked at strategic moments in almost every aspect of our personal and public lives. The consent form for federally-funded sterilization operations includes this prominent statement: "I UNDERSTAND THAT THE STERILIZATION MUST BE CONSIDERED PERMANENT AND NOT REVERSIBLE. I HAVE DECIDED THAT I DO NOT WANT TO BECOME PREGNANT, BEAR CHILDREN OR FATHER CHILDREN."[3] Similar concerns underlie our discussion of abortion, capital punishment, environmental hazards, and even commercial advertising ("Final Closeout! Prices Will Never Be This Low Again!").

The sense of caution aroused by a forewarning of the irreparable poses two questions for the rhetorical scholar: What is the basis for this strong evocation? And, what implications does this commonplace have for social judgment? In what follows, I intend to elaborate Perelman and Olbrechts-Tyteca's treatment of the *locus* of the irreparable as one of several "lines of argument relating to the preferable,"[4] and, second, to ground this account in Heidegger's general interpretation of human existence as *Ek-sistenz*—"the standing beyond oneself."[5] In the final section I will trace certain strategic and ethical implications that a forewarning of an irreparable occurrence has for individual and collective decision-making.

The Irreparable and Loci Communes

Perelman and Olbrechts-Tyteca observe that agreement upon common values often yields a divergence of opinion as soon as we move from general to specific references. Thus, our discussion of liberty, justice, or truth must be accompanied by an attempt to interpret and define these values in the particular contexts of judgment. In doing this, we resort to ideas regarding what is desirable, good, or preferable. Such common conceptions, *loci communes*, function as the constitutive principles of our discourse, i.e., as the bases for our interpretation of general values in situated moments of decision and action.

Though indebted to Aristotle's description of the common topics, the authors of *The New Rhetoric: A Treatise on Argumentation* insist their conception differs in two respects: First, identification of particular classes of *loci* is not tied to any metaphysical system; and, second, they refer only to *loci* of the preferable—"premises of a general nature that can serve as the bases for values and hierarchies."[6] Aside from these differences, however, Perelman and Olbrechts-Tyteca claim that arguments relating to the preferable are not unlike the subjects Aristotle treats under the heading "accident" in *Topics* III, 116a-119a. There the dialectical problem is whether one of two things is better or more worthy of choice than the other.[7] Aristotle explains: "[T]he inquiry we are making concerns . . . things that are nearly related and about which we commonly discuss for which of the two we ought rather to vote, because we do not see any advantage on either side as compared with the other. Clearly, then, in such cases *if we can show a single advantage, or more than one, our judgment will record our assent that whichever side happens to have the advantage is the more desirable.*"[8]

Much of Book III provides a description of the principles by which a judgment of advantage can be made. Although not listing a topic of the irreparable per se, for example, he advises the dialectician to judge by the destructions, losses, or contraries of things: "for a thing whose loss or whose contrary is more objectionable is itself more desirable."[9]

In a similar fashion, Perelman and Olbrechts-Tyteca set forth a series of premises useful in establishing an object, act, or situation as having greater value than something else. They classify these principles under six general headings: *loci* of quantity, quality, order, the existing, essence, and the person. As part of this topical arrangement, then, the *locus* of the irreparable becomes a principle for securing agreement with an audience concerning a value or hierarchy of values.

In a sense, of course, all choice is irreparable: We can never experience precisely the same moment again. And the loss of certain things, though irreplaceable, may be of little or no consequence in themselves. For Perelman and Olbrechts-Tyteca, however, this *locus* gains importance when considered in light of the dialectical question Aristotle poses: How can we decide between two referents which seem to be of equal value, or demonstrate the advantage of one which is believed initially to have lesser value than another? The *locus* of the irreparable assists the rhetor in discovering arguments that accentuate the value or hierarchical ordering of one referent vis-a-vis another referent.

Specifically, Perelman and Olbrechts-Tyteca suggest the basis for the attention of the irreparable is linked to *loci* of quality: the unique or exceptional, a contrapuntal emphasis to what is usual, customary, or easily replaceable in human experience. "To be irreparable, an action must be one that cannot be repeated: it acquires a value by the very fact of being considered under this aspect."[10] The *locus* of the irreparable is a way of organizing our perceptions of a situation involving decision or action; its use calls attention to the *unique* and *precarious* nature of some object or state of affairs, and stresses the *timeliness* of our relationship to it.

Uniqueness

The object or act which qualifies as irreparable is necessarily unique. Human life and aspects of experience and the environment which cannot be restored, if "lost," are seen in their singularity—as distinct, original, rare, or exceptional. Such topical equations are often voiced explicitly: In its March/April 1981 newsletter, for example, the Nature Conservancy announced plans to safeguard a portion of "the *unique* and *priceless* riverine woodlands and streams that comprise the heart of the Deep South." Failure to act, the newsletter stressed, would lead to irreparable loss: "Gone with these forests will be the rich variety of flora and fauna they support. The Florida panther, the swallow-tailed kite, the green pitcher plant, and the untold number of less familiar plant and animal species *will have disappeared forever.*"[11] In this case, the irreparable acquires significance by being linked to that which is unique, for the "unique cannot be priced, and its value is increased by the very fact that it cannot be estimated."[12]

Loss of the unique is even more poignant when juxtaposed against the usual, the ordinary, the vulgar, that which is fungible or interchangeable.[13] This dialectic is quite explicit, for instance, in the appeal of the Center for Environmental Education for protection of the ocean's whales: "Why are these magnificent animals being killed? To produce mink food, fertilizer, cosmetics and lubricating oil." Thus, that which is exceptional—"these awesome, highly-intelligent marine mammals"—is sacrificed for the ordinary and the common. Is this practice necessary? "Although there are cheap, plentiful substitutes for all these products, the needless slaughter continues."[14]

Much of the potency of arguments regarding the irreparable derives from the value of what is unique or singular, and from the contrast between that and some fungible alternative.

Precariousness

Since what is unique (singular) may be lost, its constancy is open to challenge—its very existence, precarious. It is principally in terms of this quality that

Perelman and Olbrechts-Tyteca define the irreparable: "as a limit, which accentuates the *locus* of the precarious. . . ."[15] That which is precarious, in turn, gains significance from its contrast with *loci* of quantity, with what is plentiful, permanent, or enduring. For, "as we know, anything that is threatended acquires great value: *Carpe diem*."[16]

There is, nevertheless, some ambiguity in the identification of the irreparable with the *locus* of the precarious. For the urge to "enjoy the day" invites a sense of inevitability—an absence of choice or ability to affect the future. In this sense, precariousness refers to what is transitory, fleeting, or ephemeral, e.g., a special season, encounter, or state of affairs which cannot intrinsically be sustained; even with our intervention, its special status cannot be preserved or its existence lengthened. "Loss" is inevitable. Yet, the association which Perelman and Olbrechts-Tyteca seem to draw between the irreparable and human choice supposes that that which is threatened *need not be lost if one acts as the rhetor requests*.

This second sense of precariousness is captured in references to what is (1) fragile and (2) established, stable, or secure, but threatened by radical intrusion. That which is fragile requires protection or an agent's active intervention to ensure its continued existence. Perelman and Olbrechts-Tyteca illustrate this sense in citing the peroration of St. Vincent de Paul's appeal to women patrons for support of the orphans under his protection: "You have been their mothers by grace since the time when their mothers by nature abandoned them. Consider now whether you too wish to abandon them forever . . . ; their life and death are in your hands. . . . If you continue to give them your charitable care, they will live; but I tell you before God, they will all be dead tomorrow if you forsake them."[17]

Second, the established, stable, or secure may itself be threatened by disease, accident, or the actions of a powerful agent. The identification of the irreparable with this sense of precariousness incorporates a wide range of references—from capital punishment (human life), abortion and sterilization (reproductive processes), to whaling and clear-cutting of rain forests (natural resources).

An act, object, or condition gains value in our eyes when it is seen in any one of the foregoing senses—as transitory, fragile, or as secure but now threatened by radical action. The precarious becomes identified with the *locus* of the irreparable, however, when that which is threatened *need not be lost*, when choice is possible. The irreparable is offered as a defining limit to the precarious, for if choice is foresaken what is "lost" cannot be restored. "Extinction," declares the Center for Environmental Education, "is the ultimate crime against nature. Extinction means forever."[18]

Timeliness

Our experience with precarious reality places value upon the timeliness of choice or action. Though Perelman and Olbrechts-Tyteca do not associate this quality with the irreparable, timeliness seems both a natural and logical outcome of its claims. In *The New Rhetoric* the *locus* of timeliness is derived from Aristotle's discussion of transitory existence. The authors observe, "by making value dependent upon a transitory state of affairs, we lay stress on the precariousness of this value and, at the same time, increase the store set on it while it lasts."[19]

With regard to claims of finality, however, timeliness assumes other dimensions: in the caution evoked in contemplating an irreparable consequence, and in the urgency of action that is required to save something rare and irreplaceable. In the first instance, caution is elicited when one's own actions may be cause for an irreparable occurrence, as in a juror's vote where the death penalty is mandatory upon conviction for a capital offense. A similar concern also arises in what might broadly be termed *decisions of renunciation*, e.g., the decisions facing the potential expatriate, kidney donor, or person considering surgical sterilization. For the value of what we may normally take for granted is accentuated by images of death, denial, separation, or loss. In other cases, urgency of choice and action occurs when what we perceive as fragile or essential to our well-being is threatened; hence, we act to forestall or oppose forces that would do irreparable harm, to save what is exceptional. It is this dimension of timeliness which the Democratic National Committee draws upon in attacking the policies of U.S. Secretary of the Interior James Watt: "*Because* the destruction to our environment cannot be undone. . . . *Because* our fragile wilderness areas once desecrated by senseless development are lost forever. . . . *Because* the insensitive, dangerous, and irreverisble decisions by Secretary Watt will devastate the air we must breathe, the water we must drink, the soil we must live upon . . . we, *as a nation, must act immediately to stop the senseless waste.*"[20] If allowed to go unchecked, the Secretary's policies will do irreparable damage to the nation's natural resources. Thus, action is "timely": "Therefore, the Democratic National Committee is immediately forming a special fund—unique in our 132-year history—to make certain that Mr. Watt and the special interests he represents are stopped from irrevocably ruining our lands, water, and wildlife."[21]

Approached from the viewpoint of its topical associations, the *locus* of the irreparable functions in a *nomos*-building capacity, i.e., as a principle governing our interpretation of experience. A speaker's claim of irreparableness helps to structure a situation in which an auditor perceives X as being of heightened value. Such a claim assumes: (1) X is a referent whose quality is considered vis-a-vis some other referent (usually "not-X"); (2) X is *unique* (exceptional, rare, or original); further, (3) X's status is *precarious*, threatened by some agent's actions or because its survival cannot be assured without our intervention; thus (4) choice or action regarding X is *timely*. In relation to these attributions, then, the *locus* of the irreparable presents itself as a defining limit: Its rhetorical appeal occurs as a *forewarning*, an opportunity to act in appropriate ways before it is too late. Once "lost," X cannot be restored, the consequence of choice being irreversible, final.

Beyond these topical dimensions, there seems to be a more fundamental dimension which assigns value to X. For the notion of an irreparable act anticipates some state that is *subsequent* to the act, *a-time-when* choice cannot be repeated or X restored. The value we assign to the irreparable, in other words, presupposes our experience of time and our valuing of an object or act in this dimension.

Time and the Irreparable

Perelman and Olbrechts-Tyteca themselves suggest that temporality comprises a basis for the value of the irreparable. They link this dimension specifically to *loci* of quantity: "the infinity of time which will elapse after the irreparable has been done or established, the certitude that the effects, whether or not they were wanted, will continue indefinitely."[22] They do not, however, develop this idea further in *The New Rhetoric*. This is unfortunate because the topical traits of "length" and "duration" capture only part of our experience of time. We can also regard time as an ontological dimension, as a necessary condition for our forming any judgments of value at all.

From an ontological perspective, the appeal of the irreparable emerges from the interaction between our perception of time—especially future time—and human meaning. For, in temporalizing, we structure our existence in relation to certain ends—in relation to purposes which are realizable *within* time. We experience time as "opportunity" as in the Greek *kairos*, "the knife edge of chance, a choice point of fortune."[23]

Heidegger develops this idea more fully in *Being and Time* in his general interpretation of human existence as *Ek-sistenz*—literally, the "standing beyond oneself." The meaning of our experience is rooted, not in a succession of particular Nows, but in a field or temporal spread of Future-Present-Past. Heidegger calls this basic temporality "*ectases*" for in experiencing the Present we are already "standing outside" of it.[24] The unifying thread in this temporal field is *future* time; it is our anticipation of future (potentiality-for-Being) which constitutes and informs our present understanding.

Within this structuring framework of time, we are able to establish our lives meaningfully; we can entertain hope, make plans, act, or organize projects. "Project" (*Entwurf*) is a central word in Heidegger's ontology. Barrett explains: "Not only do we plan specific projects for today or tomorrow, but our life as a whole is a project in the sense that we are perpetually thrown-ahead-of-ourselves-toward-the-future."[25] Our experience of the future, then, is more than mere foretelling of what will occur; it is, in Cassirer's words, *an imperative of human life*: "to think of the future and to live in the future is a necessary part of [our] nature."[26]

This fact, nevertheless, confronts us with an existential dilemma: The symbolic capacity which allows us to "stand beyond" ourselves also brings us face to face with our finitude. As humans, we know that in the future we will die. Such knowledge, in turn, emphasizes the precarious investment of our existence: accident or disease may strike unexpectedly; the death of a friend or loved one wrenches from us a vital part of ourselves.

Loss, separation, and death, then, transform our experience of time. We experience the future as closed. When this happens, time becomes threatening; the future becomes a source of anxiety and dread. The human dilemma is inescapable: Whether in turning away or in resolving to face the future, we risk irreparable loss. In turning from the future as a way of reducing anxiety, we choose an "inauthentic" existence.[27] Yet, in forming projects, in opening ourselves to the future, we expose ourselves to the possibilities of suffering and loss, including our own death.

Thus, knowledge of the irreparable is rooted in *self*-knowledge, in an awareness of our own end—the absence of human possibility and of Being itself. "Madness and death," Camus reminds readers in *The Myth of Sisyphus*, "are [our] irreparables."[28] *Death* is the archetypal symbol of the irreparable event. In mythology, religion, and art, images of death effectively embody both the topical qualities and experience of time which an irreparable act evokes. One who has "died" spiritually, for example, suffers a radical severance or separation from God—the negation of the "wholly other" (*ganz endere*).[29]

Unlike religious promises of grace (restoration), the irreparable does not offer hope. That which is "fallen" cannot be undone, its effects lasting an infinity of time. Such a conception of time, Eliade suggests, separates us from the sacred. "*By its very nature sacred time is reversible in the sense that . . . it is a primordial mythical time made present.*"[30] Sacred time is "indefinitely recoverable, indefinitely repeatable;" it does not "pass," "does not constitute an irreversible duration."[31] By contrast, an irreparable event constitutes not only radical severence—an altered state or condition—but also the ceaseless experiencing of its consequence. It is perhaps this "fall" into temporality that prompts Perelman and Olbrechts-Tyteca to observe: "Whether the results of it be good or evil, the irreparable event is a source of terror for man."[32]

Because we "stand beyond" ourselves in time, we recoil at its loss; to lose the opportunity for meaningful choice is to lose something vital in ourselves. By calling upon such powerful psycho-emotional sources, the *locus* of the irreparable creates what Solomon terms an "effective rhetorical vision." Such visions "(and those least amenable to logical refutation)," she suggests, "draw from a reservoir of myth, a complex of psychic and cultural associations of enormous nonrational persuasion."[33]

Strategic and Ethical Implications

A rhetor's claim that an act is irreparable has both strategic and ethical implications for human deliberation and decision-making. When choice cannot be repeated or its consequences later reversed, actors may adapt in ways that depart from ordinary decision processes. Such *strategic* adaptations include: (1) an expansion of the time frame in which choices are considered, (2) heightened information-seeking, (3) invocation of a minimum condition rule, and, ironically, (4) the warranting of extraordinary measures. In addition, actors confront an ethical responsibility for informed choice when doing that which cannot be undone later.

Strategic Implications

An Expanded Time Frame. The portrayal of a possible alternative as irreparable fundamentally alters the time frame which informs actors' deliberation. For the basis of this *locus*, Perelman and Olbrechts-Tyteca remind us, derives *inter alia* from "the infinity of time which will elapse after the irreparable has been done or established...."[34] Alternative courses of action, conceived as tentative or temporary measures, must now be considered in terms of long-term, permanent effects.

A focus upon the irreversible effects of an act specifically renders inappropriate a strategy of incremental decision-making. Such a strategy concentrates only upon marginal differences among alternatives. The effects of a decision are adjusted in a series of incremental, exploratory, and remedial moves. Thus, an actor need not be "right" on any one move: "If his move fails or is attended by unanticipated adverse consequences, he assumes that someone's (perhaps even his own) next move will take care of the resulting problem."[35] Neither long-term consequences nor the future per se plays much of a role in those adjustments. If, however, an actor is persuaded that a projected consequence will be irreparable, he or she cannot then assume there will be a "next move;" for the effect—whether or not it was wanted—cannot be undone. This expanded "scene" (in Burke's vocabulary) imbues an individual's act with qualities of permanence, finality.

Heightened Information-Seeking. The irrevocability of certain decisions increases actors' need to be accurate, correct, or right in their actions. For, should things turn out to be other than expected, the decision cannot be undone or its consequences set aside. In such circumstances, we would expect that actors would seek more information (and more accurate information) about the possible outcomes of alternative courses of action before making their decision. Based on their conflict model of decision-making, Janis and Mann hypothesize that such actors are more likely to become open-minded, less inclined to selective exposure, and less biased in assimilating the information to which they are exposed.[36] Mann and Taylor have reported some experimental evidence supporting this hypothesis. When forewarnings were provided that their decisions (involving preferences among art prints) would be irrevocable, subjects took longer to decide and engaged in more "vigilant" patterns of information processing.[37] Such findings seem to underscore the importance of actors' *talk*: though their decision cannot be undone once actually implemented, actors' verbal projections of a course of action and its consequences are revocable—their imagining of what may happen can be revised as different alternatives are contemplated.

Where increased information-seeking does not offer a sufficient basis for action, the decision-makers may postpone choice or act in a way that does not unduely restrict choice at a later time. Such are the alternatives facing a physician who, after trying to discern the preference of a terminally ill patient, must decide whether procedures serving only to artifically prolong life should be ended. "In some cases we don't have enough information," concedes a physician with University Hospitals of Cleveland. "If we don't know what the patient's life was like, we have to be supportive *because not being supportive is irrevocable.*"[38]

A Minimum Condition Rule. If the consequences of a course of action cannot later be reversed, a decision-maker may be inclined to invoke a strategy of risk-avoidance. Such a strategy differs from usual conceptions of maximizing one's values or utility. In the latter situation, the decision-maker accepts the possibility of negative outcomes on any one occasion on the expectation of a greater return "over time."

In severe-risk situations, however, an individual or society may not be able to "lose" even once; hence, Blackstone's dictum that it is better that ten guilty individuals should go free than one innocent person be convicted. A pleading of irreparable consequences in such cases presents a minimum condition for choosing: *a course of action whose consequences turn out to be "unacceptable" must be remediable.* Such a method closely resembes Savage's criterion of "regret" or minimization of the maximum likely harm (*minimax*)[39] and Lee's rule for lexicographic ordering of preference dimensions. The latter requires that the bases for evaluating the outcomes of a decision be ranked in importance. Preference among alternative courses of action, Lee explains, "is determined by the utility magnitudes for *the most important dimension alone.*"[40] Similarly, adoption of a minimum condition rule requires that prospective actions be evaluated against a threshhold criterion: that the capacity to "undo" consequences that are unacceptable be preserved. Alternatives satisfying this criterion would then be evaluated along other, subordinate dimensions to arrive at a final decision.

Opponents of high-risk courses of action thus have available a *locus* that is grounded in a fundamental presumption of society: the preservation of future choice. The West Virginia Highlands Conservancy found this to be an appropriate source of arguments in opposing the U.S. Office of Surface Mining's proposal to allow coal mining in environmentally sensitive areas: "The line of argument which in theory would be most effective in compelling a designation of unsuitability would concentrate on the likelihood of irreversible damage from mine subsidence, landslides, destruction of endangered plant and animal species, and loss of habitat for native trout, black bear and other species."[41]

Strategically, the invocation of a minimum condition rule allows actors to subsume other potentially conflicting values in the "remediable" alternatives. Such seems to be the intention in some environmentalists' plea: "Preserving land and water resources today still allows for development at some future time. Uncontrolled development now leaves few options for the future."[42] In other words, if *X*, then never *Y*; however (if the minimum condition rule is invoked), if *Y*, then, if necessary, *X*. A *Washington Post* editorial develops this line of reasoning in support of the Alaskan Lands Act. To allow exploitation of energy and timber resources in disputed wilderness areas would irreparably damage critical wildlife habitats and other wilderness qualities: if *X* (resource exploitation), then the loss of *Y* (original habitat/ecosystem). But, the *Post* pointed out, "the wilderness designation should not be regarded as totally irreversible. Its purpose is to preserve for the future as much unspoiled acreage as the nation can now afford. . . . Surely future members of Congress will not believe themselves unable to open the range . . . if the time comes when the resources they contain are needed desperately."[43] Pleadings in support of remediable action are especially likely to succeed if the "*X*" option is characterized as fungible or easily substituted for, e.g., energy resources can be located elsewhere, or alternative sources such as solar or conservation can be utilized.

Warrant for Extraordinary Measures. Because the irreparable lasts "an infinity of time," actors may feel justified in going to extreme lengths to block or forestall the loss of something rare, precious, or unique. On the other hand, one may find comfort in claims of finality, in the acceptance of the inevitable. Hence, an actor may knowingly undertake irreparable measures or declare his or her decision to be irrevocable in an attempt to ensure the occurrence of a desired outcome. In either event, the *locus* of the irreparable may be said to warrant "extraordinary" measures—actions which go beyond the usual, customary, or what most people would approve.

The former occasion arises when an actor invokes the minimum condition rule. Logically, the rule may be satisfied in either of two ways: (1) suitable modification or abandonment of alternatives posing irreparable damage; or, failing this, (2) radical intervention—the adoption of action designed to prevent the consequences of such alternatives from occurring. Because the minimum condition rule is a *minimum* condition—else the unique (priceless) lost, the "unacceptable" allowed—actors may undertake extraordinary measures. In recent times, these have included: obstructing nuclear weapons facilities, resisting the draft, firebombing an abortion clinic, or kidnapping of sons and daughters whom parents believe have been brainwashed by religious cults. In announcing her decision to "refuse to pay Internal Revenue [sic] that 32 percent of my taxes which the budget applies to current military expenditures," the writer of a letter-to-the-editor of a local newspaper explains: "There may still be time to choose between life and death on this planet earth of ours."[44] Certainly, in the minds of the individuals involved, each of these interventions poses less danger than loss of what is irreparable. "After all," such a person may reason, "what else have I if 'all' is lost?"

Warrant for extraordinary action can also occur under very different circumstances. A paradigm case is Caesar's action, in 49 B.C., in leading his favorite Thirteenth Legion across the Rubicon, the stream forming the frontier between Gaul and Italy. Suetonius reports him as saying Iacta est alea—"the die is cast."[45] Caesar was now openly committed in his opposition to the Roman Senate and Pompey's armies. In taking an irrevocable step (as Caesar in crossing the Rubicon), one is committed, in a sense, *to seeing the act through*. Such a commitment removes (or alleges to have removed) any further choice: "We have no alternative but to do *X*" (continue toward Rome), "now that the alternative for doing not-*X* has been passed over."

The commitment of what can be called the Rubicon Ploy is of course a *social*—not logical—commitment. For choice is seldom literally between *X* and not-*X*; one may choose to do *R, S,* or some other action depending upon social and physical constraints. Nevertheless, the announcement that a decision is irrevocable tends to imbue action associated with it with a certain presumption. We feel compelled by what is inevitable, by what seems foreordained. In classical oratory this aspect of the irreparable underlies much of what Demosthenes says about resisting Philip. In *On the Crown*, he tells his audience: "The only choice, and the necessary choice, left to you was justly to oppose all his unjust actions against you."[46]

Demosthenes' use of this commonplace illustrates the phenomenon of actors' *post*-decisional bolstering of their behavior. This need to rationalize actions that cannot now be undone is vividly displayed in what Childs terms the "exile mentality" of some refugees. Such individuals feel compelled to picture what is happening in their former homelands as worse than it is "to *justify their departure and the renunciation of their birthright*."[47]

Thus, individuals may find warrant for extraordinary measures in both the fear and consolation of finality, of that which cannot be undone or changed.

Ethical Implications

Somewhat more complex questions arise when we turn to the ethical implications of irrevocable decisions: Is it unwise, irrational, or wrong to do knowingly that which cannot be undone?

In one sense, the commission of an irreparable action presupposes what the act's consequences deny—the possibility of further choice. This consideration implies that a presumption exists in favor of remediable alternatives. Nevertheless, the fact that its consequences will be permanent does not in itself render all irreparable action unethical; for an individual or society may pursue other ends whose utility presumably is greater than that which may be damaged or lost as a result. And each may find assurance in customs, practices, or rituals whose forms are unchanging or which provide a sense of permanence.

Ideally, then, ethical considerations should take into account the irreversibility—the finality—of a decision's consequences while not *a priori* ruling these consequences "unacceptable." At a minimum a decision to undertake an irreparable course of action should be an *informed* choice. Increasingly, the concept of informed choice serves as a guide when individuals must routinely undertake or counsel irreparable actions: voting, jury deliberation, regulatory permit-granting, marriage or problem pregnancy counseling. The Hastings Center's Institute of Society, Ethics, and the Life Sciences raises this consideration specifically in regard to sterilization. It notes that while technology alone seldom determines the ethics of a biomedical procedure, "the virtually irreversible nature of surgical sterilization makes the choice a more drastic one than it might be otherwise."[48] Ethically, what must be preserved in such circumstances is, not any "right to procreate" per se, but an individual's right "to control her or his own body and to decide, in a fully informed and conscious way, what sorts of interventions may be made into bodily processes, including the biological capacity to procreate."[49]

But what must a choice include to be "fully informed?" In guidelines governing jury decision-making, research using human subjects, and sterilization, the following factors seem to be recognized: (1) Awareness of any irreversible consequences of a contemplated course of action; (2) Evaluation of alternatives to this course (if any), including knowledge of the potential consequences of each course; (3) Sufficient time in which to consider each of the above and to arrive at a decision; and (4) Absence of coercive factors, i.e., that the resulting decision be voluntary.[50]

Obviously, requirements for informed choice work best in instances of individual decision-making where both time and access to relevant information are readily available. Federal regulations for surgical sterilization, for example, require a mandatory 30-day waiting period between the date of informed consent and the actual operation. The purpose of this waiting period is to ensure, insofar as possible, that "the individual reflects carefully on the consequences of the proposed sterilization and makes a decision that he or she will not later regret, since the procedure must be considered irreversible."[51]

When pressures for a decision mount, however, actors may find it more difficult to fulfill the requirements for fully informed choice. Or, as members of a strongly cohesive group, individual actors may feel less responsible for—or more invulnerable to—possible adverse consequences of their actions.[52] To the degree actors restrict the time frame informing their choices or fail to evaluate alternative courses of action, their potential for error and disappointment grows. Thus, requisites for informed choice and the constraints of time and resource limitations pose a dilemma: At what stage should deliberation be suspended and a decision made? The answer may tell us much about an individual's or group's confidence (rightly or wrongly) in its capacity to affect the future.

Conclusion

What then is the value of the foregoing analysis for the rhetorical scholar? Elsewhere I have suggested Perelman and Olbrechts-Tyteca's conception of *loci communes* makes several important contributions to critical methodology.[53] Understanding of the topical and ontological bases of the *locus* of the irreparable adds, I believe, further support for this view.

Such understanding, in particular, reveals two important aspects of social judgment: First, occurrence of this commonplace in discourse points the critic to key "objects of agreement" shared by members of a group or culture.[54] In characterizing choice as irrevocable, a rhetor also signifies what he or she believes an audience values as unique, exceptional, rare, or original. Such claims "encompass," in Burke's terminology, certain types of situations in the sense that they "name their structure and outstanding ingredients, and name them in a way that contains an attitude toward them."[55]

Second, rhetorical occurrences of the irreparable may offer some understanding of the ways a culture views its own future. The critic, for example, may ask: What are the deliberative occasions in which actors knowingly undertake an irrevocable action? What do such actors count as "good reasons" for the acceptance of irreplaceable loss? And what sense does a culture generally have of its own efficacy? Does it believe that it possesses the authority or necessary resources to affect those aspects of the future upon which its well-being rests?

Perhaps we shall find rhetorical uses of the irreparable only in a culture that is confident of its ability to address the future. A culture as much as an individual "stands beyond" itself in time, in its ability to act in the future. Without this confidence, the irreparable has little power to persuade. Indeed, in a culture for which the future is closed, the foretelling of loss does not function in a *rhetorical* sense at all. It is not an impetus for action, but only the fatalistic announcement of forces over which it has no control.

Notes

1. Ch. Perelman and L. Olbrechts-Tyteca, The New Rhetoric: A Treatise on Argumentation, trans. John Wilkinson and Purcell Weaver (Notre Dame: University of Notre Dame Press, 1971), p. 92.
2. The Complete Writings of Thucydides: The Peloponesian War, trans. R. Crawley (New York: The Modern Library, 1934), p. 336.
3. Rosalind Pollack Petchesky, "Reproduction, Ethics, and Public Policy: The Federal Sterilization Regulations," The Hastings Center Report, 9 (1979), 34.
4. Perelman and Olbrechts-Tyteca, p. 66. Recent discussions of commonplaces and the problem of invention include: Manual Bilsky, McCrea Hazlett, Robert E. Streeter, and Richard M. Weaver, "Looking for an Argument," College English, 14 (1953), 210-216; John F. Wilson and Carroll C. Arnold, Public Speaking as a Liberal Art, 2nd ed. (Boston: Allyn and Bacon, 1968), p. 115; Karl R. Wallace, "Topoi and the Problem of Invention," Quarterly Journal of Speech, 58 (1972), 387-395; and Ralph T. Eubanks, "Axiological Issues in Rhetorical Inquiry," Southern Speech Communication Journal, 44 (1978), 11-24. Eubanks outlines eight values (health, creativity, wisdom, love, freedom, justice, courage, and order) which define the demands of the "right" and the "good."
5. William Barrett, "The Flow of Time," in The Philosophy of Time, ed. Richard M. Gale (Garden City, N.Y.: Anchor, 1967), p. 356.
6. Perelman and Olbrechts-Tyteca, p. 84.
7. Aristotle does not explicitly define what he means by a topic. De Pater suggests that he is actually using the term in two senses: (1) as a formula or rule for conducting an argument, and (2) as a principle upon which the formula is founded. Walter de Pater, "La Fonction du lieu et de l'instrument dans les Topiques," in Aristotle on Dialetic. Proceedings of the Third Symposium Aristotelicum, ed. G. E. L. Owen (Oxford: Clarendon Press, 1968), p. 165.
8. Aristotle, Topica and De Sophisticis Elenchis, trans. W.A. Pickard-Cambridge, In The Works of Aristotle, ed. W. A. Ross (Oxford: Oxford University Press, 1928), I, 116a 4-13. Emphasis added.
9. Aristotle, Topica, 117b 6-7. In this and other topics in Book III, Aristotle uses "topic" to refer to a principle, rather than a formula. For further discussion, see Eleanore Stump, "Dialectic and Aristotle's Topics," in Boethius's De topicis differentiis, trans. E. Stump (Ithaca: Cornell University Press, 1978), p. 169.
10. Perelman and Olbrechts-Tyteca, p. 92.
11. William D. Blair, Jr., "The Conservancy's Richard King Mellon Grant: GREAT EXPECTATIONS," The Nature Conservancy News, 31 (March/April 1981), 5. Emphasis added.
12. Perelman and Olbrechts-Tyteca, p. 90.
13. Perelman and Olbrechts-Tyteca, p. 90.
14. "Will the Whales Survive?" Letter received from the Center for Environmental Education, 17 July 1980.
15. Perelman and Olbrechts-Tyteca, p. 91.
16. Perelman and Olbrechts-Tyteca, p. 91.
17. Cited in A. Baron, De la Rhétorique ou de la composition oratoire et Littéraire, 4th ed. (Brussels and Liège, Belgium: Libraries polytechniques de Deaq, 1879), quoted in Perelman and Olbrechts-Tyteca, p. 91.
18. "Will the Whales Survive?"
19 Perelman and Olbrechts-Tyteca, p. 91. Aristotle observes: "everything is more desirable at the season when it is of greater consequence; e.g., freedom from pain in old age more than in youth: for it is of greater consequence in old age." Topica, III, 117a 26-29.
20. Letter received from Cecil D. Andrus for the Democratic National Committee, 27 October 1981.
21. Letter from Cecil D. Andrus.
22. Perelman and Olbrechts-Tyteca, p. 92.
23. John Cohen, "Time in Psychology," in Time in Science and Philosophy, ed. Jiří Zeman (New York: Elsevier, 1971), p. 163.
24. Martin Heidegger, Being and Time, trans. John Macquairie and Edward Robinson (New York: Harper and Row, 1962), p. 377, n. 2.
25. Barrett, p. 361.
26. Ernst Cassirer, An Essay on Man: An Introduction to a Philosophy of Human Culture (New Haven: Yale University Press, 1962), pp. 55, 53.
27. Commenting on Heidegger's use of this term, Barrett states: "The inauthentic individual, . . . cowering before his own possibilities, lets time slip away and experiences it only as a passive flow of his being." p. 362.

In their study of the relationship between death anxiety in elderly persons and future time orientation, Bascue and Lawrence report that "the elderly may turn away from the future as a way of controlling death anxiety." L.O. Bascue and R.E. Lawrence, "A Study of Subjective Time and Death Anxiety in the Elderly," Omega Journal of Death and Dying, 8 (1977), 81.

28. Albert Camus, The Myth of Sisyphus and Other Essays, trans. Justin O'Brien (New York: Vintage, 1955), p. 47.

29. Rudolf Otto, Das Heilige (Breslau, 1917), cited in Mircea Eliade, The Sacred and the Profane: The Nature of Religion (New York: Harvest, 1959), p. 9.

30. Eliade, p. 68.

31. Eliade, p. 69.

32. Perelman and Olbrechts-Tyteca, p. 92.

33. Martha Solomon, "The 'Positive Woman's' Journey: A Mythic Analysis of the Rhetoric of STOP-ERA," Quarterly Journal of Speech, 65 (1979), 263.

34. Perelman and Olbrechts-Tyteca, p. 92.

35. David Braybrooke and Charles E. Lindblom, A Strategy of Decision: Policy Evaluation as a Social Process (New York: The Free Press, 1963), p. 123.

36. Irving L. Janis and Leon Mann, Decision Making: A Psychological Analysis of Conflict, Choice, and Commitment (New York: The Free Press, 1977), p. 302.

37. L. Mann and V.A. Taylor, "The Effects of Commitment and Choice Difficulty on Pre-Decisional Processes," Journal of Social Psychology, 82 (1970), 225.

38. Matt Clark, Mariana Goshall, and Dan Shapiro, "When Doctors Play God," Newsweek, August 31, 1981, p. 51. Emphasis added.

39. Leonard J. Savage, "The Theory of Statistical Decision," Journal of the American Statistical Association, 46 (1951), 55-67.

40 Wayne Lee, Decision Theory and Human Behavior (New York: Wiley, 1971), pp. 98-99. Emphasis added.

41. Bard Montgomery, "'Blatant Errors,' Ignored Issues . . . ," The Highlands Voice, March 1981, p. 5. Emphasis added.

42. Peter Stoler, "The Trouble with Watt," Time, May 11, 1981, p. 51. This also appears to be the rationale for the choice of a naval blockade in the 1962 Cuban missile crisis. Secretary of Defense Robert McNamara, in particular, argued a blockade constituted "limited pressure" which left the U.S. still in control of events. Such an option allowed contingency adjustments and, importantly, did not foreclose stronger measures should the blockade have failed. Robert Kennedy, Thirteen Days: A Memoir of the Cuban Missle Crisis (New York: New American Library, 1969), p. 34.

43. "Saving the Best of Alaska," The Washington Post, July 21, 1980, p. A18.

44. "U.S. Citizens Must Resist Trend Toward Violence," Chapel Hill Newspaper, August 3, 1980, sec. C, p. 3.

45. Gaius Suetonius Tranquillus, The Twelve Caesars, trans. Robert Graves (London: Penguin, 1957), p. 27.

46. Demosthenes' On the Crown, ed. James J. Murphy with trans. by John J. Keaney (New York: Random, 1967), p. 73.

47. Robert P. Newman and Dale R. Newman, Evidence (Boston: Houghton Mifflin, 1969), p. 63. See, Marquis Childs, "Behind the Errors on Cuban Invasion," The Washington Post, April 26, 1961, p. A18. Emphasis added.

48. Petchesky, p. 29.

49. Petchesky, p. 29.

50. Partially because of past abuses with surgical sterilization, similar criteria have been promulgated as a condition for federal funding of agencies performing such operations. Petchesky notes: "Not only must the person be given information about 'available alternative methods of family planning and birth control,' a complete explanation of the procedure to be used and all of its known risks and benefits, and explicit notice of its irreversibility, but this information must be provided orally, in the person's preferred language, and in a mode accessible to blind, deaf, or otherwise handicapped individuals" (p. 33).

51. The Federal Registrar, 43: 217 (Nov. 8, 1978), p. 52151, cited in Petchesky, p. 33.

52. Wallach et al. suggest that selection of risky options results from the tendency of groups to engage in a "process of diffusion or spreading of responsibility as a result of knowing that one's decisions are being made jointly with others rather than alone," M.A. Wallach, N. Kogan, and D.J. Biem, "Group Influences on Individual Risk Taking," Journal of Abnormal and Social Psychology, 65 (1962), 85.

Cline and Cline report recent experimental support for this "diffusion-of-responsibility" theory; see, Rebecca J. Cline and Timothy R. Cline, "A Structural Analysis of Risky-Shift and Cautious Shift Discussions: The Diffusion-of-Responsibility Theory," Communication Quarterly, 28 (Fall 1980), 26-36. See also, Irvin L. Janis, Victims of Groupthink (Boston: Houghton Mifflin, 1972): "An important symptom of groupthink is the illusion of being invulnerable to the main dangers that might arise from a risky action in which the group is strongly tempted to engage. Essentially, the notion is that 'if our leader and everyone else in our group decides that it is okay, the plan is bound to succeed. Even if it is quite risky, luck will be on our side'" (p. 36).

53. J. Robert Cox, "Loci Communes and Thoreau's Arguments for Wilderness in 'Walking' (1851)," Southern Speech Communication Journal, 46 (1980), 1-16.

54. Perelman and Olbrechts-Tyteca, p. 67.

55. Kenneth Burke, The Philosophy of Literary Form, 3rd ed. (Berkeley: University of California Press, 1973), p. 1.

Conservationism vs. Preservationism: The "Public Interest" in the Hetch Hetchy Controversy
by Christine Oravec

When naturalist John Muir in 1890 drew a map of what would eventually be Yosemite National Park and included an area called "Hetch Hetchy Valley" in its boundaries, he set the conditions for the greatest controversy in the conservation movement until that time. The features so highly praised by such preservationists as Muir—the high walls, the narrow outlet, the continual flow of the snow-fed river—made Hetch Hetchy an ideal site for constructing a municipal dam, according to officials of the city of San Francisco.[1] By 1901 the city put in a claim for the valley, and the ensuing struggle between the aesthetic and practical values of Hetch Hetchy influenced environmental debate long after the dam was approved in 1913.[2]

Seldom before the Hetch Hetchy controversy did values of aesthetics and practicality clash so directly within the movement for conservation. One might expect that the central argument of the debate would focus on standard topics of beauty and economy. But at its foundation, the debate also hinged upon differing presumptions concerning the nature of the "public" and its relationship to the natural environment. As historian Samuel P. Hays observed, the "public interest" was the "crux of the controversy" over the Hetch Hetchy.[3]

The controversy reflected two differing views of the "public interest," one of which eventually predominated over the other. Conservationists, endorsing the utilitarian principle of "the greatest good for the greatest number," argued that the material needs of numbers of identifiable individuals represented "the public interest," hence their support for the dam. Preservationists, on the other hand, argued that to save the beauty of the valley served a more generally defined "national" interest. Not incidentally, these two views of society corresponded to the two poles of the American self-image that had been linked in uneasy union throughout the later nineteenth century—progressivism, or America as a collective population of individual units, and nationalism, with America viewed as an organic nation, the whole greater than its parts.[4] However, progressivism began to predominate by the advent of the Roosevelt administration in 1901, and by 1913 conservationists won the battle over Hetch Hetchy.

A study of the Hetch Hetchy controversy illustrates how these prevailing social and political presumptions, as well as the immediate exigencies of the debate, determined the outcome of deliberations. Specifically, I argue that the fate of Hetch Hetchy rested upon the increasing legitimacy of the conservationists' concept of the "public interest," brought about by the ascendency of progressivism in the early 20th century in America. To support this interpretation, I review the competing nationalist and progressive views of the "public interest," as expressed in preservationist and conservationist discourse; show the effect of an increasingly progressive social and political climate upon the debate; and finally examine the manner in which the two sides defended their claims to legitimate representation of the "public." Such an analysis should demonstrate that the significance of the Hetch Hetchy controversy was not limited to its importance as an acute yet circumscribed conflict over the environment. Rather, the debate signaled the defeat of one view of society and the rise of another that has retained its force for much of the twentieth century and still greatly affects our concepts of the "public" and the "public interest."[5]

The "National" and the "Public" Interest: Two Views

The concept of preservationism came before conservationism in the history of America. Reserving large tracts of land for their inherent or aesthetic values was viewed as the only effective response to relentless private appropriation; later it was followed by government conservation in the form of "wise use" and "effective management." But from 1890 to 1900, as conservation and preservation became distinct positions, more and more economic interests advocated conservation both in terms of humane social policy and sound business sense. Finally, after 1901, the start of the Hetch Hetchy controversy, conservation generally became the policy of the progressive Roosevelt administration. The preservationists' position, once the only voice against unregulated development of the wilderness, became a voice of dissent within the conservation movement which was endorsed by both business and government.[6]

From the beginning, the preservationists advocated a difficult position: there was no opposition between aesthetics and public utility. The original Yosemite park grant, the Sierra Club argued, in its first resolution intended that "this great natural wonderland should be preserved in pure wilderness for all time for the benefit of the entire nation."[7] In turn, its authors did "not believe that the vital interests of the nation at large should be sacrificed and so important a part of its National Park destroyed to save a few dollars for local interests."[8]

By basing the arguments for Hetch Hetchy upon the "national" interest, preservationists used a concept which both supported their belief in the value of the wilderness and which dominated American political thought nearly to the end of the nineteenth century.[9] In the words of historian and political theorist John W. Burgess, the "Nation" itself was a "mystic body endowed with a spirit," which should never be reduced merely to its numerical equivalent, a particular "population."[10] But beyond this basic nationalism, the preservationists implied that the unity of Yosemite corresponded symbolically with the unity of the nation itself, and the integrity of the two entities transcended the claims of any of their constituent parts.

Thus Yosemite existed as a symbolic representation of the nation itself, inspiring national feeling through its very existence as an organic whole. This specifically nationalist appeal appeared as a minority statement delivered at the Governors' Conference on Conservation in 1908, by J. Horace McFarland, President of the American Civic Association. In his address, McFarland attributed the very existence of patriotic sentiment to the physical beauty of the landscape: "It is the love of country that lights and keeps glowing the holy fire of patriotism. And this love is excited primarily by the beauty of the country." He further described the precise sensation of the patriotic-aesthetic response in the words of an old familiar hymn:

> My native country, thee,
> Land of the noble, free
> Thy name I love;
> I love thy rock and rills;
> Thy woods and templed hills
> My heart with rapture thrills,
> Like that above.[11]

McFarland held that destroying natural scenery debilitated the country. "We can not destroy the scenery of our broad land," he said, "but we can utterly change its beneficial relation to our lives, and remove its stirring effect upon our love of country." He cited the examples of the Grand Canyon, Niagra Falls, and the Hetch Hetchy valley.[12] McFarland's address appeared frequently in subsequent campaign materials, indicating that preservationists found his elaboration of the "national" interest particularly appropriate and useful.[13]

Yet the preservationists' concept of the national interest did not originate in the discourse of partisan advocates. Rather, McFarland and the other preservationists referenced an earlier legal document central to the debate, the Hitchcock decision of 1905. On October 16, 1901, officials for the city of San Francisco filed a request for reservoir rights on Lake Eleanor and Hetch Hetchy, and were denied by Secretary of Interior E. A. Hitchcock.[14] They tried again, and again were denied. In his second denial, Secretary Hitchcock introduced his own concept of a "national" interest in the park:

> Presumably the Yosemite National Park was created such by law because of the natural objects . . . within its boundaries . . . like Hetch Hetchy and Yosemite Valley. It is the aggregation of such natural scenic features that makes Yosemite Park a

wonderland which the Congress of the United States sought by law to preserve for all coming time as nearly as practicable in the condition fashioned by the hand of the Creator—a worthy object of national pride and a source of healthful pleasure and rest for the thousands of people who may annually sojourn there during the heated months.[15]

Significantly, Hitchcock placed the defense of Hetch Hetchy upon two facets of national interest; the response of nationalism induced in all people by the natural beauty of one's country and the direct benefits of exposure to natural scenery upon future visitors.[16] As we shall see, the preservationists later struggled with the implications of social utility in the latter argument. Nevertheless, from 1901 to 1908, the preservationists related the social and the aesthetic realms in their view of the national interest. In so doing, they anticipated two requirements of the situation; that of addressing a general audience potentially responsive to the traditional ideas of aesthetics and nationalism influential in the last decade of the previous century, and that of countering the conservationist position on the public interest.

Conservationists were also aware of the invigorating qualities of the nation's resources. But they needed to redefine the public interest according to their own interpretation, particularly since the request by San Francisco to acquire park lands was filed under the DeVries act of 1901 specifically making deposition of the park subject to "the public interest."[17] They did so by applying the political philosophy of progressivism. For progressives, the public was a political collective, which depended upon the cooperation of individual units, any one of which could, under special conditions, represent the interests of the whole.[18] The people of San Francisco, who needed fresh water, could, by virtue of their apparent needs and clear identification, speak for the entire public.

In his response to the Hitchcock decision, San Francisco City Engineer Marsden Manson redefined the public interest. First, Manson separated the interest of a "few hardy mountaineers" in untouched scenic beauty from the interests of the public in a healthy water supply, thereby disassociating the features of the valley itself from his conception of the general public: "When these common and minor features are modified (but rendered none the less attractive to the few hardy mountaineers who reach the regions in summer) to furnish an element of health to the homes of millions for all time, the public interests are best served by the modification."[19] With this move, Manson elevated pragmatic value over aesthetic value.

More importantly, Manson countered the legal problem of locating a dam in the national park by claiming exclusive rights to the use of the term, "public interest." Public interest, was, of course, primary; his definition of public interest meant the domestic use of water; therefore, domestic use of water took priority over the intentions of the Yosemite Park bill:

It is a principle of statutory construction that words should be given their broad and natural meaning.... If, in the act of October 1, 1890 [the Yosemite Park act], the words "public interest" had been used they would naturally be connected with the park and the purpose for which it was created; but, being used in the act of February 15, 1901, the words must naturally refer primarily to the public interest in the granting and exercise of the privileges therein provided for.[20]

With this interpretation, Manson anticipated political conditions as they stood in 1905. The government's policies of conservation were increasing in strength and the public interest would come to mean the right of the people, as represented by a particular local community, to own and use natural resources to supply domestic needs.[21]

No better illustration exists of the process by which the public interest became successfully appropriated by the conservationists than Secretary of the Interior James R. Garfield's decision not to block the city's request on May 11, 1908. Garfield's statement determined the meaning of "public interest" in language strikingly similar to Manson's petition of 1905:

> In construing the words of a statute, the evident and ordinary meaning should be taken, when such meaning is reasonable and not repugnant to the evident purpose of the law itself. On this broad principle the words "the public interest" should not be confined merely to the public interest in the Yosemite National Park for use as a park only, but rather the broader public interest which requires these reservoir sites to be utilized for the highest good to the greatest number of people. If Congress had intended to restrict the meaning to the mere interest of the public in the park as such, it surely would have used specific words to show the intent.[22]

Later in the decision, Garfield defined the highest use of water as the "domestic use" and answered the preservationists by declaring, "I am convinced . . . that 'the public interest' will be much better conserved by granting the permit."[23]

With the conservationist appropriation of the meaning of "public interest," the controversy became one over social philosophy, not of the inherent values of wilderness or the aesthetics of the valley. As such, the conservationist position, with its premises grounded in social progressivism, had an inherent advantage against a preservationism which was concerned as much with nature as with humanity. However, the first public test of these concepts in the Congressional hearings of 1908-09 demonstrated that antagonists' presumptions concerning the composition of the public had yet to be matched with a specific demonstration of public support as well as a prevailing philosophy. The validity of that very demonstration of support depended in turn upon established notions of the "public."

The Congressional hearings of 1908-09 were the first clashes to center national attention upon Hetch Hetchy. The hearings were occasioned by House Resolution 184 (later 223) to exchange lands not under city patent within the valley for lands outside the valley, effectively making the valley a city enclave within the park. Both conservationist and preservationist groups viewed the resolution as a key step toward effectuating the Garfield permit.

To support the renewal of their request, the city of San Francisco ran a municipal bond election which resulted in a six-to-one ratio of voters in favor of the project (despite John Muir's statement that nine-tenths of San Francisco's residents were against it); the preservationists in turn launched a national publicity campaign larger than any previously involving preserved lands. This campaign, along with the publicity of the hearings, resulted in a wave of interest in the Hetch Hetchy issue which overwhelmed the conservationists' more private lobbying efforts.[24] Interestingly, the nature of the respective campaigns reflected certain elements of the antagonists' theories; the preservationists planned to elicit massive nationwide support, while conservationists used personal lobbying, plus the presumption that progressive ideas weighed more heavily in Congress than old-fashioned nationalism.

The success of a single publication illustrates the tactics of the preservationist campaign. Two days after the opening of the hearings in 1909, the Sierra Club released the first edition of a widely distributed pamphlet, *Let All the People Speak and Prevent the Destruction of the Yosemite Park.*[25] It included a reprint of John W. Noble's letter to the House Committee extolling John Muir's "patriotic foresight," and it encouraged "public opinion" in favor of preservation. Further, Charles Lummis was cited as stating: "Anybody American enough to object to this sort of infamy should write at once . . . and may also consult with that Prince of the California Mountains, John Muir, at Martinez, Cal."[26] Historian Holway Jones attributes the strength of the letter writing campaign primarily to such publications as *Let All the People Speak;*[27] participants in the hearings repeatedly referenced the number of letters supporting the preservationists. The eventual outcome depended more upon an unquestioned outpouring of support than close debate in the congressional hearings. Thus, the national appeal, at least in the hearings, aided the preservationists cause.[28]

In sharp contrast to these tactics, conservationists did not make a general public appeal until after their setback in the 1909 hearings. Instead, their campaign took the form of personal lobbying of Washington politicians by civil engineers and city officials representing the Bay area. Although they were fully represented in the hearings, they did not counter the preservationists' nationwide campaign, nor did they effectively demonstrate an overriding public need for the water of Hetch Hetchy. Instead, they chose to argue its desirability over other suggested supplies, assuming that "the public interest" was self-evident. The following argument by former Mayor Phelan, of San Francisco, is representative:

> Hetch Hetchy is the best.... It is the most available, it does not involve us in any litigation, it is not used for beneficial purposes, and there seems to be every reason why we should use it. Of course we could take water from the Tuolumne, the Yuba, or any of those streams. I do not say that they are ample, but I will assume that there are ample supplies elsewhere, by paying for them.[29]

In contrast to the preservationist's national appeal, the conservationist position may have seemed based upon the self-interest of the people of San Francisco, as witnessed by city-wide referendum and the pleadings of their elected officials.

The lack of engagement on the issue of public interest led to postponment of the land exchange and an effectual stalemate that, given the political climate, was a considerable accomplishment for the preservationists.[30] Reflecting their conviction that the preservationist position would fail if they justified their conception of the public interest more convincingly, the conservationists renewed their efforts. From this date the conflict over the Hetch Hetchy would be a public struggle over two opposing views of the meaning of "public."

Justifying Claims to the "Public Interest" in a Progressive Climate

After 1909, conservationists increasingly publicized arguments on both the quantity and the character of the "public" to be served by the dam. A primary argument rested on the issue of number; how many people were to be affected by the decision to dam Hetch Hetchy? This issue intrinsically favored the conservationists, for unlike the preservationists, their political philosophy was expressed in numerical terms: "the greatest good for the greatest number." The Division of Forestry's *Use Book* for 1911 stated that "the welfare of the community or the number of people benefitted should be the factor determining a higher use" for forest lands in dispute.[31] And one historian has noted that in conflicts over use of public lands, "the test of numbers would be a sufficient guide to the exercise of . . . discretion and judgment."[32]

As if confident of the defensibility of their position, conservationists repeatedly compared the numbers of tourists to Hetch Hetchy and the population of the city. Mayor Phelan made the point:

> The highest use of water is the domestic use, and the eight hundred thousand people living in San Francisco and on the opposite shore of the Bay are certainly . . . entitled to the consideration of the country. . . .

By yielding their opposition, sincere lovers of nature will turn the prayers of a million people to praise for the gifts bestowed upon them by the God of Nature, whom they cannot worship in his temple, but must perforce live in sweltering cities. A reduced death rate is a more vital consideration than the discussion of the relative beauties of a meadow or a lake.[33]

Although he boosted the population of the Bay area by two hundred thousand in the space of several paragraphs, Phelan estimated the population of the city in numbers, which in a discussion of quantities may have appeared more credible than an amorphous concept of the nation enunciated by preservationists.

Conservationists also took the offensive in characterizing the kind of people that would be most affected by the dam project. In part of a series of articles in *The California Weekly,* Phelan disassociated the class interests of the average city-dwelling worker from those of the mountaineering and leisure population: "To paraphrase a classification . . . modern society may be divided into three classes—wealth-producers, stock-jobbers, and fox-hunters. The wealth-producers—the toiling millions—and the other two classes—predatory and parasitic—consciously or unconsciously, obstruct the wheels of progress. Let them make way!"[34]

The economic analysis and the mention of classes in Phelan's statement indicated the influence of socialist political philosophy, and there is no doubt that some of the ideas of socialism influenced both progressives and conservationists.[35] However, Phelan did not need to go this far afield for his language. Henry D. Lloyd's *Wealth Against Commonwealth* had stated:

> Two classes . . . study and practice politics and government: place hunters and privilege hunters. America has grown so big—and the tickets to be voted, and the powers of government, and the duties of citizens, and the profits of personal use of public functions have all grown so big—that the average citizen has broken down. No man can half understand or half operate . . . it . . . except the place hunter and the privilege hunter. Government, therefore—municipal, State, national—is passing into the hands of these two classes.[36]

By borrowing the readily available language of social reform, proponents of the dam combined the qualitative as well as quantitative dimensions of the "public" into a uniform whole. The "public" became a mass, numerically strong and materially deserving. The conservationists then proceeded to disassociate the preservationist's unified concept of the "nation" into two parts, an idealistic dream and an elite minority.

Arguments accusing the preservationists of sentimentality, idealism, and elitism in their effort to protect the rights of a few mountaineers came quickly after Phelan's attacks. Marsden Manson, for instance, ironically contrasted the able but selfish mountaineer, capable of enjoying the valley in its wild state, with the laboring masses:

> Not one-tenth part of the [park] area is accessible to any but the hardiest mountaineer. . . . It is full of temples, placed by the hand of the Almighty . . . in order that only those devotees whose worship is pure shall ever reach their gates, shut out forever from the weak, gaping crowd, who have not the energy nor the soul to appreciate their grandeurs.[37]

Indeed, Manson once again polarized the preservationists' aesthetic perspective in a way which appealed to an American popular self-image. "Typical Americans" shunned the cultivated arts; in fact, this neglect was a special virtue, because the arts would not then interfere with the art of politics. John Burgess had written:

> Not all nations, however, are endowed with political capacity or great political impulse. Frequently the national genius expands itself in the production of language, art or religion; frequently it shows itself too feeble to bring even these to any degree of perfection.[38]

Marsden Manson's private comment that preservationism attracted "short-haired women and long-haired men" corrborated this view, even in a nation awakened for some time to the beauties of nature.[39]

In response, the preservationists searched for arguments supporting their vision of the "national" interest, while countering attacks labelling their campaign elitist and nonsocial. Their most important response was a positive characterization of the much maligned nature lover. Although the solution was obviously a reaction, it was very nearly prophetic; the mountaineer of the future was to be a typical working person:

> The wage earners and wealth producers may not all be able to visit the Yosemite National Park, but many of them have already done so and many more will follow. In time, I predict that the wage earners of this state will be doing as the citizens of Germany now do—deprive themselves of luxuries and save throughout the year in order that they may spend a few days of rest and recreation with their families in the scenic regions of Europe.[40]

In an unprecedented move, preservationists developed a utilitarian argument of their own, based upon the number of future visitors to the Sierra regions. When the population of California should have increased abruptly (as intimated in Phelan's argument), E. T. Parson predicted that "those tillers of field and vineyard will look to the mountains as a place of refuge."[41] Parsons estimated the number of visitors would increase to 10,000 from the then present level of 1,000 bringing a million dollars of revenue to the state each year.[42] Discussion of a future tourist industry allowed the preservationists to address the issue in quantitative terms, though in doing so they incorporated their opponents' own form of argument. By entertaining the idea of thousands of future visitors, they exposed themselves to the strength of their opponents' definition of the "public interest," as well as legitimized a profit motive for defending the parks.

The preservationists' tactic resembled conservationists' attempts to appropriate the argument for natural beauty themselves. Conservationists had long claimed that roads and facilities, a necessary by-product of the dam project, made the beauty of the valley more appealing to the average tourist. As early as 1903, and until the end of the campaign, supporters of the dam argued that the attractiveness of a beautiful, though artificial, lake would be made more accessible to the public by a road extending to and across the Hetch Hetchy dam.[43] This conception of natural beauty in the "public interest" provided an opportunity to incorporate massive changes in the valley itself. Both sides, then, tried to appropriate the opposing argument, but the conservationists' view of the public dominated. Preservationists' arguments extolling what today would be termed the "intrinsic" wilderness values of the valley simply could not function in a climate of "public" debate established by progressivism. Neither could preservationists argue for their view of the public interest without using the same vocabulary as the conservationists.

Thus, as the Hetch Hetchy debate moved from the legislative forum to the public arena, argument shifted from the definition of the "national" and "public" interest to debate over the "public" represented by each contending group. At first, preservationists chose to express themselves with sublime language and a political philosophy which was passing out of popular favor. Then, under conservationist pressure, they characterized the "public" in a manner essentially foreign to their implicit social theory. At the same time, the conservationists, riding a wave of increasing support for progressive politics, developed a unified yet quantifiable theory of the "public."

Once the respective political philosophies of the preservationists and conservationists became an issue, their ultimate persuasive strengths depended upon a political climate which assumed the benefits of civilization and continued social progress.[44] From 1909 to 1912, progressivism was increasingly on the upswing, and the older image of an undifferentiated nation led by a natural elite could no longer accommodate the future. The politically aware middle and upper-middle class, espousing reformist attitudes informed but not dominated by, nationalist sentiment, would more probably respond to the conservationist than the preservationist vision.[45] Moreover, conservationists had argued that the identifiable beneficiaries of preservationism did not represent the "public" as they themselves had defined it. The conservationists' success in this argument is illustrated by the preservationists' failure to withstand attacks against the nature of their adherents in the congressional hearings of 1912-13.

Demonstrating "Public" Support: The Presumption of Progressivism

By 1912 the battle for the Hetch Hetchy centered once again in congressional hearings, this time on a series of amended and reamended items collectively called the Raker bill.[46] However, the preservationists now faced stiff federal opposition. The new Democratic administration retained the aid of Gifford Pinchot on the issue, who prominently associated himself with the cause of the city. With the agreement of the secretaries of Agriculture and Interior, Chief Forester Henry Graves, and the directors of the Geological Survey and Reclamation Service, the bill giving leave to the city to build a dam in Yosemite Park officially became an administration proposal.[47]

Stating that "there is no use of water that is higher than the domestic use," Gifford Pinchot accused the preservationists before the House Committee on Public Lands of excluding the mass of the public from using the park. He claimed that only the improvement of access as a side product to building the dam could increase tourist traffic to the area:

> The presence of these additional means of communication will mean that the national forest and the national park will be visited by very large numbers of people who can not visit them now. . . . If we had nothing else to consider than the delight of the few men and women who would yearly go into the Hetch Hetchy Valley, then it should be left in its natural condition.[48]

During the questioning, Pinchot challenged the trustworthiness of the bill's opponents by implying that the apparent groundswell of popular support received by the committee represented the creation of an artificial public:

Mr. Graham. When this matter was up before I received a great many telegrams, most of them from ladies in my district, protesting against any interference with the beauty of the valley, and I wondered if the place was inaccessible, whether they spoke from observation or whether they had been influenced in some other way?

Mr. Pinchot. A very small number of people have been in the valley.[49]

To conservationists, the argument for retaining the untouched beauty of the valley in itself disproved the legitimacy of its support: no "public" of any numbers could enjoy a place it had not physically seen.

By 1913 the preservationists were required to demonstrate the "public" nature of their support or risk the appearance of being a mere special interest group. Yet demonstrating the support of the "nation," as the preservationists had defined it, was impossible in the heyday of progressive politics. All the preservationists could do was count letters, and even the numbers turned against them, since many of the letters were from members of activist women's clubs and nature groups.[50] Ironically, the preservationists' actual list of active supporters was filled by names from the "elite" politically active middle and upper-middle class who provided the conservationists with consistent support on other issues.[51]

The relative effectiveness with which the opposing sides demonstrated their support in 1913 differed radically from 1909. Preservationists still depended upon individual contact and active response through private mailings directed at select targets such as the American Civic Association, a tactic which was working against them. In contrast, the conservationists by this time could claim broad but passive consensus demonstrated by official government publications and press releases which reached all segments of the reading public.[52] Through the diffusion of state-sanctioned mass media, the conservationist's cause appeared both national and empirical, while the preservationists' claim seemed increasingly idealistic, idiosyncratic, and ultimately unwarranted.

As the Senate hearings continued, pressure grew stronger. To at least one senator, the flood of public response generated by the stepped-up preservationists' campaign represented propaganda and little else:

Senator Norris. But, Mr. Johnson, there has been some organized propaganda carried on from some central point manufacturing this sentiment, because when I wrote to these men they replied: "Well, I don't know anything about it; I heard that they are going to destroy something there and give it to a Water Power trust. . . ."

Before I went into the effect of it I thought there was some great big Water Power Trust, but it seems to me that if we are giving to San Francisco this immense water power we are doing what everybody concedes is the true interest of the country and the true interest of conservation.[53]

During House debate, Finley H. Gray of Indiana discussed his own process of coming to a decision: "Mr. Chairman, much as I admire the beauties of nature and deplore the desecration of God's Creation, yet when these two considerations come in conflict, the conservation of nature should be yielded to the conservation of human welfare, health, and life."[54] And William Kent, a personal friend of John Muir, decided that upon this issue Muir was "a man entirely without social sense."[55]

Despite the continuing conflict, the rhetoric of the antagonists had little effect in the final phases of the debate. Muir's friend and supporter Robert Underwood Johnson persisted in drafting letters to the *New York Times,* citing the "fundamental rights of the whole people," as if his right to claim the support of the people had never been questioned.[56] But the presumption of progressivism was just too strong. Pinchot implied as much when he admitted that after ten years of conflict, the only possible termination was to pass the bill.[57] Finally, a decision needed to be made, and a dam in the Hetch Hetchy valley was built in 1923 as a result of the passage of the Raker bill.[58]

After twelve years of discussion, a public decision appeared to ratify, not only a particular proposal, but a vision of the nature of the public itself. Further, the progressive's vision of the public prevailed in decision making about the environment for decades after the immediate controversy ended. To evaluate the outcome of the Hetch Hetchy controversy, then, is to evaluate the very notion of "the public interest."

Conclusion

One plausible explanation of the outcome of the Hetch Hetchy controversy involves the preservationists' use of arguments associated with the opposing side. By advocating turning Hetch Hetchy into a popular tourist attraction, the preservationists appeared to endorse conservationist argument based on social utility. This inconsistency would have been avoided, so the explanation goes, if preservationists instead had emphasized the purely intrinsic worth of wilderness. Thus the preservationists' loss may be assigned to an error in tactics which played into the hands of the opposing side.[59]

However, such an explanation, while certainly reasonable, does not fully account for the larger constraints upon public persuasion. Rhetoric conducted in the public forum is seldom "pure"—it entails presumptions of the nature of its own domain of conduct, whether explicit or implicit, adopted or imposed. The preservationists' failure lay, not in their choosing to make arguments based on social factors (which they scarcely could have avoided), but instead in conceiving of a public too idealistic for a progressive age.

The preservationists' shift to utilitarian arguments based on tourism in the middle phases of the debate may have proved to be a tactical coup, by incorporating within the preservationists' aesthetic vision an unanswerable pragmatic benefit. As Secretary Hitchcock wrote: "a source of healthful pleasure and rest for . . . thousands." Instead, the conservationists benefited by the preservationists' move, and also were able to incorporate a preservationist argument for natural beauty within their utilitarian position. Each argument was inconsistent, by strict standards. However, the advantage of the conservationists lay, not in the intrinsic consistency of the positions they held, but in their image of the public. Adding aesthetic arguments to the conservationists' position would only serve to strengthen, not to weaken, their case because it already dominated the social field. And preservationists, forced to specify their conception of the "nation," could do so only in the very terms of specificity dictated by the progressivist notion of the "public."

To conclude that arguments of preservationism failed as much because of the strength of their presumptions about the public as their argumentative tactics implies that preservation itself was inherently contrary to the prevailing social system, and implied a radical social critique. The highest evaluation of nature, as preservationists interpreted it, presumed a rejection of a form of public life advocated by a materialist and progressive democracy, and an exaltation of a form of ideal social unity. Indeed, their very mode of argument was inimical to what progressives considered rational decision making in the public forum, demanding as it did that intuitive, largely symbolic proposals be ratified without conventional statistical consensus. To advocate a policy of preservationism was to espouse what appeared to be radically un-American values in form and content to the public view.

The public view, however, was a conservative one, regardless of the "progressive" nature of the times. While preservationists strived to reconcile what seemed to be the contradiction between "spiritual" values and public action, conservationists argued for the remediation of more immediate practical difficulties. Not surprisingly, representatives of the "public," once offered a clear choice, supported the policy explicitly based on premises ameliorating, but not changing, the existing social order. And, by portraying the American public as passive rather than active, progressives encouraged their constituency to accept their designated role as endorsers of the prevailing view.

Despite decades of inactivity, however, preservationism as an environmental policy and as a social theory reemerged, but in a new guise. Starting in 1953, when preservationists successfully used the Hetch Hetchy dam as counter-evidence for the building of a dam in Dinosaur National Monument, wilderness preservation had come to challenge conservation as an official government policy.[60] More tellingly, the preservationists' implicit social critique has addressed a fundamental issue of contemporary environmentalism—that is, the effect of urbanized and industrial development on the quality of life on this planet. The "national" interest may now apply to the "ecological community," but the unified and organic social implications of preservationism remain.[61] The reemergence of preservationism indicates that new concepts of the social order as yet unformed are succeeding the progressive view.

The controversy over Hetch Hetchy shows that such notions as "the public interest," "the national" interest, and perhaps the "public" itself, are rhetorical notions shaped in response not only by the immediate context of debate, but also by the legitimizing force of predominant social and political presumptions. These presumptions, in the case of the failure of the preservationists, determined the very domain of public discussion. No "public" could appear to endorse the preservationists which had not already been admitted by progressive social theory. Thus, claims for the "public interest" must be examined for their substantive content as well as their demonstrated effect. Action taken "in the public interest" may be, as in the case of the Hetch Hetchy dam, the product of decisive presumptions about the nature of persons who comprise the "public," presumptions which have the effect of defining the very context of debate and the final outcome of public controversy.

Notes

1. Those who were against the dam constantly compared the beauty of the Yosemite and Hetch Hetchy valleys. For examples, see *To All Lovers of Nature and Scenery,* San Francisco, California, 21 Dec. 1908, in *Pamphlets By and About the Sierra Club,* General Collection, Bancroft Library, University of California, Berkeley. Proponents of the dam minimized the aesthetic similarities between Yosemite and Hetch Hetchy, and argued that preservation of two similar natural features wasted natural resources. For examples, see page 7 of William F. Colby's typescript copy of Secretary of the Interior James R. Garfield's decision on the Application for Lake Eleanor and Hetch Hetchy Valley Reservoir Sites, 15 Feb. 1901, Francis P. Farquhar Papers, C-B 517, Carton 3, Group 42, Folder 4, Bancroft Library; and James D. Phelan, "Why Congress Should Pass the Hetch-Hetchy Bill," *Outlook,* 13 Feb. 1909, p. 340. The Farquhar Papers are hereafter cited as FP.

2. For a review of the early applications for water rights in the Hetch Hetchy, see Holway Jones, *John Muir and the Sierra Club: The Battle for Yosemite* (San Francisco: Sierra Club, 1965), pp. 86-91. Jones' book is an invaluable source of material on the activities of the Sierra Club prior to 1913.

3. Samuel P. Hays, *Conservation and the Gospel of Efficiency* (New York: Athenum, 1975), p. 193.

4. Apparently, a conflict between conceptions of the "nation" and the "people" (or later, the "public"), has existed in American political thought at least since the disagreement between nationalist Francis Lieber and John C. Calhoun, who advocated states' rights: "Lieber agreed with Calhoun that sovereignty was indivisible and could not be located in government. However, for Calhoun the 'people' meant the people of the several states, while for Lieber the term denoted the national society in its totality." Barnard Edward Brown, *American Conservatives: The Political Thought of Francis Lieber and John W. Burgess* (New York: Columbia University Press, 1951), pp. 36-38.

5. This study owes much to discussions of the "public," "public knowledge," and "social knowledge" by Lloyd F. Bitzer, "Rhetoric and Public Knowledge," in *Rhetoric, Philosophy, and Literature: An Exploration,* ed. Don M. Burks (West Lafayette, In.: Purdue University Press, 1978), pp. 67-93; Thomas B. Farrell, "Knowledge, Consensus, and Rhetorical Theory," *Quarterly Journal of Speech,* 62 (1976), 1-14; and Michael Calvin McGee and Martha Anne Martin, "Public Knowledge and Ideological Argumentation," *Communication Monographs,* 50 (1983), 47-65. Based on the present study, I would suggest that the "public" might well be usefully conceived in terms of "publics" or "versions of the public." Since use of the phrase "the public interest" to signify the concerns of the social-political collectivity derives much of its contemporary force from progressivist social theory, a critic should be careful not to apply the phrase to anything more concrete than a position in a debate.

6. Many books record the story of the conservation movement and its dual emphases on preservation and conservation, but two of the best are Hays, cited above, and Roderick Nash, *Wilderness and the American Mind,* rev. ed. (New Haven: Yale University Press, 1973). See also Christine Oravec, "John Muir, Yosemite, and the Sublime Response: A Study in the Rhetoric of Preservationism," *Quarterly Journal of Speech,* 67 (1981), 245-58.

7. Jones, pp. 94-95.

8. Jones, p. 95.

9. Henry Steele Commager, *The American Mind: An Interpretation of American Thought* and *Character Since the 1880's* (New Haven: Yale University Press, 1950), p. 313.

10. Hans Kohn, *American Nationalism: An Interpretive Essay* (New York: Macmillan, 1957), pp. 126-27; Bert James Lowenberg, *American History in American Thought: Christopher Columbus to Henry Adams* (New York: Simon and Schuster, 1972), p. 362.

11. *Proceedings of a Conference of Governors in the White House,* Washington, D.C., May 13-15, 1908 (Washington: Government Printing Office, 1909), p. 153. Those attending the conference may have recognized in McFarland's reference to "rapture" an evocation of the sublime response. See Oravec, pp. 248-49.

12. *Proceedings,* pp. 153, 156.

13. See, for example, *Let All the People Speak* [1909], p 3; *Let Everyone Help* (1909), p. 12; and in a similar vein, *More Light on the Destructive Hetch Hetchy Scheme,* 2 page edition [1913], p. 2; in FP, Carton 3, Group 42, Folder 4.

14. Jones, p. 91.

15. See the transcript of Hitchcock's ruling in *San Francisco and the Hetch Hetchy Reservoir: Hearings Held before the Committee on the Public Lands of the House of Representatives, January 9, and 12, 1909, on H.J. Resolution 233,* in U.S. Cong., *San Francisco and the Hetch Hetchy Reservoir: Hearings,*

1908-09 (Washington, D.C.: Government Printing Office, 1909), p. 12. Hereafter cited as *House Committee Hearings,* 9 and 12 Jan. 1909.

16. The Hitchcock decision was repeatedly cited in publications, testimony, articles, and bulletins throughout the campaign. See, for example, John Muir, "The Tuolumne Yosemite in Danger," *Outlook,* 2 Nov. 1907, p. 488; *The Yosemite* (1912; rpt. Garden City, New York: Anchor-Doubleday, 1962), p. 199; *Let All the People Speak and Prevent the Destruction of Yosemite Park,* 12 Jan. 1908 [1909], p. 13; *Let Everyone Help to Save the Famous Hetch-Hetchy Valley and Stop the Commercial Destruction which Threatens our National Parks,* Nov. 1909, p. 10, both in FP, Carton 3, Group 43; Society for the Preservation of National Parks, California Branch, *More Light on the Destructive Hetch Hetchy Scheme,* 4 page edition [1913], p. 3, in the Robert Underwood Johnson Papers, C-B 385, Box 8, Bancroft Library. The Johnson Papers are hereafter cited as JP.

17. There is an extensive examination of legal precedent for the application of the city for water rights in the Hetch Hetchy in the *House Committee Hearings,* 9 and 12 Jan. 1909, pp. 8-16, which focuses upon the interpretation of "public interest" in the DeVries act of 1901.

18. Ideally, according to progressive thinking, the nation was constituted through "specialization, organization, and group participation" of individual units in the collective. This position, though it emphasized group cohesion on the highest level, allowed for relatively less intermediate private or group organization, a policy which has been called "social atomism." Thomas L. Hartshorne, *The Distorted Image: Changing Conceptions of the American Character Since Turner* (Cleveland: Case Western University Press, 1968), p. 31; Hayes, pp. 269-70.

19. Marsden Manson, *A Brief in the Matter of Reservoir Rights of Way for the City and County of San Francisco,* 27 July, 1907, Appendix B, p. 14; in Marsden Manson, *Efforts to Obtain a Water Supply for San Francisco from the Tuolumne River* (San Francisco, 1907).

20. Manson, p. 14.

21. Hays, pp. 38-44, documents Gifford Pinchot's efforts to place federal forests under a conservation rather than a preservation policy, culminating in the establishment of the Bureau of Forestry in 1905. Such areas of resource management as water and range use followed suit, with the conservationists gaining full public recognition by 1908 (Hays, p. 122).

22. Garfield decision, p. 4. See also Jones' account of the impact of the Garfield decision, pp. 99-101.

23. Garfield decision, pp. 5, 7.

24. See, for example, the numerous telegrams and letters reprinted in the *House Committee Hearings,* 9 and 12 Jan. 1909, pp. 118-234.

25. Significant portions of *Let All the People Speak* [1909], reappeared in the November 1909 edition of *Let Everyone Help,* and also made up good portions of at least two editions of *Let Everyone Help,* [1913]. The latter two editions were produced by the Society for the Preservation of National Parks, California Branch, a lobbying organization for the more militant members of the Sierra Club. Composed of short quotations, excerpts of articles, and reprinted editorials linked by boldface headings and numerous photographs, the original editions of *Let All the People Speak* and *Let Everyone Help* were easily recomposed to meet the demands of rapid production and distribution.

26. *Let All the People Speak* [1909], pp. 4 and 8.

27. Jones, pp. 102-03.

28. The House Committee report noted that "there has been an exceedingly widespread, earnest, and vigorous protest voiced by scientists, naturalists, mountain climbers, travelers, and others in person, by letters, and telegrams, and in newspaper and magazine articles," Nash, pp. 168-9.

29. *Senate Committee Hearings,* 1909, pp. 112-13; see also Garfield decision, as quoted in the *House Committee Hearings,* 16 Dec. 1909, p. 12, both in *San Francisco and the Hetch Hetchy Reservoir: Hearings, 1908-09.*

30. The House Committee issued a split decision in favor of the conservationists; the Senate Committee did not report for lack of a decision (Jones, p. 103). Both preservationists and conservationists were able to use the indecisiveness of the congressional committees as argument for their position, in effect prolonging the controversy. See James D. Phelan, "Why Congress Should Pass the Hetch-Hetchy Bill," p. 340; and R.U. Johnson, "The Yosemite National Park," *Outlook,* 13 Feb. 1909, p. 506.

31. Grant McConnell, *Private Power and American Democracy* (New York: Vintage-Random, 1966), p. 46; see also Pinchot's testimony in U.S. Cong., *Hearing Before the Committee on Public Lands, House of Representatives,* 63rd Cong., 1st sess., on H.R. 6281 (Washington, D.C.: Government Printing Office, 1913), in which he weighs the aesthetic value of Hetch Hetchy against the interest of the "most" people.

32. McConnell, p. 46.

33. Phelan, "Why Congress Should Pass the Hetch-Hetchy Bill," pp. 340-1.

34. James D. Phelan, "Hetch-Hetchy for the Wealth-Producer," *The California Weekly,* 26 March 1909, p. 283. (All *California Weeklys* cited can be located in the Farquhar Papers, Carton 3, Group 42, Folder 4).

35. Richard Hofstadter, *The Age of Reform: From Bryan to F.D.R.* (New York: Knopf, 1959), p. 238; J. Leonard Bates, "Fulfilling American Democracy: The Conservation Movement, 1907 to 1921," *The Mississippi Valley Historical Review,* 44 (1957), 30.

36. Cited in Commager, p. 330.

37. Marsden Manson, "Hetch-Hetchy: The Law and the Facts," *The California Weekly,* 18 June 1909, p. 478

38. Hartshorne, p. 22.

39. Nash, p. 169.

40. E.T. Parsons, "Reply to Mr. Phelan on Hetch-Hetchy," *The California Weekly,* 16 Apr. 1909, p. 332.

41. E.T. Parsons, "Proposed Destruction of Hetch-Hetchy," *Out West,* July 1909, p. 611.

42. Parsons, "Proposed Destruction of Hetch-Hetchy," p. 612. Travel to Hetch Hetchy in 1909 was estimated by a preservationist as "nearly a thousand persons per year," and projected as ten thousand in several years. However, estimates varied with the argument. Congressman Raker, a conservationist on the issue of the dam, estimated visitors to Hetch Hetchy as no more than 25 to 75 for the year 1913 (*Cong. Rec.,* 29 Aug. 1913, p. 3902). Total visitation to Yosemite in 1909 was approximately 13,000 and no separate figures were taken for Hetch Hetchy (*Report of the Director of the National Park Service to the Secretary of the Interior for the Fiscal Year Ended June 30, 1923 and the Travel Season, 1923* [Washington, D.C.: Government Printing Office, 1923], p. 99).

43. Manson, *A Brief in the Matter Reservoir Rights of Way,* p. 24. See also Garfield decision, p. 7; Nash, pp. 169-70; Jones, p. 139 and picture facing p. 112; and *House Committee Hearings,* 1913, p. 28.

44. A belief in social progress reached almost universal proportions in the first decade of the century, becoming almost a secular religion; see, for example, Henry F. May, *The End of American Innocence: A Study of the First Years of Our Own Time, 1912-1917* (New York: Knopf, 1969), pp. 9-14.

45. Support for progressivism in the decade 1900-1910 drew strongly from the rising middle class: "little businessmen, professional men, well-to-do farmers, skilled artisans . . . middle-class country-town citizens," Hofstadter, pp. 131-32.

46. Jones, p. 155.

47. Jones, p. 157; Nash, p. 176. The Wilson administration's support of the dam may have secured his reelection in 1916, for California determined the outcome of the presidential race in a close vote.

48. *House Committee Hearings,* 1913, p. 26. Pinchot's argument was referred to persistently throughout the subsequent House floor debate. As Congressman Ferris stated: "As the matter now stands only rich and well-to-do people can visit the park at all. It is an expensive proposition to journey there. You have to go on burros, pack trains, and so forth, and there is no railroad or street car line that would enable you to go any other way except by pack train. San Francisco concurs in this bill, that this bill exacts of the people of San Francisco as a condition precedent to build street car lines and roads and trails and railroads, so that the poor can visit the park." *Cong. Rec.,* 29 Aug. 1913, p. 3894; see also pp. 3903 and 3906. Comparing Ferris' remarks with the characterization of tourist travel in *The Truth About the Hetch Hetchy,* p. 14, indicates the fundamental differences in the opposing sides' conception of the popularity of horse-drawn and motorized travel.

49. *House Committee Hearings,* 1913, p. 30.

50. Nash describes the public reaction as originating from "women's groups, outing and sportsmen's clubs, scientific societies, and the faculties of colleges and universities, as well as from individuals," p. 177.

51. Hays, pp. 142-44, and Jones, pp. 102-03, 108, 159.

52. The conservationists' general publicity campaign, which for a time made resource policy the most discussed issue in the Roosevelt administration, employed pamphlets, tracts, letters, speeches, and pictures in educational and journalistic formats. The broadly based target audience for the campaign included farmers and business people, Easterners and Westerners, and children in the public schools. See Harold R. Pinckett, *Gifford Pinchot: Private and Public Forester* (Urbana: University of Illinois Press, 1970), p. 81; and M. Nelson McGeary, *Gifford Pinchot: Forester-Politician* (Princeton, NJ: Princeton University Press, 1960), p. 98. Preservationists claimed that Pinchot even used government frank to distribute pro-dam materials after he was out of public office; see Society for the Preservation of National Parks, Western Branch, *Hetch Hetchy—A Reply to Mr. Gifford Pinchot,* 1913, JP Box 8.

53. *Hetch-Hetchy Reservoir Site: Hearing Before the Committee on Public Lands, U.S. Senate,* 63rd Cong., 1st sess., on H.R. 7207 (Washington, D.C.: Government Printing Office, 1913), p. 41.

54. Nash, p. 172.

55. Nash, p. 174.

56. Robert Underwood Johnson, "The Hetch Hetchy Crisis: A Call to the Colors," typescript of two letters, one addressed to the editor of the *New York Evening Post*, the other to the editor of the *New York Times*, JP Box 7. Similar letters appeared regularly in these two newspapers toward the end of the campaign; see Jones, p. 156.

57. *House Committee Hearings*, 1913, p. 31.

58. Nicholas Roosevelt, *Conservation: Now or Never* (New York: Dodd, Mead, 1970), p. 35.

59. Roderick Nash has argued that the preservationists considerably weakened their position by describing Hetch Hetchy as a "scenic wonder" and a "public playground." By neglecting the valley's value as pure wilderness and emphasizing the public benefits of the area, they allowed the opposition to promise "improvement" of the valley by providing an artificial lake, roads, and access for boats (Nash, p. 170). Similarly, Holway Jones denigrated the preservationists' argument that the watershed would be closed to campers for sanitary reasons. He proposed that a less pragmatic argument, based upon preserving the sheer beauty of the valley, may have been more effective and consistent (Jones, pp. 104, 112-113, 140-141), though he called the argument from tourism "perhaps the most prophetic and in many ways the strongest" argument used by preservationists (p. 143).

60. Jones, pp. 112-113, discusses the impact of the Hetch Hetchy precedent on the Echo Park dam controversy, which in 1953 became the first national battle in a renewed preservationist movement.

61. Preservationist philosophy and ecological sciences were united in Aldo Leopold's notions of the "land ethic" and the "biological community," as expressed in *A Sand County Almanac* (New York: Ballantine Books, 1966), pp. 237-79. Leopold's concepts provided the intellectual bases for the Wilderness Act of 1964, a key indicator of the resurgence of a modern preservationism. See Susan L. Flader, *Thinking Like a Mountain: Aldo Leopold and the Evolution of an Ecological Attitude Toward Deer, Wolves and Forests* (Lincoln: University of Nebraska Press, 1974), p. 16.

The Discourse of "Environmentalist Hysteria"

by M. Jimmie Killingsworth and Jacqueline S. Palmer

Naturam expellas furca tamen usque recurret (you can throw out Nature with a pitchfork, but she'll always turn up again).

> —Latin saying, quoted and translated by C. G. Jung, *The Undiscovered Self* (29)

Freud would certainly have made a perfect impassioned idealist had he not devoted himself to the other, in the form of the hysteric.

> —Jacques Lacan, *The Four Fundamental Principles of Psycho-Analysis* (28)

Dismissing concern over the possibility of global environmental catastrophe, the conservative columnist Warren Brookes has condemned authors like Paul Ehrlich, "Stanford University's doomsday biologist," for "stirring up of environmentalist hysteria" (Brookes A4). Brookes's judgment, while harsh, is neither new nor unique. In 1962, Rachel Carson's *Silent Spring*—the book that ushered in the modern environmental movement, according to historian Kirkpatrick Sales—was denounced as the work of a "hysterical fool" by its opponents in agribusiness and the chemical industry; and again, in 1978, the epithet "hysterical" figured in the condemnation of Lois Gibbs, the activist housewife of Love Canal (Sales 3-4; also Hynes).

What is it in the message and style of Ehrlich, Carson, and Gibbs that could lead their opponents to label them "hysterical"? Different as they are, the three activists do share a common ethical and political purpose—the commitment to an environment fit for life, not only for the present, but also for future generations. Thus stated, however, the purpose is highly abstract and hardly even controversial; few public figures would deny its importance. More significant perhaps is that, in raising issues of specifically *human* health, Ehrlich, Carson, and Gibbs propose that there is more at stake in the environmental movement than the preservation of wild nature. Not just owls and old-growth timber but *people* are directly affected—gravely affected—by problems like overpopulation and the misuse of natural resources and chemical technologies. For them, environmentalism is a matter not only of "land ethics," to use Aldo Leopold's much-cited term, but of ethics as traditionally defined—a concern with human values, questions of right and wrong, good and bad, the search for a good life. And, since rhetoric has traditionally been understood as a "productive art enabling ethical and political action" (Porter 210), it is not surprising that the discourse of Ehrlich, Carson, and Gibbs also has a common generative core—an acceptance of the need to bring into the public forum information and perspectives that ultimately challenge the value and direction of technological development.

If the aim of this discourse is thus to disturb the order of things—or at least to call attention to already existing disturbances (the damaged environment)—the charge of "environmentalist hysteria" represents an attempt by opponents in the environmental debate to defuse the threat and maintain the stability of the social order as it is. Toward this end, the antienvironmentalists borrow from popular psychology a code for political enmity that uses cultural stereotypes to belittle the character or evidence of their opponents. The implication is that, for now, the danger to the earth is "all in the minds" of the environmentalists, but that, if not contained, environmentalist concern might spread, developing into an epidemic of "mass hysteria" comparable to, for example, the irrational passion for Naziism in Weimar Germany or the "red scare" that captured the public imagination in America during the 1950s (see Levin). The label "hysterical" means that, from the perspective of writers like Brookes (or Dixy Lee Ray or Ronald Bailey—two more conservative critics of contemporary environmentalism), only an aberrant imagination could see trouble brewing in the progressive development of Western civilization. And yet, there must be some semblance of reality in the warnings of the environmentalists for the antienvironmentalists to fear a general acceptance of their opponents' views. Thus the charge of hysteria itself contains a measure of defensiveness, worry, and pathos.

In this essay, we pursue these threads of analysis, using the charge of "environmentalist hysteria" as a heuristic for exploring the emotions invested in the public debate over environmental degradation. Borrowing upon the method of "genealogy" as developed in Michel Foucault's work (especially in the *History of Sexuality*), we examine the significance of "hysteria" in its historical contexts, searching for variant meanings of the term as they relate to different perspectives on what constitutes normal and aberrant behavior in Western culture. We suggest that the pejorative connotations of terms like "mass hysteria" and "environmentalist hysteria" date back to pre-Freudian medical practice. Nineteenth-century physicians, for example, were inclined to dismiss the symptoms of hysterical women as the result of overwrought imaginations rather than as signs of either real organic illnesses (for which there was no evidence) or repressive social conditions (which were screened by an ideology unconsciously defended by the medical establishment). We find a counterpoint to this diagnosis in the early work of Sigmund Freud. Though hardly a feminist himself, Freud provided the foundation for a feminist critique of the earlier understanding of hysteria by arguing that the illness arose (and receded) as a result of a systematic triadic interchange between a *patient*, the patient's social and physical *environment*, and a *discourse*, the medium of exchange between patient and environment. According to Freud's interpretation, hysteria occurred when repressed information in the unconscious—which could not be acknowledged by the socially conscious ego—appeared in coded expressions, usually in the form of bodily symptoms. The analyst, by "breaking the code" and allowing the repressed information to enter into conscious conversation, could (at least in theory) effect a "talking cure" that eliminated the bodily symptoms.

As a model for social relations during environmental crisis, we argue, hysterical discourse opens new avenues of understanding and action. If, as a number of ecological philosophers suggest, the human mind can be viewed as the consciousness of the earth's body, then in a psychoanalytical view of environmentalist hysteria, a technological or instrumental understanding of earthly existence can be said to represent only the conscious mind, the *ego* of Western civilization. While driving the action and shaping the character of public interchange, all the time focusing on its own spectacular accomplishments, the technological ego turns away from the shortcomings or "side effects" of technological practice. Ultimately, the neglected effects appear as "symptoms" in the earth's body (including the human body and the whole of physical existence) ranging from the stink of overloaded landfills to the fever of global warming. The environmentalist and the nature writer, in becoming "voices for the earth" (Gilliam; Brooks), thus represent the return of the repressed, the coming into consciousness of that which, having been avoided for far too long, has created an illness within the mind-body system of earthly existence. If the fervor of environmentalism seems irrational, that is because, in the view of the environmentalists, an ostensibly rational public discourse has neglected the signs of trouble for so long that only a cry of pain can break the public habit of inattention.

Our aim in what follows is not to create an accurate, one-to-one correspondence in the analogy between the discourse of environmental crisis and the discourse of hysteria (thus "essentializing" the category of hysteria), but rather to use the psychoanalytic model to display and examine the emotions at work in the environmental debate. As a medical and social problem, hysteria has inspired a large and sophisticated literature, but the literature on the discourse of environmental policy has only recently begun to appear. By interweaving the themes of the two literatures, we hope to advance the work of rhetorical criticism in the newly founded subfield of environmental rhetoric.

We begin by fleshing out the model of hysterical discourse; then we apply the model to an analysis of the charges and countercharges of "environmentalist hysteria." We give special attention to the book that drew the earliest accusations of hysteria, Carson's *Silent Spring*. Finally, we offer some brief observations on the nature of participation in environmental politics as it emerges in this analysis—from the perspective of both the activist and the rhetorical analyst.

The Hysterical Turn

In classical psychoanalysis, hysterical discourse involves two characteristic actions: a turning away, as if from an object of disgust, and an extension of the boundaries of psychic experience. These movements are open not only to psychoanalysis—which attempts to re-turn attention to what the mind has rejected and re-view old boundaries and transgressions—but also to rhetorical analysis, which traditionally includes the study of figures and tropes. The very word *trope* derives from the Greek *trópos*, which means *turn*. A trope turns away from the conventional denotations of a word and follows its connotations into new semantic territories. The semantic displacement inherent in the trope (the subject of rhetorical analysis) parallels the displacement of psychic energy in hysteria (the subject of psychoanalysis).

In ancient times, hysteria was believed to be caused by the movements of the empty and dissatisfied womb, which, breaking free from its normal anatomical position, turns away from its life-giving work of conception and wanders about in the woman's body, spitefully affecting diverse parts of the body with illnesses and discomforts. Etymology confirms the ancient etiology: the word *hysteria* derives from the Greek word for *uterus*. By the nineteenth century, physiology had rejected the old theory of causation, but the burgeoning medical science of the day kept the name and continued to recognize manifestations of the disease, which included various paralyses, neuralgias, and impairments of bodily functions (see Veith).

When Charcot came to dominate the discourse on hysteria late in the nineteenth century, the disease was understood to be capable of striking male as well as female victims, though women suffered most frequently. Charcot followed the positivist inclination of the day in hypothesizing a neurological cause. Logically, organic symptoms must arise from organic causes. Other physicians, disregarding the impressive but rather too sensational demonstrations arranged by Charcot, accused hysterics of faking and denied the reality of the organic symptoms. After studying with the French master and treating patients of his own, Freud eventually split the difference between the divergent views of hysteria and then totally reconstructed the clinical picture. He sided with Charcot on the reality of the symptoms, but sought the causes in the power of the mind; he reinterpreted hysterical manifestations as the work not of a wayward womb or a neurological lesion, but of a frenetic mind driven by an unsatisfied libidinal charge. As the womb in the old physiology of hysteria migrated from place to place within the body of the victim, the hysterical mind, in Freud's theory, affected the body by discharging energy in various somatic locations, creating symptoms that baffled organically oriented diagnosis (see David-Ménard; also Evans).

In the Freudian scheme, the mind and the body join in a single affectional system. Whereas in Cartesian dualism, the ego becomes the boss of the worker body, rationally directing it this way and that, in Freudian psychology the mind becomes a dynamo whose energy can be only partly diverted for the purposes of the ego, rational and otherwise. The dynamo is above all a pleasure machine. Its pleasure-seeking charge prompts the ego to construct a "pleasure-body" through which it may be discharged (David-Ménard 4-5). The physical body may well be a willing partner, but the ego, unable to manage the size of the dynamo's demands, falters. The surplus energy proves overwhelming, and the ego turns away in horror, as a person turns away in disgust from a loathsome object. The residue of the unsatisfied or partially satisfied drive is what Freud calls the *unconscious*, a mental constituent that, with the ego, shares access to the body. As the ego attempts to carry out its conscious purposes in life, the unconscious exacts a toll, which becomes larger and larger as long as the affect remains unsatisfied, eventually blocking purposeful action altogether.

The first great insight of psychoanalytic technique was that, if the affect cannot be discharged physically but can be talked through, it can thereby be satisfied (see Freud, *Five Lectures*, Lecture I). Hence the famous "talking cure," a phrase invented by the founding patient of psychoanalysis, the hysterical Anna O. Instead of a physical arena for pleasure, Freud learned that, in collaboration with the hysteric, he could construct a body of discourse through which the charge arising in the unconscious could be released. The physical body continued to play a role as well. Above all else, the early psychoanalyst was a medical man and the proof of his cure—the glory of Breuer and Freud's *Studies on Hysteria*—was the disappearance of the hysterical symptoms from the organic body of the patient. Anna O. mastered her hallucinations and dispensed with her nervous cough; she left her invalid's bed and eventually became a successful social worker and a leader in the Austrian feminist movement.

The mind-body distinction, though weakened by psychoanalysis, therefore remained crucial. What was new was the discursiveness introduced by Freud. The symptoms of the hysteric—the loss of voice, the nervous cough, the inability to walk, the pain in the abdomen, the tic and the grimace—have meanings that elude explanations based upon the organic body constructed by the positivism of modern science just as surely as they escape the conscious control of the hysteric. Freud's concept of repression coupled with his topography of drives and inhibitions provides the missing link. In a famous letter of 1897 to his friend Wilhelm Fliess, Freud writes, "In the same manner as we turn away our sense organ (the head and the nose) in disgust, the preconscious and the sense of consciousness [of the hysteric] turn away from the memory. This is *repression*" (*Letters to Fliess* 280). Because the memory "stinks," as Freud says, the ego attempts to bury it while simultaneously averting attention from it. The analogy works. If you cannot see what you are trying to bury, you cannot do an adequate job. No wonder, then, that what is repressed returns, haunting the body. The voice, the legs, the digestive system, finally even the sense organs themselves give way, as the hysteric suffers visual, aural, and olfactory hallucinations in the advanced stages of the illness—sights, sounds, and smells which represent the inadequately buried memory, but which the beleaguered ego cannot interpret as such because of its insistence on turning away.

Enter the psychoanalyst, whose work becomes a kind of "archaeology," "clearing away the pathogenic psychical material layer by layer," as if "excavating a buried city" (Breuer and Freud 139). The physical symptom is exposed as "a memory-symbol of the operation of certain (traumatic) impressions and experiences . . . a substitute . . . for the reactivation of those traumatic experiences by association" (Freud, *Dora* 149). The state of the body thus represents an unarticulated or unspeakable state of mind that the consciousness refuses to acknowledge. Desires like Elisabeth von R.'s unseemly attraction to her brother-in-law at the time of her sister's death or Dora's homosexual longing for her father's mistress, a desire coupled with an incestuous wish to possess the father, haunt the hysterical soul and accumulate new associations. The intensity of the repressed desire grows; what was a single edifice becomes a buried city that ultimately protrudes into the life of the hysterical body. By the time it shows as a symptom, it is "overdetermined," as Freud says, the product of multiple associations and links to experience. It speaks through the body, but it speaks in a symbolic idiom that escapes the understanding of the hysteric and her doctors.

The body of the hysteric, then, is eloquent, but the mind cannot interpret its meaning. The psychoanalyst who listens to the voice of the ego gets nowhere and must listen instead to the body. In the case of Elisabeth von R., Freud says, for example, that he made little progress in his analysis until "the painful legs" of his patient "began to 'join in the conversation'"; then he could "use such pains as a compass" to guide him (Breuer and Freud 148). As the patient tells her story, the analyst probes with questions, trying to create a new associative avenue or, in his words, "a new vein of ideas, the contents of which [he] gradually extract[s]" (Breuer and Freud 145). The movements and contortions caused by the leg pains let him know when he gets warm, there to probe the deeper.

In his early writings, Freud suggested that the extraction of the repressed material itself was enough to effect a cure. Later he realized that his success in curing hysterics lay not just in bringing into the light of consciousness the hidden layers of the repressed memory, but in creating a new kind of consciousness, an analytical outlook, an interpretive frame of mind built upon a linguistic base. The patient does not immediately arise to enlightenment but must be carefully led through the stages of resistance and transference. In the first stage (resistance), the patient attempts to keep the old habits of turning away intact, refusing to own the buried city revealed by the analyst; in the second stage (transference), the patient attempts to bring the analyst into the pantomime or fantasy that keeps the memory buried, casting the analyst into the role of father or lover, who can be embraced or rejected according to habits the ego has developed to keep the unwanted desires at bay. Once worked through, however, these stages yield to acceptance, and the analyst and patient join in a scene constructed partly of memory and partly of interpretation, a place that the mind and body find peaceable enough, for the toll of the unexpended charge has been paid.

The Hysterical Woman—and Man: Issues of Power

Freud's hysterical women turn away from a situation in which their fathers hold the central authority but are somehow inadequate in wielding their power. All of Freud's most famous cases of hysteria—Anna O., Elisabeth von R., and Dora—involve bright young women who, lacking a socially sanctioned outlet for their intelligence and energy, find themselves nursing sick fathers. Out of a sense of duty and a repressed reluctance to give up their independence to marriage, they flee the very possibility of sexual exchange, but are actively pursued by a masculinized unconscious, an unknown demon that overtakes their bodies and rules their lives. The psychoanalyst intervenes, identifies himself with the demon, and joins the hysteric in producing a discourse in which the demon discharges its power—and disappears. Freud teaches his patients not to turn away, but to look within themselves at the thing they loath. Again, though, this process is not a mere uncovering. They must reconstruct the demon and accept it as their own creation. What they behold in psychoanalysis is therefore not the thing itself, neither the original demon nor the abusive father, but the demon transfigured by adult memory, adult language, and the analytical process. Now instead of an awful parent, they face the father they have reconstructed with Freud, a father within the discourse of hysteria, a part of themselves that, though repulsive, can be known and thereby mastered.

The male neurotics Freud encountered share with the female hysterics an initial powerlessness in the face of their demons. All three of the major cases—the Wolf-Man, the Rat-Man, and Schreber—fall ill because of the father complex. Toward their fathers they feel a profound affection that alternates with an impulse verging on murderous. As the deep love for the parent seeks to overwhelm the conventional boundaries of filial attraction, drifting toward homosexual desire, the neurotic turns away and experiences an unspeakable hatred for the father. Of the male cases, though, only the Wolf-Man takes the typically hysterical path of retreat by converting his homosexual longings into somatic symptoms (manifested as "intestinal trouble"). The others take the royal road of obsessional neurosis. As Freud explains, "The language of an obsessional neurosis—the means by which it expresses its secret thoughts—is, as it were, only a dialect of the language of hysteria; but it is a dialect . . . more nearly related to the forms of expression adopted by our conscious thought than is the language of hysteria," which permits a "leap from a mental process to a somatic innervation" (*Three Case Histories* 17). Yet obsessional neurosis is no less difficult to understand; for, while it maintains the usual boundaries of psychic movement, expressing itself in word and deed rather than in somatic symptoms, the results confound ordinary language use and experience. Above all, the obsessive person seems to expend more energy on a particular thought or action than it deserves, so that "the affect [appears] too great for the occasion"; but psychoanalysis shows that the affect *is* justified, not by the current occasion or object, but by some other content *symbolized* by the occasion or object (*Three Case Histories* 35).

Thus, for the Rat-Man, *rat* becomes a "complex stimulus-word" whose tropic power knows few bounds; it represents money, his father, the penis, and even himself (*Three Case Histories* 68-72). His wishes and his fears crystallize around the symbol, enlarging its significance, so that upon the concept of ratness he constructs an entire mental world. Here he displaces his deepest feelings and wastes untold measures of psychic energy, crippling himself morally. In Freud's view, however, this crippling is not so much the effect as the cause of his illness. Unable to face the conflicts of his life—especially the decision of whether to marry the woman he loves against the wishes of his dead father—he turns away, wishing his lover were dead and his father (already dead) banished to the hell of forgetfulness. The cycle of suffering is completed when he punishes himself with guilt over these hateful wishes. The suicidal direction of the Rat-Man's thoughts—his obsessional fantasy of cutting his own throat as he shaves—represents his need to remove himself from conflict, to put an end to the frustrating cycle of love, hate, and self-loathing. Ironically, his neurosis proves too strong to be overwhelmed even by the suicidal impulse, as his throat-cutting fantasies are merely absorbed into his obsessional routines as another obstacle to action.

The Rat-Man, like Anna O., Elizabeth von R., Dora, and the Wolf-Man, suffers from repetition. A repressed event, bodily state, or disturbing vision continually asserts itself in the mental world of these tormented souls, distracting their attention and absorbing their energy. In a recent study of hysterical patterns in fictional narratives, Robert Newman writes, "In hysterical discourse . . . repetition becomes compulsive, demonic. And the need for alleviation on the part of hysterics . . . is indicated by the prevalence of the apocalyptic in their discourse and the discourse concerning them. Thus, the annihilation of order which hysterics and their discourse effect becomes also a revelation of the desire for self-annihilation, for a final transgression that will end all transgressions" (7).

Nowhere is this tendency clearer than in the case of the paranoid Dr. Schreber, a high official in the courts of Dresden, who, during a remission in 1903, published an autobiographical account of his terrifying psychosis. Freud's analysis of Schreber's book focuses again on the neurotic's ill-sorted relation with his father, which the patient projects first onto his doctor and then onto God. As a defense against repressed homosexual impulses, he experiences a vision of "a great catastrophe, of the end of the world" (*Three Case Histories* 171). Freud explains that such visions are common among both psychotics and neurotics: "The patient has withdrawn from the persons in his environment and from the external world generally the libidinal cathexis which he has hitherto directed on to them. Thus all things have become indifferent and irrelevant to him, and have to be explained by means of a secondary rationalization. . . . The end of the world is the projection of this internal catastrophe; for his subjective world has come to an end since he has withdrawn his love from it" (173).

In one sense, this apocalyptic trend of obsessional neurosis—a rhetorical scheme shared with environmentalist discourse—is merely an exaggerated version of the modernist temper, which, in the provocative formulation of Edward Said, despairs of generativity, the will and the ability to transmit a cultural and personal legacy to the next generation. The very notion of the modern implies the end of the old ways. If we have the passing of the world of the fathers, the death of God, and the end of the age, why not then the death of the self or the end of nature— "life as we know it," according to the current cliché?

Whether they project the end of the world or only the end of personal involvement in the world (the debility of the body), the discourses of obsessional neurosis and hysteria demonstrate an attitude that is ultimately aggressive and power-seeking. Though hysterics may turn violently away from what offends their deepest sensitivities, they also attempt to extend the range of their personal power, to take charge of a situation they have been unable to control. In this sense, their illness is a reaction against powerlessness; and, and in the Freudian scheme, neurosis in general is "a form of denial of certain weaknesses," as Phillip Rieff has said (Introduction to Freud, *Three Cases* 8). Though Freud took hysterical symptoms seriously, dismissing the charges of malingering that his colleagues often leveled against hysterics, he nevertheless recognized that illness represented a definite gain for these sufferers, a kind of freedom and even pleasure. Early on, in *Studies on*

Hysteria, he noted that hysterical patients seemed to take pride in the inability of their doctors to cure them. Moreover, they may have responded as well as they did to psychoanalysis because, for once, they commanded the attention of an intelligent and interested man.

Obsession and Objectivity
in Antienvironmentalist Arguments

Freud's neurotics anticipate ecological activists in many ways, most notably perhaps in their use of end-of-the-world scenarios, such as we find in the famous prologue to *Silent Spring*, entitled "A Fable for Tomorrow," and in the dire predictions of famine in Ehrlich's *Population Bomb*. In the rhetorical tradition established by Carson, environmentalist writers and speakers resort to what at first glance appear to be desperate measures in the hope of capturing the attention of an indifferent or uninformed audience (See Killingsworth and Palmer, *Ecospeak*; also "Millennial Ecology").

It is on this basis that Warren Brookes rejects the prophesies of an ecological holocaust as an unethical and disingenuous attempt to "stir up environmentalist hysteria" (Brookes A4). He wants to dismiss all predictions of environmental disaster as the empty fantasies of confused leftists. It's all in their minds, he argues, citing the failure of Paul Ehrlich's 1969 prophesy of world-wide famine to materialize in the 1980s and warning Al Gore and other "naive" politicians to beware of similar predictions about global warming.

With this dismissive attitude, Brookes brings to mind Freud's nineteenth-century colleagues who refused to accept the reality of hysterical illness because they could find no organic basis for it. And Brookes is not alone in taking this narrow view. It is a common attitude among "risk specialists" who, in distinguishing between "perceived risk" and "actual risk," attempt to bring a hard positivist outlook into the discourse of environmental politics. This perspective fails to distinguish between what the philosopher Neil Evernden calls "physical pollution" and "moral pollution" and refuses to countenance psychological and extrascientific significance (*Social Creation of Nature* 4-5). In the popular book *Technological Risk*, for example, H. W. Lewis concludes that a broad range of "sources of technological risk . . . pose almost imperceptible threats to most of us—the vast majority of us are doomed to die of far more mundane causes than strange chemicals, pesticides, or radiation" (332). While admitting that "the risk is there, sometimes lurking as a risk-in-waiting, with little threat now but the potential for real problems later," Lewis complains that most risks are exaggerated by a melodramatic media and a shady element out to make a fast fortune or satisfy some dark passion—like revenge or greed. He warns us to "beware of pseudo-experts with a mission and a grudge, especially if they are lawyers pretending to be scientists" (334-36). With his own impeccable credentials, Lewis wants to set strict limits on the discourse of environmental risk. He wants the discourse conditioned by the demands of empirical science and controlled by certified experts. He wants above all to leave aside moral questions and confine the definition of risk to that which kills or causes definite organic illnesses.

Scientists like Lewis, despite their commitment to public service, have little patience for politics. When they go public, they expect not so much to argue but rather to "educate." "In the end, there is no substitute for education," Lewis concludes (336). Turning away from melodramatic rhetoric and the open plying of interests that all politicians must face, he prefers to set himself at a cool distance from the heat of debate; he wants to remake the public forum into a classroom in which the scientist lectures and the newspeople, the lawyers, the politicians, and the general public politely take notes.

What's missing in Lewis's picture of the politics of risk is a clear perspective on the benefits that accrue to the scientific expert himself. It would be easy enough to show that, no matter how measured and objective Lewis's approach is, his argument still betrays the physicist's vested interests—evident, for example, in the preferred status he grants nuclear power throughout his book. To offer such a critique would be to suggest that scientific discourse, for all its objectivity, is still rhetorical, still geared to the service of special political interests.

To criticize Lewis's argument simply on the grounds of political interest, however, requires that we diminish the importance of objectivity as a value. (He may be right about nuclear power after all, despite his vested interest.) A more powerful critique—one which rescues objectivity, at least in a modified form, and which is more suggestive of the psychology of argument—is supplied by the feminist scientist and philosopher Evelyn Fox Keller. Keller defines objectivity as "the pursuit of a maximally authentic, and hence maximally reliable, understanding of the world around oneself" (116). There are, she says, two forms of objectivity—dynamic and static. Dynamic objectivity embraces a "form of knowledge that grants to the world around us its independent integrity but does so in a way that remains cognizant of, indeed relies on, our connectivity with that world" (117). It thus can include empathy with the objects of study. Philosophically, it approximates Hilary Putnam's concept of pragmatic or "internal" realism: "The mind and the world," says Putnam, "jointly make up the mind and the world" (1). According to this view, discourse plays a crucial role in mediating self and world, as does the body. By contrast, static objectivity pursues a knowledge that "begins with the severance of subject from object" (Keller 117). It ignores the existence of the self, treats discourse lightly as a transparent (and barely necessary) vehicle for scientific thought, and acts as if a pure separation of mind and body were possible or that emotion and other subjective responses could be eliminated entirely from the objective outlook of the scientist. Keller's thesis is that, far from eliminating emotion, static objectivity, like every other human response to the world, satisfies the emotions of a certain type of individual. Keller does not go as far as Ernest Schachtel, who claims that the static objectivity to which science all too typically aspires is based upon an obsessive-compulsive dogmatism, a pathological longing to control the world and protect the self from intense emotional involvements. In Freudian analysis, we recall, the obsessive neurotic "has withdrawn from the persons in his environment and from the external world generally the libidinal cathexis which he has hitherto directed on to them" so that "all things have become indifferent and irrelevant to him" (*Three Case Histories* 173). Keller stops short of such a severe diagnosis, but she does argue that "a science that advertises itself by the promise of a cool and objective remove from the object of study" tends to recruit—or unconsciously "selects for"—people who take "emotional comfort" in the prospect of objective distance (124).

Dynamic Objectivity
and Emotional Intensity in Silent Spring

The practitioner of static objectivity, who takes emotional comfort at a cool distance from the object of study, was precisely the kind of scientist who took offense at Rachel Carson's *Silent Spring* when it first appeared in 1962, launching a new era of environmental activism. Carson's presentation of the facts, said its scientific opponents, was "exaggerated" (Hynes 13), the same term Lewis uses in dismissing popular accounts of technological risk. "Exaggerated" appears to be a code word that implies more than mere rhetorical hyperbole. It suggests an unacceptable emotional involvement on the part of the author, a subjective engagement that offends the limits set by static objectivity. Drawing on the work of Keller, we might more accurately say that, from the perspective of static objectivity, "exaggeration" satisfies the emotions of the wrong psychological type, the kind of person who courts dynamic objectivity.

Along such lines, Patricia Hynes argues that Carson's willingness to write with a "feeling mind and thinking heart" accounts for both the success and the controversy surrounding *Silent Spring*. As Hynes notes (3-4), Murray Bookchin's book *Our Synthetic Environment* appeared in print six months before *Silent Spring* (under the pseudonym of Lewis Herber) and relayed much of the same information, but failed to elicit the overwhelming response that greeted Carson's book. Bookchin himself has attributed the difference to the power of Carson's "superb prose" to win popular attention. He had directed his book, he said, to "a small, specialized audience . . . the technically trained" while she sought a broader audience (qtd. in Hynes 3). "Ironically," Hynes notes, "of the two [authors] Carson was the technically trained scientist; and her work had more scientific rigor than his." Thus, the difference must be "more than one of writing style." In Hynes's view, "it is the difference between rational and passionate thinking. In [Bookchin's] work we are critical onlookers. . . . In [Carson's] work we enter into the problem" (3-4). In short, Carson had achieved Keller's ideal of dynamic objectivity.

One of the keys to the controversial nature of Carson's book, and its success, is its reliance upon apocalyptic rhetoric. As with the apocalyptic trend among Freud's neurotics, Carson's rhetoric arises out of disgust and a sense of powerlessness, which simultaneously refuses to be constrained any longer. In this mood, she begins her book with a bleak vision of the future that awaits a now prosperous nation. The famous prelude tells of "a town in the heart of America where all life seemed to live in harmony with its surroundings" until one day the town awakened to a "strange blight" that "silenced the rebirth of new life." The fairy-tale aura of the story dissipates abruptly when the narrator reveals that "no witchcraft, no enemy action" had precipitated the "mysterious maladies" that killed the animals and plants on which the community depended. Rather, "the people had done it themselves" (13-14).

This little tale, barely two pages long, produced an immediate and highly emotional response with its recrafting of the generic features of the fable for the purposes of sociopolitical exhortation (Killingsworth and Palmer, *Ecospeak*, 64-78). Placed on the defensive, the chemical industry tried to anticipate the public response by producing future visions of its own. The Monsanto Chemical Company, for example, issued "The Desolate Year," a story of famine and chaos unleashed upon a future world deprived of the benefits of agricultural chemicals (Graham 65). On the side of ecological activism, Carson's fable became a virtual template for the literature of protest and awakening. From Paul Ehrlich's *Population Bomb* of 1969 to Stephen Schneider's *Global Warming* of 1989, authors drew freely upon the model of Carson's success. And, despite Warren Brookes's attempt to associate the doomsday motif with "environmentalist hysteria," the enemies of environmentalism have regularly devised apocalyptic narratives of their own, from James Watt's vision of scarcity-driven chaos caused by irresponsible government interference in the late 1970s to Dixy Lee Ray's almost classically hysterical enumeration of fears over the possible return to a rural world that stinks of "horse manure, human sweat, and unwashed bodies."

What makes Carson different from the authors she has influenced on both sides of the environmental debate is the depth to which she explored the prophetic ethos. She was interested not just in actions and effects, in behavior and policy, but in character. She rejects the morality of "the chemical salesmen and the eager contractors" (69) and looks to the new science of ecology for hints about self-definition. Just as ecology searches for answers in whole systems, she responds to chemical pollution with the fullest possible resources of human character, producing a discourse that expresses emotions freely and calls upon her reader to respond in like manner. She openly appeals to the childlike fear of loss and danger implicit in "A Fable for Tomorrow" and her many references to witchcraft and sorcery. Her appeals are clearly directed to stir a new awareness in the minds of nonparticipants who have always left policy matters to the experts. Like the birds and plants eradicated by pesticides, Carson treats the ordinary citizen as a blameless victim. "Lulled by the soft sell and the hidden persuader, the average citizen is seldom aware of the deadly materials with which he is surrounding himself," she writes (157), reserving prophetic wrath for the scientists in the chemical industry, who should know better. As if it were not enough to condemn them for their "primitive" paradigm of science, Carson goes on to metaphorize their work as black magic, the ancient enemy of science, supposedly eradicated with the Enlightenment. Their chemicals are "brewed" like witch's broth (17) and sprayed across the earth as a "chemical death rain" (21), the polar opposite of Nature's nourishing waters (64). In opposition to the hypnotic advertising, benighted science, and crude engineering of the pesticide industry, Carson issues the cry for ordinary people to stir themselves to consciousness and action.

Even with her emphasis on character, though, Carson does not fall into the rhetorical stridency that suggests, with Wendell Berry, that "moral ignorance and weakness of character" are the only causes of environmental crisis, as if moral uprightness could do without technical support in restoring the environment (Berry 13). Carson does not deny the possibility of technical solutions to environmental problems. Her hope is rather to reunite the moral, the aesthetic, and the technical imagination of humankind. Her aim is to conquer the whole person for the service of nature, including human nature. Her appeals to the intellect—her ample research and documentation, not to mention her established authority as a science writer and educator—balance her appeals to emotion, with the result that *Silent Spring* effectively realizes Keller's ideal of dynamic objectivity, a concept that fits nicely with Carson's holistic approach to a reunified mind and body of nature.

Carson's holism recalls the psychoanalytical interpretation of hysteria. Freud learned from his hysterics that the mind and the world have a more dynamic relationship than positivistic medical science can allow. Organic symptoms may be the signs of psychic disturbances. Likewise, Carson suggests that, behind the measurable effects of chemical pollution upon the earth's body, there lies a wrong attitude toward the world, according to which the earth is seen not as the medium of life, but as an object to be controlled and conquered. "The 'control of nature,'" Carson argues, "is a phrase conceived in arrogance, born of the Neanderthal age of biology and philosophy, when it was supposed that nature exists for the convenience of man. . . . It is our alarming misfortune that so primitive a science has armed itself with the most modern and terrible weapons, and that in turning them against the insects it has also turned them against the earth" (261-62). Not only is such science morally contemptible in Carson's estimation, it is bad science as well. In one study she cites, for example, "investigators conducting an experiment with DDT on volunteer subjects dismissed the complaint of headache and 'pain in every bone' as 'obviously of psychoneurotic origin'" (173). Again we have the convenient division of mind and body that permits defensive practitioners of medical science to protect themselves against their powerlessness to understand or to cure by placing the blame on the ill, by saying, "It's all in your head."

And we have a parallel division, equally convenient, that separates human beings from nature. But Carson cuts off this line of retreat, reminding her readers that "man, however much he may like to pretend to the contrary, is part of nature" (169). In seeking to control that which he is a part of, "man" (the prefeminist form is appropriate) can succeed only in turning nature against himself. For him, the earth is already a dead thing. The alternative perspective brought forward in *Silent Spring* insists that the earth is a live body not unlike, and indeed intimately related to, the human body. Carson mourns over the "health of the landscape" (69), the "scars of dead vegetation" (70), the "weeping appearance" of trees (71). While abandoning scientific strictures against anthropomorphism, this alternative view, Carson claims, can be reconciled with science—not the "Neanderthal" science of control as practiced by researchers and engineers in the chemical industry, but rather the holism of the new ecology, which Carson introduced to a popular readership for the first time in *Silent Spring*. Seen from this perspective, "The phrase 'health of the environment' is not [merely] a literary convention. It has a real biological meaning, because the surface of the earth is truly a living organism" (Dubos 27).

The Earthly Unconscious

If, as holists like Carson suggest, the earth has a body, a body continuous with the human body, then (remembering the model of hysteria) we should pause to qualify the notion that human consciousness is the mind of the earth. In its simplest form, this concept represents no real advance over the Cartesian outlook on the ego's relation to the rest of creation—an outlook explicit in the conservative reaction to *Silent Spring* and in the concept of static objectivity, in which the human mind maintains sovereignty over the body and the material world. A cosmology that separates human consciousness from the material body of the earth could still support arguments that charge Carson and the holistic camp with confusing their own outsider ethos with the condition of the earth. Out of their own powerlessness, the argument would run, they project ill health onto the body of the earth when in fact there is little or nothing to worry about. It's all in their hysterical minds.

But Carson's dynamic view of the human relation to the earth will countenance no such separation. For her, the earth itself appears as a living being with a consciousness and a will. All of creation is subject to "nature's control," as she puts it, "that relentlessly pressing force by which nature controls her own" (219, 220). According to the cosmology of *Silent Spring*, then, the minds and bodies of human beings are continuous with the mind and body of nature. To separate any of the components is a prelude to violence against the earth and ultimately against oneself.

Following this analogy, we can say that the earth itself has grown hysterical under the abuses of technological man. In the "body" of the earth, organic symptoms present themselves that have not been accounted for (or predicted) in the standard systems of explanation. If the mind of technological man is understood as the consciousness, the ego of earthly life, then the "mind" of the earth appears as the great unconscious, the unknown reserve of information and power which can neither be fully comprehended nor totally mastered by human science—the "it" (id). Thus, in a recent exploration of the psychological implications of environmentalism, Theodore Roszak can lament modern culture's repression of the "ecological unconscious" (13-14, 301-305).

In seeking to understand what the earth is "saying," Carson, like Freud before her, left aside the old Cartesianism and came to see the mind and the body as nodes in an overall energy system driven by both conscious and unconscious forces. Freud drew upon geographical and archaeological metaphors in his attempt to map the discourse of hysteria, turning the body-mind-language system into a landscape to be surveyed by the analyst. Carson reverses the metaphor, projecting human characteristics upon the landscape—the scarred vegetation and weeping trees—in an attempt to win back wayward human sympathies. She then reverses the field of her metaphor again, describing the body in terms normally reserved for the earth. "There is also an ecology of the world within our bodies," she explains, and this inward ecology is deeply connected to the world outside our bodies through the cycles of energy exchange (170-86). She thus creates a dynamic interplay between the two terms of the metaphor—the earth and the human body.

The symptoms of illness in this body, the signs of pollution and misuse, are neglected or explained away by the object of Carson's critique—"Neanderthal" science, an approach to the world that may well be founded upon an unconscious wish to control by overwhelming, overpowering, and subduing the body. Now a mainstay of ecofeminism, this critique was once again anticipated by Freud in his darker moments. In *Civilization and Its Discontents*, for example, he writes, "Man has, as it were, become a kind of prosthetic God. When he puts on all his auxiliary organs"—when he arms himself with his various tools and extensions—"he is truly magnificent," but "those organs have not grown on to him and they still give him trouble at times"; indeed "we cannot remove all suffering," for "a piece of unconquerable nature may lie behind" (33, 39).

The traces of the bad fit between man and his own technological creation appear as symptoms in the earth's body, the signs that something is wrong: There are fewer birds singing in the Spring after the fields have been sprayed with pesticides. The technological ego denies the trouble, rationalizing it as a risk worth taking. But the ecological ego represented in Carson's work, which identifies the human body with that of the earth, experiences pollution and death in nature as a form of pain. The cry of pain emanating from *Silent Spring* distinguishes it from the more familiar political anger represented in writers like Murray Bookchin. The cry of pain is what is most controversial and most disturbing about *Silent Spring*. It says to technological man, your chemicals are not helping me; they are killing me, depriving me of what I love most in life. Carson's ecological activism—much like the ecofeminist movement that springs from Carson's legacy—confronts the technological ego with the "piece of unconquerable nature" that the prosthetic god would sooner forget. Repeated again and again in successive environmental catastrophes and in the environmentalist outcry that accompanies them, the cry of pain signals the return of the repressed, the earthly unconscious.

Accounting for Otherness
in Political Practice and Rhetorical Analysis

"Psycho-analysis," says Jacques Lacan "is neither a *Weltanschauung*, nor a philosophy that claims to provide the key to the universe. It is governed by a particular aim, which is historically defined by the elaboration of the notion of the subject" (77). In one sense, the same is true of modern environmentalism, which, inspired by the work of Rachel Carson, redefines the boundaries of the modern Western ego. It attempts to reintegrate the human mind with the natural body. And it expands the appeals of scientific rhetoric to include not only a broad "general audience," but also a broader conception of the human being as a creature of thoughtful feeling. This reformed identity serves as an alternative to the disembodied Cartesian intellect or the "prosthetic God" so proud of his meager knowledge and so dependent upon his technical devices that he loses track of all that he has repressed, only to find it returning to haunt him, first in the form of a vague discontent (Freud) and then in the form of environmental pollution (Carson).

In another sense, though, it is not environmental activism per se but rather rhetorical analysis of environmental discourse that shares with psychoanalysis an interest in *elaborating* the notion of the subject. Like any political position, environmentalism seeks to restrict access to certain subject positions just as surely as it opens access to others. While granting the beauty and challenge of Carson's accomplishment, then, we must on final analysis admit that there remains a trace of unresolved hysteria in the rhetoric of *Silent Spring*, which, if left unexamined, is liable to prove detrimental to the health of the emerging environmentalist ego. Behind Carson's impressive vision of a reunified human spirit lies a frightful wish—the desire for the dead body of the political opponent. While cultivating the sensibilities and courting the sympathy of the presumably neutral and poorly informed general public, *Silent Spring* makes no effort to rehabilitate or convert the other side. Rather, it makes war upon the chemical industry and its dependents.

Here, then, is a more disturbing legacy of the discourse of environmentalist hysteria: The apocalyptic prophets who warn of the ultimate environmental disaster—Carson's silent spring, Ehrlich's population explosion, Schneider's greenhouse century—if they are considered politically, seem to stand at the opposite end of the spectrum from risk specialists who tell us not to worry, that the benefits of technology far outweigh the risks, that risk is more a matter of perception than a thing of reality. Considered psychologically, however, the reassuring expert who demands silence in the audience and the impassioned environmentalist who calls for the passing of the "Neanderthal" scientist (an extinct life form) share a fundamental trait—the desire for the relief of tension that assumes the form of a death wish.

In this desire, both sides bring to mind the beleaguered hysterics described in classical psychoanalysis. Just as Freud's famous neurotics built elaborate defense mechanisms and projected end-of-the-world scenarios out of their need to escape the pain of the present, so the risk apologists and millennial ecologists seem to imagine a world beyond conflict, a world without politics. The pressure to overcome conflict and to negate difference thus drives a reactionary rhetoric that threatens to undermine an ostensible commitment to "make the world a better place."

Though such rhetoric meets well the need to build and support communities of advocacy, it fails to meet the continuing need for dialogue, deliberation, and consensus-building—the need to keep the other in the foreground and to adjust one's position accordingly. Rhetorical analysis, therefore, may illuminate the workings of each position in relation to its other, but must finally stop short of advocacy, just as psychoanalysis produced a discourse large enough to accommodate the voice of the hysteric, but left the way open for feminism to take up the hysteric's cause (see Evans). Freud's willingness to engage the hysterical other, in Lacan's shrewd judgment, prevented (or "saved") him from becoming "a perfect impassioned idealist" (Lacan 28). Likewise for the rhetorical analyst, the path to idealism is ever blocked by the presence of the political opponent, who demands to be given voice and engaged.

Notes

1. In addition to the works of Killingsworth and Palmer on rhetoric and environmental politics, there are essays and articles by Socolow, Oravec, Killingsworth, Miller, Peterson, Killingsworth and Steffens, Throgmorton, and Lange, as well as the papers published in Proceedings of the 1991 Conference on the Discourse of Environmental Advocacy (edited by Oravec and Cantrill). Forthcoming works include collections of essays by Oravec and Cantrill and by Stuart Brown and Carl Herndl. A fast-growing literature on media and the environment is developing in the communications field, a good foothold for which is offered in the collection of articles by LaMay and Dennis. The related literature on risk communication has grown large very quickly in the last ten years but is beset by difficulties, not the least of which is the problem of defining *risk*. Instructive in this regard are Krimsky and Plough; also Kasperson and Stallen. The study of nature writing is a bit more fully developed than the rhetorical criticism and the work on risk communication, but not much. Work in this area ranges from the impressionistic survey by Brooks to the relatively sophisticated criticism of Hynes and Slovic. The historical studies of both Merchant and Berman, the philosophical works of Evernden and Oelschlaeger, and the essays of the biologist Botkin all take a strong interest in discourse. Luhmann's *Ecological Communication* represents the bravest attempt thus far to theorize the concept of the environment in relation to discourse. His choice of general systems theory as his base of operations leaves something to be desired, however, especially for those of us skeptical about the relevance of neopositivism to the study of discourse.

2. Our reading of the discourse on hysteria owes most to three outstanding critical studies: Monique David-Ménard's *Hysteria from Freud to Lacan: Body and Language in Psychoanalysis* (1989), Martha Noel Evans's *Fits and Starts: A Genealogy of Hysteria in Modern France* (1991), and Hannah S. Decker's *Freud, Dora, and Vienna 1900* (1991). David-Ménard and Evans draw heavily upon the work of Jacques Lacan, but, for us, the most important primary sources remain Breuer and Freud's *Studies on Hysteria*, the letters of Freud to Wilhelm Fliess, Freud's later case histories, especially the cases of Dora and Schreber, and Lectures I and II of Freud's *Five Lectures*. In the background of almost every sentence we write about Freud is the work of Peter Gay, whose historical studies renewed our interest in Freud and whose magisterial biography convinced us of the continuing relevance of Freudian thinking for our times.

3. Likewise in the case of the Wolf-Man, whose "intestinal trouble . . . represented the small trait of hysteria at the root of an obsessional neurosis," Freud says, "his bowel began, like a hysterically affected organ, to 'join in conversation'" (218).

4. We are indebted to Robert Newman for directing us to the case of Schreber as the most important instance of the connection between suicidal impulses and apocalyptic visions. In a turn of mind similar to Schreber's, the Rat-Man reinvents the relationship between his interior world and the external world of nature and society. Rather than following Schreber's path of depriving the world of value, though, the Rat-Man is inclined to "overestimate the effects of his hostile feelings upon the external world"; he finds his own emotions "overwhelming," but he reverses the direction of the affect. Instead of fearing that he will be destroyed by the world, he worries that he will destroy the world. Freud concludes that obsessional neurotics "need the help of the possibility of death chiefly in order that it may act as a solution of conflicts they have left unresolved. Their essential characteristic is that they are incapable of coming to a decision . . .; they endeavor to postpone every decision, and . . . choose as their model the old German courts of justice, in which the suits were usually brought to an end, before judgement had been given, by the death of the parties to the dispute. Thus in every conflict which enters their lives they are on the look out for the death of some one who is of importance to them" (*Three Case Histories* 91).

5. Not that Freud himself liked hysterics. Nor was he immune to impatience toward his hysterical patients. In the Dora case in particular, he submitted to the temptation to let his interest in science overwhelm his responsibility as a therapist. He rushed his interpretation, forcing his shocking revelations upon his young patient, and subsequently botched the transference. Dora suspected all along that Freud was merely the tool of her manipulative father, who insisted on her treatment and begged Freud to convince her of the absurdity of her fantasies; so, when Dora saw that Freud was using her case to further the interests of his own science, thereby reenacting her father's tendency to use her as a means of fulfilling his own passions, she bolted. See Decker; also Gay.

6. On Watt, see Killingsworth and Palmer, *Ecospeak*, 36-40; for Ray's views, see her *Trashing* the Planet 14-18. Besides Brookes, a number of antienvironmentalist commentators have associated the apocalyptic

fervor of the movement with its lack of trustworthiness. See, for example, Ronald Bailey's recent book. A fuller treatment appears in Killingsworth and Palmer, "Millennial Ecology."

7. This concept, which is implicit in the work of cultural historian Thomas Berry, is made explicit in the work of the physicist and New Age philosopher Brian Swimme. See Berry's *The Dream of the Earth* and Swimme's *The Universe Is a Green Dragon*. The latter is a dialogue between the author and a figure of the wise man based upon Thomas Berry.

8. While taking Freud's id as his starting point, however, Roszak ultimately leans toward Jungianism, arguing, "Of the theoretical apparatus we inherit from mainstream modern psychology, Jung's often elusive and always controversial notion of a collective unconscious may prove to be the most serviceable in the creation of an ecopsychology" (301-302). Our position is that neither the Freudian nor the Jungian concept of the unconscious can be directly applied as an explanatory theory of the human relation to the rest of nature. But, while neither is "serviceable" in quite this way, both offer highly suggestive models for conceiving of what is wrong with the modernist view of human interaction with the earth. The great advantage of Freud, we think, is his emphasis on the unconscious as the other, the thing, the "it." Jung's collective unconscious seems tamer by comparison, too "human," not altogether unlike the great cultural inheritance theorized by traditional humanism. Freud's theory is also superior in its emphasis on discursive formations, which in Jung's mysticism are essentialized and reified in ways that can only strike the post-scientific reader as naive in the extreme.

9. In his later years, growing frustrated in his efforts to comprehend the psychology of woman, Freud again resorted to geographical metaphors. In a 1928 letter to Ernest Jones, he admitted that "everything we know of feminine *early development* appears to me unsatisfactory and uncertain" and that, moreover, "the sexual life of the adult woman" remains for psychoanalysis "a *dark continent*" (qtd. in Gay 501). The (unconscious?) reference to Africa and the failure of European colonialism—the dark continent that would not yield to light—may suggest to the feminist critic the sexual imperialism of Freudian theory—and its self-admitted failure.

10. As Keller vividly shows, "In the effort to 'master' nature, to 'storm her strongholds and castles,' science can come to sound like a battlefield. . . . Problems, for many scientists, are to be 'attacked,' 'conquered,' or 'licked'" (123).

11. As Gay shows, Freud himself was suffering from cancer of the mouth and struggling with an ill-fitting prosthetic device when he wrote this famous passage. It is a tragically ironic conincidence that Carson also produced her most prophetic environmentalist work in the last years of her life, after a lump was discovered in her breast, the first signs of the cancer that killed her.

12. Three authors we have already cited are key figures in ecofeminism—Merchant, Keller, and Hynes. See also the collections of essays by Plant and by Diamond and Orenstein and the special issue of *Hypatia* edited by Warren. The essay by Bullis represents a starting point for a critical discussion of the characteristic discourses of ecofeminism.

Works Cited

Bailey, Ronald. *Eco-Scam: The False Prophets of Ecological Apocalypse*. New York: St. Martin's, 1993.

Berry, Thomas. *The Dream of the Earth*. San Francisco: Sierra Club, 1988.

Berry, Wendell. *Unsettling of America*. San Francisco: Sierra Club, 1988.

[Bookchin, Murray]. Herber, Lewis (pseudo). *Our Synthetic Environment.* New York: Knopf, 1962.

Botkin, Daniel B. *Discordant Harmonies: A New Ecology for the Twenty-First Century*. New York: Oxford UP, 1990.

Breuer, Josef, and Sigmund Freud. *Studies on Hysteria*. Trans. And ed. James Strachey. New York: Basic, 1957.

Brookes, Warren T. "Stirring Up Environmentalist Hysteria." *Memphis Commercial-Appeal 17* Sept. 1989: A4.

Brooks, Paul. *Speaking for Nature: How Literary Naturalists from Henry Thoreau to Rachel Carson Have Shaped America*. San Francisco: Sierra Club, 1980.

Bullis, Connie. "Retalking Environmental Discourses from Feminist Perspectives: The Radical Potential of Ecofeminism." In Oravec and Cantrill. 346-59.

Carson, Rachel. *Silent Spring*. New York: Fawcett, 1962.

David-Ménard, Monique. *Hysteria from Freud to Lacan: Body and Language in Psychoanalysis*. Trans. Catherine Porter. Foreword by Ned Lukacher. Ithaca: Cornell UP, 1989.

Decker, Hannah. *Freud, Dora, and Vienna 1900*. New York: Free Press, 1991.

Diamond, Irene, and Gloria Feman Orenstein, eds. *Reweaving the World: The Emergence of Ecofeminism*. San Francisco: Sierra Club, 1990.

Dubos, René. "The Limits of Adaptability." *The Environmental Handbook*. Ed. Garrett De Bell. New York: Ballantine, 1970. 27-30.

Ehrlich, Paul R. *The Population Bomb*. San Francisco: Sierra Club, 1969.

Evans, Martha Noel. *Fits and Starts: A Genealogy of Hysteria in Modern France*. Ithaca: Cornell UP, 1991.

Evernden, Neil. *The Natural Alien: Humankind and Environment*. Toronto: U of Toronto P, 1985.

Evernden, Neil. *The Social Creation of Nature*. Baltimore: Johns Hopkins UP, 1992.

Foucault, Michel. *The History of Sexuality: Volume 1, an Introduction*. Trans. Robert Hurley. New York: Pantheon, 1978.

Freud, Sigmund. "The Case of the Wolf-Man." *The Wolf-Man by the Wolf-Man*. Ed. Muriel Gardiner. 1971. New York: Hill and Wang, 1991. 153-262.

Freud, Sigmund. *Civilization and Its Discontents*. Trans. and ed. James Strachey. New York: Norton, 1962.

Freud, Sigmund. *The Complete Letters of Sigmund Freud to Wilhelm Fliess, 1887-1904*. Trans. and ed. Jeffrey M. Masson. Cambridge: Harvard UP, 1985.

Freud, Sigmund. *Dora: An Analysis of a Case of Hysteria*. Ed. Philip Rieff. New York: Collier Macmillan, 1963.

Freud, Sigmund. *Five Lectures on Psycho-Analysis*. Trans. and ed. James Strachey. New York: Norton, 1977.

Freud, Sigmund. *Three Case Histories*. Ed. Philip Rieff. New York: Collier Macmillan, 1963.

Gay, Peter. *Freud: A Life for Our Time*. New York: Anchor, 1988.

Gilliam, Ann, ed. *Voices for the Earth: A Treasury of the Sierra Club Bulletin*. San Francisco: Sierra Club, 1979.

Graham, Frank, Jr. *Since Silent Spring*. Boston: Houghton, 1970.

Hynes, H. Patricia. *The Recurring Silent Spring*. New York: Pergamon, 1989.

Jung, C. G. *The Undiscovered Self*. Trans. R. F. C. Hull. Boston: Little, Brown, 1958.

Kasperson, Roger E. and Pieter Jan M. Stallen. "Risk Communication: The Evolution of Attempts." *Communicating Risks to the Public: International Perspectives*. Ed. Kasperson and Stallen. Dordrecht: Kluwer, 1991. 1-12.

Keller, Evelyn Fox. *Reflections on Gender and Science*. New Haven: Yale UP, 1985.

Killingsworth, M. Jimmie. "Can an English Teacher Contribute to the Energy Debate?" *College English* 43 (1981): 581-86.

Killingsworth, M. Jimmie, and Dean Steffens. "Effectiveness in the Environmental Impact Statement: A Study in Public Rhetoric." *Written Communication* 6 (1989): 155-80.

Killingsworth, M. Jimmie, and Jacqueline S. Palmer. *Ecospeak: Rhetoric and Environmental Politics*. Carbondale: Southern Illinois UP, 1992.

Killingsworth, M. Jimmie, and Jacqueline S. Palmer. "How to Save the World: The Greening of Instrumental Discourse." *Written Communication* 9 (1992): 385-403.

Killingsworth, M. Jimmie, and Jacqueline S. Palmer. "Millennial Ecology: The Apocalyptic Narrative from *Silent Spring* to Global Warming." *Green Culture: Environmental Rhetoric in Contemporary America*. Ed. Carl G. Herndl and Stuart C. Brown. Madison: U of Wisconsin P, forthcoming.

Krimsky, Sheldon, and Alonzo Plough. *Environmental Hazards: Communicating Risks as a Social Process*. Dover, MA: Auburn House, 1988.

Lacan, Jacques. *The Four Fundamental Concepts of Psycho-Analysis*. Ed. Jacques-Alain Miller. Trans. Alan Sheridan. New York: Norton, 1978.

LaMay, Craig L. and Everette E. Dennis, eds. *Media and the Environment*. Washington, DC: Island Press, 1991.

Lange, Jonathan I. "Refusal to Compromise: The Case of Earth First!" *Western Journal of Speech Communication* 54 (1990): 473-94.

Leopold, Aldo. *A Sand County Almanac*. New York: Ballantine, 1966.

Levin, Murray B. *Political Hysteria in America: The Democratic Capacity for Repression*. New York: Basic, 1971.

Lewis, H. W. *Technological Risk*. New York: Norton, 1990.

Luhmann, Niklas. *Ecological Communication*. Chicago: U of Chicago P, 1989.

Merchant, Carolyn. *The Death of Nature: Women, Ecology, and the Scientific Revolution*. San Francisco: Harper and Row, 1980.

_____. *Ecological Revolutions: Nature, Gender, and Science in New England*. Chapel Hill: U of North Carolina P, 1989.

Miller, Carolyn R. "Genre as Social Action." *Quarterly Journal of Speech 70* (1984): 151-67.

Newman, Robert D. *Transgressions of Reading: Narrative Engagement as Exile and Return.* Durham: Duke UP, 1993.

Oelschlaeger, Max. *The Idea of Wilderness: From Prehistory to the Age of Ecology.* New Haven: Yale UP, 1991.

Oravec, Christine. "Conservationism vs. Preservationism: The Public Interest in the Hetch-Hetchy Controversy." *Quarterly Journal of Speech* 70 (1984): 444-58.

Oravec, Christine. "The Evolutionary Sublime and the Essay of Natural History." *Communication Monographs* 49 (1982): 215-28.

Oravec, Christine. "John Muir, Yosemite, and the Sublime Response: A Study in the Rhetoric of Preservationism." *Quarterly Journal of Speech* 67 (1981): 245-58.

Oravec, Christine L., and James G. Cantrill, eds. *The Conference on the Discourse of Environmental Advocacy.* Salt Lake City: University of Utah Humanities Center, 1992.

Peterson, Tarla Rai. "The Rhetorical Construction of Institutional Authority in a Senate Subcommittee Hearing on Wilderness Legislation." *Western Journal of Speech Communication* 52 (1988): 259-76.

Peterson, Tarla Rai. "The Will to Conservation: A Burkeian Analysis of Dust Bowl Rhetoric and American Farming Motives." *The Southern Speech Communication Journal* 52 (1986): 1-21.

Plant, Judith, ed. *Healing the Wounds: The Promise of Ecofeminism.* Philadelphia: New Society, 1989.

Porter, James E. "Developing a Postmodern Ethics of Rhetoric and Composition." *Defining the New Rhetorics.* Ed. Theresa Enos and Stuart C. Brown. Newbury Park, CA: Sage, 1993. 207-26.

Putnam, Hilary. *The Many Faces of Realism.* LaSalle, IL: Open Court, 1987.

Ray, Dixy Lee (with Lou Guzzo). *Trashing the Planet.* Washington, DC: Regnery Gateway, 1990.

Roszak, Theodore. *The Voice of the Earth: An Exploration of Ecopsychology.* New York: Simon and Schuster, 1992.

Said, Edward W. *The World, the Text, and the Critic.* Cambridge: Harvard UP, 1983.

Sales, Kirkpatrick. *The Green Revolution: The American Environmental Movement 1962-1992.* New York: Hill and Wang, 1993.

Schachtel, Ernest G. *Metamorphosis: On the Development of Affect Perception, Attention, and Memory.* New York: Basic, 1959.

Schneider, Stephen H. *Global Warming: Are We Entering the Greenhouse Century?* San Francisco: Sierra Club, 1989.

Slovic, Scott. *Seeking Awareness in American Nature Writing: Henry David Thoreau, Annie Dillard, Edward Abbey, Wendell Berry, Barry Lopez.* Salt Lake City: U of Utah P, 1992.

Socolow, Robert H. "Failures of Discourse: Obstacles to the Integration of Environmental Values into Natural Resource Policy." *When Values Conflict: Essays on Environmental Analysis, Discourse, and Decision.* Ed. Laurence H. Tribe, Corinne S. Schelling, and John Voss. Cambridge, MA: Ballinger, 1976. 1-33.

Swimme, Brian. *The Universe Is a Green Dragon: A Cosmic Creation Story.* Santa Fe: Bear, 1983.

Throgmorton, James A. "Passion, Reason, and Power: The Rhetorics of Electric Power Planning in Chicago." *Journal of Architechtural Planning and Research* 7 (1990): 330-50.

Throgmorton, James A. "The Rhetorics of Policy Analysis." *Policy Sciences* 24 (1991): 153-79.

Veith, Ilza. *Hysteria: The History of a Disease.* Chicago: U of Chicago P, 1965.

Warren, Karen, ed. Special Issue on Ecofeminism. *Hypatia 6* (1991).

Perils of a Modern Cassandra:
Rhetorical Aspects of Public Indifference
to the Population Explosion
by Craig Waddell

In *De Oratore*, Cicero claims that "no man can be an orator complete in all points of merit, who has not attained a knowledge of all important subjects and arts" (Cicero, 1942: I.vi.20). More recently, however, C. P. Snow has argued that "the intellectual life of the whole of western society is increasingly being split into two polar groups. . . . Literary intellectuals at one pole—at the other scientists" (Snow, 1964: 3-4). Michael Halloran has argued that, in an age where information increases exponentially, the ideal of the Renaissance man or woman, and hence, of the polymath-orator, is impossible to achieve (Halloran, 1976: 238; see also Snow, 1964: 61).

Unfortunately, our ability to address successfully many of the most pressing problems we face today—problems such as global warming, ozone depletion, habitat destruction, and hazardous-waste disposal—requires sophistication in both scientific and humanistic disciplines. A few intrepid scientists have attempted to bridge the two cultures by venturing out of the field or laboratory and into the public-policy arena. However, many of these scientists have been frustrated in their attempts to arouse public or governmental support for their concerns. In 1988, Paul Ehrlich and John Holdren edited a collection of sixteen papers from the Cassandra Conference.[1] In their introduction to this volume, Ehrlich and Holdren claim that like Cassandra, whose prophecies were never believed, scientists who attempt to warn their governments and fellow citizens about the hazards of the human predicament "often remain unheard or unheeded by those whose decisions are charting the course of the United States and the rest of the world" (Ehrlich and Holdren, 1988: x).

Plato's Gorgias reminds us that experts have long been frustrated in their attempts to persuade apparently inexorable audiences. In defending his art against the challenge presented by Socrates, Gorgias suggests a solution to this problem:

On many occasions in the past, in the company of my brother and other physicians, I have made calls on patients who were unwilling to take their medicine or submit to an operation or a cautery; and though their doctor could not persuade them, I did so, by no other art than rhetoric. (Plato, 1952: 456)[2]

If they are to be effective public-policy advocates, contemporary scientists must master this same art. In 1976, Philip Wander described two forms of rhetoric of science. One concerns itself "with the efforts made by scientists to persuade one another"; the other concerns itself with the place of science in the deliberation of public policy (Wander, 1976: 226-227). A significant body of literature has since developed with respect to the former, but much less has been done to enhance our understanding of the latter (see Harris, 1991).[3] Hence, I hope to broaden the discussion of the rhetoric of science policy[4] by examining the rhetoric of Paul Ehrlich's *The Population Bomb* (Ehrlich, 1968).

Paul Ehrlich is Bing Professor of Population Studies at Stanford University and a member of the National Academy of Sciences. He is the author of several hundred scientific papers and the author, co-author, or editor of more than twenty books. In 1989 Ehrlich received the first Science in the Service of Humankind prize, awarded by the American Association for the Advancement of Science; and in 1990 he shared with Harvard entomologist E. O. Wilson the Crafoord Prize, a $240,000 award administered by the Royal Swedish Academy of Sciences to recognize areas not covered by the Nobel Prizes. Ehrlich is also the co-founder (in 1968) and honorary president of Zero Population Growth (ZPG), an organization that works to achieve a sustainable balance between population, resources, and the environment.

In 1968 Ehrlich published *The Population Bomb*,[5] in which—echoing Thomas Malthus—he argued that if the human population were not quickly brought under control by humane and rational means, the job would be done for us by war, pestilence, and famine (69ff.; 45ff.).[6] The book was revised in 1971, and by 1989 there were over 2 million copies in print. Nevertheless, in their 1990 book *The Population Explosion*, Paul and Anne Ehrlich contend that "Remarkably little has been accomplished in population control in the twenty years since *The Population Bomb* appeared" (Ehrlich and Ehrlich, 1990: 214). In fact, between the publication of *The Population Bomb* and that of *The Population Explosion*, the human population grew from 3.5 billion to 5.3 billion, an increase of over 50 percent in just twenty-two years (Ehrlich and Ehrlich, 1990: 9).[7] Ehrlich and Ehrlich go on to claim that "The alarm has been sounded repeatedly, but society has turned a deaf ear" (Ehrlich and Ehrlich, 1990: 10); that "many of the world's leaders and perhaps most of the world's people still don't believe that there are compelling reasons" to end population growth (Ehrlich and Ehrlich, 1990: 16); and that "One of the toughest things for a population biologist to reconcile is the contrast between his or her recognition that civilization is in imminent serious jeopardy and the modest level of concern that population issues generate among the public and even among elected officials" (Ehrlich and Ehrlich, 1990: 13).[8]

Ehrlich and Ehrlich suggest that a major reason for the lack of response to concerns raised in *The Population Bomb* and elsewhere "lies in the evolutionary history of our species," which they claim "has profoundly shaped every human being's general view of the world" (Ehrlich and Ehrlich, 1990: 186):

> Biological evolution has made us primarily "sight animals." Thirty million years ago, our ancestors were jumping around in trees. Judging the distance to the next branch by sight is much more efficient than doing it by smell or hearing. . . . Our perceptual systems only take in perhaps a billionth of the possible stimuli that are "out there," and they give emphasis to those detectable with the eyes. . . . [9]

> A second thing that our biological evolution did for our sensory systems was design them to respond strongly to "events": the charge of a lion, the snap of a breaking branch. . . . In order to make these important occurrences stand out, evolution also seems to have made our minds perceive the environmental backdrop as constant. [10] (Ehrlich and Ehrlich, 1990: 186)

Hence, Ehrlich and Ehrlich conclude that although slower changes such as climate alteration and population growth "are much greater threats to most people than stalking predators," we have evolved as a species that does not readily perceive such changes or the threats they represent (Ehrlich and Ehrlich, 1990: 187-189).[11]

To the extent that it is a factor at all, "the evolutionary history of our species" is part of the background against which Ehrlich and Ehrlich and other public-policy advocates must work. We cannot change evolutionary history, but provocative books can influence and have influenced public sentiment and public policy. American examples include *Common Sense, Uncle Tom's Cabin, The Jungle,* and *Silent Spring.*[12] Why, then, has *The Population Bomb* failed to have a similar influence? One reason, I think, lies in Ehrlich's rhetorical strategies.

In appealing to evolutionary constraints to explain "the modest level of concern" that population issues have generated, Ehrlich accepts no responsibility for the failure of his own rhetoric. As Aristotle says, "the function [of rhetoric] is not simply to succeed in persuading, but rather to discover the means of coming as near such success as the circumstances of each particular case allow" (Aristotle, 1954: 1355b10-11).[13] By his own admission, Ehrlich has failed to persuade the public; however, this failure is shaped less by the Darwinian factors to which he appeals than it is by the way in which he has constructed his audience and by the way in which this construction shapes his rhetoric.[14]

At the end of the first chapter of *The Population Bomb*, Ehrlich describes his audience and his rhetorical strategy:

> You will note that my discussion of man's environment has not dwelt on the themes that characterize the pleas of conservationists. . . . I've shed no tears here for the passenger pigeons, now extinct, or for the California condors, soon to join them. . . . Instead, I have concentrated on things that seem to bear most directly on man. The reason is simple. In spite of all the efforts of conservationists, all the propaganda, all the eloquent writing, all the beautiful pictures, the conservation battle is presently being lost. . . . for two powerful reasons. The first, of course, is that nothing "underdeveloped" can long stand in the face of the population explosion. The second is that most Americans clearly don't give a damn. They've never heard of the California condor and would shed no tears if it became extinct. Indeed, many

Americans would compete for the privilege of shooting the last one.[15] Our population consists of two groups; a comparatively small one dedicated to the preservation of beauty and wildlife, and a vastly larger one dedicated to the destruction of both (or at least apathetic toward it).[16] I am assuming that the first group is with me and that the second cannot be moved to action by an appeal to beauty, or a plea for mercy for what may well be our only living companions in a vast universe.[17] (65-66; 43-44)

This audience analysis shapes not only Ehrlich's discussion of the environmental effects of overpopulation, but his entire appeal for population control.

I suspect that Ehrlich, like fellow biologist and Darwinian Garrett Hardin, whom he cites, believes that "It is a mistake to think that we can control the breeding of mankind by an appeal to conscience" (Hardin, 1968: 1246).[18] Hardin bases this argument on the claim by Charles Galton Darwin (grandson of Charles Robert Darwin) that to the extent that such appeals were successful, "the variety *Homo contracipiens* would become extinct and would be replaced by the variety *Homo progenitivus*" (Darwin, 1960: 469). This position leads Hardin to reject "persuasion" and to "prefer the greater candor of the word coercion"; albeit a coercion that is "mutually agreed upon by the majority of the people affected" (Hardin, 1968: 1247). This same position may have inclined Ehrlich to avoid appealing to "a comparatively small [audience] dedicated to the preservation of beauty and wildlife" and to appeal, instead, to "a vastly larger [audience] dedicated to the destruction of both."

Whether or not Ehrlich arrives at his approach to his audience by way of the Darwinian arguments presented by Hardin and C. G. Darwin, his approach is problematic for at least five reasons. First, most of those who comprise an audience that "cannot be moved to action by an appeal to beauty, or a plea for mercy" are unlikely to read *The Population Bomb*. Second, if Ehrlich actually expects this audience to read his book, it is probably counterproductive for him to characterize its members as he has. Third, those in this audience who do read or otherwise learn about *The Population Bomb* are liable to use its arguments for their own racist and xenophobic ends; to some extent, this has already happened. In a footnote to his 1978 update of *The Population Bomb*, Ehrlich says that "The idea that blacks make a disproportionate contribution to population problems in the United States is 180 degrees from the truth. So is the notion that population control is a genocidal plot against blacks, but the idea is given credence by the racism of some advocates of population control" (223; see also 171-174). Fourth, Ehrlich simply indulges and makes no effort to reconstitute this audience; that is, he makes no effort to convert this audience from one dedicated or apathetic to the destruction of beauty and wildlife to one dedicated to the preservation of both (see Antczak, 1985: 8-10). Finally, by tailoring his argument to this audience, Ehrlich too often appeals to a lower rather than to a higher common denominator; thus, he risks alienating the more humanistic and ecologically oriented audience that might respond constructively to arguments about the need for population control.

In opposition to Ehrlich, I would define those who are "dedicated to the preservation of beauty and wildlife" and who *can* "be moved to action by an appeal to beauty, or a plea for mercy" as the appropriate rhetorical audience in this situation; that is, as the audience that consists of people who, as Lloyd Bitzer says, are "capable of being influenced by discourse and of being mediators of change" (Bitzer, 1968: 8).[19] In assuming that this audience is already with him, Ehrlich fails to distinguish between conviction, the intellectual acceptance of an idea, and persuasion, the commitment to act on the basis of our beliefs (see Perelman and Olbrechts-Tyteca, 1969: 26-27). Hence, he leaves this audience convinced but unmotivated.

Lloyd Bitzer contends that "Prior to the creation and presentation of discourse, there are three constituents of any rhetorical situation": the exigence ("an imperfection marked by urgency"), the audience, and the constraints ("persons, events, objects, and relations which are parts of the situation because they have the power to constrain decision and action needed to modify the exigence") (Bitzer, 1968: 6-8). In rejecting what he calls Bitzer's "Platonist *Weltanschauung*" (Vatz, 1973: 155), Richard Vatz suggests that exigences, like meanings, are not discovered in situations, but are created by rhetors (Vatz, 1973: 155-158). Vatz goes on to say that "If one accepts Bitzer's position . . . then we ascribe little responsibility to the rhetor with respect to what he has chosen to give salience. On the other hand if we view the communication of an event as a choice, interpretation, and translation, the rhetor's responsibility is of supreme concern" (Vatz, 1973: 158). Scott Consigny takes a middle ground between these two positions, arguing, in effect, that the exigence is *underdetermined* by the particularities of the situation:[20]

> Bitzer correctly construes the rhetorical situation as characterized by "particularities," but misconstrues the situation as being thereby determinate and determining. . . . Vatz correctly treats the rhetor as creative, but he fails to account for the real constraints on the rhetor's activities. The rhetor cannot create exigences arbitrarily, but must take into account the particularities of each situation in which he actively becomes engaged. (Consigny, 1974: 176)

Borrowing from all three of these arguments, I believe that—taking into account the particularities of the situation in which he or she becomes engaged—the rhetor constructs not only the exigence, but also the audience (e.g., those who would compete to kill the last California condor) and the constraints (e.g., the evolutionary history of a species); hence, the rhetor bears responsibility for all three constituents of the rhetorical situation.

As any political strategist would attest, if rhetors construct the wrong audiences for their discourse and then adapt their discourse to those audiences, they risk alienating the audiences that are most apt to respond favorably to more appropriate appeals. Appeals to reason, emotion, and character are most effective when they are consonant with one another and—with an important exception, which I will describe shortly—with the beliefs and values of the audience. For example, an astute politician would not employ xenophobic appeals in attempting to gain liberal support for the reduction of trade deficits; and an appeal to compassion is more effective when delivered by a compassionate rather than by an apparently callous speaker or writer. Ehrlich, however, fails to achieve such consonance, or at least he fails to achieve it with a more humanistic or ecologically oriented audience.

In indulging an audience that "cannot be moved to action by an appeal to beauty, or a plea for mercy" for other species, Ehrlich repeatedly appeals to fear rather than to compassion, even when attending to the plight of his own species. For example, in the first chapter of *The Population Bomb*, Ehrlich outlines the problem his book will address. He says that although he has understood the population explosion intellectually for a long time, he "came to understand it emotionally one stinking hot night in Delhi" when he visited the city with his wife and daughter (15; 1). He proceeds to offer the following description of "a crowded slum area" that he and his family passed through in their taxi:

> The streets seemed alive with people. People eating, people washing, people sleeping. People visiting, arguing, and screaming. People thrusting their hands through the taxi window, begging. People defecating and urinating. People clinging to the buses. People herding animals. People, people, people, people. As we moved slowly through the mob, hand horn squawking, the dust, noise, heat, and cooking fires gave the scene a hellish aspect. Would we ever get to our hotel? All three of us were, frankly, frightened. (15; 1)

Here, on the first page of his first chapter, Ehrlich has an opportunity to establish a theme of compassion for the masses of people who suffer most directly from the ravages of overpopulation. However, instead of focusing on the plight of the poor, he focuses on his own demophobic anxiety. This focus on those who are, for the time being, only indirectly affected by the most severe effects of the population explosion recurs elsewhere in the text. In chapter 4, for example, Ehrlich says that if the underdeveloped countries should "sink," those of us in the overdeveloped countries would "at the very least have to put up with the spectacle of their drowning and listen to their screams. . . . we will be treated to the sights and sounds of mass starvation on the evening news" (132; 128). He goes on to say that we would be unlikely "to get off with just our appetites spoiled and our consciences disturbed" since the people of these countries would be unlikely to just "starve gracefully, without rocking the boat" (133; 128). This focus on fear *of* rather than fear *for* the most oppressed peoples of the world might sway an audience that cannot be moved to action by a plea for mercy, but it is dissonant with the prevailing values of Ehrlich's rhetorical audience.

A second area in which Ehrlich's rhetoric is dissonant with the values of his rhetorical audience is in his support (sometimes tacit, sometimes explicit) for compulsory birth control. He makes his position on this clear from the outset. In the prologue, he says that "We must have population control at home, hopefully through a system of incentives and penalties, but by compulsion if voluntary methods fail" (11; xii).[21] After describing a proposed compulsory sterilization program in India for all men who were fathers of three or more children, Ehrlich raises concerns about the *logistics*, but not the *ethics*, of such a plan, arguing that "it would take 1,000 surgeons or parasurgeons operating eight hours a day, five days a week, a full eight years to sterilize the candidates who exist today" (86; 82). He later suggests that the United States should have volunteered logistical support for this program "in the form of helicopters, vehicles, and surgical instruments" (166; 151). He continues: "We should have sent doctors to aid in the program by setting up centers for paramedical personnel to do vasectomies. Coercion? Perhaps, but coercion in a good cause" (166; 151-152). He also suggests that compulsory sterilization might be enacted in the United States by "the addition of temporary sterilants to water supplies or staple food" (135; 130-131). He adds, however, that "thanks to the criminal inadequacy of biomedical research in this area," no such sterilants exist, and that even if we had them, "society would probably dissolve before sterilants were added to the water supply by the government" (131; 136).

Ehrlich goes on to justify this argument, which he admits "sounds very callous" (165; 151), by drawing an analogy between human population growth and cancer:

> We must shift our efforts from treatment of the symptoms to the cutting out of the cancer. The operation will demand many apparently brutal and heartless decisions. The pain will be intense. But the disease is so far advanced that only with radical surgery does the patient have a chance of survival. (166-167; 152)

Although any analogy between human beings and cancer is potentially offensive, such an analogy *could be* persuasive if presented by someone who consistently appeals to compassion and, in the process, develops a compassionate *ethos*, both of which Ehrlich fails to do.[22] Instead, he seems almost to welcome the prospect of what he calls a "death rate solution" to the population problem, and he presents three death-rate scenarios, of war, pestilence, and famine, respectively (69; 45). He closes the second scenario, in which the world's population has been decimated by Lassa fever, with a report on a fictional UN resolution: "The loss of nearly half of the world's children was an immeasurably profound tragedy. . . . *Nevertheless*, the opportunity to establish population stability for the next two generations must be grasped" (72, revised edition [my emphasis]). At the close of the final scenario, Ehrlich claims that "This scenario has considerably more appeal than the others, even though it presumes the death by starvation of perhaps as many as half a billion people" (80). In the revised edition, this number is increased to a billion people (77). From the perspective of the rhetorical audience, it seems incomprehensible that a scenario that presumes the starvation of half-a-billion to a billion people could be referred to as appealing.

There are other ways in which Ehrlich's appeals are dissonant with the values and beliefs of his rhetorical audience, such as his bio-evolutionary reductionism, sexism, and inappropriate humor. One example illustrates all three of these problems. In chapter 1, Ehrlich explains that in order to allow for the assimilation of a growing body of cultural information, human brains and, hence, human heads expanded. Since there were practical limits on the size of a woman's pelvis, human infants were born at a developmental stage at which their heads were still relatively small and, hence, at which they were still in need of a prolonged period of nurturance. This leads Ehrlich to make the following observations:

> How could the mother defend and care for her infant during its unusually long period of helplessness? She couldn't, unless Papa hung around. The girls are still working on that problem, but an essential step was to get rid of the short, well-defined breeding season characteristic of most mammals. . . . [and replace it with the] year-round sexuality of the human female. . . . (30-31; 13-14)

There seems to be no place in this stark, evolutionary vision for human emotions or for ethical commitments. More could be said about the shortcomings of Ehrlich's appeals, but let us now turn to some constructive alternatives.

A long tradition in rhetoric insists that the goal of rhetoric must not only be to persuade, but also to uplift. For example, Plato claims that a noble rhetoric entails "a genuine attempt to make the souls of one's fellows as excellent as may be, a striving always to say what is best, whatever degree of pleasure or pain it may afford the audience" (Plato, 1953: 503). In *Institutio Oratoria*, Quintilian argues that

> Too much insistence cannot be laid upon the point that no one can be said to speak appropriately who has not considered not merely what it is expedient, but also what it is becoming to say. . . . these two considerations generally go hand in hand. For whatever is becoming is, as a rule, useful, and there is nothing that does more to conciliate the good-will of the judge than the observance or to alienate it than the disregard of these considerations. Sometimes, however, the two are at variance. Now, whenever this occurs, expedience must yield to the demands of what is becoming. . . . the end which the orator must keep in view is not persuasion, but speaking well, since there are occasions when to persuade would be a blot upon his honour. (Quintilian, 1922: XI.I.8-11)

And in *Thought and Character: The Rhetoric of Democratic Education*, Frederick Antczak argues that rhetors should reconstitute, rather than indulge, their audiences (Antczak, 1985: 8-10). That is, rather than simply indulge the audience's baser sentiments, the rhetor should strive to raise the level of discussion and engage the audience through the highest common denominator. One way in which Ehrlich might reconstitute his audience would be by emphasizing the positive aspects of population-control strategies. In *The Population Explosion*, Ehrlich and Ehrlich claim that significant research suggests that "The critical prerequisites to reduced fertility are five: adequate nutrition, proper sanitation, basic health care, education of women, and equal rights for women" (Ehrlich and Ehrlich, 1990: 215-216). It would be far easier to rally the rhetorical audience behind these goals than it would be to rally it behind demophobia and forced sterilization. Hence, the advocates of population control might focus their audience's attention on goals that most reasonable people would endorse, regardless of population pressures. As Ehrlich himself says in the final chapter of *The Population Bomb*,

> To cover [the possibility that I might be wrong], I would like to propose an analogue to Pascal's famous wager. Pascal considered the only safe course for a man was to believe in God. If there was no God, it made no difference, but if there was, you ended up in heaven. In other words, play it safe. If I'm right, we will save the world. If I'm wrong, people will still be better fed, better housed, and happier, thanks to our efforts. (197-198; 179)

Ehrlich is a prolific writer, and it is difficult to say whether he has significantly changed his rhetorical strategies over the past quarter of a century. In *The Population Explosion*, Ehrlich and Ehrlich suggest that if we do not control the human population ourselves, the job may be done for us by population-density-dependent, or population-density-related, diseases. Citing the opinions of two Nobel laureates, they speculate that the AIDS virus might mutate into a virus that could be "spread by casual contact, by inhalation, or through eating contaminated food" and that it might even mutate into a virus that "might be transmissable [sic] through coughs" (Ehrlich and Ehrlich, 1990: 148). Given the discrimination already suffered by AIDS patients, this speculation seems rather irresponsible, and it suggests that Ehrlich's rhetorical strategies have not changed. Nevertheless, there is some reason for optimism. In "Biodiversity Studies: Science and Policy,"[23] Ehrlich and Edward O. Wilson claim that

> The loss of biodiversity should be of concern to everyone for three basic reasons. The first is ethical and esthetic. Because *Homo sapiens* is the dominant species on Earth, we and many others think that people have an absolute moral responsibility to protect what are our only known living companions in the universe. . . . human beings gain great esthetic rewards from those companions (and generate substantial economic activity in the process).
>
> The second reason is that humanity has already obtained enormous direct economic benefits from biodiversity in the form of foods, medicines, and industrial products, and has the potential for gaining many more. . . .
>
> The third reason, perhaps the most poorly evaluated to date, is the array of essential services provided by natural ecosystems, of which diverse species are the key working parts. Ecosystem services include maintenance of the gaseous composition of the atmosphere, preventing changes in the mix of gases from being too rapid for the biota to adjust. (Ehrlich and Wilson, 1991: 760)

Perhaps because of the audience, perhaps because of his co-author, but perhaps simply because he has reassessed the broader public and his rhetorical strategies, Ehrlich here presents a more sophisticated array of appeals than those he presented in *The Population Bomb*. Note the shift in his position from the claim that most Americans "cannot be moved to action by an appeal to beauty, or a plea for mercy for what may well be our only living companions in a vast universe" (*Bomb*, 66; 44), to the above claim that many people believe "that people have an absolute moral responsibility to protect what are our only known living companions in the universe."[24]

Carolyn Merchant's three-part taxonomy of environmental ethics provides a useful means of mapping Ehrlich's appeals. Merchant's three categories of appeals are egocentric, homocentric, and ecocentric. According to Merchant, "An egocentric ethic is grounded in the self. It is based on an individual ought focused on individual good. In its applied form, it involves the claim that what is good for the individual will benefit society. . . . in the United States, it has been the guiding ethic of private entrepreneurs and corporations. . . ." (Merchant, 1990: 46).[25] Merchant describes a homocentric (or anthropocentric) ethic as one grounded in society: "A homocentric ethic underlies the social interest model of politics and the approach of environmental regulatory agencies that protect human health" (Merchant, 1990: 52). Finally, Merchant says that "An ecocentric ethic is grounded in the cosmos. The whole environment . . . is assigned intrinsic value. . . . Of primary importance is the survival of all living and nonliving things as components of healthy ecosystems" (Merchant, 1990: 57).

Most of the appeals in *The Population Bomb* are either egocentric or homocentric. As Ehrlich says, "my discussion of man's environment has not dwelt on the themes that characterize the pleas of conservationists. . . . Instead, I have concentrated on things that seem to bear most directly on man" (65; 43). In "Biodiversity Studies," however, Ehrlich shifts away from egocentrism to a more solidly homocentric ethic, one that flirts with ecocentrism. Ehrlich and Wilson claim that our moral responsibility to other species is "deep, beyond measure, beyond conventional science for the moment" (Ehrlich and Wilson, 1991: 760). Nevertheless, the attraction of a homocentric ethic is powerful, and they follow this observation by noting that our aesthetic appreciation of nature has generated "substantial economic activity" (Ehrlich and Wilson, 1991: 760).

This juxtaposition (or orchestration) of motives, however, may be one of the best ways in which to appeal to a more sophisticated audience while simultaneously reconstituting a less sophisticated one. Although Plato, Quintilian, Antczak, and others have called for a noble or a reconstitutive rhetoric, they have provided little specific advice about how such a rhetoric might succeed. Indeed, after arguing that the noble rhetorician must "say what is best, whatever degree of pleasure or pain it may afford the audience," Plato (through Socrates) says he knows of no rhetorician who practices such rhetoric (1952: 503). Quintilian promotes noble rhetoric, but is willing to concede defeat when there is a conflict between what is "expedient" and what is "becoming," arguing that "there are occasions when to persuade would be a blot upon [the rhetor's] honour" (Quintilian, 1922: XI.I.8-11). Antczak does a little better, arguing that any definition of rhetorical success must always include persuasion: "While 'successful' rhetoric may well involve moral standards, by definition it involves persuading the audience too" (Antczak, 1985: 90). Hence, a principled and provocative speech that leaves the audience unpersuaded and perhaps even more adamantly opposed cannot be defined as a rhetorical success (Antczak, 1985: 90); it may leave the rhetor feeling righteous, but it has failed to meet Plato's criterion of improving "the souls of one's fellows." Beyond this, Antczak offers little advice about how a rhetor might successfully reconstitute an audience. Following Donald Bryant (1953: 413), however, Antczak does say that "A rhetor's success in democratic education will involve adjustments of ideas to people and people to ideas—a mutual reconstitution of thought and character" (Antczak, 1985: 11).

Although Lawrence Kohlberg has been criticized for a variety of reasons—for not including women in his research sample, for suggesting that his stages of moral judgment are universal and invariant rather than socially constructed and historical, and, hence, for taking an ethnocentric approach to moral development—he has provided at least one interesting insight into the problem of reconstituting an audience.[26] Before discussing this insight, however, let me first suggest an alternative, socially constructed framework within which some of Kohlberg's empirical observations might be situated.

In *Practical Criticism*, I. A. Richards describes three realms of knowledge: "subjects . . . which can be discussed in terms of verifiable facts and precise hypotheses"; "subjects which can be handled by rules of thumb and generally accepted conventions"; and

> the vast *corpus* of problems, assumptions, adumbrations, fictions, prejudices, tenets; the sphere of random beliefs and hopeful guesses; the whole world, in brief, of abstract opinion and disputation about matters of feeling. To this world belongs everything about which civilized man cares most. I need only instance ethics, metaphysics, morals, religion, aesthetics, and the discussions surrounding liberty, nationality, justice, love, truth, faith and knowledge to make this plain. (Richards, 1929: 5)

This is largely the realm that Aristotle describes as contingent knowledge—the realm of rhetoric (Aristotle, 1954: 1357a4-7; 1357a24-27).[27] Richards argues that "as a subject-matter for discussion, poetry is a central and typical denizen of" this third realm. Hence, he suggests that poetry serves "as eminently suitable bait for anyone who wishes to trap the current opinions and responses of this middle field for the purpose of examining and comparing them, and with a view to advancing our knowledge of what may be called the natural history of human opinions and feelings" (Richards, 1929: 5-6).

Richards describes an "experiment," conducted over a number of years while he was a lecturer at Cambridge and elsewhere, in which he asked students in his undergraduate literature classes to comment (or write "protocols") on poems, the authorship of which he did not reveal to them. Hence, Richards claims that *Practical Criticism* is, in part, "a record of a piece of fieldwork in comparative ideology" (Richards, 1929: 6). That is, he suggests that he has used responses to anonymous poetry as a projective test to excavate contemporary beliefs and values within his cultural context.

Although Kohlberg suggests that his moral-dilemma experiments have revealed universal and invariant stages of moral development, it may be more useful to consider the results of his research in terms similar to those described by Richards; that is, as an excavation of contemporary beliefs and values within a particular cultural context. Hence, rejecting the theoretical implications that Kohlberg draws from his empirical findings does not necessarily entail rejecting the empirical findings themselves. Given this qualification, let me now turn to one of Kohlberg's observations that is relevant to the problem of reconstituting an audience.

In describing his stage-theory of moral judgment, Kohlberg notes that a series of empirical studies have suggested that "children and adolescents comprehend all stages up to their own, but no more than one stage beyond their own. And importantly, *they prefer this next stage*" (Kohlberg, 1968: 30; see also Turiel (1966); Rest *et al.* (1969); and Blatt and Kohlberg (1975)). Unlike Kohlberg, I would argue that any hierarchy of moral judgment is socially constructed. As I have argued elsewhere, however, even from a social-constructivist perspective, we can still define general principles that transcend immediate contexts because these immediate contexts are themselves situated within a larger and more stable cultural context, what Gadamer calls our "thrownness" (Waddell, 1990: 393-394). That is, we are born (or "thrown") into a historical context, a culture, a tradition in whose values, prejudices, and presuppositions we are steeped. What understanding we have, we gain not by *freeing* ourselves of these prejudices, but by *applying* them; for we understand only by virtue of the questions we ask, and those questions are framed by our prejudices. We distinguish appropriate from inappropriate prejudices when we expose our prejudices to the test of experience (Gadamer, 1982: 236-237).

Hence, the prevailing values and presuppositions of a culture transcend immediate contexts and apply in a wide range of cases much as universal principles would. Unlike moral absolutes, however, our values and presuppositions are socially constructed and, hence, mutable. The ideal rhetor both embodies and appeals to what his or her society deems the best and most noble of its sentiments and prejudices. When the times require it, the ideal rhetor helps the society to adapt to new and changing circumstances by helping it to define values that are appropriate to the issues raised by these new, often more complex, conditions, or by reinterpreting old values in new and more appropriate ways.

The social construction of appropriate values, however, is not just a process of noble rhetors enlightening their audiences; it is a process of rhetors and audiences together co-creating meaning and values through the give and take of the rhetorical enterprise. Thus, like the ideal rhetor, the ideal audience embodies, responds to, and—when the times call for it—*helps to determine* the society's best and most noble sentiments.

If it is indeed possible to reconstitute an audience by appealing to the next higher stage in Kohlberg's hierarchy of moral judgment, the same approach might apply to Merchant's taxonomy of environmental ethics. In this case, the normative characterization *higher* can be replaced (if one chooses to do so) with the more descriptive characterization *more comprehensive*, since concern for the species can be said to encompass concern for the individual member of the species, and concern for the biosphere can be said to encompass concern for the species. When situated within a social-constructionist framework, Kohlberg's work suggests that we are culturally conditioned to value more comprehensive approaches to problem solving. Kohlberg contends that "the core of each [of his stages of moral reasoning] is an underlying conception of justice, and that each higher stage is better for resolving justice problems" (Kohlberg, 1981: xiv). Rest *et al.* suggest that people prefer reasoning from the next-higher stage "under conditions of disequilibrium, i.e., in problems where own-stage thinking breaks down or is self-contradictory" (Rest *et al.*, 1969: 241).

The appeal of the more comprehensive allows for a dynamic system, as opposed to a stagnant conventionalism. This appeal is not limited to our ethical frameworks. In the history and philosophy of science, Thomas Kuhn suggests that, "Probably the most prevalent claim advanced by the proponents of a new paradigm is that they can solve the problems that have led the old one to a crisis. When it can legitimately be made, this claim is the most effective one possible" (Kuhn, 1970a: 153). Stephen Littlejohn argues that theoretical scope—a theory's comprehensiveness or inclusiveness—is one of the principal criteria by which theories are evaluated (Littlejohn, 1983: 23-24).

If we can develop a complex repertoire of strategies or behaviors that allows us to meet a range of needs, we tend to prefer that repertoire over a less comprehensive pattern. As Abraham Maslow says, when a person is dominated by a certain need, his or her whole philosophy of the future also tends to change. For [a] chronically and extremely hungry man, Utopia can be defined simply as a place where there is plenty of food. . . . Freedom, love, community feelings, respect, philosophy, may all be waived aside as fripperies that are useless, since they fail to fill the stomach. Such a man may fairly be said to live by bread alone. . . . But what happens to man's desires when there is plenty of bread and his belly is chronically filled? *At once other (and higher) needs emerge* and these, rather than physiological hungers, dominate the organism. (Maslow, 1970: 37-38)

Since the "lower needs" are never extinguished, we are only able to invest our energies in addressing "higher needs" by developing more efficient means of meeting our lower needs.[28]

It would be difficult for a middle-class environmentalist to persuade a starving Brazilian peasant that slash-and-burn agriculture violates the inherent rights of the other species that inhabit the rain forests. However, if that same environmentalist could show the peasant how to make a living by sustainably harvesting the forests, he or she might simultaneously be able to invest the peasant with a sense of respect for the forest and its biodiversity. Thus, the egocentric and homocentric are not *replaced* by the ecocentric; they are *encompassed* by it.

Note that reconstituting an audience does not *necessarily* mean challenging the audience's values. It might, instead, mean challenging the audience to think in new ways about how values it already holds (e.g., justice or caring) might be extended such that they apply in a new context. Abolitionists, for example, struggled to persuade a reluctant America that the principle "all men are created equal" was not limited to European Americans; and suffragists argued that this principle was not limited to *men*. When we extend a principle that we have applied to ourselves such that it applies to a wider circle of beings, we reconstitute our ethical judgment. Lincoln pointed this out when he said "I know slavery must be wrong because no man would wish it upon himself." And John Stuart Mill argued that "the rules and precepts for human conduct" should be extended "so far as the nature of things admits, to the whole sentient creation" (Mill, 1985: 16). If we extend principles of caring and reversibility to other species, we move from a homocentric to an ecocentric ethic.[29]

The appeal of the more comprehensive suggests not elitist imposition of the rhetor's standards of judgment, but, as Donald Bryant says, the adjustment of "ideas to people and people to ideas" (Bryant, 1953: 413).[30] Wayne Booth defines rhetoric as "the art of discovering warrantable beliefs and improving those beliefs in shared discourse" (Booth, 1974: xiii). Hence, rhetoric is the exercise of symbolic induce-ment within the marketplace of ideas. People must *decide* whether or not they are persuaded—they must be *convinced*. To be human is to have values; to speak or to act is to *assert* those values. A good rhetor, however, is someone who provides us with a better vision of ourselves and suggests ways in which we might more closely approximate that vision. Rest *et al.* contend that a person who is influenced by a higher stage of moral reasoning "may be able to prefer and comprehend material one or two stages above his own, even though he cannot spontaneously produce such material and hence is not at that stage himself" (Rest *et al.*, 1969: 242). Emerson makes a similar point when he says that an orator will persuade his or her audience when he or she says "that which they recognize as part of them but which they were not yet ready to say" (Emerson, 1966: 57). Hence, in arguing from a more comprehensive framework, the rhetor might articulate values, motives, or reasons of which we have a tacit grasp, but which we may, as yet, be unable to articulate ourselves.

There would seem to be a contradiction between my earlier claim that a rhetor should employ appeals that are consonant with one another and with the beliefs and values of the audience, and the claim that a rhetor should appeal to a higher or more comprehensive ethical framework than that generally employed by his or her audience. The resolution of this contradiction may already be apparent.

Whether or not the rhetor's appeal should be consonant with the values and beliefs of his or her audience depends upon whether or not that audience already shares the values and beliefs to which the rhetor would appeal. In the case of population control, I have suggested that Paul Ehrlich should take as his primary rhetorical audience those whom he defines as caring deeply about the preservation of beauty and wildlife, and I have suggested that his appeal should be essentially consonant with the beliefs and values of this audience. I have *not*, however, suggested that Ehrlich or other advocates of population control abandon those whom Ehrlich says "clearly don't give a damn." Instead, I have suggested that they strive to reconstitute this audience. Such an effort might entail appeals that are dissonant with the prevailing values and beliefs of this audience, or it might entail challenging the audience to interpret and apply old values in new ways.

Although a rhetor does not need to reconstitute the *values* of an audience if that audience already shares the values to which the rhetor would appeal, the rhetor may still need to persuade the audience to *act* on the basis of these values, and he or she may also need to persuade the audience of which action is appropriate. Thus, three things are necessary to persuasion: first, a set of values to which the rhetor can appeal; second, something that will move an audience to act on the basis of those values; and third, some basis upon which an audience might determine which action will most likely achieve the desired result. I suspect that the dominant appeals in these three aspects of persuasion are, respectively, *ethos*, *pathos*, and *logos*.[31]

Kohlberg's work suggests that when an appeal is "downwardly dissonant" (that is, when it is from a lower stage or a less comprehensive framework than that of the audience), it will tend to be rejected; when an appeal is consonant, it will tend to be accepted, but it may leave the audience where it found it; and when an appeal is "upwardly dissonant," it should both appeal to and help to reconstitute the audience, as long as it is not so dissonant as to be incomprehensible to the audience.[32] As Antczak says, "every effective form of persuasion moves from previously held beliefs to new ones that seem somehow more satisfying extensions or conclusions of the original beliefs" (Antczak, 1985: 101).

By constructing an audience of people who "cannot be moved to action by an appeal to beauty, or a plea for mercy," and then by indulging rather than attempting to reconstitute that audience, Ehrlich has created an essentially egocentric appeal, one that has failed to move an audience motivated primarily by a homocentric or an ecocentric ethic. With a more skillful combination of appeals from all three of Merchant's categories, proponents of population control should be able to engage homocentric and ecocentric audiences and simultaneously reconstitute the egocentric audience.

Notes

1. The Cassandra Conference was sponsored by the Colleges of Geoscience, Liberal Arts, and Agriculture of Texas A&M University, where the conference was held from May 6-7, 1985. Approximately 350-500 people participated.
2. Although he allows Gorgias to make few good points, Plato does not, of course, allow Gorgias' sophistic vision of rhetoric to prevail against Socrates' philosophic challenge, even though this challenge is itself at times explicitly rhetorical (see, for example, Kennedy, 1980: 45-52).
3. Given contemporary interest in epistemology (as opposed to ethics), the attention paid to rhetoric of science vs. rhetoric of science policy should not be surprising. There may, however, be a developmental sequence at work, with rhetoric of science policy developing out of rhetoric of science. Carolyn Miller suggests that understanding rhetoric of science is crucial to the rhetoric of science policy (Miller, 1991).
4. For other studies in the rhetoric of science policy, see Bantz (1981), Farrell and Goodnight (1981), Gross (1984), Killingsworth and Palmer (1992), Miller (1982), and Waddell (1990).
5. In my citations of *The Population Bomb* [e.g., (69ff.; 45ff.)], the first page reference is to the original, 1968 edition, and the second page reference is to the relevant passage in the revised, 1971 edition, to which an update was appended in 1978. Unless otherwise indicated, all quotations are from the original edition; in some cases, minor changes were made in the revised edition.
6. In the first edition (1798) of *An Essay on the Principle of Population*, Thomas Malthus cited three checks on the human population: war, pestilence, and famine. He acknowledged moral restraint as a viable population check only as an afterthought in the revised (1803) edition.
7. Although addressed primarily to an American audience (65-66; 43-44), *The Population Bomb* might influence population control in other countries in at least three ways: (1) through foreign distribution of the book, or at least of its main arguments; (2) through the influence of the American example that the book might inspire; and (3) through the book's effect, or lack thereof, on US foreign policy. With respect to the last of these factors, Ehrlich says that President Reagan's "irrational position" on population control "was translated into action when his administration withdrew funding from the International Planned Parenthood Federation in 1985 and in 1986 ended all American support of the United Nations Fund for Population Activities (UNFPA), because those organizations supported the right of women to have abortions, even though, because of the American government's concerns, they don't fund abortion activities directly" (Ehrlich and Ehrlich, 1990: 194-195). It would seem that the American public was not sufficiently aroused by the population-control movement to prevent these policies from being implemented.
8. Contrary to these pessimistic pronouncements, Ehrlich elsewhere claims to have had a modest impact. In the 1978 update of *The Population Bomb*, he suggests that his book "may have" played a role in raising public concerns about family size and quality of life (204). In *The Population Explosion*, Ehrlich and Ehrlich claim that many people "did pay attention to *The Population Bomb*" (Ehrlich and Ehrlich, 1990: 183); and in an endnote, they add that "Literally thousands have written or told us in person that reading *The Population Bomb* led them to have smaller families. Needless to say, this is not a scientific sample, but it does convince us that the book had an impact" (Ehrlich and Ehrlich, 1990: 296).

There is some evidence, however, that Ehrlich's pessimism is better founded than his optimism. For example, in his 1978 update of *The Population Bomb*, Ehrlich predicted that "the U.S. population will stop growing around the year 2025, with a peak population of about 250 million" (204). However, the 1990 US census reported the US population to be 248.7 million, and an officially acknowledged undercount of 5.3 million brings the 1990 US population to approximately 254 million.

Ehrlich suggests that a major factor in this misprediction was immigration (Ehrlich, 1992). The annual rate of immigration per 1,000 US population between 1961 and 1970 was 1.7 percent; between 1971 and 1980, the rate was 2.1 percent; and between 1981 and 1989, the rate was 2.7 percent (US Bureau of the Census, 1991: 9).

9. Keith Stanovich notes that "Social and cognitive psychologists have studied what is termed the *vividness effect* in human memory and decision making. When faced with a problem-solving or decision-making situation, people retrieve from memory the information that seems relevant to the situation at hand. Thus, they are more likely to employ the facts that are more accessible to solve a problem or make a decision. One factor that strongly affects accessibility is the vividness of the information" (Stanovich, 1989: 66). If we are, in fact, primarily "sight animals," then visual representation of information should make that information more vivid for us. Nevertheless, although the Sierra Club edition of *The*

Population Bomb was illustrated, neither the Ballantine Books edition of *The Population Bomb* nor the more recent *The Population Explosion* includes a single graph or photograph.

10. Essentially, this same argument is made in *The Population Bomb*: "Sadly, man's evolution did not provide him with a nervous system that readily detects changes that take place slowly, not in minutes, hours, or days, but over decades. It was important for early man and his nonhuman ancestors to be able to detect rather sudden changes in their environments" (58; 36).

For a more detailed account of this view, see Robert Ornstein and Paul Ehrlich's *New World, New Mind* (1989).

11. Note that Ehrlich and Ehrlich claim that the evolutionary pressures they describe have *shaped* our world views, not *determined* them. If our world views were determined by these pressures, the arguments in *The Population Bomb* and *The Population Explosion*—if they could be conceptualized at all—would be moot. As Aristotle pointed out, "The subjects of our deliberation are such as seem to present us with alternative possibilities: about things that could not have been, and cannot now or in the future be, other than they are, nobody who takes them to be of this nature wastes his time in deliberation" (Aristotle, 1954: 1357a5-6).

Note also that although it may be the case, as Ehrlich and Ehrlich claim, that humans are primarily "sight animals," linguists have argued that humans are nearly unique in our ability to engage in displaced communication; that is, in our ability to communicate about things that are remote in space or time or both (see, for example, Hockett, 1960: 90).

12. Note also rapidly changed public perceptions in recent years of, for example, African Americans, women, smoking, and the former Soviet Union.

13. Aristotle also claims that "things that are true and things that are just have a natural tendency to prevail over their opposites, so that if the decisions of judges are not what they ought to be, the defeat must be due to the speakers themselves, and they must be blamed accordingly" (Aristotle, 1954: 1355a21-24). Today, of course, we would acknowledge a range of significant variables; however, the nature of the rhetoric is still a principal concern.

14. Scientists who enter the public-policy arena always function as rhetoricians, for they always appeal—skillfully or not, deliberately or not—to reason, emotion, and character. Scientists, however, are more accustomed to working in genres in which—despite recent work in the rhetoric of science—many practitioners believe that appeals to emotion and character are irrelevant and inappropriate. Hence, the transition from scientist to policy advocate can be arduous.

15. Note that these "two powerful reasons" do not include the aforementioned reasons for our failure to address population problems; i.e., that humans are "sight animals" who respond to events. I assume, however, that these reasons are implicit in the "two powerful reasons" described here.

16. Ehrlich here conflates the hostile audience with the apathetic audience. Although there are occasional, dramatic examples of conversion of hostiles—e.g., Paul's conversion from a persecutor of Christians to their greatest proselytizer—the apathetic are more likely to be persuaded than the hostile. Hence, it is probably a mistake to lump these two audiences together.

17. Note that although Ehrlich elsewhere complains that environmentalists do not pay enough attention to population issues, at this point, he himself separates environmental concerns from population issues.

18. There are other indications that Ehrlich and Hardin endorse one another's work. For example, Hardin has the lead essay in *The Cassandra Conference*, which was edited by Ehrlich and John Holdren; and when Hardin closes the second (1969) edition of his anthology *Population, Evolution, and Birth Control* with his famous essay "The Tragedy of the Commons," he prefaces this essay with an excerpt from *The Population Bomb*.

19. Henceforth, I will refer to this audience—which Ehrlich assumes is already with him (65-66; 43-44)—as the rhetorical audience. Once this audience is moved to action, its actions may bring about the secondary persuasion of a still larger audience. Furthermore, as I will suggest below, with a more skillful combination of appeals than Ehrlich constructs, it might be possible to persuade simultaneously both this audience and the audience Ehrlich has actually targeted.

20. Compare Mary Hesse's assertion that "It was realized from an early stage in the scientific revolution that there is a logical problem about the inference of theories from observations, because this cannot be made logically conclusive: there are in principle always an indefinite number of theories that fit the observed facts more or less adequately" (Hesse, 1980: vii-viii).

Hesse goes on to define the "by now fairly uncontroversial proposition that all scientific theories are *underdetermined* by facts": "Theories are logically constrained by facts, but are underdetermined by them: that is, while, to be acceptable, theories should be more or less plausibly coherent with facts, they can neither be conclusively refuted nor uniquely derived from statements of fact alone" (Hesse, 1980: 187).

21. In the revised edition, "through a system of incentives and penalties" is replaced by "through changes in our value systems."

22. As Aristotle says, *ethos* "may almost be called the most effective means of persuasion [a rhetor] possesses" (Aristotle, 1954: 1356a13-14).

23. Biodiversity and human population are clearly linked in Ehrlich's work. As he and Wilson claim in this article, if population growth continues at its current rate, "most of the world's biodiversity seems destined to disappear" (Ehrlich and Wilson, 1991: 760).

24. Other evidence of a more positive audience analysis can be found in *Extinction* (1981) and *Healing the Planet* (1991), both co-authored with Anne Ehrlich.

25. Consider, for example, GM executive Charles Erwin Wilson's famous, 1952 pronouncement before the United States Senate that "what's good for General Motors is good for the country."

26. For a critique of Kohlberg's work, see Kurtines and Grief (1974); Blasi (1980); Gilligan (1982); and Harre (1984).

27. As Carolyn Miller has pointed out, however, "Over the centuries, we have become less certain than Aristotle was about many things, and what we call the *new rhetoric* reflects the extension of uncertainty to matters other than Athenian civic affairs—beyond ethics and politics to philosophy, science, and the academic disciplines generally" (Miller, 1990: 162).

28. On a societal level, one example of developing a more efficient means of meeting our needs might be the agricultural revolution.

29. Kohlberg's ethic of justice as reversibility and Carol Gilligan's ethic of caring might be synthesized, just as appeals to reason (*logos*) and emotion (*pathos*) have traditionally been synthesized in rhetoric.

30. According to Aristotle, some modes of persuasion are artistic in that they are invented by the speaker and are provided through speech. Other modes of persuasion are inartistic in that they are there at the outset (e.g., power differential) (Aristotle, 1954: 1355b, 35-40). Thus, the imposition of belief through, for example, intimidation is not artistic and hence, by definition, not rhetorical.

31. Edwin Black has argued that in order to change, rather than simply reinforce, beliefs, it is often necessary to create emotional dissonance, which the audience may then reduce by adopting new beliefs, possibly those offered (implicitly or explicitly) by the rhetor (Black, 1978: 138-146).

32. Note that in responding to his critics, Kuhn points out that when he says that a revolutionary paradigm is incommensurable with the paradigm that it displaces, he does not mean to say that the two paradigms are incomparable (Kuhn, 1970b: 267).

Works Cited

Antczak, F. J. (1985), *Thought and Character: The Rhetoric of Democratic Education,* Iowa State University Press, Ames.

Aristotle (1954), *The Rhetoric* (trans. W. R. Roberts), Random House, New York.

Bantz, C. R. (1981), "Public arguing in the regulation of health and safety," *Western Journal of Speech Communication,* 45; 71-87.

Bitzer, L. F. (1968), "The rhetorical situation," *Philosophy and Rhetoric,* 1: 1-14.

Black, E. (1978), *Rhetorical Criticism: A Study in Method* (1965), University of Wisconsin Press, Madison.

Blasi, A. (1980), "Bridging moral cognition and moral action: A critical review of the literature," *Psychological Bulletin,* 88: 1-45.

Blatt, M. M. and Kohlberg, L. (1975), "The effects of classroom moral discussion upon children's level of moral judgment," *Journal of Moral Education,* 4: 129-161.

Booth, W. C. (1974), *Modern Dogma and the Rhetoric of Assent,* University of Chicago Press, Chicago.

Bryant, D. C. (1953), "Rhetoric: Its functions and its scope," *Quarterly Journal of Speech,* 39: 401-424.

Cicero (1942), *De Oratore,* Books I-II (trans. E. W. Sutton and H. Rackham), Harvard University Press, Cambridge.

Consigny, S. (1974), "Rhetoric and its situations," *Philosophy and Rhetoric,* 7: 175-186.

Darwin, C. G. (1960) "Can man control his numbers?" in S. Tax (ed.), *The Evolution of Man,* University of Chicago Press, Chicago, pp. 463-473. [Vol. 2 of *Evolution After Darwin,* 3 vols.]

Ehrlich, P. R. (1968), *The Population Bomb,* Ballantine, New York. Revised 1971, 1978.

Ehrlich, P. R. (1992), Letter to the author. 3 January 1992.

Ehrlich, P. R. and Ehrlich, A. H. (1981), *Extinction: The Causes and Consequences of the Disappearance of Species,* Ballantine, New York.

Ehrlich, P. R. and Ehrlich, A. H. (1990), *The Population Explosion,* Simon and Schuster, New York.

Ehrlich, P. R. and Ehrlich, A. H. (1991), *Healing the Planet: Strategies for Resolving the Environmental Crisis,* Addison-Wesley, New York.

Ehrlich, P. R. and Holdren, J. P. (1988), *The Cassandra Conference: Resources and the Human Predicament,* Texas A&M University Press, College Station.

Ehrlich, P. R. and Wilson, E. O. (1991), "Biodiversity studies: Science and policy," *Science* 253: 758-762

Emerson, R. W. (1966), "Literature," in S. E. Whicher, R. E. Spiller and W. E. Williams (eds.), *The Early Lectures of Ralph Waldo Emerson,* Vol. 2, Harvard University Press, Cambridge, pp. 58-68.

Farrell, T. B., and Goodnight, G. T. (1981), "Accidental rhetoric: The root metaphors of Three Mile Island," *Communication Monographs,* 48: 271-300.

Gadamer, H. G. (1982), *Truth and Method,* Crossroads, New York, trans. of *Wahrheit und Methode,* 1960.

Gilligan, C. (1982), *In a Different Voice: Psychological Theory and Women's Development,* Harvard University Press, Cambridge.

Gross, A. G. (1984), "Public debates as failed social dramas: The recombinant DNA controversy," *Quarterly Journal of Speech,* 70: 397-409.

Halloran, S. M. (1976), "Tradition and theory in rhetoric," *Quarterly Journal of Speech,* 62: 234-241.

Hardin, G. (1968), "The tragedy of the commons," *Science* 162: 1243-1248.

Hardin, G. (1969), *Population, Evolution and Birth Control,* W. H. Freeman, San Francisco.

Harre, R. (1984), *Personal Being: A Theory for Personal Psychology,* Harvard University Press, Cambridge.

Harris, R. A. (1991), "Rhetoric of science," *College English,* 53: 282-307.

Hesse, M. (1980), *Revolutions and Reconstructions in the Philosophy of Science,* Indiana University Press, Bloomington.

Hockett, C. F. (1960), "The origin of speech," *Scientific American,* 203.3: 89-96.

Kennedy, G. A. (1980), *Classical Rhetoric and Its Christian and Secular Tradition from Ancient to Modern Times,* University of North Carolina Press, Chapel Hill.

Killingsworth, M. J., and Palmer, J. S. (1992), *Ecospeak: Rhetoric and Environmental Politics in America,* Southern Illinois University Press, Carbondale.

Kohlberg, L. (1968), "The child as a moral philosopher," *Psychology Today,* September: 25-30.

Kohlberg, L. (1981), *The Philosophy of Moral Development,* Harper & Row, New York.

Kuhn, T. S. (1970a), *The Structure of Scientific Revolutions,* 2nd ed., University of Chicago Press, Chicago.

Kuhn, T.S. (1970b), "Reflections on my critics," in I. Lakatos and A. Musgrave (eds.), *Criticism and the Growth of Knowledge,* Cambridge University Press, Cambridge.

Kurtines, W. and Grief, E. B. (1974), "The development of moral thought: Review and evaluation of Kohlberg's approach," *Psychological Bulletin,* 81: 453-470.

Littlejohn, S. W. (1983), *Theories of Human Communication,* 2nd ed., Wadsworth, Belmont.

Malthus, T. R. (1978), *An Essay on the Principle of Population* (1798), W. W. Norton, New York.

Maslow, A. H. (1970), *Motivation and Personality,* 2nd ed., Harper & Row, New York.

Merchant, C. (1990), "Environmental ethics and political conflict: A view from California," *Environmental Ehtics,* 12: 45-68.

Mill, J. S. (1985), *Utilitarianism* (1861), Macmillan, New York.

Miller, C. R. (1982), "Public knowledge in science and society," *Pre/Text,* 3: 31-49.

Miller, C. R. (1990), "The rhetoric of decision science, or Herbert A. Simon says," in H. W. Simons (ed.), *The Rhetorical Turn: Invention and Persuasion in the Conduct of Inquiry,* University of Chicago Press, Chicago, pp. 162-184.

Miller, C. R. (1991), Letter to the author. 5 April 1991.

Ornstein, R. and Ehrlich, P. (1989), *New World, New Mind: Moving toward Conscious Evolution,* Doubleday, New York.

Perelman, C. And Olbrechts-Tyteca, L. (1969), *The New Rhetoric: A Treatise on Argumentation* (trans. J. Wilkinson and P. Weaver), University of Notre Dame Press, Notre Dame.

Plato (1952), *Gorgias* (trans. W. C. Hembold), Macmillan, New York.

Qunitilian (1922), *The Institutio Oratoria* (trans. H. E. Butler), Harvard University Press, Cambridge.

Rest, J., Turiel, E., and Kohlberg, L. (1969), "Level of moral development as a determinant of preference and comprehension of moral judgments made by others," *Journal of Personality,* 37: 225-252.

Richards, I. A. (1929), *Practical Criticism: A Study of Literary Judgment,* Harcourt Brace Jovanovich, New York.

Snow, C. P. (1964), *The Two Cultures and A Second Look* (expansion of the 1959 version), Cambridge University Press, Cambridge.

Stanovich, K. E. (1989), *How to Think Straight about Psychology,* 2nd. Ed., Scott, Foresman and Co., Glenview.

Turiel, E. (1966), "An experimental test of the sequentiality of developmental stages in the child's moral judgment," *Journal of Personality and Social Psychology,* 3: 611-618.

United States Bureau of the Census (1991), *Statistical Abstract of the United States:1991,* 111th edition, Government Printing Office, Washington.

Vatz, R. E. (1973), "The myth of the rhetorical situation," *Philosophy and Rhetoric,* 6: 154-161.

Waddell, C. (1990), "The role of *pathos* in the decision-making process: A study in the rhetoric of science policy," *Quarterly Journal of Speech,* 76: 381-400.

Wander, P. C. (1976), "The rhetoric of science," *Western Journal of Speech Communication,* 40: 226-35.

Accidental Rhetoric:
The Root Metaphors of Three Mile Island
by Thomas B. Farrell and G. Thomas Goodnight

Mankind, which in Homerss time was an object of contemplation for Olympian gods,
now is one for itself. Its self-alienation has reached such a degree that it can experience
its own destruction as an aesthetic pleasure of the first order.

—Walter Benjamin, *Illuminations*

The events at Three Mile Island 2, an electrical power-generating plant on the
Susquehanna River, riveted national attention for five days in late March of 1979.
State and local officials, federal bureaucrats, technologists and politicians, activist
groups and media representatives, as well as "accident victims," and the mass
audience all seemed to converge, each frantically attempting to explain and evaluate
a mysterious "happening": the melting of fuel rods, the appearance of a hydrogen
bubble, and the release of radiation near several small communities in Pennsylvania.
Since those feverish days, there has been an abundance of discursive analysis. The
journalistic community has examined and confirmed the balanced objectivity of its
reportage.[1] The regulatory agencies have examined and tightened their standards
for technical safety and social coordination.[2] The energy industry itself has been
forced to re-examine its own practices, the result of which has been a reordering of
public relations to confirm the superior safety and efficiency of nuclear energy.[3]
Although each particular faction invokes the "public" as the warrant and benefactor
of its analysis, the rhetorical practices of all who co-opt the public prerogative,
speak in its name, and make its decisions have yet to be examined. For this reason,
no commission, agency, industry, or interest group has been able to explain how
this "extremely small and unimportant malfunction," of a nuclear reactor "turned
into an event of momentous impact, with repercussions felt over most of the
world."[4] It is our belief that the answer may be found by examining the discourse
surrounding the accident at "Three Mile Island 2" as a rhetorical crisis.

Communication practice typically serves to reinforce the ongoing construction of social reality.[5] Interchanges among government functionaries and private citizens flow within traditional, institutional channels. Routine, transparent, and utterly predictable, these soon-to-be-forgotten transactions constitute patterns of life within a culture. Even those few communications which ascend to the more rarified sphere of public discourse tend to reinforce the ordinariness of these patterns. While attended to and diffused by mass media, these communications punctuate individual lives with "news" about events played out on a grander but still familiar scale. Thus institutional advocates and "anchors" report the comings and goings of celebrities, high political dramas, or the quantitative indicators of social well-being. Even the voices of conflict (reported by surrogates for the public) do not so much address and engage society as quietly reinforce confidence in its existing patterns of communication. Discourse unsettling, urgent, and timely enough to warrant widespread uncertainty and alarm is rare indeed.

A rhetorical crisis occurs when discourse fails to fulfill ordinary epistemological and axiological expectations. Previously functional practices of communication and techniques of persuasion break down, proliferating disbelief when informed consensus is demanded, foreclosing options when cooperative action is seen as vital. In some instances, the crisis may be the product of cultural fragmentation: too few share commitments to common terms to sustain a fund of social knowledge or direct a course of public action. In other instances, loss of public competence combines with an anomaly of the natural world to thwart effective discourse.[6] But in each case, rhetors search awkwardly for language capable of defining, explaining, and assimilating urgent events. Audiences struggle to understand information, set criteria for policy evaluation, and locate viable options for action. Unlike a rhetorical exigence, the crisis does not so much "invite" discourse as defy it.[7]

That the discourse employed at Three Mile Island constituted such a crisis is underlined again and again by the self-reports of all concerned. Reporters were unable to judge the validity of technical statements. Technicians often could not sense the relevance of reporters' questions. Government sources, frequently at odds with one another, could not decide what information to release or what action to take. Some representatives of the nuclear power industry made misleading statements. Still others did not speak at all. The people of Middletown and Londonderry did not know whom to believe. Many simply fled. The larger public audience waited, only to receive still more fragmentary reports from the scene. No one understood all that was going on. No source was entirely credible throughout the crisis. The very pervasiveness of flawed discourse suggests that the causes of the rhetorical problems were systemic failures, emanating from deep-seated contradictions in contemporary theories and practices of communication.

Our central contention is that the technological failure at Three Mile Island extended beyond the faulty machinery. In many respects, the crisis was generated and sustained by the failure of technical reasoning to inform adequately public deliberation. By technical reason, we mean those modes of inference that are characteristic of specialized forums, wherein discourse is coded to fit functional demands of particular information fields and evaluated according to an array of state-of-the-art techniques. Its counterpart, social reason, employs inferences that are prompted through the pressing contingencies of ordinary life, wherein the claims of advocates are affiliated with the interests of related others and grounded in the generalizable convictions of a competent audience. In the best of all possible worlds, each type of reasoning would perform separate, but complementary, functions. The crisis at Three Mile Island, however, augurs that present communication practices may actually impede public deliberation. In particular, we contend that long before the crisis itself, technical reasoning had usurped the role of social reasoning; that during the crisis, technical and surrogate[8] discourse were inadequate to the task of informing public judgment; that, therefore, the events at Three Mile Island mark the failure of technical reasoning and concomitant communication practices to master contemporary rhetorical demands.

Lacking communication principles adequate to encompass the crisis, several of the specialists and agency representatives at Harrisburg referred to themselves as being among the accident's victims. The implied claim—one we fully share—is that technology has imposed limits upon the practical capacity of discourse to adjudicate problems within the public sphere. However, this claim presents a special problem of judgment. How can "accidental rhetoric," discourse that could not realistically have been other than it was, be evaluated fairly? Yet the options of discourse are almost never clear during the moments of its unfolding. And the discourse of crisis, like Sartre's "situation," must, "evolve on the eve of great events which transcend predictions, frustrate expectations, upset plans." Even as the characters are "in movement—dragged along by the action itself that is interpreted,"[9] still they must be judged. Our governing conviction—developed throughout this essay—is that discursive limits and contradictions, whether avoidable or not, must be acknowledged. This is the responsibility of the rhetorical critic. And, with a self-reflection afforded by history, it becomes the responsibility of the advocates themselves.

Our study of accidental rhetoric proceeds in three stages of analysis. First, in order to perceive the discourse at Three Mile Island as clearly as possible, we begin by tracing several contingent world views which—together—allowed technical reasoning to solidify its cultural dominance over the problem of nuclear power. Our contention is that three successive forms-of-life—industry, ecology, and energy—gradually sedimented the discourse thought competent to address the nuclear question, thereby removing this issue from public view. Second, in order to recreate the discourse at Three Mile Island, we reconstruct the attempts of multiple actors, agencies, and specialists to explain and encompass the accident throughout the various stages of its unfolding. Our contention is that the discourse of Three Mile Island, when viewed from the broader conceptual horizons marking its origins, comprises a narrative of failed anticipations and an inadvertent struggle for deliberative rhetorical form. Third, in order to judge this material fairly, we will offer a tentative appraisal of the technical communicative discourse at Three Mile Island, not in terms of its real historical audiences, for this discourse rarely addressed anyone directly; rather, our aim is to construct those visions of the public implied by "accidental" rhetoric and to judge its acquired quality of vision. Our contention is that the limits of technical communicative discourse are severe, recurrent, and perhaps irreparable. This evaluation proceeds from a traditional and somewhat prescriptive sense of what rhetoric is capable of being: as an art preoccupied with the formation of public discourse; as defining practical questions for prudential reason and conduct; and as the counterpart of dialectic, the reflective critique of reason in politics and ethics.

Antecedents of Rhetorical Crisis

The antecedents of rhetorical crisis reside deep within the hidden ambivalences and uncertainties of a culture. Consequently, in order to understand the potential for crisis, it is necessary to explore the technical and social concerns underlying nuclear power. In this section, we hope to accomplish the task by developing two parallel positions. First, we shall argue that three successive visions of nature and man—captured by the root metaphors of "industry," "ecology," and "energy"—extended the preeminence of technical reason, while, at the same time, they imposed severe restrictions on forms of social life.[10] Second, we wish to demonstrate that the ultimate dream of technology—nuclear power—came to be seen as an important but uncertain factor in resolving dilemmas posed by these visions.

Industry as a Precondition for Social Life

Central to the expansionist culture of late nineteenth-century America was the form of life of industry. In mythic intent, if not fact, industry marked the trek of American civility westward and the taming of its savage wilderness. With industry came the city and the city's most visible nineteenth century sign: the factory. Operating together, the city and the factory promised a higher standard of living and all the cultural benefits that prosperity must bring: such as libraries, museums, symphonies, and monuments to the socially significant. Perhaps less visibly, however, industry forged an unlikely alliance with the public—now defined as a "work force"—as well as with the latest promises of technological invention. Long after the warnings of Malthus and others—that nature was finite, that growth must one day end—Frederick Taylor and Henry Ford answered with the nation's first purely technical philosophy: scientific management, social engineering and the assembly-line. And when problems of the "work force" (wages, health, safety) understandably became *public* problems, the philosophers of industry allied their philosophy with the avant-garde of liberal progressivism. The precondition of progress had now become an agent of progressive reform. By the 1920's, the major consumer products of the new technologized industry had become the automobile and the radio. Technology was reproducing itself. As Charles Beard has observed:

> [Technological civilization] rests fundamentally on power-driven machinery which transcends the physical limits of its human directors, multiplying indefinitely the production of goods. . . . The day of crude invention being almost over, continuous research in the natural sciences is absolutely necessary to the extension of the machine

and its market, thus forcing continuously the creation of new goods, new processes, and new modes of life.[11]

While there were countervailing tendencies throughout the flourishing of industry as form of life (Teddy Roosevelt's advocacy of the "strenuous life," the Boy Scouts), often such tendencies merely applied the values of industry itself to unexamined contexts. The arguments of naturalists did not challenge significantly the dominant vision of nature as a resource to be used by an industrial order.[12] Some questioned the city and its values, and national parks were singled out as protected areas. But by the 1940's, the American war culture had come to depend upon the technical coordination of consumer behavior and full production by increasingly specialized industries.[13]

Ecology as a Precondition for Social Life

It was not until the late 1950's that a major challenge to the preeminent order of industrial values emerged: from the work of biologist, Rachel Carson. More than attacking pesticides, Carson's book, *Silent Spring*, offered a chilling indictment of industrial logic and its related technology.[14] Carson's perspective conceded what industrial advocates had proclaimed all along: that technological innovation could use and even reconstitute nature. But what was questioned, in the strongest terms, was the direction and reversibility of technological change. Pesticides, Carson claimed, had posited a "chain of evil" that already infected our living tissues: "In this now universal contamination of the environment, chemicals are the sinister and little recognized partners of radiation in changing the very nature of the world—the very nature of its life."[15] In the form of life of ecology, then, nature and human culture are both inseparable and finite. Moreover, time itself can no longer be assumed as a neutral ally of progress. Once flawed by the poisons of technique, the path may be marked *for all time*. For Public Health official, David Price, the worst-case scenario finds the environment corrupted to the point, "where man joins the dinosaurs as an obsolete form of life." But Carson took special note of his conclusion: "that our fate could be sealed twenty or more years before the development of the symptoms."[16]

The ecological form of life engendered, for a time, a new way of interpreting the natural and social world—a vision threatened by the industrial view of nature. But perhaps more striking, because more observable, was the appearance and then abatement of a powerful ecological movement within the political forums of the late 1960's and early 1970's. Not surprisingly, the limits of the ecological form of life are revealed most dramatically in these attempts to engage a politically active public.

While ecology discourse was apocalyptic in tone, it remained highly esoteric in its patterns of inference. The enemy was often invisible and its harms virtually inscrutable to the ordinary person. Yet the "public" to be engaged by such discourse was completely ordinary: the "man on the street." Indeed, ordinary life concerns themselves framed the dominant statements of threat. For this reason, the difficult questions of *how* and *by whom* technology was to be controlled were never addressed by this discourse. Instead, experts in various specializations were brandished and balanced in the most manichean fashion: scientists who were "friends of the earth," versus scientists who, presumably, were otherwise. As forums and causes for offical regulation expanded, the public seemed to retreat to what James Bowman termed the stance of "victim."[17] And thus, by the middle 1970's, ecology had become a kind of leisurely avocation of a privatized social class.

Energy as the Precondition for Social Life

Even as industrial and ecological forms of life remained radically conflicted, a new ultimate term—energy—transformed these visions into partisan stances. The centrality of energy to both the factory and environmental safety was far from obvious initially. From the great demands for fuel during World War II to the development of the Arab oil reserves, from the shifts in geopolitical production patterns to the continuing ritual of oil cartel diplomacy, concern for energy steadily moved from technical forums of decision-making to become a central public concern. The concern was well-founded; if energy ran out, the wheels of the factory would stop, and the ecology would remain unredeemed.

First dramatized by the OPEC oil embargo, the energy form of life filled technical and public communication channels throughout the 1970's. The resulting array of possible futures suggested by various trade-offs bewildered experts and interest groups alike. Some sources predicted a quick, catastrophic fuel decline; others proclaimed that shortages were a figment of artificial restrictions. Die-hard environmentalists took the opportunity to support reduced industrialization. Everyone supported conservation, at least in name. But when it became apparent that diminished growth meant fewer jobs, the public-as-worker and the public-as-victim were finally opposed, and still other alternatives were demanded. Unfamiliar technologies loomed as the wave of the future, promising to reshape American life into a hydrogen economy, a solar economy, or a wind-mill and wave economy. And as the complexity of tradeoffs among industry, ecology, and energy grew, the public's projected ability to attend to, let alone adjudicate this proliferation of technical communication declined.

The preceding narrative of successive root metaphors helps to advance and clarify our initial claim: that the invention of advanced technology has had the unintended effect of technologizing rhetorical invention. Such a thesis is not, in itself, novel. Jeremiads of the machine age had warned of a technical future throughout the Forties and Fifties. From Chaplin's *Modern Times* to Skinner's *Walden II,* future fantasies threatened or beckoned with a precisely coordinated social environment. Yet even as this vision was prophesied in the abstract, our view is that it was being realized in the concrete. Technical reasoning finds its optimal operationalization in the control over a natural environment. And as long as such a mission was confined to an environment thought to be objective, neutral, and infinitely malleable, the reasoning of technique offered merely a mystifying alternative to social intuition. But the notion of a technological ultimate—one that could obliterate its own creators—confirmed the growing sense that nature was finite, while placing progress itself in the most severe jeopardy. In William Barrett's words:

What has happened is nothing less than the transformation of human reason itself, an event that consequently transforms all subsequent history. Reason takes up a new stand and posits new goals for itself in the face of all that is. The change reaches into every cranny of human existence. . . . Technology embodies physically what science has already done in thought when science sets up its own conditions as a measure of nature. The new science is in its essence technological.[18]

The bomb was, in the words of its creators, the ultimate gadget. And the culture that resulted promised both a realized future and (the worst fear) a future without reality. The atom bomb may have ended the pragmatic practice of entertaining live hypotheses by rendering life itself vulnerable as an ongoing proposition. As the embodiment of technical reasoning, the bomb drew the lines and the limits for all future disputes among forms of life.[19]

Nuclear Power, the Uncertain Solution

When the peaceful use of the atom first received attention, nuclear power was heralded as a great advance in technology, an advance that reaffirmed faith in the traditional promise of industry and science. It was predicted, for example, that soon even meters for measuring energy use would not be necessary. Thus, early in its development, the "atomic furnace" was likened to other inventions (the telephone, automobile, airplane), all inventions portentous of progress, and all overcoming what had seemed to be a limitation of nature. Nuclear power was analogous, but with a major difference: no other invention in the history of mankind had demonstrated as great a potential for mass destruction (and perhaps mass salvation) as had atomic energy. However, it was hoped that as technical thinking had discovered nature's secret to virtually unlimited energy, so this same thinking could perfect its safe use. "Atomic energy as used in bombs could destroy our civilization," explained a children's reader in the 1950s. "Atomic energy as used in an atomic furnace can be as safe as gasoline used in a car. It can make our lives easier and help give us leisure for the greater enjoyment of living."[20] Over the past 30 years the development of nuclear power has not been as rapid or happy as early proponents predicted.

The development of nuclear energy was rarely engaged directly as a deliberative issue. Its history and difficulties were formed by the prevailing forms of life we have discussed.[21] Nuclear energy developed first as an industry. Early on, the federal government took unprecedented steps to propagate and control the nuclear industry; financial support was available for research, even as economic incentives made the development of power plants attractive. Even though the technology expanded throughout the Cold War, it remained troubled by controversies.[22] These included several small accidents, passage of the Price-Anderson Act which limited the liability of the nuclear industry, and disclosures that the Atomic Energy Commission (a federal agency charged with both the promotion and regulation of the industry) had suppressed information of significant consequence and had loaded its procedures in favor of industrial developmental.[23] For a brief period of time nuclear power became the focus of ecological concern. "The National Environmental Policy Act of 1969 was being debated in the Congress and the Administration had officially committed itself to environmental restoration. This led to a confluence of issues, the parameters of which included the quality control in construction, environmental impacts, radiation exposure and its cumulative impact, and the possibility of accidents, all juxtaposed with an apparently growing demand for electricity."[24] But, unlike other movements of the era, the nuclear power opponents never achieved much national prominence.

"The protest movement initially was made up mostly of local groups in various areas that intervened in the licensing process to slow down and occasionally block construction of a nuclear power plant."[25] Local protest, at first discouraged by AEC decision-making rules, was rendered more effective by the Supreme Court Calvert Cliffs decision which expanded the National Environmental Policy Act to include demands for environmental impact statements, giving anti-nuclear advocates greater recourse through the courts. In addition, the safety functions of regulation were given to a new agency, the Nuclear Regulatory Commission, which initiated some moves toward greater public involvement in the siting of reactors.[26] Thus debate over the expansion of nuclear power was translated into local and regional contests.

The special forums containing the nuclear issue (business, courts, regulatory agency, and the scientific establishment) were geared gradually to evolve social consensus. Yet, public ambivalence in the late 1970s seemed only to grow deeper. Technical journals reflected rancorous dissent within the scientific community. Legal battles, providing questionable conclusions of the desirability of nuclear power *per se,* embittered both sides. Local communities, enticed by the benefits to industry and appalled by the potential environmental damage, made tentative decisions.

Despite general fears and disagreements, growing predictions of energy shortfalls presented nuclear power as the only practical alternative for the maintenance of social life. But, late in the winter of 1979, a series of incidents underscored the fact that atomic power was far from a certain solution. Five nuclear reactors were shut down because of design flaws which potentially imperiled public safety. WASH-1400, a major study supporting the safety of nuclear power, was repudiated by the Nuclear Regulatory Commission. The Karen Silkwood case proceeded to a stormy conclusion, replete with charges that a worker protesting nuclear power had been murdered by agents bent on protecting the industry. And then, days before the accident, these isolated incidents were given coherence and visual substance by the film: *The China Syndrome.*

Superficially, at least, *The China Syndrome* was a hybrid artifact, deriving from the two most prominent genres of the 1970s: disaster (*Meteor, Earthquake, The Swarm*) and conspiracy (*The Parallax View, Executive Action, All the President's Men*). Familiar to both plotlines (and present in *The China Syndrome*) were the themes of public victimage, political corruption, technical heroism, and a sense of consuming suspicion and evil. These representative anecdotes portrayed a world in which the dream of human perfectibility was abandoned: evil was regarded as something ineradicable that pervades—even defines—the body politic itself. It seems that when the succession of industry, ecology, and energy further attenuated prospects for social life, fears of the end began to surface and were dramatized. Neil Smelser confirms this conclusion. "When a shortage of energy or power threatens, the initial psychological impact is to create a feeling of powerlessness, of helplessness, of anxiety, of death—as though that which has been sustaining us is being exhausted. The prospect of everything running out can excite the strongest and most primitive psychological fantasies of desertion and destruction."[27] If the atom bomb presented an ultimate horizon framed by ultimate power, at least it admitted a possibility for rational control. But, if power runs out, so do alternatives. Mankind is left at the mercy of punitive nature.

What was so alarming about *The China Syndrome* was its glaring departures from the Seventies prototypes. Although this film is ostensibly the story of a disturbed reactor programmer who takes increasingly drastic action to warn of an impending nuclear catastrophe (*The China Syndrome*), the accident itself never actually occurs. The viewer is left with the impression that it "is only a matter of time." And, because this prospective disaster will be technical rather than natural, the technical elite of society (news anchors, regulatory officials, nuclear scientists) are not the heroic figures of typical disaster/conspiracy films. In *The China Syndrome,* even the most sympathetic characters are portrayed as powerless to ward off or control their own creations. Finally, and most striking, the problems of communicative competence—by both specialists and "public"—are heightened in this film to an almost surreal extreme. There are almost no ordinary people at all who are not functionally inarticulate. Protesters wear black gags at a public hearing. Workers are killed or "silenced" before they can testify. Other than such cases of failed communication, the landscape of *The China Syndrome* is depopulated. Nor is anyone else able to speak competently on the public's behalf. Neither the crazed programmer nor the sympathetic reporter is able even to explain to a television audience what has happened. And the cameraman's film of an earlier disturbance at the plant is silent. While the dramatic tension in ordinary disaster/conspiracy artifacts is generated by the search to find someone who will listen, the dramatic tension of *The China Syndrome* is generated by the continuing struggle to find anyone who can speak. Although melodrama provides an imaginative portrayal of hopes and fears, a crisis which would disclose the true extent of our predicament had yet to appear.

Failed Anticipations:
A Reconstruction of Crisis Discourse

Middletown, Pennsylvania must have seemed an unlikely backdrop for an encounter with the global implications of nuclear technology. Yet Middletown, like Londonderry and other small towns, had quietly come to depend upon a source of power few had ever questioned. On the morning of March 28, 1979, at 4:00 AM, a series of alarms began to ring inside the reactor facilities at Three Mile Island—so many that a plant operator, Faust, did not know which to obey. One hundred minutes into the accident the technicians knew that a serious problem existed on site. Five days into the accident, an ever-widening array of specialized and public demands had met with conspicuous confusion and failure. We now explore that discourse, throughout its narrative problems in describing, naming/reassuring, assessing, and assimilating the accident.

1. The Accident

Even the simplest reconstruction of the accident at Three Mile Island must confront the technical confusions responsible.[28] In the belated judgment of the Nuclear Regulatory Commission, there were initial failures of two pumps essential to the plant's secondary cooling system. When the primary facility had no outlet, it began to overheat—blowing open a safety valve which then could not be shut. A large quantity of gas and water escaped. Because the valves remained open, the coolant in the reactor core also dropped, exposing part of the core itself. When this damage extends to the entire reactor core, it is called a meltdown—the China Syndrome. There was considerable debate about how long portions of the core were exposed and how much damage actually resulted. In any case, related "judgment" problems did not ease the situation. An emergency cooling pump was shut down; company officials released sizeable quantities of radioactive gases into the atmosphere without warning. And, company officials pumped twelve to fifteen thousand gallons of escaped radioactive coolant into an adjoining building which (it turns out) had no containment system. The vapors in this coolant escaped through the company's ventilation system into the air outside. The NRC concluded that the company officials did not know what they were doing. In this sense, the accident at Three Mile Island deviated from the typical disaster storyline from the first day.[29] It began with *blame*—because it simply was not supposed to happen.

The accident involved much more than a simple mechanical failure. For five days, the status of the reactor remained unclear. The ambiguous signs it emitted suggested everything from cold shut-down to catastrophe. Experts predicted, calculated, and enacted technical decisions. But each act and explanation assumed the burden of a public judgment because the potential consequences to wider audiences could not be ignored. Here, in summary form, are the events and choices that created and extended the crisis.

Wednesday, March 28, 1979
AM Metropolitan Edison declares general emergency, due to reactor shutdown; monitoring of radiation release begins.
PM Metropolitan Edison officials attempt to explain accident; public and regulatory officials are called in.

Thursday, March 29, 1979
AM Metropolitan Edison dumps contaminated waste water into the Susquehanna River; controversy over reliability of industry and government sources continues throughout the day.
PM Plant and public officials announce that the crisis is over.

Friday, March 30, 1979
AM   Metropolitan Edison vents radioactive gas; a partial evacuation is recommended; hydrogen bubble in reactor is discovered and announced.
PM   Fears of meltdown mount; partial evacuation continues; Harold Denton of the NRC assumes control of press briefings.

Saturday, March 31, 1979
AM   Periodic press briefings from on-site experts, the Nuclear Regulatory Commission, and Governor Thornburgh on status of hydrogen bubble; technical debate over its explosive potential and immediate dangers continues.
PM   Press releases conflicting stories on explosive potential; Governor's press office stormed by reporters seeking to determine the status of the reactor.

Sunday, April 1, 1979
AM   Denton and advisors meet to dispute the safety of the reactor while the presidential plane is landing.
PM   President and Mrs. Carter tour the facility; Carter and Governor Thornburgh hold press conference; media attention intensifies throughout the day.

Monday, April 2, 1979
PM   Reactor "stabilizes," bubble continues to shrink, crisis recedes.[30]

In general, the accidental rhetoric at Three Mile Island, however inconsistent and tension-ridden, was a continual attempt to depersonalize the accident itself while reassuring the public sector as to its human costs. The overriding root metaphor of container and thing-contained often is applied to something hidden and mysterious. This is still more fashionable in an era preoccupied with conspiracy and clandestine behavior. Yet the archetype of disaster requires more discernible signs of resolution. It did not help that the advocates at Three Mile Island had specialized ends to serve, that they were less than familiar with the larger demands of public discourse, and that no one—media surrogates included—had command of the full picture. We now attempt to reconstruct the successive phases of the crisis in order to illustrate how the burdens of public address were fulfilled by the crisis actors.

2. Naming and Reassuring

It is interesting that the earliest stage of the rhetoric from Three Mile Island had some special reasons for being on the "outside looking in." Recall that some malfunctions had occurred. But not only was the company already issuing conflicting reports, it had also begun to reassure the public that all was under control. Because no one in the so-called public sphere really knew what was going on inside the plant, attention and media discourse focused upon effects outside the plant. But here, too, the media were stuck. Disasters—even their technical mutations—are usually visible. But the radiation that had escaped was not. The early attempts at naming the accident and effects had to depend upon experts and company officials. Their flirtations with opposite poles of discourse—the esoteric and the mundane—are of more than passing interest. While NRC official Charles Gallina acknowledged a "serious contamination problem on site,"[31] Charles Blaisdell of the Pennsylvania Emergency Management Agency was being reassuring. He said, "Our word is that people have nothing to worry about. The radiation level is what people would get if they played golf in the sunshine."[32] When plant officials okayed the discharge of 400,000 gallons of radioactive waste water from the plant into the Susquehanna River, the Department of Environmental Resources was finally called in. But here, too, the outside message was one of reassurance. Another surrogate, DER spokesman David Milne, said: "Most of it will be dissipated like bubbles in soda pop."[33] The problem that had forced the discharge was also described in comfortably domestic terms. Accumulated lethal radiation in the plant's turbine room was announced thusly: "Plutonium has taken up residence in the building."[34] We note, in passing, that the regulatory officials at the power plant won the Doublespeak Award for 1979.[35] Yet there is a tradition dating back to the early 1950s of domesticating America's ultimate threats. As then, at Three Mile Island much remained hidden.[36] Dangerous human decisions were defined as a "happening." The accident remained officially an "incident." Most important, the language of domestication and sanitizing assumed a portentous rhetorical burden. In attempting to reassure prematurely, those who employed such language assumed, or rather hoped, that the chain reaction of faulty system relays, turbine trips, and exposed fuel rods had been terminated quietly in the technical sphere, even as their ramifications were being hidden from the social sphere.

3. Failed Reassurance

In the second phase of the accident, technical reassurance continued, amid growing uncertainty as to whether the accident was really over. The NRC and plant management said that it was but with varying degrees of qualification. According to Commissioner Hendrie of the NRC, "At this time, the danger is over for people off-site. . . . Our readings show radiation levels have dropped significantly."[37] Company officials were even more adamant in their denials: "We didn't injure anybody in this accident, we didn't seriously contaminate anybody, and we certainly didn't kill a human soul."[38] Note a couple of things about director Herbein's statement: first, the incident has now become an *accident*. Here is at least some partisan acknowledgement that some aspect of the plant's operations was outside the control of management. Second, Herbein does not deny contaminating anybody (but rather, "seriously" contaminating anybody). Because the measurements were incomplete, and the effects of low level radiation contestable, Herbein's statement is not entirely assuring. From this vantage, it became impossible to prove anyone was *not* seriously injured or killed. The accident continues even if it is over. Reporters distrusted any single official source, and still they needed someone to blame. They were not well-informed about radiation. But many had seen *The China Syndrome*—in which they emerged as protagonists. These facts, plus the continuous discharge of radioactive materials on the second day, may help to explain the equally conspicuous failure of early reassurance.

We have two examples of this failure. First, because no one had yet seen the inside of the plant, everyone was free to speculate. This allowed the press and other partisans to impose less than soothing interpretations upon conditions inside the reactor facility. The NRC representative mentioned earlier was asked by several subcommittee members how he could be sure that overheating had only broken up the fuel rods and not melted them. We underline this portion of the *Washington Post* article:

> He was asked if he had seen the film, *The China Syndrome,* whose plot is about a possible accident in which a nuclear power plant core melts down so completely that it eats its way through the Earth to China. . . .

Hendrie's reply is interesting:

> I can't be absolutely sure that parts of the fuel haven't melted, but we think we'd see more and different fission products if the fuel had melted. . . . As for the China Syndrome, we were nowhere near it, nowhere near it.[39]

In the midst of all the changes in tense, Hendrie's reply must acknowledge the uncertainty of his own removed vantage from the reactor plant. And yet, his very candor about the limits of expertise undermined the conviction of this last statement.

A second indication of failed reassurance may be found in the media's premature attempts to summarize the human costs through the discourse of town residents near the power station. This is a traditional step in the disaster narrative for assimilating bad news into the regularities of ordinary life. This time, however, the repeated interviews with the residents of Londonderry and Middletown were tempered by a nagging sense that life here might never be quite normal again.

Recall, to begin, that disaster narrative defines the proper role for ordinary members of the public to be that of victim. A *Washington Post* article initiated this theme by inquiring whether the "blessing" of island power plants had turned into a "curse"; of course, neither imposed state of affairs suggested a large number of personal options.[40] As soon as we turn to the discourse of these people, our suspicions are confirmed. One old lady was quoted as saying: "I don't like it. I don't like it at all. . . . It's almost enough to make me want to sell out and move."[41] Indeed, this seems to have been the most extreme among the range of options available. More limited changes of conduct were described as follows: "One woman said she decided not to hang her laundry outside. One old man put off plowing his garden for a week. And the Londonderry Elementary School didn't let children go out for recess all day."[42] Thus far, we find very limited alterations in the pattern of private conduct. Moreover, all the examples offered were cases of people *not* doing everyday things that they typically do. Such negation of ordinary activity suggested an even more severe retreat into private life. When pressed as to their most fundamental choices, these "victims" passively reflected the technical decision-making arena. James Engle said, "I'm more afraid of that highway out there, and the crime that goes on around here, than that plant across the river."[43] Rita O'Connor said, "I don't worry about it. . . . You see these lights burning in this house? As long as I want to keep them burning, there have to be plants like this someplace."[44]

Monica Drayer was rather philosophical: "If you are going to go, you're going to go. Life is one big gamble. That plant's as safe as anything else." And then, "I really don't think the government would let them do anything to endanger our health."[45] In composite, the responses suggest the archetypal consumer-victim of technological decision-making. Life is a constant gamble, a world of trade-offs, where necessary evils balance trained consumer habits. When it gets too bad, you go inside, or you just go. We all have to.

Yet, we suggested that there is failed reassurance here; and this is because even the resignation to a world of risks and trade-offs does not seem to be enough. Monica Drayer was forced to add a note of blind faith in government's capacity to regulate foreseeable risks. In fact, not one person voiced a positive personal motive to guide conduct; all sought to adjust to the risk, to minimize evil. The *Post* article ends:

> Now the woman, like so many other people here, said she was going to have to do some real nitty gritty soul searching. "Now that it is down to the real nitty gritty, I want to know more about what goes on in there," she said.[46]

However, as subsequent events would demonstrate, even the options for personal adjustment would become more limited.

Thus far, we have seen the disaster narrative straining to encompass an "incident" and then an "accident" within its own schematic frame of anticipations. Within this framework, the experts were losing confidence, due—we think—to their inability to explain the incident, or agree upon its costs. The public officials found their own attempts at reassurance unsuccessful, given the non-accountability of plant management, and the increasing frustration of media surrogates with the dispersion of information. Governor Thornburgh expressed this official dilemma graphically in his Thursday press briefing:

> I believe, at this point, that there is no cause for alarm, nor any reason to disrupt your daily routine, nor any reason to feel that the public health has been affected by events on Three Mile Island.
>
> This applies to pregnant women; this applies to little children; and this applies to our food supply.
>
> I realize that you are being subjected to a conflicting array of information from a variety of sources. So am I.[47]

The media anchors were not faring well either. They found the technical information difficult to translate into a public language, and they still had nothing visual to convey, given the invisibility of the central phenomenon and the accident's dependence upon technology itself.

The White House became concerned about something called, "the echo effect," a loss of credibility which "occurs when technical experts talk about the same phenomena in slightly different terms; as a result, different stories come out in the media."[48] The consequence of this expressed concern was swift but unpredictable. The Bethesda information center was closed until further notice, under the assumption that a simple absence of information could stop the echos. But it could not.

For their part the reporters exchanged anomalies with the elite sector. (Reporter: "Do you know what you are doing?" Denton: "I think we know what we are doing, but. . . .")[49] They reinterviewed the same residents, who reflected back again what the technical experts and officials and the media had told them. The system of discourse was giving way from the strain; even as it reconfirmed its most tenuous assumptions, it passed along its weaknesses from part to part.

4. Crisis

By Friday, neither technical knowledge nor narrative anticipation could hold the volatile mixture of events. And in their struggle to do so, a moment of unintended reflection emerged. Several cumulative developments contributed to the crisis atmosphere. The deliberate release of radioactive gases by the Metropolitan Edison Company forced renewed attention upon the technical measurement of risks. No longer were management, experts, or regulation agency representatives claiming that a meltdown was impossible. Put simply, no one knew what to expect from a much more primitive hydrogen-oxygen reaction developing in the reactor core; a hydrogen bubble had been trapped there. The further down the bubble reached, the more it threatened to expose the reactor core ("The China Syndrome"!). The closer it reached to the top of the reactor, the more it appeared likely to detonate. Related to these intensified developments was a decision by Governor Thornburgh to evacuate, from within a five-mile radius of the plant, pregnant women and young children. Finally the media had hit upon an iconographic anchor for its faltering narrative: the huge cooling towers of the plant itself.[50] Because the crisis itself was still largely invisible, the media story would become the subject of its own narrative. The result would yield associations and oppositions that were surely beyond all conscious intent.

The samples of discourse encountered during this crisis period seem even more fragmented and inconsistent than what had come before. In a world robbed of practical public options, the technical control of nature had at least provided the illusion of reassurance. Now apparently the most sophisticated and specialized forms of expertise were unable to anticipate or control the most primitive combination of elements within the reactor facilities. If the repercussions to health and safety were too far-reaching for the conventional measurements of scientized decision-making, the reactor's own momentary changes in configuration were so sudden and spontaneous as to defy even the obsessive immediacy of news. The resulting network of discourse seemed to place everyone on the periphery of the phenomenon's elusive center.

Here, then, are some glimpses from this suddenly rarified horizon of action and events. On Friday evening, Walter Cronkite seemed to sense the range of thematic associations in these opening lines of his newscast:

> We are faced with the remote but very real possibility of a nuclear meltdown at the Three Mile Island atomic-power plant. The danger faced by man for tampering with natural forces, a theme familiar from the myths of Prometheus to the story of Frankenstein, moved closer to fact from fancy through the day.[51]

If remarks such as these did not represent "the way it was" in a technical sense, they at least suggested a realization that a more animistic metaphor for nature (ecology) remained close at hand.

On this same day, there was an unpleasant press conference exchange with Metropolitan Edison Chairman John Herbein. As noted earlier, Herbein had authorized a considerable release of radioactive gases (the exact amount is unknown) that morning without consulting either public agencies or (one senses) the press. In an atmosphere where everyone else seemed to be reacting, measuring, or adapting, Herbein's behavior was conspicuous by contrast. His response to a somewhat hostile press corps did little to arouse sympathy: "I don't know why we need to tell you each and every thing we do specifically. . . . We certainly feel a responsibility for people who live around our plant, and we need to get on with our job."[52] Interestingly enough, this workmanlike appeal depends upon a sense of authority that was fast becoming suspect, considering the growing appearance of technical uncertainty. Inside the reactor, the bubble continued to expand. Outside the reactor, an evacuation siren sounded accidently. And, for a time, there was confusion and panic.

Much of the discourse throughout March 31, and the days following, represented an attempt by the growing number of specialists at Three Mile Island simultaneously to resolve their technical problem, even as they sought to reassure the "public." Yet from the perspective we have sketched thus far such attempts could only fail. Indeed, the technical and social communicative demands facing the experts and advocates at Three Mile Island proved to be incompatible. Because no one had anticipated quite the primitive combination of ingredients forming in the reactor bubble, technical problem-solving required that still more professional opinions be consulted. But amid growing media speculation, this only increased the "echo effect." Furthermore, no technical specialist—nuclear or otherwise—was prepared to speak beyond the margins of precision in his or her own discipline. No single representative or scientist at Three Mile Island would risk speaking generally, or pronouncing definitively on matters that remained technically uncertain. But while such precautionary measures preserved "guarded optimism" in each specialized sector, they appeared more and more unsettling with every qualifier. Consider the following account of the news media's most trusted spokesman, Harold Denton of the NRC:

> Harold Denton of the Nuclear Regulatory Commission said last night that, based on his agency's calculations, the total exposure to residents of the surrounding area amounted to 1,000 man-rems. Referring to studies that show 10,000 to 20,000 man-rems would result in one to two excess cases of cancer in future years, he said that one could estimate that the exposure in the Three Mile Island area would cause one-tenth to two-tenths of one cancer case that would not otherwise have occurred. But he admitted that the 1,000 man-rem figure he mentioned was a "crude estimate."[53]

Even the most reassuring of specialized pronouncements tended to undermine their suasory force, by conceding the uncertainty of a particular situation. Nuclear scientist, Zenons Zudans urged the public: "You must remember that the people best trained for this situation are working on it. Give them time to decide." Then he added: "There will only be one chance."[54]

Perhaps the most important incompatibility, then, was between the real uncertainty and apparent disagreement of the specialists and their own felt need to persuade. With a proliferation of technical pronouncements, disagreement became equal to the diversity of expression. Later, one of the chief participants was to recall, "We were like a couple of blind men staggering around making decisions."[55] And at the time, Roger Mattson, the NRC's director for safety systems, commented over the telephone: "We don't have a solution. We've got the best you got, Joe, and they are not coming up with answers."[56] When actual consensus begins to erode, the proclamations of technical authority are made to seem hollow. And as this discourse seemed to struggle with itself for a sense of audience, it is not surprising that the news media moved in to fill the gap.

But here, again, a certain trained incapacity seemed to be the rule. We have found the widespread claims for news media "balance" and reliability during this crisis period especially interesting, in light of the media's historic dependence upon the agreement of reliable sources. It is true that reporters converted Harold Denton to "Doctor" Harold Denton (although he had not received a doctorate). But claims for media balance have ignored reliability. David Rubin's study of press coverage during Three Mile Island concluded that the media performance was "balanced" because a content analysis of their coverage found a relative stand-off in the numbers of "reassuring" amid "alarming" statements.[57] Of course, reassuring statements typically derived from the official or expert community, and indicated that the plant was safe. However, alarming statements typically indicated that information about the accident—expert and otherwise—was unreliable. Remarkably, the *Public's Right to Information Task Force* concluded that any such reassuring statement should be accorded the same credence as a statement undermining the authority of the aforementioned reassuring statement. In the Commission's own statistics, 99% of the statements in the category of "Information" were found to be "alarming"; i.e., they undermined the informational quality of the reassuring statements. We are, therefore, less sanguine about the performance of both the news media and its social science interpreters during the crisis and its aftermath.

As the crisis deepened, then, technical consensus tended to erode, uncertainties multiplied, and contingencies for action seemed disengaged from real persons. It is no wonder that the world of ordinary life seemed frightening and insecure. What were social actors to make of the following exchange?

REPORTER: Which option will you take?
   DENTON: Well, I would hope there would be a consensus of experts before we make a decision.
REPORTER: Who decides finally at the very end?
   DENTON: I think the NRC would make the final decision.
REPORTER: Is any option a gamble?
   DENTON: Well, they all have pros and cons and different experts advocate different ways and. . . .[58]

It remained, then, for the media to frame the drama with more primitive symbolism. If the world of nuclear technology lacked a way of clearly naming and forecasting unlikely actualities, the media did not. Unlikely actualities were called *news.* Once Governor Thornburgh had evacuated pregnant women and preschool children from the plant's immediate vicinity (even as he was insisting that the reactor was "stable"), it became possible for the news media to connote visually the magnitude of a yet invisible event. Three Mile Island became a spectacle: something to behold dramatically from without, something to witness without cognitive understanding.

We turn now toward an illustration of the discursive fragments that the media employed to characterize the crisis period. Our text is an inner page from the highly respected newspaper *The Washington Post,* a page that seems to capture both intended and subliminal features of news narrative. There is, it seems, a special kind of irony at work in the ultimate terms of nuclear radiation; over and over, participants in the crisis referred to the ambiguity of an accident that could not be verified or disconfirmed by the senses. The sense of dread aroused by the invisible brings forth the world positivism refuted but never really left behind; it was last encountered in the post-war era of the 1950s. Then, its black and white characters reminded us, the world could be rendered malevolent enough to be completely destroyed; an enemy that could not be seen made everything that was visible illusory and expendable. Nuclear radiation is that sinister still (in some people's minds at least); and even precautionary measures tend to accentuate its evils. In evacuating pre-school children and mothers with their unborn, Governor Thornburgh was being a responsible public official. But he also allowed the media to portray those who were innocent, vulnerable, and most closely associated with the generation and renewal of life as the first victims of nuclear radiation.

In the excerpted page of headlines and captions[*], it is difficult to know with precision what first captures the reader's attention. But in case there is serious doubt, we have the semiotic of the newspaper headline to guide us: *Day Few Believed Possible Arrives in Atomic Age.*[59] Roland Barthes has concluded that the literal, denotative function of press headlines is less important than their iconographic directions for reading the connotative messages of press photographs. But even from a literal view, the headline itself is arresting. These are ultimate terms: *Day* with *Age* (surely, an unusual bit of scanning from the deadline chronology of journalism); *Possibility/Impossibility* with *Belief.* The *Few,* of course, could be the prophets of doom, those who dream of the epoch. And there is also (with the *Arrival*) the almost Biblical sense of a foretelling, of something coming to pass on its own accord. And perhaps there is more.

Consider the photographs. We read from left to right; and to our left are the ominous cooling towers in the upper portions of the graphic. One wonders why they are placed so far above eye level. The caption helps to explain; it reads: "Some residents in homes like these in a five-mile radius . . . have been urged to leave and have gone to Hershey sports area, right."[60] Other iconographic features of the towers now emerge: they are huge, and seem to dwarf the little box-like homes in the foreground. The towers are highly visible as well; they stand out against the gray horizon, giving us the sense that we can look upon and ponder the entire event.

---

[*]Editor's Note: Not reproduced here.

We now follow through on the caption's directions. The towers are just above the faces of the very frightened looking woman with children on the right. This is a truly remarkable image. The woman is looking up—as if to "watch the skies." She cradles her suckling infant in a gesture of warmth and protection; her glasses intensify her expression. She is an intelligent, but terrified Madonna. Over her right shoulder is a still younger infant, and . . . those demonic towers. In actuality, the towers were not a vehicle of damage; in fact, they were there to cool the steam and to protect the environment. But their impact in this graphic is that of pure connotation. The era of the apocalypse and disaster may have invited its own logic of disbelief; and in that logic, the towers have acquired the emblem of mushroom clouds from an earlier decade. Symbolic values are no easier to confirm than they are to discount, but this radical opposition of terms and images would not seem to require further interpretation. At this stage of the crisis, it is at least safe to say that the containers of the nuclear age, discursive and technical, would no longer absorb the public issues created here.

Another headline story every bit as revealing comes to us from the *Philadelphia Inquirer*. The uppermost headline read: *What Hath Man Wrought? Worshippers Ask.*[61] The story is thematically consistent with the science fiction films of the fifties: ultimately machinery runs on faith. The congregation of the Glad Tidings Assembly of God believed that it was all over:

> "I believe," said their minister, the Reverend Steven Sparks, when the hand-clapping had died down, "we are living in the last days." There were murmurs of approval. "I'm not saying that to scare anybody," the minister went on. "I'm just saying what the Bible tells us."[62]

Moving out to the suburbs, we hear from Rev. John Bestwick of a Catholic church in Harrisburg. The priest advised his congregation to "stay calm, cool, and collected and pray for Almighty God to grant the inspiration and technology to do what is necessary."[63] On this same Sunday, Jimmy Carter tested his own faith by appearing inside the reactor facilities for twenty-five minutes. But based upon the excerpts we have studied, it appears that ordinary human beings were in need of a higher authority.

By three o'clock Sunday afternoon, one NRC staffer later recalled, "We're convinced we've got it. It's not going to go boom." And by Tuesday the crisis atmosphere had eased. The bubble, rather than bursting, was getting smaller, and the plant was pronounced stable by a consortium of authorities. It was later reported by the President's Commission that the NRC wanted to find some more or less concrete event to use as a symbol, and visually to punctuate the ending of the crisis. But none could be found.

Implications of the Crisis for Communication and Rhetorical Theory and Practice

On the evening of April 3rd, Governor Dick Thornburgh delivered an address, televised state-wide, to assure the people of Pennsylvania that the week-long crisis was nearing an end, and to tell the "brave and innocent people" who were evacuated that they might soon, "indeed, go home again." Reflecting upon "the most danger-ous days of decision that any Governor has had to face in this century," Thornburgh expressed a widely shared viewpoint: "Not all the promotion in the world can erase the memories of central Pennsylvania as the place where the worst fear of modern man almost came to pass."[64] But while dedicating his administration to the propo-sition that "what never should have happened in the world today" should "never happen again," the question of how the public could act was left just as unclear as at the peak of crisis. "Nuclear opponents, who would shut down every reactor in the country tonight simply are not in touch with our needs for tomorrow," the Governor opined, "but nuclear advocates, who pretend that nothing was changed by our vigil at Three Mile Island simply are not in touch with reality."[65] Thus, even as Thornburgh and his national counterparts made personal commitments to refine the system of control through new investigations, reviews, and procedures, the actual role of the public remained obscure. "There is much that has changed and much that remains the same"; he concluded, "we" must only "sacrifice more . . . work harder . . . help one another . . . and stay calm in the face of a storm."[66] In spite of these and similar reassurances of future safety, to many the crisis at Three Mile Island called for much more than a stoic renewal of commitment to failed practice. As one NRC commissioner put it, Three Mile Island meant "the need for addressing the fundamental question of can the system work."[67]

In order to answer this question we now explore three distinct levels of critique: first, the communication problems reported by those directly involved in the crisis; second, communication problems discerned by a more comprehensive and impar-tial review; and, third, a critical analysis of the optimal communication practices implied by the foregoing interpretations. By evaluating the discourse at Three Mile Island against successively broader horizons (from institutional obligations to communication use values to deliberative choice), we hope to approximate the limits of rhetoric in a technological era.

Partisan Claims

While Governor Thornburgh may not have captured all the dilemmas suggested by the crisis, still his own views of the quality of discourse are important. As a central decision-maker he had to "weigh the potential risks of Three Mile Island against the proven hazards of moving people under panic conditions." Then, he had to inform the public. On the question of communication adequacy, he was quite specific, characterizing the discourse as an "unending flow of rumors," "a kaleido-scope of signals," and an "unending avalanche of misstatements and second-guess-ing from virtually everyone who had an opinion."[68] From his perspective, the chief difficulty was not the amount of information but its variable quality. He concluded it was virtually impossible to sift out "facts from fiction, hyperbole from analysis, cant from candor, and guesswork from solid reporting."[69] The source of this problem he attributed to "some erroneous, some alarming and some irresponsible reports carried by the media." But he also added that it was "easy to understand how five different stories could come out of a single press conference" given "the nuclear trade jargon, the clamor of competing experts, and the garble gap between Harrisburg and Washington."[70]

Most assessments of the problems at Three Mile Island are similar to Thornburgh's accusations of incompetence. Local officials, conceding errors in judgment (such as setting off the civil defense sirens on Friday), blamed state officials for a lack of information.[71] State officials, while confessing that their judgments about evacuation were tentative, found the Federal government to be at fault for inadequate co-ordination of information and expertise.[72] Elected Federal officials, acknowledging that nuclear power demanded certain tradeoffs between risks and benefits, found the NRC responsible for inadequate emergency planning and poor licensing reviews.[73] The NRC, in turn, claimed that the staff of Metropolitan Edison was not thoroughly trained or adequately equipped, even while admitting that a report indicating the potential failure of the reactor had "slipped through the cracks."[74] Representatives of the industry, while purporting "to have learned our lesson" at Three Mile Island, nevertheless blamed the press for sensationalism and fringe elements for using Three Mile Island to try to deny the benefits of nuclear power to the American people.[75] The news establishment, although conceding that the staff sent to cover the story was not expert in the nuances of nuclear technology, accused Metropolitan Edison of lying and the NRC of covering up.[76] It seems that representatives of each institution admitted some inadequacy in its own performance but attributed the essential causes of communication failures to events and people beyond its immediate responsibility and control.

Whoever or whatever was to blame, the net result was failed communication. As one post-investigative report concluded:

> The local residents who testified told us they received such conflicting reports they had no idea what to believe or whom to believe. They opinioned [sic] that they could believe nothing told them by the state, NRC or Met-Ed officials from March 28 until Sunday or Monday of the following week.[77]

Therefore, assessment of the communication problems must take into consideration the generic causes of failure, the reasons why the whole system became entangled in the web of crisis.

A Systemic Analysis

A Presidential Task Force investigating the crisis concluded that the communication incompetence was so widespread that popular explanations ("that the utility lied, that the NRC covered up . . ., or that the media engaged in an orgy of sensationalism") were not credible. Concluding that "The public's right to know during the accident was ill served by Met Ed, the NRC, and most of the other institutions involved,"[78] the Task Force focused its report on the lack of systematic planning, delegation of authority, and preparation for technological emergencies.

The root cause of the crisis to members of the Task Force resided in the novel aspects of the reactor accident. Unlike other incidents at Fort St. Vrain and Browns Ferry, accidents that were over before reported, Three Mile Island invited popular coverage of "a potentially serious accident *as it was happening,*" thus creating a unique environment of "drama and urgency." Because the consequences of a major accident were predicted even by conservative estimates to be catastrophic, and because the phenomena at the center of the reactor core remained enigmatic (a matter subject to changing predictions), the requests for information and the demands for action proliferated, exposing the weaknesses of the communication system.[79]

If the communication networks in place before the accident were unable to anticipate problems or prepare suitable spokespersons to present "timely, accurate and understandable information," the question remains what is the ultimate reason for lack of preparation. Here the Task Force was less forthcoming, stating rather tersely that members of the nuclear establishment were *"victims"* of their own reassurances.[80] The NRC's Peter A. Bradford, under Senate cross-examination, better elaborated this idea: "There has been reluctance bordering on embarrassment to look hard at evacuation questions, to look hard at certain types of accidents because they seemed so unlikely, because the precautions were expensive, because they tended to remind people that a nuclear accident, however, [sic] unlikely, could be catastrophic."[81] The result of this logic of disbelief was a myopia which led Bradford and his nuclear colleagues to see "events considered highly unlikely as actually impossible."[82]

Many criticisms of Three Mile Island seem to converge upon this central claim that the bureaucratic establishment, the energy industry, the mass media, and the affected citizens were all victims of the crisis. The thesis has some merit. After all, the unstable and uncertain conditions of the reactor defied all authoritative technical and social discourse. Unfortunately, those who hold to their hypothesis foreshorten critique by failing to reflect carefully upon the world view contributing to their assumptions. Transforming the accident into partisan capital, advocates have sought to attribute blame without asking the fundamental question of whether even well-motivated, competent people could prevent crises. Systems analysts, seeing the incident as an opportunity to improve existing practice, have applied state-of-the-art communication concepts without inquiring as to whether these may be part of the problem. However, the events at Three Mile Island could offer something more than an opportunity for partisan ascendancy or reification of existing communication concepts. If we are to understand the nature of the crisis completely, the underlying conceptions of prevailing practice need to be critiqued.

Three Mile Island, The Limits of Rhetoric

If the initial hypothesis of the study is correct, then the communication failures at Three Mile Island should point to the limits of rhetorical practice in the modern age. Under ordinary circumstances, such limits are difficult to ascertain because communication practices develop in a fragmented manner, thereby concealing their implications from rhetorical choice. Only when representatives of specialties are drawn together to talk directly to a general public can we know the degree to which these variations inhibit communication and constrain rhetoric. Thus far, a variety of commentaries have been presented on the nature of failed communication at

Three Mile Island. In this section, we hope to trace the implied limits of contemporary discourse by contrasting the views of the public suggested by the practices at Three Mile Island with an ideal conception of the public as a knowledgeable and responsible collection of citizens, making prudential judgments. Such a critique is appropriate because it is to the public that all actors claimed to speak, and it is from the public that they were forced to draw ultimate authority and responsibility. Such a critique is necessary if understanding is to advance beyond partisan awareness or systemic coherence and toward a reflective knowledge of the practical dilemmas faced by speakers in a technological age.

The Accidental Public

In many respects, the discourse at Three Mile Island seemed to be governed by a conception of the public itself as accident, an audience extrinsic to the community of technologists, indirectly addressed only during times of expert dissensus. This conception of the public affirms distinctions, drawn by an earlier study, between social and technical reasoning.[83] Technical reasoning, interested in prediction and control, employs non-reflexive procedures in order to solve puzzles integral to specialized codes. By contrast, social reasoning focuses upon situation-dependent problems, employing self-criticism in order to inform choice and guide conduct toward a more perfect society. At Three Mile Island the lack of actual consensus within the technical community seemed to compel actors to address a wider and less familiar audience, the public. But even as speakers attempted to formulate statements of deliberative function, they appeared to be trapped. The insulated terminology, limited inference structures, sanitized language, and complicated divisions of status and authority within the nuclear power community worked at cross purposes with the perceived need to make timely, clear statements guiding public action.

Recognizing that competence in technical discourse does not imply competence in social discourse, a number of industries in a variety of technological fields since the accident have endeavored to train "scientist-explainers" to talk to "Joe Lunch Pail," the stereotype of the public offered by some public relations experts. In addition to holding "debates" with local interest groups, the goal of the new effort is to "develop special teams that can be 'parachuted' into a 'high risk situation' such as Three Mile Island." Those trained "are urged to speak simply, use simple analogies" and to employ "calm facial expressions" in order "to turn an adversary from emotional to rational."[84]

Although this attention to the requirements of social discourse may be superior to the almost completely accidental manner in which the public was addressed by the technical community during the crisis, the problems of formulating a deliberative rhetoric go far beyond those of teaching scientists public speaking. If the public is to be revitalized, then the language, the modes of decision-making, and procedures for establishing consensus must be discovered for both experts and generalists alike. Yet, the accident implies that the values of technological communication are such that language use proliferates arbitrarily, if not by deliberate sanitization; that inference structures relating technical and social judgments remain inaccessible; and, that knowledgeable consensus remains subordinated to shifting configurations of technical innovation. It seems that even as technical reasoning encompasses an increasing array of social questions, its very logic precludes its practitioners from full social responsibility. Thus, what Whitehead has called the "tragic" vision of science, "the vision of fate, remorseless and indifferent, urging a tragic incident to its inevitable issue,"[85] seems to be irreconcilable with the Utopian requirements of a vital public that demands by its very nature a vision of social wisdom and acknowledgement of moral accountability. So long as technical reasoning remains at odds with and ascendant over social reasoning, deliberative rhetoric remains accidental.

The Public as Spectator

It would be incorrect to conclude that only the accidental vision of the public contributed to the crisis. Implicit in much of the discourse is a vision of the public as spectator. Evidence for this conclusion is derived from inspecting the form of the Three Mile Island "story" produced by the mass-media, that of a natural disaster. The problem was that the technological accident varied with the script. First, the duration and significance of natural disasters are fairly well known. Nuclear power is unique and hence far more uncertain. Second, natural disaster reporting depends upon the traditional techniques of balancing good news and bad, alternatively piquing interest and assuaging fears. This ritual proportionality only heightened the phantasmagoric dimensions of a new and possibly catastrophic event. Third, reporters appear to be more knowledgeable than the general public, or at least knowledgeable enough to sort out good sources from bad. Yet, the traditional social techniques of cross-questioning hampered expert efforts at best and relied upon second-hand guesses at worst. In short, by following its traditional narrative form, the media became embroiled in the crisis.

For a short period afterwards, the mass-media, riding a wave of "public interest" featured a plethora of stories pertaining to nuclear power. Investigations were urged by editorials, and the hearings were initially covered with traditional fanfare. Anti-nuclear protests were anticipated, and such were dutifully covered, mainly as nostalgia pieces, featuring rock-singing, sign-carrying, protestors playing out their roles.[86] Some of the old technical controversies were even resurrected, complete with elided expert statements on complicated issues concerning waste and safety.[87] Interest abruptly halted in early summer. The crash of Flight 191 presented a new, more immediate disaster. Subsequent reports on nuclear power were consigned to the back pages. Thus does the public remain a spectator to a parade of endless catastrophes.

What passes for "public communication" today is frequently the news as spectacle. Although the news media seem to value the theme of popular participation—the public itself as an active agency—news formats mark the erosion of actual participation as media give news primacy to brute visual happenings to be named, explained, assessed, and assimilated. In such a format, the public finds its own role reduced to that of a passive receiver.[88] With the burgeoning of news formats, the "participatory" communication format for the public is that of ritual. And here, the goal of social decision is subordinated to the patterns of cultural nuance and preservation. Participation, in other words, is vicarious and stylized. In political ritual, the sacred and profane each have their place in a pageantry of image. The symbols of community affiliation are repeated in mock-heroic style while formal expectations are dramatized and fulfilled. Not all ritual is empty, of course. But as the news dramatizes the surface features of public issues without inviting knowledgeable action, often form alone remains. For this reason, even while witnessing the traditional dramas of social controversy, the mass-audience remains without impulse, knowledge of alternatives, or direction.

The Public as "Standing Reserve of Energy"

Although neither the technological nor mass-media institutions have apparently found a place for the public as an active agent, at least one of the prominent visions of the public acknowledges a role for discourse to change attitudes and mark improvement in public opinion indicators. Such a view conceives the public to be a natural resource full of potential power waiting to be harnessed. This vision was not much in evidence during the crisis. The voice of public relations was weak and stilled after the first couple of unfortunate days. Since the accident, however, the nuclear industry, predictably responding to public ambivalence over nuclear power, has launched a campaign to cultivate opinion.[89]

Following the modern format of political advertisements, many of the appeals are framed in terms of psychological primitives. Women are depicted as especially afraid of radiation, so a commercial features a mother with babe cooing over the benefits of a respirator with a stable power source. The language of protest is depicted as angry and demagogic, so special "advocates" are obtained to distribute bumper stickers, the technological equivalent of hand-made placards, reading "Feed Jane Fonda to the Whales," "More People have Died in Ted Kennedy's Car Than in Nuclear Accidents," and "A Little Nukey Never Hurt Anyone." Finally, many advertisements are worded in the language of pseudo-science. "I was the only victim of Three Mile Island," testifies Edward Teller in a Mobil Oil ad claiming that the physicist had a heart attack testifying before so many investigations.[90] The general aim of the public relations campaign has been to re-orient attitudes about the accident—to prove the system worked, not that it failed.

Yet, if the conclusion of the Atomic Energy Commission is correct, that only luck has prevented more serious accidents from occurring,[91] we wonder whether influencing attitudes only serves to deepen the potentiality for crisis. The Task Force concluded that the perceived need to protect the image of the nuclear industry may have been one of the causes for underestimating the potential significance of the breakdown.[92] Even if the industry is completely forthcoming, would not the credibility problems be even greater the next time, especially if the attitudes were shifted in a strongly pro-nuclear direction? It seems, then, that the techniques of mass manipulation practiced by the nuclear industry would transform citizens into aggregate attitude capital in order to advance the industry itself. Ironically enough, such practices as these continue to define a world where the public is forced to endure an unsteady relationship with technology and the environment.

In conclusion, we contend that the failures of Three Mile Island suggest the extent to which the art of deliberative rhetoric is constrained by prevailing conceptions of the public. Of course, it could be maintained that few eras discovered vital rhetorics for addressing knowledgeable publics. Disillusioned with the ideological wranglings of the nineteenth century, Kierkegaard concluded: "The qualification, 'public,' is produced by the deceptive juggling of an age of reflection."[93] The American pragmatic philosopher John Dewey was equally pessimistic about the early twentieth century. He wrote: "In spite of attained integration, or perhaps because of its nature, the Public seems to be lost; it is certainly bewildered. If a public exists, it is certainly as uncertain about its own whereabouts as philosophers since Hume have been about the residence and make-up of the self."[94] What distinguishes this era, however, is the manner in which questions of public address are bypassed altogether. Whether preoccupied with orientations of self and other, message-transmission, or the fulfillment of specialized roles and formats, ordinary communication patterns proliferate, apparently without much reflective choice.

Even as technical concepts of communication have receded from ordinary audiences, the practical art of rhetoric has become more remote. Indeed, because the practices of more specialized forms of inquiry have tended to fragment problems to fit each branch of expertise, there has been little need to consult general audiences. As the general audience itself has become transformed into the mass audience, issues of potential public consequence are processed for ritual consumption. Accordingly, most contemporary forms of communication do not display their patterns of inference; still fewer permit external audiences to participate volitionally, to help adjudicate the messages. So long as the assumptions, procedures, expectations, and formats of technical communication and surrogate discourse operate within undisturbed patterns, they are virtually self-confirming. And the once-esteemed art called rhetoric is abandoned altogether.

Paradoxically enough, it is only in the midst of crisis that such habituated patterns of discourse may be interrupted and exposed to contingency. With a breakdown of actual consensus, a contest of specialized interests, and an intermittent search for social confirmation, the discourse at Three Mile Island could no longer replicate itself. While the crisis confronted the communicators with incompatible, even tragic choices, nevertheless it revealed the most fundamental limitations of present conceptions of public discourse.

Of late, it has become fashionable to collapse the distinction between social and technical discourse. Intent upon expanding the role of rhetoric to fill the horizons of human knowledge and action, scholars have obscured longstanding distinctions between those areas bound by science and those by other forms of symbolization. In this view, rhetoric's limits are only those of the human imagination. While such soaring visions are no doubt inspiring, our analysis has proceded from a different vantage. We see the domains of the social and the technical as grounded in an historical dialectic, formed by social actors who must choose to regard some instances of knowledge as derived from science pertaining to facts in the natural world, and others as bounded instances of practical wisdom. When a crisis erupts, the limits of rhetoric and science as historical practices are made apparent. The study of Three Mile Island becomes important precisely because it allows us to see the limits of rhetoric for our own age.

Notes

1. Peter M. Sandman and Mary Paden, "At Three Mile Island," *Columbia Journalism Review,* 18 (1979), 43-58; Mark Bowden, "Nuclear Power and the Reporter's Plight," *Technology Review,* 84 (1981), 8-10; Sharon M. Friedman, "Blueprint for Breakdown: Three Mile Island and the Media Before the Accident," *Journal of Communication,* 31 (1981), 116-128; David M. Rubin, "What the President's Commission Learned About the Media," unpublished paper, Department of Journalism and Mass Communications, New York University, n.d., pp. 1-23.

2. U.S. Nuclear Regulatory Commission, *The President's Commission on the Accident at Three Mile Island,* full report (Washington, D.C.: GPO, Oct. 1979), esp. pp. 30-200; Lewis Battiste, et al., *Population Dose and Health Impact of the Accident at the Three Mile Island Nuclear Station: Preliminary Estimates Prepared by the Ad Hoc Interagency Dose Assessment Group,* U.S. Nuclear Regulatory Commission (NUREG-0558; Washington, D.C.: GPO, May 1979), pp. 1-77; U.S. Nuclear Regulatory Commission, *Three Mile Island—Two Lessons Learned: Task Force Report and Short Term Recommendations* (NUREG-0578; Washington, D.C.: GPO, July 1979), pp. 1-20; National Academy of Sciences, *Energy in Transition 1985-2010: Final Report of the Committee on Nuclear and Alternative Energy Systems* (San Francisco: W. H. Freeman and Company, 1980), pp. 460-461.

3. Among the many materials available, one might consult "Three Mile Island-2: A Babcock & Wilcox Perspective," a press-package introduced by John H. Macmillan, Vice President, Nuclear Power Generation Division, Lynchburg, VA, June 5, 1979. See also Commonwealth Edison, "Radiation and the Future of Kimberly Michelle Mayberry," *Chicago Tribune,* 12 Oct. 1980, Sec. 17, p. 2; "Exploding Three Mile Island," *Chicago Tribune,* 18 March 1980, Sec. 2, p. 6; "Investigating the Harrisburg Hoax," *Fusion: Magazine of the Fusion Energy Foundation,* 2 (1979), 8-16; Richard C. Hyde, "Three Mile Island: PR's Balaklava," *Public Relations Journal,* 35 (1979), 10-14.

4. John G. Kemeny, "An Extremely Small Malfunction . . . And Then Something Terrible Happened," *Dartmouth Alumni Magazine,* 72 (1979), 30.

5. A growing body of scholarship has stressed this "epistemic" function of rhetoric. Much of this scholarly literature is reviewed and summarized in Robert L. Scott, "On Viewing Rhetoric as Epistemic: Ten Years Later," *Central States Speech Journal,* 27 (1976), 258-266; and in Michael C. Leff, "In Search of Ariadne's Thread: A Review of the Recent Literature on Rhetorical Theory," *Central States Speech Journal,* 29 (1978), 73-91.

6. See John Angus Campbell, "Historical Reason: Field as Consciousness," in *Dimensions of Argument: Proceedings of the Second Summer Conference on Argumentation,* ed. George Ziegelmueller and Jack Rhodes (Annandale, Virginia: Speech Communication Association, 1981), pp. 101-113.

7. See Lloyd F. Bitzer, "The Rhetorical Situation," *Philosophy and Rhetoric,* 1 (1968), 1-14. It is not our claim that Three Mile Island, as a complex of incidents and events, is sufficient to undermine Bitzer's instrumental view of rhetorical practice. Rather, what we have called a rhetorical crisis will confront any theory of discourse with limits that disclose its most basic assumptions: its philosophy of communication.

8. For the origin of this distinction, see Thomas B. Farrell, "Knowledge, Consensus, and Rhetorical Theory," *Quarterly Journal of Speech,* 62 (1976), 2-8. By surrogates we mean those who "stand in" for the larger public and invoke its interests in order to perform their own specialized responsibilities. Examples might include reporters or regulatory officials.

9. Jean-Paul Sartre cited in "The Literature of Extreme Situations," *Aesthetics Today,* ed. Morris Philipson and Paul J. Gudel (New York: New American Library, 1980), p. 24.

10. Richard Sennett, *The Fall of Public Man: On the Social Psychology of Capitalism* (New York: Vintage Books, 1978); Christopher Lasch, *The Culture of Narcissism: American Life in an Age of Diminishing Expectations* (New York: W. W. Norton & Co., 1978); Alvin W. Gouldner, *The Dialectic of Ideology and Technology: The Origins, Grammar, and Future of Ideology* (New York: Seabury Press, 1976). The reasons we offer for the decline of the public idea and the rise of other forms of discourse depart from each of the above commentaries. Yet we find it interesting that sources of such divergent method and ideological stance have reached similar conclusions.

11. Charles A. Beard, "Whither Mankind," cited in *A Modern Reader,* ed. Walter Lippman and Allan Nevins (New York: D. C. Heath & Co., 1936), p. 136.

12. Martin Heidegger, "The Question Concerning Technology," in *Basic Writings,* ed. David Farrell Krell (New York: Harper and Row, 1977), p. 296. Heidegger isolates the predominant approach, or way of seeing nature that has come to typify the Western epoch. "The revealing that rules modern technology

is a challenging *[Herausfordern]*, which puts to nature the unreasonable demand that it supply energy which can be extracted and stored as such. But does not this hold true for the old windmill as well? No. Its sails do indeed turn in the wind; they are left entirely to the wind's blowing. But the windmill does not unlock energy from the air currents in order to store it.

In contrast, a tract of land is challenged in the hauling out of coal and ore. The earth now reveals itself as a coal mining district, the soil as a mineral deposit. The field that peasants formerly cultivated and set in order appears different from how it did when to set in order meant to take care of and maintain. The work of the peasant does not challenge the soil of the field. In sowing grain it places seed in the keeping of the forces of growth and watches over its increase. But meanwhile even the cultivation of the field has come under the grip of another kind of setting in order, which sets upon nature. It sets upon in the sense of challenging it. Agriculture is now mechanized food industry. Air is now set upon to yield nitrogen, the earth to yield ore, ore to yield uranium, for example; uranium is set upon to yield atomic energy, which can be released for either destruction or for peaceful use."

13. As Roosevelt repeatedly urged the domestic sector following Pearl Harbor, "There are now two fronts in this war." The result was a degree of industrial coordination and consumer management unprecedented in American history. See William Manchester, *The Glory and the Dream: A Narrative History of America* (Boston: Little, Brown and Company, 1974), esp. Ch. 10, "The Home Front."

14. Rachel Carson, *Silent Spring* (Boston: Houghton Mifflin Co., 1962). For a discussion of Carson's contribution to the ecology movement see Joel Primack and Frank von Hippel, *Advice and Dissent: Scientists in the Political Arena* (New York: Basic Books Inc., 1974), pp. 38-48.

15. Carson, p. 6.

16. Carson, p. 188.

17. James S. Bowman, "The Environmental Movement: An Assessment of Ecological Politics," *Environmental Affairs,* 5 (1976), 650.

18. William Barrett, *The Illusion of Technique: A Search for Meaning in a Technological Civilization* (Garden City: Anchor Press, 1978), p. 182.

19. G. Thomas Goodnight, "The Rhetoric of War in a Nuclear Age," Central States Speech Association Convention, Chicago, Illinois, 1977.

20. John Lewellen, *You and Atomic Energy and Its Wonderful Uses* (n.p.: Children's Press, 1949).

21. Carroll L. Wilson, "Nuclear Energy: What Went Wrong," *The Bulletin of the Atomic Scientists,* 35 (1979), 15.

22. Wilson, pp. 16-18.

23. Daniel F. Ford and Henry W. Kendall, "Nuclear Misinformation," *Environment,* 17 (1975), 19. More recently, a study by dissident Soviet scientist Zhores A. Medvedev, *Nuclear Disaster in the Urals* (New York: Vintage Books, 1980) offers persuasive evidence that the Atomic Energy Commission suppressed information about the 1957-58 Soviet nuclear accident.

24. Steven Ebbin and Raphael Kasper, *Citizen Groups and the Nuclear Power Controversy: Uses of Scientific and Technological Information* (Cambridge: MIT Press, 1974), p. 12. See also K. S. Schrader-Frechette, *Nuclear Power and Public Policy: The Social and Ethical Problems of Fission Technology* (Dordrecht, Holland: D. Reidel Publishing Company, 1980), pp. 153-156.

25. *New York Times,* 7 May 1979, p. B13. See also James T. Ramey, "The Role of the Public in the Development and Regulation of Nuclear Power," U.S. Cong., House, Subcommittee of the Committee on Appropriation, Pollution Control and Power Development and Atomic Energy Appropriations Bill 1979, *Hearings* (Washington, D.C.: GPO, 1979), p. 559.

26. Ebbin and Kasper, p. 104. Public consensus continues to be a concern of the nuclear establishment. Various alternative methods for public input into decision-making have been suggested before and after the incident. For example, James Schlesinger reported that "Today the public may not consider itself a full fledged partner in the siting and licensing process." U.S. Cong., Senate, Committee on Environment and Public Works, Subcommittee on Nuclear Regulation, Nuclear Siting and Licensing Act of 1978, *Hearings* (Washington, D.C.: GPO, 1978), p. 46.

27. Neil J. Smelser, "Energy Restriction, Consumption, and Social Stratification," supporting paper 5, in *Sociopolitical Effects on Energy Use and Policy,* ed. Charles T. Unseld, Denton E. Morrison, David L. Sills and C. P. Wolf, (Washington, D.C.: National Academy of Sciences, 1979), p. 225. For a critical review of the technical accuracy of "The China Syndrome" see Samuel McCracken, "The Harrisburg Syndrome," *Commentary,* 67 (1979), pp. 27-39.

28. This account of the actual incidents contributing to the accident is taken from *The President's Commission on the Accident at Three Mile Island* full report, pp. 101-110.

29. *President's Commission,* pp. 38-39. Rather than imposing these phases of naming, reassuring, balancing, and assimilating upon the body of discourse at Three Mile Island, we have consulted the typical narrative steps of disaster story-line in both film genre and news. See, for news narrative, Harvey Molotch and Marilyn Lester, "News as Purposive Behavior: On the Strategic Use of Routine Events, Accidents, and Scandals," *American Sociological Review,* 39 (1974), 107-9; Erving Goffman, *Frame Analysis* (New York: Harper Colophon Books, 1974), esp. on the "documentary frame," pp. 448-477; Peter Braestrup, *Big Story* (Garden City: Anchor Press, 1978); "What is News," *Journal of Communication,* 26 (1976), 86-123. It is through the attempts of the principle actors in this crisis to impose narrative categories upon their own anticipated discourse that the stages of this troubled period begin to take on recognizable form.

30. See, in addition to notes 1-3, the following sources: U.S. Cong., Senate, Committee on Environment and Public Works, Subcommittee on Nuclear Regulation, "Three Mile Island Nuclear Powerplant Accident," *Hearings,* 96th Cong., 1st sees., Part I [April 10, 23, 30, 1979], Part II [Oct. 2, 3, 1979], and Part III [Nov. 8, 9, 1979] (Washington, D.C.: GPO, 1979), hereafter referred to as Subcommittee on Nuclear Regulation, *Hearings,* Part I, II, or III; U.S. Cong., Senate, Committee on Science and Technology, Subcommittee on Natural Resources and Environment, "Three Mile Island Nuclear Plant Accident," *Hearings,* 96th Cong., 1st sess. [June 2, 1979] (Washington, D.C.: GPO, 1979), hereafter referred to as Subcommittee on Natural Resources and Environment, *Hearings.* And, on the question of media objectivity, see Edwin Diamond and Leigh Passman, "Three Mile Island, How Clear Was TV's Picture?" *TV Guide,* 4 Aug. 1979, p. 6.

31. Thomas O'Toole, "Radiation Spreads 10 Miles from A-Plant Mishap Site," *Washington Post,* 29 Mar. 1979, p. A1.

32. O'Toole, p. A1.

33. Associated Press, "A-Plant's Contaminated Water Discharged into Susquehanna," *Washington Post,* 29 Mar. 1979, p. A2.

34. Casey Banas, "Nuclear Firm Generates Optimized Jargon," *Chicago Tribune,* 26 Nov. 1979, p. 6.

35. Banas, p. 6.

36. An interesting account of this use of discourse is supplied by Douglas T. Miller and Marion Nowak, *The Fifties: The Way We Really Were* (Garden City: Doubleday and Co., 1977), pp. 43-55.

37. Thomas O'Toole and Bill Peterson, "Pa. Reactor Mishap Called Worst in U.S. History," *Washington Post,* 30 Mar. 1979, p. A2.

38. John Herbein as cited by Bill Richards, *Washington Post,* 30 Mar. 1979, p. A2. (We have corrected the text slightly through a tape recording of the original statement.)

39. O'Toole and Peterson, p. A2.

40. Articles and interviews by Bill Peterson, "Nuclear Accident Turns a Bonanza Into a Mixed Blessing," *Washington Post,* 29 Mar. 1979, p. A2.

41. Peterson, p. A2.

42. Peterson, p. A2.

43. James Engle, cited by Peterson, p. A7.

44. Rita O'Connor, cited by Peterson, p. A7.

45. Monica Drayer, cited by Peterson, p. A7.

46. Monica Drayer, cited by Peterson, p. A7.

47. Governor Richard Thornburgh, *Press Conference,* transcript, 29 March 1979, 10:20 p.m., Governor's Press Office, 401-R.

48. David Rubin, *The Public's Right to Information Task Force* (205071; Washington, D.C.: GPO, 1979), p. 160.

49. Governor Richard Thornburgh, Lt. Governor William Scranton III, Harold Denton, *Press Conference,* transcript, 30 March 1979, 10:00 p.m. Pt. II, p. 1a.

50. Beginning on Thursday evening the three major news networks began to use the cooling towers as visual anchors to all their voice reports. Several national magazines also featured photographs of the towers.

51. Diamond and Passman.

52. John Herbein, cited in "Evacuation," *Washington Post,* 31 Mar. 1979, p. A9. The plant engineers were also at odds with the press. "'My statements are technical,' one of them said, 'They [the press] would not understand. They distort! That's how they operate.'" "President's Commission Confronts the 'Truth,'" *Nuclear News,* 22 July 1979, p. 26.

53. Walter Pincus, "Monitoring of Radiation Levels Has Been Haphazard," *Washington Post,* 31 Mar. 1979, p. A8.

54. Jane Shoemaker, "What Scientists Must Deal With," *Philadelphia Inquirer,* 2 Apr. 1979, p. 1.

55. House Interior and Insular Affairs Committee, transcripts, cited in *Chicago Sun-Times,* 13 Apr. 1979, p. 3.

56. Roger Mattson, cited in House Interior and Insular Affairs Committee, transcripts, p. 26; Denton, himself, said afterwards that communication with the site "was like looking down a black hole," "President's Commission Confronts the Truth," p. 26.

57. Rubin, *The Public's Right to Information Task Force,* pp. 200-210.

58. Thornburgh et al., *Press Conference,* p. 3A.

59. Our sample includes the *New York Times,* the *Washington Post,* the *Chicago Tribune* and *Sun-Times,* the South Jersey *Bulletin,* the *Philadelphia Inquirer.* All these papers moved their science sections to the front pages throughout the weekend 30 March to 1 April. Subsequent citations and analysis are based upon *Washington Post* headlines, photos, and captions, 31 March 1979, p. A9.

60. *Washington Post,* 31 Mar. 1979, p. A9. Both *Newsweek* and *Life* featured pictures of the cooling towers on the covers of their issues following the accident.

61. William Ecenbarger, Josh Friedman, and Art Carey, "What Hath Man Wrought? Worshippers Ask." *Philadelphia Inquirer,* 2 Apr. 1979, p. 1.

62. Ecenbarger et al., p. 1.

63. Ecenbarger et al., p. 1.

64. Richard Thornburgh, *Press Conference,* transcript, 2 Apr. 1979. It was not until April 9 that the crisis was brought to an official end by a joint press conference held by state and federal officials. See Richard Thornburgh, *Press Conference—Three Mile Island Incident,* transcript, 9 Apr. 1979, 3:00 p.m., pp. 1-6B.

65. Thornburgh, *Press Conference,* 9 Apr. 1979.

66. Thornburgh, *Press Conference,* 9 Apr. 1979.

67. John F. Ahearne, quoted in Subcommittee on Nuclear Regulation, *Hearings,* Part I, p. 57.

68. Richard Thornburgh, Subcommittee on Nuclear Regulation, *Hearings,* Part I, pp. 236-242.

69. Thornburgh, Subcommittee on Nuclear Regulation, *Hearings,* Part I, p. 237.

70. Thornburgh, Subcommittee on Nuclear Regulation, *Hearings,* Part I, p. 237.

71. Casey Bukro, "Three Mile Island: The Fear was Real . . .," *Chicago Tribune,* 9 Sep. 1979, Sec. 2, pp. 1-2; "Chapter 1: How the Crisis was Managed," *Washington Post,* 8 Apr. 1979, p. A16.

72. "Chapter Twelve," *Washington Post,* 10 Apr. 1979, p. A14.

73. The events at Three Mile Island were predicted to form major issues for the upcoming 1980 elections. But apart from several state referenda, the implications of nuclear power did not play a dominant role in the Presidential campaign.

74. "Atomic Showdown," *Wall Street Journal,* 22 Oct. 1979, pp. 1, 25; Joanne Omang, "NRC Loses Study on Big Radiation Emission at TMI," *Chicago Sun Times,* 4 Aug. 1979, p. 52; John R. Emshiviller and Walter S. Mossberg "Plant in Pennsylvania Had Series of Problems over 14-Month Period," *Wall Street Journal,* 9 Apr. 1979, p. 1.

75. John T. Conway, quoted in Subcommittee on Nuclear Regulation, *Hearings,* Part I, p. 376. See also Ian Fells, "Three Mile Island and its Implications," *Engineering,* 223 (1980), 278; Michael Blake, "Three Mile Island One Year Later: GPU Perseveres, but to What Future," *Nuclear News,* 23 Mar. 1980, p. 54. Some proponents of the industry carry the issue to the level of purported general opposition to science. See Robert Nisbet, "The Rape of Progress," *Public Opinion,* 2 (1979), 2-6, 55; Samuel C. Florman, *Blaming Technology: The Irrational Scapegoat,* (New York: St. Martin's, 1981), pp. 167-68.

76. Rubin, *Public's Right to Information Task Force,* p. 5; "A Nuclear Nightmare," *Time,* 9 Apr. 1979, pp. 8-20; "Chapter 8: An Open Conflict Over Authority," *Washington Post,* 9 Apr. 1979, p. A15; "Chapter 9: The Media Corps' All-Out Invasion," *Washington Post,* 9 Apr. 1979, p. A16.

77. Kenneth Brandt, quoted in Subcommittee on Natural Resources and Environment, *Hearings,* p. 56.

78. Rubin, *The Public's Right to Information Task Force,* p. 13.

79. Rubin, *The Public's Right to Information Task Force,* p. 1.

80. Rubin, *The Public's Right to Information Task Force,* p. 3.

81. Peter Bradford, quoted in Subcommittee on Nuclear Regulation, *Hearings,* Part I, p. 57.

82. Bradford, quoted in Subcommittee on Nuclear Regulation, *Hearings,* Part I, p. 57.

83. See Farrell, "Knowledge, Consensus, and Rhetorical Theory."

84. Maria Shad, "Concerns Seeking Credibility Put Scientists in Spotlight," *Wall Street Journal,* 23 Sept. 1981, p. 1. See also Peter J. Schuzten, "Scientist and Society's Fears," *New York Times,* 9 Apr. 1979, pp. A1, D9.

85. Alfred North Whitehead, *Science and the Modern World: Lowell Lectures 1925* (New York: Macmillan Company, 1931), p. 15.

86. "The 'Movement' Moves on to Anti-nuclear Protest," *Science*, 204 (1979), 715; Wendall Rawls, "65,000 Demonstrate at Capital to Halt Atomic Power Units," *New York Times*, 7 May 1979, p. 1; Paul W. Valentine and Karlyn Barker, "The Protestors," *Washington Post*, 7 May 1979, p. 1; Tom Mathews, "Fallout From the Nuke-In," *Newsweek*, 7 May 1979, pp. 34-35.

87. "Public is 'on the Fence' about Nuclear Power," *Chicago Tribune*, 10 May 1979, pp. 1, 12; "State Fears it's a Nuclear Dump," *Chicago Tribune*, 8 May 1979, p. 1; "Nuclear Cost Estimate 2,000 Lives in 21 Years," *Chicago Tribune*, 10 May 1979, p. 12. Definitive studies on the consequences reported several months afterwards received less than thorough coverage. Terry Brown, "Study Urges New Rules to Avoid Nuclear Accidents," *Chicago Tribune*, 25 Jan. 1980, Sec. 1, p. 10; Barbara Jorgenson, "Credibility And the President's TMI Commission," *Public Relations Journal*, 36 (1980), 36-38.

88. For an interesting analysis of narrative form, see Seymour Chatman, *Story and Discourse* (Ithaca: Cornell University Press, 1978). On the functions of format itself: Herbert J. Gans, *Deciding What's News: A Study of CBS Evening News, NBC Nightly News, Newsweek* and *Time* (New York: Vintage Books, 1979), esp. chs. 3-5; Edward Jay Epstein, "Journalism and Truth," *Commentary*, 57 (1974), 36-40; Bernard Rubin, *Media, Politics, and Democracy* (New York: Oxford University Press, 1977); also the Glasgow University Media Group, *Bad News*, (London: Routledge & Kegan Paul, 1976), I.

89. On the question of public ambivalence as measured by polls see: Mark A. Schulman, "The Impact of Three Mile Island," *Public Opinion*, 2 (1979), 7-9; "Opinion Roundup," *Public Opinion*, 2 (1979), 23-26. For the latest government and industry measures responding to the crisis, see: U.S. Cong., Senate, Committee on Environment and Public Works, "Fiscal Year 1982 Budget Review," *Hearings*, 97th Cong. [February 25, 26 and March 4, 5, 6, 1981] (Washington, D.C.: GPO, 1981), pp. 44-264; and U.S. Cong., Senate, Committee on Environment and Public Works, "Nuclear Accident and Recovery at Three Mile Island: A Special Investigation," (Washington, D.C.: GPO, 1980).

90. "I Was the Only Victim of Three Mile Island," *Chicago Tribune*, 1 Mar. 1980, Sec. 6, p. 1. See also "Fear of Fission," *The Smith Kline Forum For a Healthier American Society*, Apr. 1981; "Science, Technology and the Human Prospect," *SYMPOSIUM: A Report from the Edison Electric Institute*, (Washington, D.C.: n.p. n.d.).

91. "Three Mile Island Puts Focus on the Operators at All Nuclear Plants," *Wall Street Journal*, 22 Oct. 1979, p. 1.

92. Rubin, *The Public's Right to Information Task Force*, p. 3.

93. Soren Kierkegaard, "The Present Age," in *A Kierkegaard Anthology*, ed. Robert Bretall (Princeton: Princeton University Press, 1946), p. 267.

94. John Dewey, *The Public and Its Problems* (Chicago: The Swallow Press, 1927), pp. 116-117.

Earth First! and the Rhetoric
of Moral Confrontation
by Brant Short

In 1981, a small group of disgruntled environmentalists unfurled a 300-foot long black plastic ribbon on the Glen Canyon Dam at the Arizona-Utah border. Creating the visual image of a huge crack in the dam, the plastic ribbon represented the first major act of Earth First!, an unknown group at the extreme philosophical edge of the national environmental movement (Japenga, 1985). Founded in 1980, Earth First! has been a constant thorn in the side of land developers, oil companies, logging operations, cattle ranchers, the National Park Service, the U.S. Forest Service, and even other environmental groups. Members of Earth First! allegedly have placed metal spikes in trees to prevent logging, pulled up survey stakes on land development sites, sat in trees scheduled for timber harvest, and paraded in bear costumes in Yellowstone National Park to protest lack of grizzly habitat. Basing their actions on a philosophy called "deep ecology," leaders have attacked mainstream environmentalists for being too cautious and too open to political compromise. Members of Earth First! perceive a clearly defined mission for their group. According to Howie Wolke, a founder of the group, "If you look at any social reform movement, there has always been a radical arm of that movement. We want to push the traditional environmentalists back into the roots, away from the political establishment that governs it and further toward the extreme" (White, 1984, p. A11).

The rhetoric of any social movement must create, order, and define a view of reality that enables the movement to sustain itself in times of confrontation, crises, or complacency. Members at the extremes of a movement's ideology, in efforts to articulate their unique vision of reality, often create an internal tension that either can threaten or energize the social movement. This study examines Earth First!'s agitative rhetoric and its impact on the contemporary environmental movement. Guerrilla theater, physical obstruction, and threats of sabotage, combined with more traditional forms of persuasion, provide the foundation for Earth First!'s rhetoric of confrontation. By understanding the function of agitative rhetoric[1] in the context of a social movement, this study will illuminate the continuing rhetorical events that foster, sustain, and change social movements.

Three topics guide this analysis. Initially, the rhetorical dimensions of agitation and the rhetorical characteristics of social movements will be reviewed. Next the history, philosophy, and rhetorical practices of Earth First! will be discussed and the relationship between Earth First! and the mainstream environmental movement will be considered. Finally, Earth First!'s public communication, both discursive and nondiscursive, will be examined in order to evaluate its relation to the form and structure of the environmental movement and to identify implications for the study of social movement rhetoric.[2]

Rhetorical Dimensions of Social Movements

The explosion of confrontational political behavior in the 1960s shook not only the political base but also the foundations of the academic world. Scholars of rhetoric and public address were challenged to reexamine prevailing conceptions of reasoned discourse in light of the civil rights movement, the antiwar movement, the free speech movement, and so on. As a result, a plethora of essays examining the function of confrontational rhetoric appeared in the late 1960s and early 1970s (see, for example, Andrews, 1969; Bailey, 1972; Bowers & Ochs, 1971; Gregg, 1971; Haiman, 1967; Jefferson, 1969; McEdwards, 1968; and Scott & Smith, 1969). Although critics acknowledged the rhetorical aspects of confrontation, protest, and agitation, these studies suggest that theoretical accounts of seemingly *nonrational* discourse remained linked to traditional notions of logic, rationality, and artistic proofs.

In his seminal study of the "rhetoric of the streets," Haiman (1967) reports that some observers rejected agitation as rhetoric on two grounds: It "exceeds the bounds of rational discourse" and the "new rhetoric is 'persuasion' by a strategy of power and coercion rather than by reason and democratic decision-making" (p. 102). Although reluctant to endorse "nonrational strategies of discourse," Haiman urges scholars to understand the inequalities in the balance of power that help explain the emergence of confrontational discourse. McEdwards (1968) stresses the functional aspects of agitative rhetoric and attempts to counter the pejorative connotations of agitation. Claiming that agitation is designed to gain the attention of the public, McEdwards focuses on the language used by protesters. Only when agitation arouses public attention, concludes McEdwards, "will it [the public] respond to intellectual argument" (p. 38). In a 1969 paper, Bailey (1972) argues that confrontation "represents an extension of communication not a form of anti-communication" (p. 182). Agreeing with McEdwards that confrontation is a precursor to rational interaction, Bailey concludes that confrontation "is designed to bring about bargaining, not nonnegotiable demands" (p. 191). In his study of student protests at Columbia University, Andrews (1969) agrees with Haiman that viewing rhetoric as primarily a rational process is too restrictive. Arguing that rhetoric can be viewed as persuasive or coercive in nature, Andrews suggests coercive rhetoric does not give audiences a rational choice, that it uses a rhetoric of polarization, and that it gives audiences only two choices, "one of which was consistently distorted" (15).

Only with the appearance of *The Rhetoric of Agitation and Control* did scholars fully embrace agitation and confrontation as rhetorical artifacts that were more than the attention-getting devices of protest movements. According to the authors of that book, Bowers and Ochs (1971), "We think that the central element in a persuasive attempt, if we are to call it agitation, should be the exercise of extra-discursive means of persuasion. . . . Hence, we have made our primary concern the analysis of instrumental, symbolic events that are largely nonverbal, or extra-verbal" (pp. 5-6). Their definition of rhetoric as "the rationale of instrumental, symbolic behavior" (p. 2) expands the boundaries of what constituted appropriate topics for rhetorical criticism and paved the way for a deeper understanding of nondiscursive forms of persuasion.

Study of the social movement provided a natural extension for scholars interested in the rhetorical analysis of political agitation. While social movements provide significant, numerous, and rich case studies of rhetoric in action, they also present issues of complexity, definition, and explanation. "Political movements are massive, impassioned, and ineluctable," write Simons and Mechling (1981). "Their sheer size and duration make them difficult to comprehend . . . their amorphousness and diversity render them resistant to coherent theoretical accounts" (p. 417). Because of such complexity, this study will isolate a part of a social movement, analyze its rhetorical dimensions, and assess its relationship to the movement in general.

Observing that political movements are "long-term, collective efforts in behalf of a cause," Simons and Mechling (1981) conclude that the typical movement is a "loosely coordinated collectivity consisting of one or more core organizations" (p. 418). From both perspectives, environmentalism has been an active social movement in the United States since the 1960s. It represents at least 10 million Americans who hold widely divergent political beliefs, with groups such as the National Wildlife Federation, the Sierra Club, the Wilderness Society, and others developing their own particular environmental agenda.[3] Multiple organizations form the core of the movement and articulate environmentalist positions on political action and legislation. In a recent review of the major environmental groups in the United States, Weisskopf (1990) of the *Washington Post* concludes: "Once on the political fringe of 1960s activism, environmental groups have become an integral part of the American political process, key players in the nexus of regulatory action, congressional lawmaking and executive decision-making" (p. 10). The work of Cathcart presents a useful way to identify and evaluate the function of agitative rhetoric within a social movement.[4]

Claiming that a social movement can be identified by its *"confrontational form,"* Cathcart (1978) writes that "movements are a kind of ritual conflict whose most distinguishing form is *confrontation*" (p. 235). While many critics recognize confrontation as a form of communication, Cathcart (1980) believes they view it as "an extension of communication in situations where confronters have exhausted normal (i.e., accepted) means of communication with those in power" (p. 268). As a result, confrontation has been viewed by many as primarily a way to gain attention, an instrumental function, and not as communication itself, a consummatory form

(Cathcart, 1978, p. 236). For Cathcart, confrontational rhetoric challenges the values of a political system, producing a counterrhetoric that in turn recognizes movement protesters and their potential threat to the established order. From this counterrhetoric "emerges the dialectical enjoinment which defines a collective as a social movement in the public mind" (Cathcart, 1980, p. 268). In this way, confrontational rhetoric enables the movement to define itself to its members as well as to the outside world. Agitative rhetoric also appears to serve a consummatory function within the social movement. "To study a movement," observes Griffin (1969), "is to study a striving for salvation, a struggle for perfection, a progress toward the 'good'" (p. 460). Noting that movements "begin in the stasis of indecision, and they end in the stasis of 'decision persevered in,'" Griffin concludes, "They begin with guilt and the dream of salvation. They end with the achievement, and maintenance, of a state of redemption" (p. 461). The extreme, agitative rhetoric of one element within a social movement provides an internal dialectic that forces a counterresponse *within* the movement as well as outside the movement. Such discourse demands that the movement faithfully acknowledge that salvation and redemption have not been achieved and that guilt still should drive members to act. In this manner *true believers* have a vehicle to critique and motivate other members in the social movement who seemingly have accepted the state of redemption.

For members in the social movement, agitative rhetoric serves as a touchstone for measuring their individual level of commitment to the movement and how far they will go to purify the system. According to Cathcart (1980), social movements evolve through their struggles with the establishment *and* struggles within the movement: "Confrontation involves movement members in questions about their own morality and their contribution to the evils of the existing system. Decisions over tactics raise questions about ends as well as means" (p. 271). As a result, agitative rhetoric encourages supporters to reexamine their ideological roots as well as their commitment to the movement itself. As Simons and Mechling (1981) observe, "Ideologies are expressed in the person of symbolic leaders, in symbolic acts of protest and defiance, and in legends and myths about founding fathers, martyrs and sages, and cowards and traitors" (p. 424). Such rhetoric draws attention to the movement and forces supporters either to accept or reject the extreme view of a given controversy. In either case, the larger social movement must respond to agitative discourse because silence could be interpreted as tacit approval of confrontation and coercion. An examination of Earth First! and its rhetorical practices will demonstrate that agitative rhetoric serves an important function in the life of a social movement, forcing the movement to redefine itself to its membership as well as to those in the established order.

Earth First! And Environmental Politics

History of the Movement

Starting with thirteen members, Earth First! has grown significantly as additional sympathetic followers have found the group. Seventy-five people attended a rally in 1981, and more than 400 attended a similar affair in 1982 (Kane, 1987). By 1985, more than 6,500 readers were receiving the organization's newsletter (Japenga, 1985). Throughout the 1980s the group maintained a high profile in environmental politics while politicians, developers, bureaucrats, and environmentalists attacked the radical agenda of Earth First!. To demonstrate their dissatisfaction with mainstream environmental groups and their hierarchical structure, Earth First! claims to maintain no official records, has no membership lists, operates without annual dues and officers, and refuses to be designated a nonprofit organization (Setterberg, 1986). Because subscriptions to the Earth First! journal do not clearly reflect the group's total membership, a good estimate comes from former member Fayhee (1988), who believes about 12,000 people consider themselves to be Earth Firsters (p. 21).

The narrative history of Earth First!, told by group members and published in various newspapers and magazine articles, stresses the necessity of confrontational action to save the environment from development. By supporting agitation and condoning sabotage in public forums, Earth Firsters help construct an extremist image that is an important part of the group's self-identity and mission. Without such an image, it is doubtful that Earth First! would be a regular feature in the nation's popular and environmental press.

In 1979, three disillusioned members of the mainstream environmental movement, Foreman and Koehler of the Wilderness Society and Wolke of the Friends of the Earth, resigned their staff positions in Washington, D.C., and headed for the American West in Foreman's Volkswagen van (see "For the members," 1984). Each had lost faith in the environmental movement and set off to find a different way to preserve the environment. Decrying the moderate nature of the environmental movement, Foreman claims that land developers had gained control of the wilderness debate: "The anti-environmental side had been extreme, radical, emotional. . . . Their arguments had been easily shot full of holes. We had been factual, rational. They looked like fools. We looked like statesmen. Who won? They did" (Setterberg, 1986, p. 23). Foreman believed the environmental movement had been duped by the Carter administration. Only 15 million acres of wilderness (out of more than 66 million under study) were recommended for preservation by the administration in 1979. "This was from the administration that was supposedly our friend," observes Wolke (White, 1984, p. A11). Environmentalists were losing the battle to save the environment, Foreman (1985a) charges, because they were being corrupted by the system. "While in Washington," he recalls, "I came to realize that, because of the rules we were playing by, we were *being* lobbied more effectively than we were lobbying" (p. 17). Indeed, Foreman argues that in their attempts to be "reasonable and credible and politically pragmatic," the environmental movement would "come out of those meetings having *made* all the concessions" (p. 18). The "emotional, hard-line, no-compromise approach taken by the mining, timber, and livestock industries, and by the off-road vehicle people" taught Foreman a significant lesson about environmental politics (p. 18). As a result, he offers a radically different alternative to save the ecosystem from destruction.

Foreman and the other founders of the group envisioned confrontation and agitation as a primary means of persuasion in order to shake the environmental movement out of its doldrums:

It was time for a new joker in the deck. Something more than commenting on dreary environmental-impact statements and writing letters to members of Congress. Politics in the streets. Civil disobedience. Media stunts. Holding the villains up to ridicule. Using music to charge the cause. . . . All that would be required to join us, we decided, was a belief in Earth first. ("For the members," 1984, p. G8)

A consistent theme running throughout Earth First! discourse stresses the need for militant activity to counter the softening of the mainstream environmental movement. "I sensed that we were becoming bureaucrats in gray-flannel suits, more interested in saving our jobs than in saving the environment," Foreman reports (Taylor, 1986, p. 70). The influx of new members into the mainstream environmental groups, suggested some Earth Firsters, caused in large part by the prodevelopment policies of the Reagan administration, actually hurt the movement. Arguing that most of the new members "are soft," Foreman reasons that they forced some groups to take a "more cautious attitude toward environmental activism out of fear of alienating the membership" (Baumgartner, 1986, p. 4). Besides being soft on the issues, environmentalists appeared to be out of touch with movement concerns. Roselle claims that most environmental leaders had not even seen the old growth forest in Oregon, a major political battleground in the 1980s: "Most of them are in D.C., doing lunch in their designer khakis and working out their retirement bennies. The problem is, the environmental movement isn't a calling anymore, it's a job. They think wilderness is some Disneyland you check into after you shut down your computer and lock up the condo" (Kane, 1987, p. 98).

To counter the moderate and subdued image associated with environmentalism, Earth First! promulgated a radical personae. "It was ridiculous that off-roaders were macho men and backpackers were considered wimps," Foreman observes (Taylor, 1986, p. 70). Roselle, one of the original members of Earth First!, echoes this vision and concludes, "Not all environmentalists are granola-crunching hippies. Some of us are rednecks and cowboys" (Setterberg, 1986, p. 20). Indeed, one of the group's best means of raising money is through the sale of t-shirts, caps, and bumper stickers with the logo: "Rednecks for Wilderness" (Setterberg, 1986, p. 22).

Philosophical Foundations of the Movement

The philosophical foundation of Earth First! comes from two quite different sources: *The Monkey Wrench Gang,* a novel by Edward Abbey, and the theory of deep ecology. Each source provides an integral part of the group's ideology as well as its specific political agenda. There is no doubt that *The Monkey Wrench Gang* served as a combination battle plan, manifesto, and spiritual guide for Earth First! in its origins, philosophy, and rhetoric.[5] The novel inspired Foreman and his colleagues to create a new and radical environmental group that placed wilderness protection above all else (see McKibben, 1989, pp. 177-182, and Nash, 1989, pp. 191-194). Abbey spoke at Earth First! rallies and encouraged the group to be true to its calling. He also wrote the forward to Earth First!'s controversial book, *Ecodefense: A Field Guide to Monkeywrenching* (*monkeywrenching* being the term for industrial sabotage that was borrowed by Earth First! directly from Abbey's novel).[6] Although not an active member of Earth First!, Abbey supported the group in many ways.[7] Speaking at the Glen Canyon Dam (a target for destruction by the fictional *Monkey Wrench Gang*), Abbey tells an Earth First! rally: "Oppose! Oppose the destruction of our homeland. . . . And if opposition is not enough, we must subvert" ("For the members," 1984, p. G9). In describing his support for Earth First!, Abbey tells one reporter, "When the only alternative is to give up and lose the battle outright, I'm in favor of active resistance. Even sabotage. . . . If your conscience demands it of you, then do it. And don't get caught" (McBride, 1983, p. 71).

Published in 1975, *The Monkey Wrench Gang* detailed the fictional adventures of four individuals in the American Southwest who wreaked havoc on numerous wilderness-development schemes.[8] The characters burned billboards, derailed trains, and plotted to destroy the Glen Canyon Dam. In the confines of the novel, Abbey details in precise terms the process of "ecotage," the destruction of machinery and equipment designed to develop the wilderness. The characters in *The Monkey Wrench Gang* justify their illegal actions by reasoning that nature needs a guardian to stop human assaults upon the ecosystem. Ecological sabotage, or *monkeywrenching,* is justified by Earth Firsters through arguments almost identical to those made by characters in the novel. Believing that monkeywrenching is required morally, Foreman (1985a) argues that the "all-out war being waged against ecosystems all over the world" forces environmentalists to consider "any and all means of resisting that destruction" (p. 21). For Earth Firsters, the only *moral* response to wilderness development is active resistance. Wolke, who served a six-month sentence in Wyoming for pulling up survey stakes, concludes, "When all legal remedies have been exhausted someone has got to be there to continue the fight and use tactics that the establishment won't use, such as civil disobedience" (White, 1984, p. A12).

Earth Firsters describe monkeywrenching as a nonviolent response to the excesses of industrial and urban growth. "It's directed toward inanimate objects, and never toward people or any other life-forms," observes Foreman (1985a, p. 21). Moreover monkeywrenching is not considered to be an act of mere vandalism: "While monkeywrenching is undertaken with purpose and respect, and with the highest moral standards in mind, vandalism is senseless and hurtful" (p. 21). In the opening chapter to *Ecodefense: A Field Guide to Monkeywrenching,* Foreman (1985b) presents a rationale that distinguishes "strategic monkeywrenching" from crime and vandalism. Among other features, monkeywrenching should be nonviolent, not organized, the act of individuals, targeted, timely, simple, dispersed among all regions, and fun. Most important, monkeywrenching must be "deliberate and ethical" and respect the importance of the act itself. "It is not a casual and flippant affair," concludes Foreman. Monkeywrenchers must "keep a pure heart and mind about it. They remember that they are engaged in the most moral of all actions: protecting life, defending the Earth" (pp. 11-12).

The concept of *deep ecology,* which serves as a second philosophical ground to monkeywrenching, stems from the writings of Norwegian philosopher Arne Naess (see Nash, 1989, pp. 146-150) and holds that "human beings should participate in but not dominate the natural world" (Setterberg, 1986, p. 26). Devall, co-author of a 1985 book examining the philosophical implications of deep ecology, suggests that nature should be seen as "a relationship, not an entity." According to Devall, "Deep ecologists rearticulate a minority position that envisions human beings as stewards, not masters, of the earth" (Setterberg, 1986, p. 26). As a result, Earth First! members believe nature has an inherent right to exist and should not be exploited by humans. Earth Firsters demonstrate an abiding commitment to deep ecology in their public communication. Robert Brothers, also known as "Bobcat," claims, "We have no business cutting the forests. Some places are sacred. Some places have value in their own right" (Nokes, 1987, p. A7). In a speech delivered in Sacramento, California, Foreman invokes images of deep ecology in describing his conversion to the cause:

> Why preserve a wilderness area? Because it's a nice place to go and relax? Because you can make pretty books of pictures of it? To protect a watershed? No. You protect a river because its [sic] a river. For its own sake. Because it has a right to exist by itself. The grizzly bear in Yellowstone Park has as much right to her life as any one of us has to our life. Each of you is an animal and should be proud of it. (McKibben, 1989, p. 180)

Deep ecology demands that humans reject the self-centered role that has guided wilderness management for generations. Recalling the age of primitive humans, in a 1984 speech, Foreman (1985a) concludes: "In those days, a person would have been laughed out of the tribe for inventing such a bizarre philosophy as the one that drives Western thought today—the belief that the world was created just for us, and that we are meant to have dominion over everything in it" (p. 19).

Ecodefense has served more than an instrumental function for members of Earth First!. Because of the book's wide availability (it has appeared in at least two editions), critics of Earth First! regularly quote lengthy passages from *Ecodefense* to substantiate the group's danger to society. Popular media sources that have cited the book include the *Denver Post* (Grelen & Sinisi, 1989), *Beef Today* (Mooney, 1989), *Smithsonian* (Parfit, 1990), *The Progressive* (Vanderpool, 1989), *The Nation* (Russell, 1989), and the *New York Times* (Robbins, 1989). This practice reinforces Earth First!'s public image as the radical wing of the environmental movement and provides opponents with the group's apparent blueprint of sabotage.

Easy access to Earth First!'s agenda (through its publications) has spawned a number of counterresponses from different groups. Appearing on Cable News Network's *Larry King Live* (1990), Troy Reinhart of Douglas Timber Company was asked what kind of evidence he had to prove that Earth First! had engaged in sabotage and terrorism. "Well," he responded, "they-they publicize it in all their publications, they admit it openly . . . they justify it in every publication that they do" (pp. 12-13). In a direct response to the Earth First! newsletter, the Utah Farm Bureau and the Arizona Game and Fish Department sent letters to farmers and ranchers urging them to protect their cattle from Earth Firsters who might kill the cattle and blame deer hunters ("Eco-terrorists," 1990).

Although the group never has officially sanctioned ecotage, Earth First! claims such activity may become necessary in the battle to save the wilderness. Stressing the symbolic message in tree-spiking, the practice of putting a metal spike in a tree to prevent its harvest, Foreman concludes, "These things say 'Stay out of this place. If you come in here with your machines and your industrialization . . . bulldozers are going to be decommissioned and trees will be spiked for their own protection'" (Slocum, 1985, p. 35). Even when there is no evidence of Earth First! involvement in an act of sabotage, the group maintains a high profile in the debate over development. In May 1987, for example, a logger in California was injured by a spiked tree. While timber officials suspected Earth First! of the sabotage, the group claimed that their supporters would have sent a warning letter or spray painted a large "S" on the tree. Without such warning, noted Greg King of Earth First!, tree spiking "would be worthless. They would still cut down the tree" (Stammer, 1987, p. 22). Exploiting the news coverage associated with the injured logger, Foreman uses the occasion to attack the timber industry for being the real "eco-terrorists" in the woods and to express his concern for the forests, spotted owls, wolverines, and salmon (Stammer, 1987, p. 22).

Rhetorical Practices

In its ten years of existence, Earth First! has used a variety of methods to present its message to other environmentalists as well as the general public. The group combines traditional forums for persuasion (calling press conferences, issuing news releases, presenting speeches at meetings, and appearing on television and radio programs such as CNN's *Larry King Live* and ABC's *Primetime Live*) with nontraditional methods (creating the visual crack on the Glen Canyon Dam, draping a banner on Mt. Rushmore to protest acid rain, sitting in trees intended for logging, and physically blocking land-development operations). In most cases, the two forms of persuasion merge in the group's public agitation. For example, to protest Yellowstone Park's decision to retain motel units in grizzly bear habitat, two dozen Earth Firsters and a television crew "invaded" the office of park superintendent Robert Barbee. Two members, one dressed in a bear outfit, awarded a buffalo chip to Barbee for being "Conservationist of the Year" ("Earth First! protesters invade," 1986). While such confrontations draw attention to the group's political agenda, the message of confrontation is symbolic in itself. By using acts of extremism, Earth First! calls attention to what it believes is a lack of conviction and passion in the mainstream environmental movement.

In terms of actually using monkeywrenching tactics such as tree-spiking, destruction of machinery, bombings, and so forth, Earth Firsters blur the distinction between condoning such actions and engaging in their own ecodefense of the planet. For example, *Ecodefense: A Field Guide to Monkeywrenching,* which details the spiking of trees, the sabotaging of construction equipment, and the burning of billboards, has sold more than 20,000 copies. Earth Firsters maintain that use of the book is a personal choice. "While Earth First! doesn't officially engage in monkeywrenching," writes editor Foreman (1985b), "or even officially advocate it, we also don't *not* advocate it. It's an individual decision" (p. 21). When asked directly on *Larry King Live* (1990) if he supported violence and sabotage, Earth Firster Mark Williams responded in a typically ambiguous manner:

As far as pulling up survey stakes, disabling—I think individuals who would undertake those actions with sober forethought with a commitment to not injure any living
thing, I think that is a prerogative, and I would not take any stand against them doing
that to save wild places. (p. 15)

While several Earth Firsters have served jail sentences for pulling up survey
stakes and trespassing, they had avoided prosecution for monkeywrenching until
1989 when Foreman and three others were arrested for conspiring to sabotage a
power plant in Arizona (Grelen, 1989). Foreman's arrest came at time in which
Earth First!'s public image, an important part of its overall mission, was in a
transition worthy of note.

Between 1980 and 1987, Earth First! represented the bit player in environmental
politics, often more ignored than repudiated. National attention placed greater attention
on the group's antics than on its public lands agenda. Followers of environmental
politics probably knew more about the parading in bear costumes than Earth First!'s
plan to repopulate grizzly bears in California, create a huge Great Plains buffalo
preserve, and increase the amount of wilderness in the United States by fully one-third.[9]
However, the stakes in the debate changed in 1988 when Earth First! found itself
under concerted attacks from not only industrial interests but also law enforcement
agencies, the federal government, and even other environmental groups.

While most critics have demanded that Earth First! stop its activity, environmentalists have felt forced to reject the actions but not necessarily the explicit goals of
Earth First!. Agreeing that many environmental crises face the world, Michael
McCloskey, chairperson of the Sierra Club, argues, "But this means it is time for
responsible, serious world strategies to deal with them. Protests have their place,
but they are not enough" (Stein, 1987, p. I1). Many environmentalists have feared
that the general public might link their specific groups to Earth First!, thereby
harming the larger environmental movement. John Charles of the Oregon Environmental Council warned that an injured logger might make the public decide "all
environmentalists are irresponsible and the movement would be hurt" (Slocum,
1985, p. 35). Decrying the perception among some observers that Earth First!
represents the environmental community, Jay Hair, chief executive officer of the
National Wildlife Federation, announced:

I don't even consider Earth First! part of the environmental community. They accuse
us of being ineffective, of selling out. Well, we have over 80 court cases pending right
now. That, in and of itself, is a far cry from anything Earth First! has done. How many
acres of wilderness has Earth First! had designated? None. Through our lobbying
efforts, we've helped designate millions of acres. (Fayhee, 1989, p. 21)

Although many environmental groups would like to keep Earth First! on the
fringe of publicity, the group has found itself the target of an organized counterresponse in the private and public sector. In 1988 Senator James McClure of Idaho
added a tree-spiking provision to a major congressional antidrug bill. Spiking a tree
became a federal crime that could result in fines of $500,000 and prison sentences
between five and ten years (Gamerman, 1988). In addition, Earth First! was

infiltrated by an FBI agent in 1988 who was instrumental in the arrest of Foreman and three other group members in June 1989 for attempting to cut down power lines to a nuclear power plant in Arizona (see Feldman & Meyer, 1989, and Tolan, 1989). The FBI warned cattle ranchers in 1989 to be aware of potential attacks from extremist groups like Earth First!. "It's a case of ecological terrorism," notes FBI agent Richard Whitaker. "Their basic goal is to eradicate the rancher" (Macy, 1989, p. B6). The *New York Times* reports that the FBI spent two years investigating Earth First!, believing the group to be part of a "domestic terrorism network." The investigations "yielded a flurry of charges and prosecutions, no convictions and few substantive results" ("FBI steps up pressure," 1990, p. A2). Three conservative legal groups—the Wilderness Impact Research Foundation, the Mountain States Legal Foundation, and the Pacific States Legal Foundation—sponsored a conference on "Sabotage-Ecotage: The Legacy of Edward Abbey and his Monkeywrench Gang." Planners of the conference, which was held in Salt Lake City in March 1990, wanted to help ranchers, loggers, and farmers understand the potential menace of "ecotage, or the sabotage of our resources and private property in the name of preservation" ("Wilderness conference," 1990). In addition, articles attacking Earth First! have appeared in diverse publications such as *Beef Today* (Mooney, 1989), *Livestock Market Digest* (Black, 1989), *Barron's* (Brody, 1990), and *Reason* (Postrel, 1990).

Editorials in regional and national newspapers also have taken Earth First! to task. The *Missoulian* ("New species of tree slime," 1989) called tree-spikers "no more than rural versions of the valueless human vermin that have recently terrorized New York City and shocked the nation with sprees of random violence" (p. A4), the *Idaho State Journal* ("This will be no picnic," 1990) called Earth First! the "skunk at the picnic" (p. A4), and the *Idaho Statesman* (Morgan, 1989) called tree-spikers the "eco-equivalent of neo-Nazi skinheads" (p. A4). Representing the Natural Resources Defense Fund, Robert F. Kennedy, Jr. (1990) used the editorial pages of the *Los Angeles Times* to repudiate Earth First!'s actions and refute claims that the group was simply an extension of the protest movement of the 1960s. Calling civil disobedience a time-honored and legitimate response to political and economic exploitation, Kennedy argues that it requires "nonviolent tactics, including the willingness to endure the blows of the oppressor . . . and the willingness to endure imprisonment" (p. B7). By contrast, Earth First! activists "attack at night, destroy property and machinery, endanger human life and then flee." The tactics of Earth First!, concludes Kennedy, "must be condemned as must the tactics of anyone who favors force over democratic principles" (p. B7).

In a little more than one year, from March 1989 to May 1990, Earth First! suffered a series of setbacks that threatened the group's existence. The death of Abbey, the group's infiltration by the FBI, and the arrest of Foreman and three other Earth Firsters had the group reeling (see Tolan, 1989). In May 1990 two members of the group were injured when a bomb exploded in their car in Oakland, California. Although the two said that the bomb was planted by enemies of Earth First!, the police arrested the Earth Firsters and claimed the bomb was being transported for an illegal act (Bishop, 1990). The charges were dropped later, and to date investigators have not determined how the bomb got into the car.

Although such crises could have dealt a death blow to other small and extreme groups within a social movement, Earth First! pushed ahead with its political program. The decentralized nature of Earth First! allowed the group to function even with threats to jail key leaders. According to Foreman, "The FBI thinks that if they can knock me out—since they think of me as the leader of Earth First!—then they can knock out the entire movement. But I'm not important to Earth First! in its day-to-day functioning" (Vanderpool, 1989, p. 15). More importantly, Foreman uses his arrest to warn followers that their cause may demand more than six months in a county jail for trespassing: "It ain't junior high anymore. They don't just send you to the principal's office. Some of us are going to spend a lot of time in jail. Some of us are going to die" (Parfit, 1990, p. 184).

Earth First! continued to pursue its rhetoric of confrontation after the various crises. In August 1989 Earth Firsters in six states at fifteen sites sat in trees to interrupt logging and force Americans to reconsider their consumption of forest products (Stein, 1989, p. 114). In April 1990 twelve Earth Firsters attempted to unfurl a banner reading "Save the Planet" on the Golden Gate Bridge ("Earth First! climbs," 1990, p. A21). Most important, the group continued plans for its 1990 "Redwood Summer," designed to call attention to the destruction of old-growth Redwoods in California. The goal of the summer-long protest was to recreate an equivalent of the civil-rights movement's "Mississippi Summer" of 1964. Approximately two hundred volunteers planned to spend the summer camped in the woods in an effort to disrupt logging by Louisiana Pacific (Barol, 1990, p. 60).

Agitative Rhetoric in the Social Movement

Goals and Transformations

The agitative rhetoric of Earth First! promotes the cause of environmentalism in two ways. First, agitation and confrontation draw public attention to many concerns of the larger environmental movement. In 1983, for example, Earth First! staged seven blockades in the Kalmiopsis Forest in Oregon, provoking citizen reaction to the proposed development and forcing the Forest Service to reconsider its actions (Foreman, 1985a, p. 20). In many cases, Earth First! claims to have been on the cutting edge of critical issues that gained attention from mainstream environmentalists only after Earth First! confrontation and protest. Arguing that Oregon's 1985 wilderness bill had "a couple of hundred thousand more acres of wilderness in it" because of Earth First! protests, Foreman concludes, "By taking a moral stand and facing the consequences, we have turned more people into supporters of preserving old-growth forests than any other environmental group has done by issuing press releases and making statements" (Berger, 1986, p. 21).

A second way in which Earth First! activities promote the cause is by agitation that pushes mainstream environmental groups to respond to controversial issues. According to Roselle, "Our tactics and our philosophy force the mainstream groups to answer a lot of questions that they have not typically had to answer" (Fayhee,

1989, p. 21). This counterresponse helps the movement set limits on how far it will go in opposing establishment plans as well as justifying the movement's course of action. Fayhee (1989), a former member of Earth First! who left because of the group's extremist views, claims that mainstream environmental groups are forced to respond to Earth First! in two ways: "They have to take a stand one way or the other when it comes to ecotage, plus they must articulate that stand in a way that doesn't sacrifice the moral high ground to a bunch of self-proclaimed radicals" (p. 21). In both cases, members of the social movement must reexamine their commitment to the cause as well as their particular means of achieving such goals. By responding to Earth First! and in presenting their own agenda to the general public, environmental groups may gain greater public legitimacy because of the contrast between their apparent moderate approach and the activities of Earth First!. Bradlee Walton, former leader of Friends of the Earth, observes, "Earth First! makes us look a lot more reasonable" (Setterberg, 1986, p. 23). David Brower, former leader of both the Sierra Club and the Friends of the Earth and one of the central leaders of the environmental movement in the United States, perceives Earth First!'s radical rhetoric to be part of the natural evolution of a movement. "I founded Friends of the Earth to make the Sierra Club look reasonable," he observes. "Then I founded the Earth Island Institute to make Friends of the Earth look reasonable. Earth First! now makes us look reasonable. We're still waiting for someone to come along and make Earth First! look reasonable" (Postrel, 1990, p. 22).

Ironically, in 1990, its tenth year of existence, Earth First! started to show signs of division within its ranks. Some members have made specific moves to reconceptualize the group's mission and find a place more in line with the mainstream environmental movement. In April 1990 Earth First! chapters in Oregon and California repudiated tree-spiking. According to Karen Wood of Oregon Earth First!, "we feel it is no longer effective or appropriate as a tactic" ("Are Earth First's rowdies," 1990, p. A10). At the group's annual meeting, held in July 1990 in Montana's Beaverhead National Forest, leaders announced several dramatic changes in Earth First!'s agenda. "We want to expand our horizons from dealing strictly with wilderness issues to dealing with systematic change," observes Darryl Cherney. "We have to change the way corporations do business in the world. That's the way to save rain forests and to aid natives who are displaced when the forests are logged." In addition, the group reported that it was going to expand its recruitment of minority members, that it had increased the Earth First! journal staff from four to fifteen members to "better reflect the organization's majority," and that some radical slogans ("AIDS is a cure to the population problem" and "Let Ethiopians Starve") did not reflect the group's "opinions on how to deal with the world population problems" ("Militant environmental group," 1990, p. B2). Most significant in the transformation of Earth First! was Foreman's resignation from the group in August 1990. Disagreeing with the direction the group was taking, Foreman tells one reporter, "I'm not needed. They're better off without me" (Talbot, 1990, p. 79). It remains to be seen what role Earth First! will play in the environmental movement in the 1990s.

Earth First! has succeeded in forcing the federal government, the news media, business interests, ranchers, loggers, mineral companies, and major environmental groups to acknowledge its agenda. Even when the group is not directly linked to wilderness sabotage, it remains newsworthy because of its radical image. For example, after a logger in California was injured by a spiked tree, the *Los Angeles Times* editorialized:

> One official guessed that the vandalism was the work of Earth First!, a group that conducts guerrilla warfare against those it views as enemies of the environment. Perhaps Earth First! was not responsible, but it is logical for Earth First! to come to mind. The group openly advocates the sabotaging of logging and other development in alleged defense of the environment. ("Environmental terrorism," 1987, p. 124)

Whether members of Earth First! spiked the tree becomes secondary in terms of the group's larger mission. They have succeeded in forcing a counterresponse from powerful institutions in society and have found a way to promote their views in national and regional forums.

Earth First!'s confrontational tactics are clearly rhetorical efforts designed to call attention to environmental concerns, to identify friends and foes in the public sector, and to promote action by others in the larger social movement. Earth Firsters regularly call for ecological sabotage (labeled earlier as "monkeywrenching" to demonstrate a connection to the group's collective values) to symbolize the importance of their agenda and the commitment and passion they bring to the cause. By combining the perception of supporting monkeywrenching with other acts of civil disobedience, Earth First! has found a vehicle to gain serious and sustained attention from audiences inside and outside the environmental movement. Commenting on attacks from cattle ranchers, Mike Roselle observes, "As long as [cattle ranchers] continue to profile us as a threat to their livelihood, other people will perceive that our momentum is building. If they just ignored us, we wouldn't have any effect" (Mooney, 1989, p. 13).

Implications from the Study of Earth First!

For those who study the rhetorical dynamics of social movements, the case of Earth First! and its relationship to the larger environmental movement generates at least three conclusions. First, agitation has both instrumental and consummatory dimensions when examined as a strategic and recurrent form of persuasion. By viewing Earth First's agitation in the context of its other forms of persuasion, it appears that sit-ins, pranks, and threats of *ecotage* are symbolic on their own merits. Agitation is not simply a vehicle to draw attention to rational appeals. Instead, agitation becomes a critique of the social movement and its *failure* to achieve its fundamental goals. To ensure that the movement and the public understand the message inherent in confrontation and agitation, Earth Firsters justify monkeywrenching in public meetings, media interviews, and other sources offered for public consumption. In this way, talking about agitation and actually engaging in confrontation combine to create Earth First!'s image as extremist element within the environmental movement.

Second, scholars who examine the rhetoric of fringe groups should recognize that the impact and significance of agitative discourse must be interpreted within the framework of the larger social movement. Interestingly, the moderate image of one group may be the result of the agitation of another group. The apparent failure of extremist groups in achieving their public goals may be a misleading standard in seeking to understand the group's importance within a movement. For example, although the New Right failed to enact much of its agenda in the 1980s, the rhetoric of the New Right energized the conservative movement in the late 1970s and helped Ronald Reagan become president in 1980.

Third, agitative rhetoric generated for audiences outside the social movement is received and interpreted by individuals and groups within the movement. As a result, agitation may serve dual purposes in creating a counterresponse inside as well as outside the social movement. For the agitator, the essence of being part of the social movement is confirmed through the *dialectical enjoinment* of the counterresponse. Without a specific response from moderate groups in the movement or individuals and groups outside the movement, agitative rhetoric would have no purpose beyond self-expression and self-gratification. After Senator McClure assailed Earth First! on the floor of the United States senate, calling the group's tactics "no more noble than those of hostage-takers and kidnappers," Foreman tells one reporter, "For someone like Jim McClure to acknowledge our existence and then condemn it, he couldn't give us a nicer compliment" ("McClure blasts," 1987, p. C7).

The small but vocal "Rednecks for Wilderness" have altered the terms of the wilderness debate in the United States and have demonstrated the power of confrontational rhetoric as a way to help shape public attention and attitudes. They also have shown that small groups with little public or financial support can be a significant force within a social movement. Although Earth First! probably lacks respect in most quarters of the mainstream environmental movement, the group certainly has the attention of movement leaders.

Notes

1. For the purpose of this paper, *agitative rhetoric* will be considered synonymous with Bowers and Ochs' (1971) notion of *agitation* ("Agitation exists when (1) people outside the normal decision-making establishment (2) advocate significant social change and (3) encounter a degree of resistance within the establishment such as to require more than the normal discursive means of persuasion") and *rhetoric* ("the rationale of instrumental symbolic behavior"), pp. 4, 2. Social movements typically employ confrontational rhetoric that falls within the tradition of *normal discursive behavior*. On the other hand, some elements within a social movement may employ an agitative style of rhetoric, which may involve physical actions, nonverbal messages, and other nondiscursive forms of persuasion.
2. This study evaluates the *public communication* of Earth First! and its relationship to the environmental movement. In collecting data for analysis, I have reviewed all available sources of Earth First!'s public communication, which include statements and actions intended for public consumption. To accomplish this purpose, newspapers, general and specialized periodicals, and television programs that discuss Earth First! have been reviewed and evaluated. Examples of internal communication (Earth First! newsletters, a songbook for members, and group meetings) have not been reviewed and are considered only when they have been cited in external sources of communication (newspaper and magazine

descriptions of the group). Other studies have evaluated Earth First!'s internal communication. For a study of the group's internal communication and the cultural implications related to that discourse, see Jonathan I. Lange, "Refusal to compromise: The case of Earth First!," *Western Journal of Speech Communication,* 54, (1990): 473-494. For an analysis of the group's newsletters as a means of supporting group cohesion in a time of crisis, see Robyn Croft, "The rape of Earth First!: A metaphor for crises," unpublished manuscript, Department of English, Idaho State University, Pocatello.

3. For example, the Sierra Club uses local chapters as well as the national office to address a full host of environmental issues. The Wilderness Society focuses specifically on protecting the public lands. The Izaak Walton League supports the interests of hunters and anglers. The National Audubon Society stresses preservation of wildlife and clean air. For other descriptions of the size, budget, and mission of the leading environmental groups in the United States, see Weisskopf (1990), p. 11.

4. Some theorists have questioned whether Cathcart has presented a rhetorical definition unique to the social movement (see, for example, Zarefsky, 1980, and Smith & Windes, 1976). However, I agree with Lucas (1980) that a distinct genre of social movement rhetoric need not be found "in order to construct generalizations of a theoretical order about the nature and functions of the rhetoric employed in social movements" (p. 263). Cathcart's perspective provides an approach that is useful in understanding the dynamics of rhetoric in a social movement, both internally and externally. Whether Cathcart can demonstrate a unique theory of social movement rhetoric is not necessary for this analysis.

5. According to Donald L. Rheem (1987), "'The Monkey Wrench Gang' was much more than an action novel. It became the handbook of radicalized environmentalists who had tired of writing letters or waiting for Washington to act. 'Monkeywrenchers' took their protest to the field, putting spikes in trees to damage chain saws, pouring sugar and corn syrup into bulldozer fuel tanks, and chaining themselves to trees and rocks. Although not a formal organization, a loose-knit group of monkey-wrenchers called Earth First! now has supporters all over the United States. One of Earth First!'s founders edited 'Ecodefense: A field guide to monkeywrenching'" (p. 16).

6. Endorsing the content of the book, Abbey concludes: "No good American should ever go into the woods again without this book and, for example, a hammer and few pounds of nails. Spike a few trees now and then whenever you enter an area condemned to chainsaw massacre by Louisiana Pacific and its affiliated subsidiary, the U.S. Forest Service. You won't hurt the tree; they'll be grateful for the protection; and you may save the forest" (Foreman, 1985b, pp. 4-5).

7. When Abbey died in 1989, Foreman eulogized the writer, observing, "He represented what the country could have been if it hadn't turned its back on its ideal 200 hundred years ago. Every book of Ed Abbey's, every essay, every story has launched a thousand deeds" ("Some 500 gather," 1989, p. C2). Abbey's death presented a spiritual crisis for many Earth Firsters who found solace in a special issue of their group's journal devoted entirely to Abbey and his life.

8. For a rhetorical analysis of *The Monkey Wrench Gang,* see Brant Short, "Saving the wild and the free: The 'monkey wrench' rhetoric of Edward Abbey,'" in Richard J. Jensen & John C. Hammerback, Eds., *In search of justice: The Indiana tradition in speech communication,* pp. 285-301, Amsterdam: Rodopi, 1987.

9. For example, in a 1983 article that examined the "Real Monkeywrench Gang," McBride concluded: "As the ecological Crown Prince, Earth First! has taken on the task of goosing those penny-loafered drudges back in conservation headquarters who think all there is to life is writing Congressmen about the melting polar ice caps or the latest Love Canal effluence. At first blush it is hard to take Earth First! too seriously, perhaps because they don't" (p. 37).

Works Cited

Abbey, E. (1975). *The monkey wrench gang.* New York: Avon.

Andrews, J. (1969). Confrontation at Columbia: A case study in coercive rhetoric. *Quarterly Journal of Speech, 55,* 9-16.

Are Earth First!'s rowdies finally sobering up? (1990, April 14). Lewiston Morning Tribune [Idaho], p. A10.

Bailey, Jr., H. (1972). Confrontation as an extension of communication. In H. Bosmajian, *Dissent: Symbolic behavior and rhetorical strategies* (pp. 181-193). Boston: Allyn & Bacon; reprint 1980, Westport, CT: Greenwood.

Barol, B. (1990, July 2). Eco-activist summer: Earth First! vs. the loggers in California. *Newsweek,* p. 60.

Baumgartner, M. (1986, December 23). Activists turn to violence to push ecological causes. *Christian Science Monitor,* pp. 3-4.

Berger, J. (1986, November). Tree shakers. *Omni*, pp. 20-21.

Bishop, K. (1990, May 26). Environmentalists hurt, then held in blast. *New York Times*, pp. A1, A10.

Black, B. E. (1989, April 10). On the edge of common sense. *Livestock Market Digest*, n. page.

Bowers, J. W., & Ochs, D. (1971). *The rhetoric of agitation and control.* Reading, MA: Addison-Wesley.

Brody, M. (1990, March 5). New leftist crusade radical cultists are trying to fill the growing emptiness. *Barron's*, p. 11.

Cathcart, R. (1978). Movements: Confrontation as rhetorical form. *Southern Speech Communication Journal*, 43, 233-247.

Cathcart, R. (1980). Defining social movements by their rhetorical form. *Central States Speech Journal*, 31, 267-273.

Devall, B., & Sessions, G. (1985). *Deep ecology: Living as if nature mattered.* Layton, UT: Peregrine.

Earth First! climbs bridge in protest. (1990, April 25). *Los Angeles Times*, p. A21.

Earth First! protesters invade office of Yellowstone Park superintendent. (1986, March 5). *Idaho Statesman* [Boise], p. C2.

Eco-terrorists may kill livestock, bureau worries. (1990, October 9). *Idaho State Journal* [Pocatello] p. A2.

Environmental militants gather in Montana. (1990, July 10). *Idaho State Journal* [Pocatello], p. A2.

Environmental terrorism. (1987, July 23). *Los Angeles Times*, p. II2.

Fayhee, M. J. (1988, September). Earth First! and foremost. *Backpacker*, pp. 20-23.

FBI steps up pressure against Earth First!. (1990, August 5). New York Times News Service, *Idaho State Journal* [Pocatello], p. A2.

Feldman, P., & Meyer, R. (1989, June 1). 4 held in plot to cut lines near nuclear plants. *Los Angeles Times*, pp. I1, I20.

For the members of Earth First! some things just aren't negotiable. (1984, 25 November). *Oregonian* [Portland], *Newsbank*, ENV: 91:G6-G11.

Foreman, D. (1985a, January-February). No compromise in defense of mother earth. *Mother Earth News*, pp. 17-22.

Foreman, D. (1985b). *Ecodefense: A field guide to monkeywrenching.* Tucson: Ned Ludd.

Gamerman, A. (1988, December 2). New law won't deter tree-spikers, Earth First! exec says. *Idaho State Journal* [Pocatello], p. B6.

Gregg, R. (1971). The ego-function of the rhetoric of protest. *Philosophy and Rhetoric*, 4, 71-91.

Grelen, J. (1989, June 2). Eco-terror act called trial run for flats. *Denver Post*, p. A12.

Grelen, J., & Sinisi, J. S. (1989, June 2). Earth First! radicalism defended. *Denver Post*, p. A12.

Griffin, L. M. (1969). A dramatistic theory of the rhetoric of movements. In W. H. Rueckert (Ed.), *Critical responses to Kenneth Burke* (pp. 456-478). Minneapolis: University of Minnesota Press.

Haiman, F. (1967). The rhetoric of the streets: Some legal and ethical considerations. *Quarterly Journal of Speech*, 53, 99-114.

Japenga, A. (1985, September 5). Earth First! A voice vying for the wilderness. *Los Angeles Times*, p. V-I.

Jefferson, P. (1969). The schizoid image of Stokely Carmichael. In J. J. Auer, *The rhetoric of our times* (pp. 389-399). New York: Appleton, Century, Crofts.

Kane, J. (1987, February). Mother nature's army: Guerrilla warfare comes to the American forest. *Esquire*, pp. 98-106.

Kennedy, Jr., R. F. (1990, April 19). Democracy is the way to hug a tree. *Los Angeles Times*, p. B7.

Larry King Live. (1990, July 6). Transcript, Journal Graphics, Inc.

Lucas, S. (1980). Coming to terms with movement studies. *Central States Speech Journal*, 35, 255-266.

Macy, R. (1989, December 17). Western ranchers worry about "ecoterrorists." *Idaho State Journal* [Pocatello] p. B6.

Malanowski, J. (1987, May 2). Monkey-wrenching around. *The Nation*, pp. 568-569.

McBride, S. (1983, January). The real monkey wrench gang. *Outside*, pp. 34+.

McClure blasts Earth First!. (1987, June 21). *Billings Gazette* [Montana], p. C7.

McEdwards, M. (1968). Agitative rhetoric: Its nature and effect. *Western Speech*, 32, 36-43.

McKibben, B. (1989). *The end of nature.* New York: Random House.

Militant environmental group wraps up annual gathering. (1990, July 16). *Idaho State Journal* [Pocatello], p. B2.

Mooney, R. (1989, August). The strong arm of Earth First!. *Beef Today*, pp. 12-13.

Monkeywrenching: Earth First!'s hole card. (1990, February 15). *Sacramento News and Review*, p. 18.

Morgan, C. (1989, May 16). Fanatics of right, left share same roots. *Idaho Statesman* [Boise], p. A4.

Nash, R. (1989). *The rights of nature: A history of environmental ethics.* Madison: University of Wisconsin Press.

New species of tree slime. (1989, April 30). *Missoulian* [Montana], p. A4.

Nokes, G. (1987, November 10). No Title. *Oregonian* [Portland] *Newsbank, ENV:* 73:A5-A8.

Parfit, M. (1990, April). Earth First!ers wield a mean monkey wrench. *Smithsonian*, pp. 184-190.

Postrel, V. (1990, April). The green road to serfdom. *Reason*, pp. 22-28.

Rheem, D. L. (1987, January 13). Environmental action: A movement comes of age. *Christian Science Monitor*, pp. 16-17.

Robbins, J. (1989, July 9). Saboteurs for a better environment. *New York Times*, p. E6.

Russell, D. (1989, July 17). Earth last! *The Nation*, p. 77.

Scott, R., & Smith, D. (1969). The rhetoric of confrontation. *Quarterly Journal of Speech*, 55, 1-8.

Setterberg, F. (1986, November 9). The wild bunch. *Image*, pp. 20-27.

Short, B. (1987). Saving the wild and the free. In R. Jensen & J. Hammerback (Eds.), *In search of justice: The Indiana tradition in speech communication* (pp. 285-301). Amsterdam: Rodopi.

Simons, H., & Mechling, E. (1981). The rhetoric of movements. In D. Nimmo & K. Sanders (Eds.), *Handbook of Political Communication* (pp. 417-444). Beverly Hills: Sage.

Slocum, K. (1985, November 14). Radical ecologists pound spikes in trees to scare loggers and hinder lumbering. *Wall Street Journal*, p. 35.

Smith, R., & Windes, R. (1976). The rhetoric of mobilization: Implications for the study of movements. *Southern Speech Communication Journal*, 42, 1-19.

Some 500 gather at Utah park to remember writer Edward Abbey. (1989, May 25). *Idaho State Journal* [Pocatello], p. C2.

Stammer, L. (1987, May 15). Environment radicals target of probe into lumber mill accident. *Los Angeles Times*, pp. I3, 22.

Stein, M. (1987, November 29). Earth First! "fanatics" try to keep things wild. *Los Angeles Times*, pp. I1, I14.

Stein, M. (1989, August 15). Radical environmentalists in trees disrupt logging across west. *Los Angeles Times*, p. I14.

Talbot, S. (1990, November/December). Earth first! What next? *Mother Jones*, pp. 46+.

Taylor, R. (1986, January 13). Pranks and protests over environment turn tough. *U.S. News and World Report*, p. 70.

This will be no picnic. (1990, May 10). *Idaho State Journal* [Pocatello], p. A4.

Tolan, S. (1989). How an FBI mole tunneled into Earth First!. *High Country News*, p. 5.

Vanderpool, T. (1989, September). Monkey-wrenching for planet earth. *The Progressive*, p. 15.

Weisskopf, M. (1990, April 30-May 6). Environmental groups sail the mainstream. *Washington Post National Weekly Edition*, pp. 10-11.

White, M. (1984, November 12). Earth First! leader says wilderness areas must be preserved. *Casper Star-Tribune* [Wyoming], *Newsbank*, ENV: 86:A11-A12.

Wilderness conference session to focus on "legacy" of Edward Abbey. (1990, March 5). News release from Idaho Farm Bureau Federation. (Available from Idaho Farm Bureau Federation, P.O. Box 4848, Pocatello, ID.)

Zarefsky, D. (1980). A skeptical view of movement studies. *Central States Speech Journal*, 31, 245-254.

The Logic of Competing
Information Campaigns:
Conflict Over Old Growth
and the Spotted Owl

by Jonathan I. Lange

As "the environment" has emerged as a predominant issue of the American scene, so have environmental advocacy and counter advocacy become a central political drama. *Time* magazine's identification of the earth as "planet of the year" reflected the public's concern with the increasing number and variety of interdependent ecological problems (Jaehne, 1990), particularly as the magnitude and consequences of environmental degradation, crisis, and policy-making itself became known. Nuclear accidents and waste disposal, air and water degradation, chemical and oil spills, ozone depletion and the greenhouse effect, species displacement and vanishing wilderness are only a small sample of the environmental concerns currently played out by assorted publics, interest groups, government agencies, and representatives in the theaters of American media, courts, and policy-making bodies.

Natural resource utilization is at center stage within the environmental drama; indeed, some scholars have argued that the perception of scarce resources is an essential—and therefore necessary—condition of any conflict (Coser, 1967; Hocker & Wilmot, 1991; Mack & Snyder, 1973). Since the economic health of so many communities depends on what are now dwindling natural resources, environmentalists, "counter-environmentalists"[1] and government agencies continually clash over resource utilization, allocation, replacement, and depletion. Natural resource issues have achieved a special prominence in the pantheon of environmental concerns. Resource conflict has become a quintessential feature of the American political drama.

Discursive practices inherently determine the "social construction" of any environmental conflict (Schoenfeld, Meier, & Griffin, 1979). What humans say about the issues—even how the issues are defined—will determine interpretation, treatment, and outcome of the public debate (Carbaugh, 1991). As rhetorical and communicative processes mold decisions affecting generations of human and non-human species, thorough scrutiny by communication theorists and critics is warranted. Unfortunately, although analyses of environmental problems abound in sociology and other disciplines (Cantrill, 1990), few appear in communication journals. Fewer still specify natural resource conflict.

There are notable exceptions. Oravec provided one of the earliest contributions in her rhetorical criticism of preservationism (1981). Peterson offered a Burkeian analysis of "dust bowl rhetoric" (1986) and an essay on farmer's resistance to conservation practices (1991). Media "packaging" of the Chernobyl accident drew an essay by Luke (1987). Waddell (1990) addressed the role of pathos in a policy-making process surrounding potentially hazardous recombinant DNA experiments. In 1990 I presented a cultural analysis of Earth First!, a radical environmental group known for their refusal to compromise (Lange). Short (1991) examined Earth First!'s agitative rhetoric. Risk communication with regard to incineration effects (Renz, 1992) and recycling behavior (Krendal, Olson, & Burke, 1992) was a recent object of inquiry. Analyses of "counter-environmental discourse" were provided by Huspek and Kendall (1991), who highlighted the political vocabulary of a speech community of lumber-industrial workers, as well as Williams and Treadaway (1992), who critiqued Exxon's crisis communication after the Valdez oil tanker spill.

The more specific category of natural resource conflict was first addressed by Cox (1982), who focused on the rhetorical strategy of casting an environmental decision as "irreparably" harmful to resources. Oravec (1984) investigated an early national resource dispute—over the building of the Hetch Hetchy dam—as she critiqued the different side's arguments and how "the public interest" was differentially conceived. Peterson studied how institutional authority was constructed during a government hearing on wilderness designation (1988). Cantrill, in a multi-disciplinary review and categorization of research in environmental communication, went so far as to define environmental advocacy as symbolic discourse "aimed at supporting conservation and preservation of finite resources" (in press).

Thus, there has been limited but increasing attention paid to environmental and counter-environmental advocacy as our discipline applies theoretical principles to this critical arena. The increase may be due not only to the crucial nature of the topic, but to the fact that environmental and counter-environmental advocacy invoke other, larger, and variably constituted communication contexts (e.g., information campaigns, political communication, mass media, public address, social movements, and—especially in the case of resource conflict—dispute resolution).

Given the numerous contexts involved, the study of environmental advocacy should seek to achieve the status of a "sub-area" from which contexts can coalesce and communication theory can evolve (cf., Berger, 1991). Such achievement is aided by the research cited above, as well as the Speech Communication Association's 1989 Seminar on Environmental Advocacy, its 1991 and 1993 conferences on Environmental Advocacy (Oravec & Cantrill, 1992) and its inclusion of environmental papers in its national and regional conventions. The current study explicitly attempts to merge contexts and build theory as it explores the communicative character of what is arguably the nation's most wrenching natural resource conflict of the late twentieth century, what Lemonik has termed "the hottest battleground" in the country's broader "environmental wars": the dispute over old growth forests and the spotted owl (1989, p. 58).

This descriptive, qualitative case study examines a resource conflict in which advocates' and counter-advocates' rhetorical and communicative strategies *mirror and match* one another as disputants engage in a synchronous, spiral-like "logic of interaction." Drawing from conversation analytic and systems theories, Pearce & Cronen (1980) and Pearce (1989) conceptualize interactions as having "logical force." That is, when interlocuters in a communication system address each other, intending to influence each other, their utterances evoke—almost force—specific types of responses, while delegitimating or even disallowing others. The interaction reported here differs from previous logic of interaction inquiry; this interaction is characterized by moves which, while communicative, are intended for just about anyone *except* the other party. As with other disputes, both environmentalists and industry representatives choose strategies that are dependent on and responsive to their antagonist. This analysis reveals how disputants' interactive logic—a mirroring and matching of each others' strategies—is achieved with little to no direct communication between parties. They learn of each others' tactics primarily through the mass media as they pursue duplicate or antithetical rhetorical strategies with various audiences. The logic becomes evident in an examination of the two sides' *information campaigns*, an area relatively neglected in the study of interactive logics.

Information campaigns are organized sets of communication activities intending to generate specific outcomes or effects in a relatively large number of people, usually within a specific time period (Rogers & Storey, 1987, p. 821). The information campaigns of timber and environmental groups are political, as opposed to marketing, public health or other types of campaigns. The current essay argues for application of the principles of interactive logics in future studies of political communication.

Previous researchers have alluded to mirroring, matching, and—relatedly—spiraling processes in studies of conflicting parties, finding a variety of communicative outcomes and patterns. In his seminal work outlining the course of both productive and destructive conflict, Deutsch wrote, "If each side in a conflict tends to perceive its own motives and behavior as more benevolent and legitimate than those of the other side, it is evident that conflict will spiral upward in intensity" (1969, p. 14). He showed how perceptions of benevolence and legitimacy facilitate a "negative spiral" of destructive strategies and tactics. Such perceptions additionally bias each side's idea of what would be an equitable agreement and fair compromise since differential legitimacy should be differentially rewarded. Following Deutsch's emphasis on perceptions, Pearce, Littlejohn, and Alexander (1987) examined a variety of actions and texts—primarily a debate between Senator Edward Kennedy and Reverend Jerry Falwell—and argued that the conflict between secular humanists and the New Christian Right was characterized by a process in which disputants' beliefs were bolstered by their interpretations of the responses of the other side. This led to a logic of interaction that the authors labeled a "reciprocated diatribe." "Each act by each participant elicited a louder, more shrill, and less informative response from the other; the interaction was quickly reduced to name-calling with a lot of emotion" (Pearce, 1989, p. 177). In discussions of interpersonal conflicts, Folger and Poole (1984) remarked how negative spirals can become self-perpetuating while Hocker and Wilmot (1991) argued that communication actually accelerates misunderstanding when contextualized in destructive escalatory spirals. Focusing on one set of texts from two competing information campaigns, Vanderford (1989) found the "parallel" use of "vilification" strategies. She analyzed newsletters of one "pro-life" and one "pro-choice" group, concluding that communication between the two was probably inhibited by the vilification rhetoric.

The conflict over old growth forests is shown here to evoke some of the above attributes and consequences—reciprocated diatribe, parallel vilification—as well as others. The current inquiry reveals a logic of interaction achieved with little to no direct communication between environmental and counter-environmental groups. The logic is instead revealed through the competing information campaigns, as each group mirrors and matches the other's communicative behavior across five categories. These categories are described below following sections on method and background. The essay concludes with a discussion of indirect interactive logics, particularly as they affect political and other communication contexts.

Method

In studying this conflict I followed qualitative data gathering techniques and field work recommendations offered by Glaser (1965), Lofland (1971), Spradley (1979, 1980), and Pearce (1989). I attempted to immerse myself in both environmentalist and counter-environmentalist (i.e., timber industry) culture in the three ways suggested by Lofland: through bodily presence, extensive interviewing, and examination of written materials. As part of an ongoing environmental research agenda, the fieldwork on which this essay draws occurred over four years. It included over 300 hours of direct participant observation of strategy and planning meetings, conferences, benefit concerts and events, political demonstrations, and other gatherings held by each side. I "hung out" at local environmental and timber industry offices and attended government hearings. I acted as moderator or facilitator on two occasions when representatives from both sides were present (during a public debate and at a meeting of national foresters). I was hired by a federal agency to analyze a "failed" experiment in collaborative forest management for a particular old growth basin; this involved 22 interviews with agency, environmental, timber and civic representatives. I also held six intensive interviews (Lofland, 1971) with informants, averaging 90 minutes per interview, and have "checked in" with four of these individuals on dozens of occasions, asking for their interpretation of various events. I informally interviewed dozens more. Since the primary focus of this study is the way the two information campaigns relate to each other, my examination of a wide range of artifacts was particularly important. These included: hundreds of local newsletters, press releases and miscellaneous publications written by representatives of each side; hundreds of articles reported by the Associated Press, United Press International, and local daily newspapers on timber issues and the spotted owl; dozens of analyses of old growth in the national popular "environmental press."

I attempted to structure my data gathering in such a way as to follow an interpretive/critical method designed to describe interaction between two conflicting groups (Pearce, 1989, p. 172-179). With this method, the qualitative researcher attends especially to the spiral-like "logic" that unfolds as each group interprets and responds to various acts and events (perhaps the previous response from the other party, perhaps a salient newsmaking occurrence). This type of communication inquiry investigates how the "original" interpretation and response elicits the other's interpretation and response, which then elicits another interpretation and response from the first party, and so on. However, as the fieldwork progressed, the relative lack of direct communication between groups moved me to add Glaser's "constant comparison method" (1965) as a supplementary procedure. While following Pearce's method revealed a synchronized logic, in which communicative tactics were opposite or mimicking each other, the lack of face-to-face communication made identification of specific and chronologically clear interpretations and responses infeasible. I thus turned to the constant comparison method to inductively generate categories into which the major tactics could be parsimoniously placed. This essay therefore pays less attention to chronological order of disputant interaction and more to communicative content and medium. This will become clear below as the tactics are reviewed.

In the pages that follow, I attempt where possible to use the language of industry or environmental group representatives. Those parts not referenced, particularly in the next section, are taken from interviews and *in situ* fieldwork or are conclusions drawn from daily newspaper reports. The five categories are not meant to be exhaustive or discrete. Following Glaser (1965), evidence is conveyed primarily by illustration and example. Some exemplars are shown to develop in chronological sequence; others do not indicate chronology.

Background

"Old growth" timber, located in what environmentalists call "ancient forests," has been the subject of increasing controversy for at least two decades, ever since environmental groups began efforts to reduce or prevent industry "clearcutting." Clearcutting—as opposed to select cutting—is the most economically efficient method of logging timber since every tree is cut. However, a desolate and unsightly landscape of tree stumps and cleared brush is left behind; what was once a magnificent section of forest—a complex habitat for dozens of plant and animal species—is transformed into a barren spectacle. This transformation notwithstanding, the timber industry would have to lay off thousands of workers were it unable to continue clearcutting trees; communities and regions whose economy and social fabric rely on timber would suffer dramatically. Those who oppose clearcutting mourn the loss of biological diversity, animal habitat, scenic beauty, spiritual retreat, and recreation areas previously available in the ancient forests. Reforestation efforts—only sometimes successful—produce rows of small, single species trees in monocultured "tree farms," and can not "replace" the majestic, environmentally precious and biologically diverse virgin forest. Though federal foresters offer some hope with "the new forestry," in which logging and reforestation processes are modified and improved, all agree that current forestry methods can not truly reproduce old growth. Old growth certainly can not be replaced within a single lifetime; the trees are generally between 200 and 1000 years old.

The vast majority of this country's remaining old growth (approximately 10% of the original) is on public lands, "owned" by the citizenry and "managed" by the United States Forest Service (USFS) and the Bureau of Land Management (BLM), divisions of the U.S. Departments of Agriculture and Interior, respectively. Both are charged by law to regulate the "multiple use" of the forests. The controversial policy of multiple use is designed to protect and preserve watersheds, wildlife, and wilderness, while still allowing for recreation, grazing, mining, and timber sales. Under the multiple use policy, timber is auctioned by the government to private timber companies that "harvest" logs for milling into lumber.

Over the past two decades, environmental groups have gone to the courts as part of their attempt to protect old growth ecosystems from alleged abuse by government agency or industry. Lawsuits and appeals were initiated to require correction of ill-prepared environmental assessments and environmental impact statements, to prevent "overcutting" a specified acreage, to stop logging in areas unsuitable for reforestation, to deter cutting where resultant erosion would destroy fish habitat and endanger watersheds, and so forth. Until recently, however, environmental groups usually lost in court or had suits prohibited by federal legislative riders.

The controversy over the spotted owl is overlayed on this history in a complicated way. In 1973, Congress passed the Endangered Species Act, one of this nation's most stringent environmental protection laws.[2] The act required that any threatened or endangered species be listed and that recovery plans be developed and implemented by all federal land-managing agencies. The legislative history of the 93rd Congress states that the purpose of the act was "to provide a means whereby the *ecosystems* upon which endangered and threatened species depend may be conserved, protected, or restored" (quoted in Norman, 1989, p. 12, emphasis added). A second critical law is the National Forest Management Act (NFMA) of 1976, the same law that mandated multiple use. This legislation further required the USFS to protect and maintain the diversity of species on its lands and to identify "indicator species" *representing* the health of the biotic community (since the agency could not monitor all species within a single ecosystem). For biological reasons, including its role in the food chain, the USFS chose the Northern spotted owl (*Strix occidentalis caurina*) as one of the indicator species of old growth forests. Environmental groups therefore liken the owl to the canary in the coal mine; if the owl is threatened or endangered, so too are the old growth ecosystems.

While timber advocates dispute the findings, studies by government agencies confirm that the owl's survival is dependent upon the health of old growth forests;

that is, the owl would perish without old growth. Since the drastically dwindling number of owls was well documented (Sterling, 1989), environmentalists in 1986 sought its listing as a threatened or endangered species to both protect the owl and—not incidentally—to prevent ruination of the ecosystems upon which it depends, old growth forests. In 1987, the United States Fish and Wildlife Service (USF&WS) denied the request. Twenty-six environmental groups sued. After months of expert testimony, political in-fighting, and intra-agency scandal involving suppression of evidence, the courts ordered the USF&WS to reconsider the owl's listing. In April of 1989 the agency changed its position; it proposed to list the owl as threatened. However, official listing could occur only after a period of further study, public comment, and biological assessment.

This seemed a great victory for environmental groups. It meant that at least some proposed auctions of timber from USFS and BLM old growth lands would now be enjoined by law since the lands constituted the habitat of a potentially threatened indicator species. However, the entire timber industry now brought its full might to bear on the controversy. Central to the economy of the affected geographical regions, and requiring a "steady and predictable" supply of old growth logs to survive without massive personnel layoffs and loss, members worked steadily to stave off economic damage to the industry and social turmoil in the timber-dependent regions.

The period between the proposal to list the owl and actual listing was thus characterized by intense debate, fervent lobbying, and congressional dealmaking. Both the industry and environmental groups waged extensive and intense information campaigns to gain the support of various groups and federal agencies, including the general public. The campaigns were marked by media depiction of demonstrations, counter-demonstrations, threats, and passionate rhetoric from both sides. Though occasional formal and informal events allowed for face-to-face interaction, negotiation, and attempted mediation, members of the industry and environmental groups rarely met in collaborative circumstances. The owl was officially listed in June of 1990.

A bevy of remaining issues sustains the competing information campaigns. Chief among them is how much and which old growth acreage should be set aside as owl habitat. Bitter controversy surrounds the agencies' long-term forest management plans. Congress's 1993 debate on reauthorization of the Endangered Species Act will refocus attention on old growth (as well as dozens of other natural resource conflicts). When making timber policy, the federal agencies and Congress will diligently attempt to assess and include the general public's position. As the sympathetic chair of an influential congressional committee told one environmentalist, "I agree with you, but you have to get me more letters." Despite a few recent signs of change, all of these occurrences indicate continuation of intense political communication designed to mobilize public support.[3]

Mirroring and Matching

Analysis of the information campaigns as waged through 1992 shows how both timber and environmental groups used the same five major and overlapping strategies as they mirrored or matched each other's communicative behavior: (1) frame and reframe; (2) select high/select low; (3) vilify/ennoble; (4) simplify and dramatize; and (5) lobby and litigate. The term "matching" indicates communicative behavior that copies or repeats the other party's strategy; "mirroring" describes communicative behavior that duplicates the other party's tactic by presenting antithetical, polar or "mirror image" information. On occasion, parties engage in both processes, as is demonstrated below. The five categories themselves are in no way new; rather, they are simple constructions that describe the logic of interaction. They provide an understanding of the primary features of the information campaigns. The first strategy discussed, framing and reframing, shows how disputants attempt to contextualize the entire dispute.

Frame and Reframe

Across a wide variety of communicative forums—including newsletters, financial appeals, propaganda materials, press releases, interviews granted reporters, newspaper advertisements, television commercials, legal briefs filed, letters to congresspersons, and presentations to Rotary, Kiwanis, and like groups—each side frames issues (see Goffman, 1974; Salmon, 1989, pp. 24-28) in accordance with its particular ends. Facts, explanations, and interpretations are contextualized to discursively construct a reality favorable to one's rhetorical goals. Frames are then predictably followed by a mirroring or matching strategy in which reality is *reframed*, by the other group, with an antithetical or oppositional context. Where it begins is, of course, a matter of arbitrary punctuation.

Representative examples will illuminate this category. The first involves mirroring and matching moves that focus on economic and employment issues such as lumber mill shutdowns, the resulting loss of jobs, and retraining displaced forest products workers for alternate vocations. In media cited above, environmental groups acknowledge the pain of transition, yet suggest it is inescapable: Old growth is finite; we will eventually run out; it is now time to acknowledge the inevitable reduction of timber-related work. They further argue that the problem of timber supply stems primarily from poor planning, decades of "overcutting," and increasingly sophisticated logging and milling technology. They note that increasing timber harvests have been accompanied by a decreasing work force throughout the 1970s and early 1980s—all prior to any effects of the spotted owl controversy; the bird is "only a scapegoat." They attempt to create a context in which the timber industry is framed as destroyers of the forest, out to get the last bit of old growth. They argue that the trend in work force reduction will continue inevitably as an effect of technology even apart from timber supplies. "I think the jobs issue is tragically irrelevant. . . . The jobs aren't going to be around that much longer anyway. . . . We won't have these jobs for our children, so let's slow [logging] down now" (quoted in Freeman, 1992, p. 1A). Environmentalists point out that if the industry really cared about its workers, owners would be helping with retraining efforts instead of fighting the inevitable.

An antithetical frame—or reframe—is offered by timber industry supporters at every opportunity. They attempt to make jobs the primary issue. Overcutting is sometimes acknowledged, yet they portray trees as "a renewable resource." The owl is to blame for supply problems and mill closure. They suggest that advanced technology is "only a scapegoat" in explaining jobs lost: "Automation never closed a mill. Lack of logs will close mills" (quoted in Zacoreli, 1991, p. 1). Timber workers accuse environmentalists of trying to ruin their communities. They scoff at suggestions that they give up a way of life that their fathers and grandfathers enjoyed. "Working in the woods or a mill, trucking logs, well, that can hardly be replaced with a minimum wage tourism job. And those computer jobs everyone talks about—do I look like I'm cut out for a desk job? It's easy for them to say, 'Stop logging.' but I've got a family to feed." The industry works diligently to press the jobs issue in nearly every discussion while environmentalists attempt to reframe it with equal fervor.

Three additional and representative examples further illustrate the framing and reframing process. In these cases, industry and environmentalist representatives match each other's moves with mirrored content as they react to news reports. (For brevity's sake, frames and reframes are indicated but not fully detailed.) In 1990, a press-announced "new environmental agenda" by the U.S. Forest Service was followed with: "[E]nvironmentalists are reacting with skepticism, calling the new agenda a 'public relations ploy,' and a timber industry association says the logging restrictions are too tough" (Grubb, 1990, p. 3). When a Bush administration task force announced a likely reduction in 1991 timber sales, the executive director of the American Forest Resource Alliance called the plan "unbalanced" in favor of "environmental special interests" ("Owl backers," 1990, p. 1A); the vice president of the Wilderness Society was moved to say the proposal was "a dismal display of politics over science and an attempt to undermine the Endangered Species Act and other federal laws that protect the environment" (Lamar, 1990, p. 1). Immediately following the 1992 Forest Service announcement of its plan to protect the owl (later rejected as inadequate by a federal judge), a timber representative offered this to the press: "We are extremely disappointed that the Forest Service has placed the spotted owl before tens of thousands of Pacific Northwest families" while an environmentalist spokesperson said, "This is completely inadequate. . . . This clearly can't stand on the grounds of being a credible plan for the owl." ("Forest Service adopts Thomas plan," 1992, p. 1). These frames or reframes represent hundreds of similar reactions, as offered to the press or in other media. They are further advanced and bolstered as both groups employ a second strategy, selecting high or low.

Select High/Select Low

In the contest to win public opinion, each side selects studies, "expert opinion," and interpretations of each that offer numbers that promote its point of view. Hardly a new process to the American political scene, sides select high or low numbers in accordance with their rhetorical ends while simultaneously and synchronistically rejecting the other side's offerings. Two representative though remarkable cases are offered here. The first concerns the potential number of jobs lost from mill closure. In a wide variety of public forums, timber industry representatives cite sources that herald catastrophic numbers of job loss. When environmentalists are forced to deal with numbers of jobs lost, they present contradictory information in which numbers are minimized. A deputy undersecretary in the Department of the Interior, acting as coordinator of a government task force developing plans for the owl's recovery, complained: "We've had studies [reported to us] over the past year with job losses ranging from 14,000 to 102,000 jobs" (Durbin, 1991, p. D2). The range is actually wider: "The Wilderness Society has portrayed the risk at only 12,000 jobs. At the other extreme, the industry-sponsored American Forest Resource Alliance placed the risk at more than 147,000 jobs" (Kadera, 1992, p. E5).

A second illustration involves the very definition of old growth forest itself—and therefore, the amount actually remaining. There are a number of definitions of old growth, ranging from the broadest (mature timber not yet cut) to the most narrow (an area with trees 200 years or older, 32 inches or larger in diameter with specific types and amounts of trees, tree canopies, and downed trees per acre). Environmentalists and industry groups offer different definitions depending on the purpose at hand. For example, if environmentalists want to demonstrate how little old growth is left and, therefore, especially precious, they use the narrow, more restrictive definition; if, however, they want to argue that large sections of old growth forest and spotted owl habitat must be off limits to logging, they employ a broad, inclusive one. Of course, the reverse scenario is true for the industry.

Similar processes of selecting high or low occur with nearly every other aspect of the controversy. Citing different sources, groups offer different counts on the number of owls remaining, the acreage of national lands already protected from logging, the amount of Pacific Northwest lumber needed by the nation, the success rate of tree replanting efforts, and other numerical "facts" that can be differentially found or interpreted. Each group points to the other's "misuse" of these facts as evidence of their villainous nature.

Vilify/Ennoble

In her case study of pro-life and pro-choice rhetoric, Vanderford (1989) outlines four forms and functions of vilification as a rhetorical strategy. They include formulating specific adversarial opponents, casting them in an exclusively negative light, attributing diabolical motives to them and magnifying their power. All four forms and functions are present in the environmental conflict. The counterpoint to vilification is also present, as environmentalists and timber advocates ennoble their own cause and motives. Taken together, this creates a mirror effect in which each side castigates the other while proclaiming its own virtue. The following perspectives, claims, and *ad hominem* arguments are illustrative as they recall Pearce et al.'s (1987) "reciprocated diatribe," the self-perceived greater "benevolence and legitimacy" articulated by Deutsch (1969) as well as Vanderford's description of "vilification" rhetoric.

In an industry with a volatile union-management history, the current internal solidarity owes some to management success in framing environmentalists as devil figures, particularly radical environmental groups like Earth First! The majority of workers and owner-operators now view environmentalists as "radical preservation-ists" who want to "lock up the forests" preventing their "wise use" ("Environmen-talists reject," 1990, p. 2A). These "so-called environmentalists" are actually "eco-terrorists" ("Timber task force," 1990, p. 3) using "raw generalizations, bum science, and half truths" (quoted in Macomber, 1990, p. D1) in creating conditions that will "be the death of many [Pacific Northwest] communities" ("Conservation-ists seek help," 1989, p. 8). Workers and owners both depict national environmental groups as wealthy, highly organized, outside "obstructionists" who should leave decisions about Pacific Northwest resources to those who live here; "enviros" are "East Coast carpetbaggers trying to tell us our economy is going to have to transition" (quoted in Manny, 1990a, p. 3A)). One informant, an owner of a struggling lumber company, told me that, "We can solve this conflict, but only if we keep it *local*" [emphasis added].

Many in the environmental community believe that the intent of the owners in particular is, as one informant said, to "take every last possible stick while the taking is still good." Pacific Northwesterners are being duped by an industry of "timber beasts" who, like the coal barons of Appalachia, will ruin the landscape and long-term economy after depleting the natural resources. The view of environmen-talists is perhaps best represented in a local newspaper opinion piece that said:

> The timber side is headed by a few giant corporations with almost unlimited resources, highly unified and closely associated with other large companies, including perhaps newspapers and television stations. The environmental side consists of a loose coalition of volunteer labor, not very unified or very well organized. (Cook, 1989, p. 15A)

An environmental informant told me that their best hope was to nationalize the issue:

> People in the East think national forests are like national parks and will remain untouched. They need to know that these forests are being destroyed. Then they need to write letters and complain. This is the only way we can fight an insensitive multi-million dollar industry.

As each group vilifies the other, so too does each side ennoble itself. Both sides claim they have "compromised"; both hold that "science" favors their position; both imply "morality" and "the common good" as their guiding forces (see Freeman, Littlejohn, & Pearce, 1992). Environmental groups point out that since only 10 percent of the nation's original old growth forests are left, to compromise on that paltry amount is to employ an unfair starting point. That is, a true compromise is impossible, since 90 percent has already gone to timber interests (Lange, 1990). Timber groups argue that millions of acres of potentially harvestable timber are now "locked up"; it is they who have compromised, now to the point of economic ruin. Similarly, when a federally appointed panel of scientists advised a significant reduction in timber harvests in order to save the owl from extinction, environmental supporters referred to the group as "our very best scientists" and "the bluest of blue ribbon committees" (Sonner, 1990b, p. 4A). Timber groups labeled the report "bum science" maintaining that the public is not learning the true "science of forestry" (Hill, 1990, p. 7). Finally, inferences about moral ends and the common good are made by both groups. The industry claims to be saving jobs as well as a way of life that spans generations. One industry leader marched in a pro-timber demonstration to call attention to the nation's growing number of homeless, connecting the harvesting of timber and milling of lumber to the need for additional housing. Environmentalists maintain they are preserving nature for our children's children's children. One environmentalist told me that, "History will eventually show that we were the heroes of our generation." Another says, "Environmentalists make great ancestors." Such images and slogans are characteristic of the third category as well, simplify and dramatize.

Simplify and Dramatize

A third mirroring and matching dynamic entails the simplification and dramatization of an issue of staggering complexity. Sproule's (1988) comparison of the old and new rhetorics provides two applicable constructs. He describes self-contained *slogans* as the "persuasive staples" of the new rhetoric—as compared to the enthymematic operation of the old. He further postulates images in new rhetorics as replacing the world of ideas common to the older suasion. Zarefsky (1992) argues that American audiences find complexity "unbearable" and that we "simplify what can not be avoided" (p. 412). These arguments are borne out in the two information campaigns as simple, easily absorbed, and dramatic images and slogans are substituted for analysis or explanation of phenomenally complicated issues.

Other than the images and slogans, there is little simple about the spotted owl conflict. Interrelated and inordinately complicated biological, economic, social, and political issues defy assimilation. John Turner, the head of the USF&WS, said the spotted owl is "one of the most complex resource issues in this nation's history" (Baum, 1990, p. 1). The USFS has been described by agency supervisors as "overwhelmed by change," and "out of control" (Robertson, 1990, p. 1A) in part, at least, because of this complexity. A federal judge, commenting on one of the lawsuits, said that, "This is the most complicatedly [sic] presented issue I have ever seen" ("Judges ponder," 1991, p. 1A.) Both groups' selective use of high or low numbers is at least partially enabled by an overwhelming abundance of figures. It seems impossible to differentiate between the "thousands" or "millions" or "billions" of revenue dollars lost or generated, of directly or indirectly affected jobs, of board feet milled or not milled, of board feet sold in the U.S. or exported, of profitable or below-cost timber sales, of current or lost wilderness acres, of private versus public acres, of reforested or spotted owl habitat acres or habitat conservation acres and so on. The jargon and endless acronyms further confuse. Budgets and service levels of federal, state, county, and local government agencies are substantially affected by timber sales. In 1990, a biologist warned that, "At this point, we are just looking at the tip of the iceberg with the spotted owl," since science will reveal further complications and ecosystem relationships (Sonner, 1990a, p. 3A). By 1991, the USF&WS was grappling with the extraordinary implications flowing from the listings of newly identified endangered species, including—in the Pacific Northwest—the sockeye salmon and the marbled murrelet.

Yet disputants work to simplify the issues so that they may be dramatized for mass consumption. The timber industry has at least partially succeeded in creating an "owls versus people" scenario in the media. *Time* magazine ran an eight-page cover story entitled, "Owl vs. Man," with photographs inside of an owl opposite a logger (Gup, 1990). *The Wall Street Journal* wrote that the issue "sets about 1500 pairs of spotted owls against the people who make their living cutting down trees in the Pacific Northwest" (quoted in "Other Editors Say," 1990, p. 15A). Timber supporters and U.S. Senators Hatfield, Packwood, and Gorton are repeatedly quoted on the forced choice between people and owls. For example, Gorton of Washington said that, "The difference between 2,000 pairs of owls and 1,425 pairs is not worth the loss of 30,000 jobs, the dislocation of rural families, and the destruction of small communities in often neglected parts of our state" (Sonner, 1990b, p. 4A). Environmentally inclined senators attempt to simplify, reframe, and dramatize the problem as one of mismanagement by federal agencies, the leaders of which were appointed by then-President Bush. One environmental group offered a slogan on each of its mailings: "It's not about owls."

The owls versus people sloganeering is only one example of simplification and dramatization. As the two groups "struggle for novelty" (Hilgartner & Bosk, 1988), attempting "photogenic discord" (Glasgow University Media Group, 1976, p. 19), they intentionally create additional images and slogans for mass audience consumption. Environmentalists drew television and photojournalist attention by camping on platforms placed high in old growth trees; others demonstrated at USFS offices, wearing owl costumes while carrying signs bemoaning loss of habitat. The industry held "counter-demonstrations," during which thousands of loggers and log truckers rallied in Northwest cities, driving through lumber towns with industry-symbol yellow ribbons attached to limbs, hard hats, and belts. They wore tee shirts and displayed bumper stickers offering phrases like "I Like Spotted Owls . . . Fried," and "Save a Logger, Eat an Owl." Environmental groups countered with slogans like "Owls Don't Destroy Forests, People Do," and "Save an Owl, Educate a Logger." "This Family Supported by Timber Dollars" was later mirrored with "This Family Supported by Intact Ecosystems." As environmentalists promoted the phrase "ancient forests," timber groups warned of turning "mill towns into ghost towns." Environmentalists renamed an industry-approved owl "preservation plan" to the owl "extinction plan." When a congressperson from Indiana sponsored a bill (which eventually failed) to end all logging of old growth, an Oregon congressperson proposed turning one and 1.3 million acres of rural Indiana into a national park (Manny, 1990b). Perhaps the ultimate matching behavior in the simplification and dramatization category was the petition actually submitted by the Washington Contract Loggers Association to the Department of the Interior seeking declaration of loggers as a threatened species ("Loggers seek species," 1990).

Members of both groups acknowledge the "low-level" nature of these public appeals. When I discussed this simplification and dramatization analysis with one informant—he could have been from either side—he said, "The process of raising public awareness is not centered on trying to educate the public about the details of the problem as much as it is on making the public aware that there is an injustice which needs their attention." Both groups hold workshops on "dealing with the media" in which participants practice delivering "sound bites."

Departure from the simplification/dramatization strategy occurs when audiences are perceived as better informed; in these cases there is often detailed, rich and more straightforward discussion. One such context includes antagonists' *internal* communication forums, such as meetings, conferences, newsletters, and interpersonal encounters, where simple and dramatic communication is accompanied by more complex, straightforward discussion. As Pearce notes, "Discourse *within* various groups in society is usually richer than that *between* groups (1989, p. 43). But those media are less a part of the two information campaigns and less a part of an interactive logic than two additional sites. It is in the litigation and lobbying arenas where more sophisticated audiences evoke more sophisticated rhetoric.

Lobby and Litigate

Both groups believe that the most serious theaters for the conflict are in the courts and Washington, D.C. There is intense, extensive, and sustained lobbying of members of Congress who might eventually author or support various bills. Both groups prepare and file lawsuits and appeals that ask the courts to change unfavorable decisions by an agency (i.e., USFS, BLM, USF&WS) or lower court. While lobbying and litigation processes reflect many of the rhetorical strategies discussed above, they additionally constitute what both groups view as the ultimate culmination of the information campaigns. Each process has a distinct set of attributes and rules.

Both groups have office space in the nation's capital, replete with full-time staff, media consultants and the latest office technology. The "Western Ancient Forest Campaign" is "networked" with the major national environmental groups ("The Big Ten") and many "local" or "grassroots" environmental groups in the Northwest. The American Forest Council, part of the "wise-use movement," coordinates with oil, coal, and other natural resource extraction industries as well as local grassroots timber groups. In both camps, staffers do their own lobbying and support lobbying efforts from visiting Northwesterners. At both offices, pamphlets provide information on "face-to-face lobbying," such as whom to visit, how to dress, and what to talk about. Materials to take home instruct supporters on how to hold demonstrations, conduct "outreach" and phone campaigns, what to say when making phone calls, and how to write the most effective letters to congresspersons and local newspaper editors.

While litigation used to be the sole province of environmental groups, recently, lumber companies and timber associations have matched the strategy, filing appeals that challenge timber inventory accuracy, clarity of guidelines, and even use of indicator species to test the health of a forest (e.g., "Umpqua forest plans," 1990). "We've gone to school on the way environmentalists use the courts," said an executive director of a timber association. Environmental groups continue filing appeals of agency plans; their appeals are based on violation of the Endangered Species Act, the National Environmental Policy Act, or the National Forest Management Act. And as environmentalists file lawsuits against private companies for alleged illegal logging, timber companies sue environmentalists for economic loss sustained during "downtime" caused by demonstrations at logging sites. Both sides carefully choose from dozens of potential issues for suit or appeal, as they are costly and time-consuming processes. Gain and loss are measured not only by the outcome of the issues in question, but by favorable or unfavorable publicity as well, showing the connection between these processes and the overall information campaign for public opinion.

Discussion

After delineating the background of one of America's most contentious natural resource disputes, this study described five communicative strategies in which conflicting parties' logic of interaction was reflected in synchronistic mirroring and matching behavior. The following addresses the theoretical implications and future directions of these explorations.

Beyond the description, this essay offers two theoretical contributions, both related to the nature of the communication relationship between the two parties. The first, revealed only through macro-analysis of the two competing information campaigns, stems from the fact that while these antagonists seldom address each other, their communicative behavior has its own peculiar logic. Previous research into the logic of interaction in other conflicts similarly revealed "reciprocated" or "parallel" behavior that resembled an "escalating negative spiral." These studies, reviewed above, focused on interpersonal encounters or a small subset of information campaign texts. Through comprehensive analysis of the entire campaigns of both groups, the current inquiry finds a logic of duplication and antithesis, a matching and mirroring, more like a synchronous spiral of *non-interaction*, as messages are directed not to each other, but to the public and members of government and government agencies. There is so little face-to-face interaction, one might ordinarily conclude that each group's communicative behavior has little to do with the other, with the obvious exception of preventing the other from achieving its goals. Yet both parties base communicative tactics on the predicted or previous moves of the antagonist. By examining the two competing information campaigns of this conflict, we find a logic of interaction between two groups who rarely communicate with each other.

Parties learn of each other's communicative moves through indirect means, usually the mass media, supporting the contention that media are "relied upon increasingly to let members of concerned groups know what . . . the opposition is doing and thinking" (Olien, Tichenor, & Donohue, 1989, p. 139). At least a large part of what the opposition is doing and thinking in this case is plotting how to respond to the other group. The interactive, interdependent, and almost symbiotic nature of the disputants was revealed as I listened to their internal discussions that so often focused on responding to, anticipating, or copying the other's moves. A recent meeting of one environmental group was held to determine whether or not they should "counteract the effects of " an industry-produced television commercial with one of their own in order to "set the record straight." Of course, the industry engaged in similar kinds of deliberations, as when they so often discussed, for example, how to respond to environmentalist lawsuits and appeals.

The second theoretical contribution is offered within the larger context of American political communication. Derived again through macro-analytic focus on the logic of competing information campaigns, the particular logic described here—mirroring and matching—implies a new framework for analyzing contemporary political communication. In a recent *Communication Monographs* Chautauqua, Swanson offered that "thousands of pages of scholarly work" make it clear that matters of public and political interest are routinely "oversimplified, personalized, trivialized, and dramatized" (1992, p. 397); Bennett contended that the nature of contemporary political dramas threaten the vitality of democracy (1992, p. 403); while Zarefsky argued that we have "debased" political debate (1992, p. 412). A number of insightful explanations (and remedies) are offered, yet there is little mention of how competing information campaigns interact. That the timber and environmental campaigns either match or mirror the other advances an additional explanation for understanding why it is so difficult for campaigns to rise above the current state of affairs: their co-created systems preclude it.

As noted earlier, Pearce (1989) describes logics of interaction to have assorted "senses of obligation" (p. 40); parties are compelled to respond to each other in ways determined by the system they constitute. The system is the best explanation for itself; a specific communicative act by one interlocuter practically "forces" a predetermined response by the other. Parties become locked into a systemic, self-reinforcing, patterned, and repetitive practice. With the exception of the current case, this type of analysis has not been applied to entire political information campaigns. Yet such a dynamic is clearly present here. For example, if one group vilifies the other, it is incumbent on the other to respond, refuting the charge and/or providing one's own. When timber representatives frame the major issue as job loss, environmentalists must attempt to reframe it; otherwise, a fully unfavorable context, from their point of view, would prevail. If one party neglected to lobby or litigate, the other party's practices in these areas would transform the entire conflict. The consequences of not mirroring or matching one's antagonist are untenable. Bantz (1981) showed how in one notably different but nonetheless controversial public argument, proponents favoring a ban on saccharin failed to match the dramatic and less scientific arguments of their opponents, and consequently failed to win the battle of public opinion. All of this is to suggest that the sorry state of political communication as reflected in information campaigns may partially obtain from a co-created sense of constraint, necessity, and logical force. Political communication campaigns may result more from a logic co-created with the competing candidate or group than the audience or other exigencies.

This essay has attempted to illuminate the character of natural resource disputes and contribute to theory by merging several contexts of communication inquiry—information campaigns, political communication, logics of interaction, and dispute resolution. It is hoped that future work will explore other competing political information campaigns in light of their logics of interaction, direct or otherwise. While this essay does not seek generalizable propositions, and while elements of the five categories have been previously noted—though perhaps in isolation or in different forms—it seems likely that the properties described above may typically obtain in the information campaigns of other disputes, particularly those over natural resources and those political in nature. Future investigations of oil, coal, natural gas, geothermal, various metal, and other resource extraction controversies might reveal similar logics with additional attributes. Descriptions of political candidate campaigns might reveal logical forces of different strength. If parties who create American political information campaigns are somehow locked into an inherently flawed system from which they retreat only at their peril, we have indeed reached the crisis in political communication about which Zarefsky (1992) warns.

Notes

1. Though some timber industry representatives and supporters would object to its application, I respectfully take the term "counterenvironmental" from the work of Richard Gale (1986). Recent journalistic analyses of the fast-growing "anti-environmental" or "wise-use" movement can be found in Byrnes (1992), Hennelly (1992), or Poole (1992). It should be noted here that neither "environmentalist" nor "timber industry" is a monolithic entity. For example, the "Ancient Forest Alliance" is an umbrella organization for 80 environmental groups. The timber industry has as many or more specific organizations.
2. More than 500 species in the 50 states are listed as endangered or threatened, including, in some states, "charismatic" species like the bald eagle, the grizzly bear, the wolf, and the mountain lion. However, while most of the 500 are plant species, the entire total represents only about 15 percent of the native species believed to be nearing extinction. "As many as three hundred species probably have gone extinct while either on the list or awaiting listing—and the current backlog is estimated at more than 3,800" (Watkins, 1991 p. 8).
3. The information campaigns did begin undergoing partial transition by the 1992 November elections. Candidate Clinton's promise of a "Timber Summit," along with the relative success of environmentalist litigation, altered some elements of the campaigns. For example, in preparation for what they termed the "Forest Summit," environmentalists began inviting some forest product labor groups to some of their meetings. Similarly, by early 1993, timber representatives were offering, for just about the first time, some conciliatory statements about the conflict. When President Clinton's "Forest Conference" was eventually held in April 1993, each side offered occasional acceptance of certain elements within the other's position.

Works Cited

Bantz, C.R. (1981). Public arguing in the regulation of health and safety. *Western Journal of Speech Communication, 45*, 71-87.

Baum, B. (1990, March 16). Feds seek more protection for owls. *Ashland Daily Tidings*, p. 1.

Bennett, W.L. (1992). White noise: The perils of mass mediated democracy. *Communication Monographs,* 59, 401-406.

Berger, C.R. (1991). Communication theory and other curios. *Communication Monographs,* 58, 101-113.

Byrnes, P. (1992). The counterfeit crusade. *Wilderness,* 56, 29-31.

Cantrill, J.G. (1990, November). Communicating about our environment: Why are we doing what we're doing when we barely know how to do it right? Paper presented to the annual meeting of the Speech Communication Association, Chicago.

Cantrill, J.G. (in press). Communication and our environment: Categorizing research in environmental advocacy. *Journal of Applied Communication Research.*

Carbaugh, D. (1991, August). "The mountain" and "the project": Dueling depictions of a natural environment. Paper presented to the Conference on Environmental Advocacy, Alta, Utah.

Conservationists seek help outside NW. (1989, December 7). *Ashland Daily Tidings,* p. 8.

Cook, H. (1989, October 20). Timber managers put industry first if uses conflict. *Ashland Daily Tidings,* p. 15.

Coser, L.A. (1967). *Continuities in the study of social conflict.* New York: Free Press.

Cox, J.R. (1982). The die is cast: Topical and ontological dimensions of the locus of the irreparable. *Quarterly Journal of Speech,* 68, 227-239.

Deutsch, M. (1969). Conflicts: Productive and destructive. *Journal of Social Issues,* 25, 7-41.

Durbin, K. (1991, March 6). Owl team allotted 9 months for report. *The Oregonian,* p. D2.

Environmentalists reject preservationist label. (1990, August 26). *Mail Tribune,* p. 2A.

Folger, J.P., & Poole, M.S. (1984). *Working through conflict: A communication perspective.* Glenview, IL.: Scott Foresman.

Forest Service adopts Thomas plan. (1992, March 5). *Ashland Daily Tidings,* p. 1.

Freeman, M. (1992, January 10). F&W owl ruling upsets both sides. *Mail Tribune,* p. 1A.

Freeman, S.A., Littlejohn, S.W., & Pearce, W.B. (1992). Communication and moral conflict. *Western Journal of Communication,* 56, 311-329.

Gale, R.P. (1986). Social movements and the state: The environmental movement, countermovement, and government agencies. *Sociological Perspectives,* 29, 202-240.

Glaser, B.G. (1965). The constant comparative method of qualitative analysis. *Social Problems,* 12, 436-455.

Glasgow University Media Group. (1976). *Bad news.* London: Routledge & Kegan Paul.

Goffman, E. (1974). *Frame analysis: An essay on the organization of experience.* Cambridge, MA.: Harvard University Press.

Grubb, K. (1990, February 9). Feds restrict logging in California forests. *Ashland Daily Tidings,* p. 3.

Gup, T. (1990, June 25). Owl vs. man. *Time,* pp. 55-56.

Hennelly, R. (1992, Fall). Getting wise to the "wise use"guys. *The Amicus Journal,* pp. 35-39.

Hilgartner, S., & Bosk, C.L. (1988). The rise and fall of social problems: A public arenas model. *American Journal of Sociology,* 94, 53-78.

Hill, T. (1990, March 3). "Half-truths" called damaging to timber. *Ashland Daily Tidings,* p. 7.

Hocker, J., & Wilmot, W.W. (1991). *Interpersonal conflict* (3rd ed.). Dubuque, IA: Brown.

Huspek, M. & Kendall, K.E. (1991). On withholding political voice: An analysis of the political vocabulary of a "non-political" speech community. *Quarterly Journal of Speech,* 77, 1-19.

Jaehne, D. (1990, November). From polluted environment to endangered planet: Ideology and environment in *Time, 1969-1989.* Paper presented to the annual meeting of the Speech Communication Association, Chicago.

Judges ponder owl appeals. (1991, August 30). *Mail Tribune,* p. 1A.

Kadera, J. (1992, March 14). Latest guess: Owl will cost 34,000 jobs, *The Oregonian,* p. E5.

Krendal, D.A., Olson, B., & Burke, R. (1992). Preparing for the environmental decade: A field experiment on recycling behavior. *Journal of Applied Communication Research,* 20, 19-36.

Lamar, A. (1990, September 22). White House timber plan takes flak. *Ashland Daily Tidings,* p. 1.

Lange, J.I. (1990). Refusal to compromise: The case of Earth First!. *Western Journal of Speech Communication,* 54, 473-494.

Lemonik, M.D. (1989, August 28). Showdown in the treetops. *Time,* p. 58.

Lofland, J. (1971). *Analyzing social settings: A guide to qualitative observation and analysis.* Belmont: CA.: Wadsworth.

Loggers seek species act protection. (1990, October 13). *Mail Tribune,* p. 2A.

Luke, T.W. (1987). Chernobyl: The packaging of transnational ecological disaster. *Critical Studies in Mass Communication,* 4, 351-375.

Mack, R.M., & Snyder, R.C. (1973). The analysis of social conflict-toward an overview and synthesis. In F. Jandt (Ed.), *Conflict resolution through communication* (pp. 25-87). New York: Harper & Row.

Macomber, P. (1990, March 7). Timber advocate sees bitter campaign. *Mail Tribune*, p. D1.

Manny, B. (1990a, January 11). Tree "reserves" would cut federal logging 40%. *Mail Tribune*, p. 3A.

Manny, B. (1990b, April 4). Rep. Smith vows to turn tables on Indiana old-growth advocate. *Mail Tribune*, p. 1.

Norman, J. (1989, August). USFS/BLM ignore substitutes for old-growth and trigger political bail-out that threatens U.S. constitution. *Headwaters*, pp. 12-13.

Olien, C.N., Tichenor, P.J., & Donohue, G.A. (1989). Media coverage and social movements. In C.T. Salmon (Ed.), *Information campaigns: Balancing social values and social change* (pp. 139-163). Newbury Park, CA.: Sage.

Oravec, C. (1981). John Muir, Yosemite, and the sublime response: A study in the rhetoric of preservationism. *Quarterly Journal of Speech, 67*, 245-258.

Oravec, C. (1984). Conservationism vs. preservationism: The public interest in the Hetch-Hetchy controversy. *Quarterly Journal of Speech, 70*, 444-458.

Oravec, C., & Cantrill, J.G. (Eds.). (1992). *The conference on the discourse of environmental advocacy.* Salt Lake City: University of Utah Humanities Center.

Other editors say: People suffer to help protect spotted owls. (1990, April 11). *Mail Tribune*, p. 15A.

Owl backers see plan as basis for talks. (1990, November 22). *Mail Tribune*, p. 1A.

Pearce, W.B. (1989). *Communication and the human condition.* Carbondale: Southern Illinois University Press.

Pearce, W.B., & Cronen, V.E. (1980). *Communication, action, and meaning: The creation of social realities.* New York: Praeger.

Pearce, W.B., Littlejohn, S.W., & Alexander, A. (1987). The new Christian right and the humanist response: Reciprocated diatribe. *Communication Quarterly, 35*, 171-192.

Peterson, T.R. (1986). The will to conservation: A Burkeian analysis of dust bowl rhetoric and American farming motives. *Southern Speech Communication Journal, 52*, 1-21.

Peterson, T.R. (1988). The rhetorical construction of institutional authority in a senate subcommittee hearing on wilderness legislation. *Western Journal of Speech Communication, 52*, 259-276.

Peterson, T.R. (1991). Telling the farmers' story: Competing responses to soil conservation rhetoric. *Quarterly Journal of Speech, 77*, 289-308.

Poole, W. (1992). Neither wise nor well. *Sierra, 77*, 58-61, 88-93.

Renz, M.A. (1992). Communicating about environmental risk: An examination of a Minnesota county's communication on incineration. *Journal of Applied Communication Research, 20*, 1-18.

Robertson, L. (1990, March 18). Agency chief praised, criticized. *Eugene Register Guard*, p. 1A.

Rogers, E.M., & Storey, J.D. (1987). Communication campaigns. In C.R. Berger & S.H. Chaffee (Eds.), *Handbook of communication science* (pp. 817-846). Newbury Park, CA.: Sage.

Salmon, C.T. (Ed.). (1989). *Information campaigns: Balancing social values and social change.* Newbury Park, CA.: Sage.

Schoenfeld, A.C., Meier, R.F., & Griffin, R.J. (1979). Constructing a social problem: The press and the environment. *Social Problems, 27*, 38-61.

Short, B. (1991). Earth First! and the rhetoric of moral confrontation. *Communication Studies, 42*, 172-188.

Sonner, S. (1990a, September 2). Scientists say owl only piece of bigger picture. *Mail Tribune*, p. 3A.

Sonner, S. (1990b, April 8). Owl ruling may alter timber export debate. *Mail Tribune*, p. 4A.

Spradley, J.P. (1979). *The ethnographic interview.* New York: Holt.

Spradley, J.P. (1980). *Participant observation.* New York: Holt.

Sproule, J.M. (1988). The new managerial rhetoric and the old criticism. *Quarterly Journal of Speech, 74*, 468-486.

Sterling, R. (1989, June 25). If owl is well, forest is well. *Mail Tribune*, p. 6A.

Swanson, D.L. (1992). The political-media complex. *Communication Monographs, 59*, 397-400.

Timber task force head senses emotions. (1990, July 21). *Ashland Daily Tidings*, p. 3.

Umpqua forest plans hit with appeals. (1990, December 28). *Ashland Daily Tidings*, p. 5.

Vanderford, M.L. (1989). Vilification and social movements: A case study of pro-life and pro-choice rhetoric. *Quarterly Journal of Speech, 75*, 166-182.

Waddell, C. (1990). The role of pathos in the decision-making process: A study in the rhetoric of science policy. *Quarterly Journal of Speech, 76*, 381-401.

Watkins, T.H. (1991). The protocols of endangerment. *Wilderness, 54*, 8-9.

Williams, D.E., & Treadaway, G. (1992). Exxon and the Valdez accident: A failure in crisis communication. *Communication Studies,* 43, 56-64.

Zacoreli, A.C. (1991, September 12). Timber workers frustrated. *Ashland Daily Tidings,* p. 1.

Zarefsky, D. (1992). Spectator politics and the revival of public argument. *Communication Monographs,* 59, 410-414.

Constructing Irreconcilable Conflict:
The Function of Synecdoche
in the Spotted Owl Controversy
by Mark P. Moore

During the past two decades the American timber industry has engaged in a war of words with environmentalists over the destiny of old-growth forests in the Pacific Northwest.[1] "What we have in the Northwest today," observes Jim Geisinger, president of the Northwest Forestry Association, "is absolute chaos and confusion" that is casting "an incredibly dark cloud over the stability and predictability of the future" (Barnard, 1992, p. C6). While both groups heighten confusion with conflicting "facts," they also construct competing social realities with opposing rhetorical tropes. Most recently, the controversy over proper forest management has come to the forefront of public consciousness through two divergent, synecdochic constructions of the spotted owl, as an "indicator" species by environmentalists and an economic "scapegoat" by the timber industry.[2] While each group attempts to disarm the other with their own synecdochic form of the owl, these tropes *prevent* resolution and *maintain* controversy by becoming issues in and of themselves.

This essay examines the spotted owl controversy as a public argument rooted in conflicting owl synecdoches that conceptualize competing social realities, and argues that social construction of the owl in divergent synecdochic forms generates irresolvable conflict. Though social conflict can only be managed and framed with rhetorical tropes, there are flaws in both synecdoches that negate the resolution of this controversy. By applying Burke's (1969) view of synecdoche, and extending McGee's (1980a) concept of the ideograph to views expressed in synecdochic form,[3] this essay shows how rhetorical tropes manage, articulate, and maintain conflict too threatening to resolve. It also offers a unique critical perspective on the dual, contradictory function of such symbolizing in public controversy.

Synecdoche and Social Controversy

In his discussion of the "Four Master Tropes," Kenneth Burke describes synecdoche as a rhetorical figure that is similar to metaphor, but deals in particular with matters of *representation*, not *perspective*. While metaphor identifies something in terms of something else, synecdoche expresses a relationship between "act of perception" and "thing perceived" (Burke, 1969, p. 507). To the environmentalists, the spotted owl serves as a synecdoche for the complete forest or "ecosystem." In this way, the nature or material condition of the owl, seen as something threatened, also represents the mental picture that the environmentalists have of the old-growth forest. The owl also represents the mental state of material conditions for the timber industry, but the mental state and material conditions of timber workers emanate from the economics of their industry. Thus, representations of the owl as an indicator of the endangered ecosystem by the environmentalists conflict with those of the timber industry, as a scapegoat for an endangered economic system, to provide a symbolic foundation for irresolvable conflict.

Development or "analogical extension" of the dispute by each group is "determined by the particular kind of *interest* uppermost at the time" (Burke, 1984b, p. 104, emphasis added). In other words, as a symbol that represents a part of a greater whole, the spotted owl surfaces in public discourse as the verbal parallel to a "pattern of experience," for each particular interest group (Burke, 1968, p. 152). Since experiences differ for loggers and environmentalists, a different symbolization of the owl serves as the "generating principle" for each competing group (Burke, 1968, p. 157). As a result, the owl synecdoche functions as a guiding principle in and of itself. As the owl guides the conflict, it also obscures the larger issue of preservation versus extinction, to create a separate reality for debate. Furthermore, when the real issue is supplanted by the rhetorical trope, resolution is thwarted because, in a sense, the trope has created a "meta" or contrived conflict of its own that not only distorts and obscures the issue, but replaces it as well.

Overall, the owl synecdoche functions to establish a context for debate, provide an organizing principle for its orientation, and encapsulate the opposing world views, but it does not provide a ground for resolution. Though distinctions held by the timber industry and environmentalists may arise from the "great central moltenness" of public discourse, as Burke (1969) suggests, the consequences of the debate are too great to allow "distinctions" to return to their "source," where they can be "remade," to arise again in "new combinations" (p. xix). Indeed, the distinctions represented with the spotted owl by the timber industry and the environmentalists are incommensurable. To Burke, the constant "remaking" of old tropes into newer (and better) ones would allow for the consubstantiality of *A* and *non-A*, but in the spotted owl controversy the social, political, and economic differences remain fixed, above ground, where they maintain conflict and keep it prominent in social consciousness.

As rhetorical tropes like synecdoche reflect and distinguish opposing views, they also create a reality of their own based on the ultimate, "God" terms that the tropes represent for the group as a whole. With the spotted owl, both timber and environmental groups not only reveal economic and environmental interests, they convey their views of *life* and *liberty* in concrete terms.[4] That is, while the spotted owl as indicator species ostensibly *serves* "as a barometer for the overall health of the ancient forest" for environmentalists (Butterworth, 1991), it symbolically represents extinction of the forest (life) to environmentalists and the end of the timber industry (liberty) to loggers. As such, these two groups displace the owl species as a species and transform it (in its representation of some material condition) into a *political* instrument. These different representations by environmentalists and the timber industry can therefore serve in public argument as "representational" or "figurative ideographs," that is, one-term summations of a political orientation in synecdochal form.

As McGee (1980a) notes, ideographs "exist in real discourse" and "come to be a part of real lives of the people whose motives they articulate" (p. 7). As "a group of *words* and not a series of symbols representing ideas," McGee feels that ideographs serve as the "basic structural elements" of ideology (p. 6), but like all language, they also cloud "pure thought" about ideas (p. 9). Since ideographs cloud thought yet convey meaning as abstract *and* "God" terms that represent collective commitment to a world view or political orientation (suggesting both an ambiguous and shared meaning), synecdochal form is one way to make ideographic meaning more tangible and concrete. Whereas an ideograph like "liberty" may be an "ultimate term" materialized in a culture, an ideograph in synecdochic form ("owl as indicator," "owl as scapegoat") may signify an "ultimate conflict," since differing representational forms may reflect divergent, and even incommensurable realities.

Representational ideographs can hold meaning for society at large, but they can also limit discourse to a part of the problem that does not resolve the conflict. This dual and contradictory function of symbolizing in public controversy can be described in the following way: enduring social conflicts can only be managed with and articulated through rhetorical figures and tropes, such as synecdoche and the ideograph, but their existence also creates the conditions of irreconcilability. Since this controversy is generated as well as limited by the form (synecdoche) and meaning (ideograph) of the "spotted owl" articulated by competing groups, these competing groups maintain controversy by perpetuating their individual forms and meanings of the spotted owl.

An examination of the synecdochal development of the spotted owl for each group and the weaknesses of each group's synecdochal construction reveals how rhetorical tropes can negate resolution of social controversy. In the following analysis, three separate areas of inquiry singularly and then collectively demonstrate how an ideograph in divergent synecdochic forms produces irresolvable conflict. These areas include: (1) the conflicting synecdoches of the ideograph owl as an "indicator" for the environmentalists and as a "scapegoat" for the loggers; (2) the irreconcilability of the representational ideographs; and (3) the political implications of irreconcilable conflict. The analysis begins with development of the conflicting synecdoches.

The Conflicting Synecdoches of the Ideograph Owl

Just as Burke (1970) notes that every way of knowing, seeing, or naming is also a way of *not* knowing, *not* seeing, or *not* naming, a synecdochal construction of environmental and economic reality is not complete, but limited by both perspective and language use itself. When defined as true yet conflicting representations of the problem, the synecdochal development of the owl by each group therefore will be weak or flawed in some way, making it difficult if not impossible to categorically accept either position. Thus, conflict resolution is negated by a false, either/or dilemma that is generated and sustained by conflicting synecdoches of the owl.

In form and meaning, the spotted owl constitutes a blessing to environmentalists and a curse to the timber industry. Loggers believe the owl has "deprived them of much of their prime lumber—and their livelihood," while environmentalists feel, "that may be a price worth paying for preservation" ("Environment's little big bird," 1990). The owl represents a dual and contradictory symbol of the old forest for environmentalists and loggers as a life form threatened by, and a threat to, human transformations of its natural environment. In June, 1990, the owl was listed as a threatened species and its future seemed to lie in the hands of those who control the old-growth forest. Elliot Norse (1990) of the Wilderness Society explains the literal and synecdochal role of the owl, saying, "it is just one species on the constellation of plants, animals, fungi, and bacteria that inhabit the ancient forests," but since they "require so much old-growth, protecting them will mean defacto protection for many other species with smaller requirements" (p. 83). Thus, he concludes, "the spotted owl is quite special" (p. 83).

Yet sentiment for the spotted owl varies. "We survived the dinosaur," observes one timber-town resident, "so what's the big deal about the owl?" (Gup, 1990, p. 60) Since loggers interpret the owl as a threat to economic freedom and coin the problem as one of humans versus the owls with slogans like, "Save a logger, eat a spotted owl," the timber industry identifies the owl as a scapegoat for their economic problems (Satchell, 1990, p. 27). Biologist Eric Forsman, however, responds to such sentiments by claiming, "if we continue pell-mell down the path of eliminating these old forests, we'll never have the opportunity to learn because they won't be there to study" (Gup, 1990, p. 59). While both groups view the problem as local, material, and individual, with the owl as victim or victimizer, they also describe it as generalizable, symbolic, and universal, with portrayals of life and liberty in synecdochic form. This dual and contradictory function of the owl can be identified in the discourse of each group, beginning with the environmentalists.

The Environmentalist's "Owl as Indicator"

While focusing on a part of nature to indicate the health of nature as a whole, the environmentalists construct what appears to be a legitimate case of reasoning by sign, but the weaknesses of the environmentalist's position lie in the fact that the owl synecdoche is both *misleading* and *contradictory*. This is evident not only in the environmental perspective on the conservation and preservation of life in totality, but also in the methods used to support and reinforce such perspectives. At one extreme, the owl depicts how nature can only be preserved by eliminating the human element from it, and at the other, the owl suggests that life can only be saved through active human intervention.

Since environmentalists see their spotted owl as a symbol of life threatened, saving the owl means saving life. Regarding the owl controversy, Northwest environmentalist Lou Gold believes "We have to be a *part* of a *total* community, human and non-human," for "it's about having a relationship with the Earth that we live and die on" (Durbin, 1990, p. A18). Argon Steele of the Audubon Society also contends that the survival of the ecosystem hinges on old growth and wants "to make sure that pieces" are "around in not just 10, but 100 years" (Durbin & Koberstein, 1990, p. A1). In 1973, The Department of Fish and Wildlife devised a plan to protect the owl nests by preserving sufficient old-growth for what was considered a minimum population. With three techniques available (i.e., featured species, indicator species, and ecosystem management), the agency selected the indicator species technique for what became known as The Spotted Owl Management Plan, without any consideration of the other two (La Follette, 1979).

Following the synecdochic assumption that the health of part (one species) of an ecosystem represents the health of the whole, the concept of indicator species management has been most clearly established by the Committee of Scientists Report on the proposed regulations for the National Forest Management Act (La Follette, 1979, p. 11). Key to this management system is the monitoring of a species as "the perfect paradigm or prototype" (in microcosm), which then becomes the basis for managing and saving the entire forest as a macrocosm (Burke, 1969, p. 508). That is, monitoring the reaction of one species "to management regimes is a way of 'taking the pulse' of the community" (La Follette, 1979, p. 12). Once an indicator has been identified, managers can determine the desired population level and monitor the effects.

Even though the indicator species management plan has been selected for several Department of Fish and Wildlife conservation attempts, there are three specific problems with this plan, which reveal the limitations of this type of synecdochic representation in science. First, it is onerous to determine which species does actually *represent* a given habitat. Second, there is a tendency to oversimplify wildlife management while focusing on only a few species. And third, indicator species management only accounts for biological needs of a particular species and may not provide an accurate economic assessment for the optimum amount of habitat to protect (La Follette, 1979, p. 12). Thus, an actual "integral relationship" of "convertibility" between the spotted owl and the forest that the synecdochic form of indicator species management suggests remains in question (Burke, 1969, p. 508).

Indicator species management poses a problem of authenticity that weakens the environmentalist position further still. Rather than demonstrate representativeness, the reliability of measuring the health of the forest by *monitoring* the owl is greatly reduced when habitat is altered to measure quality and increase quantity of a species. When habitat is controlled, owls cannot "indicate," and the management system defeats its purpose. Nevertheless, as a result of its attention as an indicator species, the owl became the focus of political and scientific debate. In "A Conservation Strategy for the Northern Spotted Owl," developed for the federal government, Jack Ward Thomas (1990) states the following:

> the owl is imperiled over significant portions of its range because of continuing losses of habitat from logging and natural disturbances. Current management strategies are inadequate to ensure its viability. Moreover, in some portions of the owl's range, few options remain open, and available alternatives are steadily declining throughout the bird's range. (p. 1)[5]

As an indicator of life threatened, the owl represents "the decline of the Northwest ancient forest ecosystem and the species in it" (Davis, 1991b, p. 1438). While writing for the Wilderness Society, Norse (1990) synecdochically notes that the "logging of the ancient forests is without question the biggest threat to the survival of the spotted owl" (p. 78), and the fragmentation and isolation of prime owl habitat greatly raises "the risk of extinction" (p. 77). Designated as an indicator, the owl seems to portray a contradictory symbol of life and death. Zuckerman (1991) of the Wilderness Society, for example, believes that "the owl is a good sign," because when "the owl population dwindles, it means something's wrong with the forest" (p. 51):

> This is why the U.S. Forest Service selected the owl as an indicator of the forest's health. Just as miners used canaries to indicate whether there was enough good air in a mine shaft, we can use the spotted owl to read the health of the forest. (p. 51)

While environmentalists compare the owl's health to that of a forest, they perceive efforts to save the owl as a way to save forest life. But if the spotted owl truly is an indicator of the forest's "health," like the canary in a coal mine, then, assuming that the forest is threatened, as ecologists state, it serves as a sacrifice for environmentalists in the same way that the canary is a "sacrifice" for the coal miners (Burke, 1984b, pp. 286-287). The owl must die, and be dying to "measure" death and demonstrate the need for protecting the forest. Evidence of owl extinction justifies habitat protection and the role of indicator species management is to protect threatened habitat by sustaining species threatened by habitat loss. But as the attention focused on the *indicator*, the indicator became the problem. Biologist Chris Maser (1988) explains how this misconception guides the debate:

> The spotted owl is the symbol of the old-growth forest, but what does it really symbolize? The spotted owl is called an "indicator species" because its presence supposedly indicates a healthy old-growth forest, but what does it really indicate? The spotted owl may be seen as a symbol for the survival of old-growth forests, but in reality it is an indicator species for the planned extinction of old-growth forests. (p. 152)

In Burke's (1969) terms, "the paradoxes of the synecdochic present themselves" here for critical examination (pp. 508-509). While the owl is blamed for "the run up" of lumber prices and the loss of timber jobs, "that seems not to be so," according to the ecologists (*Congressional Record*, 1991, p. S 8701). As one activist from Spokane, Washington notes, "we're not up against the spotted owl, we're up against the Pacific Ocean" (Zuckerman, 1991, p. 52). Zuckerman (1991) further claims, "the spotted owl" and "the old-growth logger" are both "endangered for the same reason—they're running out of habitat" (p. 52). The spotted owl may have been designated as an indicator species with best intentions, but such a view of the owl serves more as a way to transform a biological need into a political commitment, and then a political commitment back into a biological fact. In the first place, the attempts to save the owl by declaring it a symbol of the ancient forest are misguided, as Maser (1988) claims, "because the real issue is not the owl. The real issue is the economics of extinction," that is, "the planned liquidation of old-growth forests for short-term economic gain" (p. 152). In addition, lawsuits intending to save the owl from extinction have only set aside the "bare minimum" of old growth for species survival, which could reduce the known owl population by 50% (Zuckerman, 1991, p. 50).

The synecdochic construction of social reality in this case turns a biological need into political commitment when efforts to protect the forest concentrate more on the symbol of habitat loss than the habitat itself. With this approach, Maser (1988) feels government is "planning spotted owl habitat in terms of absolute minimums and the old-growth cut in terms of flexible maximums" (p. 153). Jerry Mires, spotted owl expert for the Bureau of Land Management, also senses a larger problem, saying, "It isn't just if we started from right now, 200 years from now we'd have this type of structure. It's a continual process. It just keeps working" (Meehan, 1990a, p. A1). He then connects ecological and economic need in synecdochic form, as he concludes, "the spotted-owl issue actually raised 20 issues . . . *it's not a piece unto itself . . . it's related to everything else*" (Meehan, 1990a, p. A1, emphasis added).[6] In particular, though, the owl represents a problem for the timber industry.

The Logger's "Owl as Scapegoat"

While environmentalists use the spotted owl to indicate both the value of and threat to life in synecdochic form, the timber industry adopts the owl as a scapegoat to affirm the value of and threat to liberty (or, lifestyle). The problem with the loggers' stance is not so much that their synecdoche is misleading or even contradictory, as in the environmentalist's view. Instead, it is *illusory*, because regardless of the fate of the owl, the logger's dilemma does not end, and if the loggers, who love their work and the forest, are allowed to do what they love unimpeded, they will inevitably lose what they love by doing what they love. Michael Satchell (1990) observes that "both the loggers' livelihoods and their cherished rough-hewn lifestyle have been under increasing pressure during the past decade" (p. 28). In this light, efforts to save both the owl and the timber industry prove increasingly incompatible. Jerry Leppell of the American Loggers Solidarity Movement asks, "How much do these preservationists want? If the owl" goes on the endangered species list, then jobs "for us will be like Boeing leaving Seattle" (Satchell, 1990, p. 28).

The owl as a threat to liberty places the timber industry's view in an ideological frame steeped in American folk tradition. As Northwest historian William Robbins (1990) notes, Paul Bunyan arrived in the Northwest along with a rich tradition of logging folklore dating all the way back to the "early timber drives in Maine" (pp. 54-56). And "in that view, the dawn-to-dusk work in the woods and the sweat and blood of the speedups in the mills are described as a composite of patriotism, apple pie, and duty to family and motherhood." It did not, however, detail the "daily reckoning with death and crippling injury," nor emphasize the "protracted periods of unemployment that have characterized the industry" (Robbins, 1990, p. 54). In part, the need for work suggests how much loggers care about their jobs, as one explains:

> Did I ever hear of getting killed on the last day of work? Well, I guess if you got killed it would be your last day of work, wouldn't it? Anyhow, you know, no matter whether you're killed or injured, they leave you there by the cold deck and take you in with the last load of the day, so you won't lose on a day's pay. And no matter what, a day's pay is a day's pay. (Robbins, 1990, p. 55)

As each lumberjack synecdochically creates a part of Bunyan, Bunyan becomes part of each lumberjack. The mythic story of the heroic tree cutter furthermore extends beyond loggers, swampers, logging camps, and log jams to illustrate a life or death struggle for the timber industry as a whole. In this "noblest synecdoche" loggers find themselves not only fighting nature, but technology, time, and progress (Burke, 1969, p. 508). Following the legend, Bunyan finally left the states for better prospects in the North Pole, but with no real place to go, many see the past and future on a collision course, as one millworker's union leader suggests:

> Who do I blame? Do I blame the industry for raping the lands in the East and raping the lands in the West 50 years ago and not replanting? Do I blame my father? . . . blame my grandfather? . . . blame myself for not reading the paper every night and not being critically involved in the issues? (Gup, 1990, p. 61)

Like Paul Bunyan, individual *liberty* in the timber industry, sustained by nature and protected by the past, is seen to be held captive by the progression of life in the present and the future. With no solution, attention thus turns to the owl. In Portland, loggers waved signs saying, "I need a job—Not the Bird" (Durbin & Bella, 1992, p. A1). Logger Bill Haire warned, "If it comes down to my family or that bird . . . that bird's going to suffer" (Gup, 1990, p. 60). Oregon State Representative Bob Smith also said he was "shocked that the courts are so concerned about owls and so unconcerned about people" (Koberstein, 1991, p. E10). Frank Backus, a forester for the SDS Lumber Company, admitted, "we'll be going out of business because of the northern spotted owl," and wanted to know, "where is the justice in this?" (Bella, 1991, p. E10). As media covered the controversy with such headlines as, "Economic woes blamed on owl" (Manzano, 1991, p. A11) and "Saving Spotted Owl Seen As Threat To Schools" (Gup, 1990, p. 60), accusations flew at an alarming rate. At a hearing with industry and labor leaders, Oregon Senator Bob

Packwood claimed that the owl crisis will result in "catastrophic failure for the region" (Manzano, 1991, p. A11). According to one report on unemployed timber workers in Douglas County (Oregon's most timber dependent county), "many are downright bitter, blaming environmentalists—'tree huggers,' they call them here—for putting the northern spotted owl before their livelihoods" (Hamburg, 1992, p. R1). Roger Kimble, a log loader from Canyonville, Oregon, summed up the problem when he declared, "the hooty owl has finished us" (Hamburg, 1992, p. R5). All this bitterness toward the owl and the environmentalists combined with fear and despair as the timber industry described their forecasts for a dismal future under spotted owl preservation. In one case, a joint Forest Service-BLM study claimed that if the "biologists" have their way, the owl recovery plan would lead to "severe cases of community dysfunction" along with "increased rates of domestic disputes, divorce, acts of violence, delinquency, vandalism, suicide, alcoholism," and other problems (Gup, 1990, p. 58).

It is not surprising, then, that the timber workers not only rejected the logic that placed owls above humans, but furthermore adopted the owl as a scapegoat for the industry's problems. With slogans such as, "I Like Spotted Owls—Fried," loggers blame the owl, however unrepresentatively, for every socio-economic problem the workers face (Satchell, 1990, p. 27). Yet ironic depictions of protecting this "little bird," while human lives are at stake, also reflect the paradoxical manner in which loggers view their work. A third generation logger, for example, told the *Oregonian* a familiar story about the trade: it was the most dangerous job in the state; it meant leaving for work at 3:00 a.m. and returning at night; it included a three hour drive to get to a logging site, which was usually pounded by rain and snow; it confronted workers with several ways to get killed or maimed. Even still, the danger and the sacrifice seem worthwhile, as the logger then said, "I enjoy getting out in the forest. . . . I enjoy getting out with the spotted owls and with the deer and the elk" (Mcchan, 1990b, p. A22).

Aside from the pleasure, "wanting the forest and cutting it too" is illusory. At a town meeting in 1991, Indiana Congressman Jim Jontz told people of Sweet Home, Oregon that "we can blame it all on the spotted owl and we can thumb our nose at the federal government, but it's not going to change" the way logging levels are going to decline in the future ("Old growth protection bill," 1991, p. B10). Instead of sharing the forest with the bird, Northwest loggers identify it as a real threat to their lifestyle and stand themselves to be sacrificed on the alter of an impending ethic. If saving the environment means protecting the owl, the region's next endangered species will be the Northwest logger, or so the argument goes. In 1990, Northwest timber companies not only had tighter supplies (some less than 50% of what they held two years prior), but less demand. Robert Ragon, executive vice president of Sun Studs Lumber Company, in Oregon, explains that competition and survival may still dictate the industry, but the owl changes everything:

A small company that has built up a position in the area and has the willpower to survive might be able to survive, if their product line is right in relation to the marketplace. . . . We have been competitive for forty years. I do not know if we will be competitive after this thing runs its course. (Church, 1990, p. A11)

The Irreconcilability of Representational Ideographs

The owl synecdoches in the controversy reveal a common fate that binds each group together, makes each group dependent on the other, and therefore prevents conflict resolution. One ideograph (the owl) produces two conflicting synecdoches with two different underlying value orientations: life or liberty. Both synecdoches are self-defeating, in part because of the relative weaknesses of each position, but also because life potentially signifies death for owls and liberty potentially conveys death for loggers, even though environmentalists seek "life" and loggers want "liberty." In this way, the rhetoric of each group virtually guarantees the outcome they are trying to avoid.

Even with "resolution," the problem that the owl represents still exists. In 1991 Federal District Court Judge William Dwyer found a Northwest timber sale program proposed by the U.S. Forest Service to be in violation of the National Forest Management Act, arguing that there are no problems with current laws, but "simply a refusal of administrative agencies to comply with them" (p. S 8699). Thus, he feels the executive branch of government stands responsible not scientists, foresters, or rangers. Only four days after the owl was placed on the threatened species list, the Bush Administration, for instance, presented a plan "to save the owl, preserve the ancient forest," and "protect timber-industry jobs, all at the same time," a plan both environmentalists and loggers dismissed as being able to do "none of the above" ("No peace for the owl," 1990, p. 60).

As the timber industry undergoes fundamental change due to modernization, product demand and foreign competition of imported logs, the federal government has not changed its way of thinking, nor met the challenge of change. *Congressional Record* notes that the entire history of the owl dispute and the reason it is before a judge, "is that neither elected branch of government has wanted to be the one to decide" (1991a, p. S 8700). Meanwhile, as Dwyer points out, the spotted owl has become a scapegoat even though "*job losses in the wood products industry will continue regardless of whether the northern spotted owl is protected*" (1991, p. S 8700, emphasis added). He furthermore stresses that the owl is not the subject of the controversy but a convenient metaphor that signals the extinction of the entire forest system. The industry is declining "for economic rather than environmental reasons that have nothing to do with the owl—but that has made the owl doubly a *symbol*" (Dwyer, 1991, p. S 8700).

The use of the spotted owl as a symbol for environmentalists and loggers grows from its ability to capture the essence of each group's political commitments and orientations concerning forest management, while constituting a real part of the forest and real part of the lives whose motives the symbol represents. Depiction of the spotted owl is unique in the sense that it represents two different interests of two competing groups embroiled in the same controversy. As a different symbol to each group, the owl raises uncertainty and clouds the public perception of the real material problem. After court rulings determined that the spotted owl was not responsible for the timber industry's problems, the Fish and Wildlife Service in 1991 emerged as only the *first* federal agency to admit that several other factors

including automation, foreign competition, and raw log exports were more responsible for timber industry woes than the owl (Sonner, 1991, p. B1). Yet the mock
owls in timber towns still hang in effigy above tavern bars, and swing, with arrows
through their heads, below truck mirrors (Gup, 1990, p. 68). In addition, environmentalists perceive the owl as a way to protect the forest even though they openly
admit that as an indicator species it "is subject to bias" and "must be viewed with
caution" (Noss, 1991, p. 233). Discordant views of the owl keep the false dilemma
of ecology *or* economy prominent in social consciousness without raising questions
about the way ecology and economy are conceptualized in the debate. Both groups
also avoid having to acknowledge their own bias and their own culpability in doing
so.

With ecology and industry, the forest is the "common ground" from which two
different socio-political commitments arise. But dispute intensifies as conflicting
synecdochic conceptions of the owl form a "killing ground" to encapsulate the
conflicting socio-political orientations. With a laissez-faire ideological frame, the
quest for profits, through cutthroat competition, overshadows the long-range social
costs of "eroded soils, cutover forestland, tax delinquency, and decaying and
impoverished communities" that have culminated today in what has been defined
as the spotted owl controversy (Robbins, 1990, p. 3).[7] Defending itself, as a part
divided by the whole, the timber industry stresses their right to economic freedom
without, claim the environmentalists, social obligations. Environmentalists justify
their efforts in the name of the whole and appear willing to sacrifice the timber
"part" to save it. With socio-political praxis, the timber industry joins their individual right to free enterprise with representations of the owl as a threat to that right,
while environmentalists pursue "justice" in the name of "balance," with representations of the owl as life "unbalanced" by unrestrained economic drive and
human neglect.

As a "container" as well as thing contained, the owl shifts from an indicator and
scapegoat to a representation of the larger problem concerning economics and the
environment. Though the owl as an indicator and scapegoat creates an either/or
situation, the larger (real) issue represents a both/and conflict (economics *and*
environment). Controversy over the owl as either an indicator *or* scapegoat can be
resolved dialectically, but such a resolution is illusory because the owl as either an
indicator or scapegoat does not resolve the larger conflict concerning economics
and ecology. This false dilemma, generated by competing synecdoches, prevents
discussion of the larger problem and negates conflict resolution.

As long as the spotted owl functions as an indicator for the environmentalists
and a scapegoat for the timber industry it will also serve as an ideograph of "life"
for the former and "liberty" for the latter (quality of life versus quantity of liberty).
Social truths created from such bases build on incongruencies, which are difficult
to overcome because "truth" is already incorporated in the social construction of
reality (Peterson, 1991, p. 305). The timber industry views the spotted owl as a
literal threat, but the owl actually shares a common fate with those involved in the
timber industry and plays a real part in the transformation of the human environment
as well as its own habitat. Moreover, if the owl can be compared to the timber
worker, then the old-growth forest can be compared to timber-dependent commu-

nities, which can only survive if given enough room to move through their economic habitat. Cutting off the supply of trees to the community equals the cutting down of trees to the owl. This inverted relationship that owls and humans share with the forest fuels controversy and heightens political incompatibility.

Political Implications of Irreconcilable Conflict

The rhetorical significance of political efforts to resolve, or even control the controversy lies in the fact that they mirror the very same dilemmas facing the groups in conflict and actually exacerbate the problem through indecisiveness, postponement, and contradiction. Since the spotted owl controversy raises concerns such as life and liberty to the environmentalists and the loggers and since each group presents the other as the cause for concern, the political discourse increases polarization and reinforces the incompatibility of efforts to save the old forest and the timber industry. Sid Morrison, from the House Agriculture Subcommittee on Forests, claims that although "the walls are closing in around us," the issue is too important for the courts to resolve (Davis, 1991a, p. 1438).

Rendering the spotted owl as a lugubrious indication of both economic and environmental "extinction" makes federal legislation all the more difficult. For as people express partisan concerns, the battle also hinges on the symbolic *political representations* of the spotted owl. On the one hand, the timber industry depicts environmentalism as "eco-mania" and its owl as a mere "surrogate" for their "real" agenda, "which is to put economically vital old-growth forests off limits, loggers and timber mills be damned" (McCarthy, 1992, p. A19). On the other, environmentalists argue that the timber industry uses their owl to protect obsolete jobs and to save their vanishing lifestyle. And extreme views of both groups support the irreconcilability of the dispute even further. "'Deep ecologists,'" for instance, "advocate a mystical view of the world as an end to itself not made for human beings" and also criticize the traditional view "for emphasizing the environment's value to people" (Postrel, 1990, p. 729). Conversely, the "Wise Use" movement among timber workers refers to environmentalism as "anti-Christian," the "third great wave of messianism to hit the planet after Christianity and Marxism-Leninism," and vows "to destroy" the movement within the next decade (Udall & Olson, 1992, p. C7).

Though expressed in either/or terms by the competing groups, the federal government responds to the controversy with both/and proposals that are unrealistic to environmentalists and loggers alike. In this way, the government prevents resolution as well, telling both groups they can "have their trees and cut them too" (Pytte, 1990b, p. 3104). Washington State Congresswoman Jolene Unsoeld says, "we are all at fault, all of us wanted the days of abundance to go on forever, but we didn't plan and we didn't manage for that end" (Gup, 1990, p. 63). Given the circumstances, Oregon Representative Ron Wyden argues that the "administration's position is sort of like going to a smorgasbord and saying you can eat it all . . . [but] you can't protect all the jobs and all the trees" (Pytte, 1990a, p. 2043). Even with the God Squad and its power to rule if economic factors outweigh species protection (which is only called into action if all other efforts to resolve the problem have failed), Oregon Representative Les AuCoin claims that Bush "hardly solved the Northwest timber crisis," and on all counts he "leaves a lot to be desired":

> So far we have seen absolutely nothing from the environmental President or . . . the pro-jobs President, when it comes to leadership on this issue, either for the environment or for the jobs from those forests. (*Congressional Record*, 1991b, p. H 7126)

The timber industry and the environmentalists each construct the spotted owl in ways which are consistent with their political commitments and orientations to land management. Moreover, as a symbol of both life and liberty, the spotted owl functions as an ideograph in synecdochic form that reveals material and political division. With this division, the owl as synecdoche encapsulates social truth for each political orientation but it also maintains conflict. Kevin Kirchner, of the Sierra Club Legal Defense fund, believes that "it's not just the owl and jobs, it gets into how we manage our public lands in general" (Pytte, 1990b, p. 3105). It is this larger view of ecology and economy that the spotted owl controversy obscures. For example, the federal government decided to protect 11 million acres in Washington, Oregon, and California for the spotted owl in May of 1990. In August, the figure was reduced to 8 million acres, and by October, under pressure and impending law suits from the timber industry, the Fish and Wildlife Service then rescinded the decision altogether (Blumenthal, 1991). With the federal government trying to save owls and timber jobs without a bonafide plan, conditions worsened for everyone (Durbin, 1991a, 1992c; Painter, 1992).

In addition to the mill closures, displaced workers, loss of local revenues, and dwindling timber reserves, some ecologists now believe the owl is in "precipitous" decline and will probably die off even if all logging is discontinued in the Northwest (Durbin, 1992a). It would be ironic to see the spotted owl vanish before this battle ends, but in politics the bird is overshadowed by its own symbolic significance. The owl was adopted conveniently as a scapegoat for the economy by Republicans during the 1992 election campaign. In his campaign, Vice President Quayle declared, "the spotted owl alone has added $3,000 to $5,000 to the price" of the new $140,000 homes he has seen (Broder, 1992, p. A11). At the Republican National Convention, Pat Buchanan said, "from the ancient forest of Oregon and Washington . . . America's great middle class has got to start standing up to the environmental extremists who put birds and rats and insects ahead of families, workers and jobs" (Mapes, 1992, p. A10).

With the controversy splitting Democrats and Republicans in the election, the failure to develop a recovery plan furthermore illustrates that the spotted owl not only shapes divergent social realities, but also prevents conflict resolution. The competing realities actually supplant long range goals. Environmentalists delay harvests with court rulings, the timber industry postpones enforcement of court rulings through legal suspension of judicial review, and the federal government delays construction of a plan with God Squad intervention. After the second God Squad hearing on the owl in less than one year, Interior Secretary Manuel Lujan determined that the recovery plan written by his own staff would eliminate too many jobs and decided in February, 1992 to appoint a new panel and devise a new plan to "protect more jobs" (Durbin, 1992d). The following month Lujan postponed another decision on the plan that involved 44 timber sales in Oregon blocked by federal court since May, 1991 (Ulrich, 1992a, 1992b). With these delays, government only adds to the "confusion" that prompted action in the first place, and leaves lawmakers with a "stark choice" between owls and jobs (Durbin, 1992b, p. A1).

Conclusions

To Burke, any act of representation automatically implies a synecdochic relationship and any synecdochic relationship implies reduction. By reducing conflict between the environment and the economy to a spotted owl, the conflict is represented within the limits of that spotted owl. Problems arise with the synecdochal constructions since they are not, as Burke would suggest, "truly representative" of the whole. That is, the owl may not indicate the actual health of the forest nor determine the fate of the timber industry. If life and liberty are material ideas or "conditions of the society into which each of us is born," (McGee, 1980a, p. 9), they are nevertheless "reduced" in the controversy by the owl (Burke, 1969, p. 508). What the foregoing analysis reveals about synecdoche and the ideograph is that the former can serve as one way to make the latter more concrete for groups, but in doing so, it distorts the conflict because it only *represents* the conflict. This extends McGee's conception of the ideograph by demonstrating how material ideas function in social controversy as the ultimate material and mental states that are reduced, represented, and then distorted in social controversy. In this manner, an ideograph in divergent synecdochic forms generates irresolvable conflict.

While instrumental in the growth and maintenance of dispute, a different view of the owl as synecdoche and ideograph can serve as a rhetorical form that may lead the groups toward a resolution or goal. As an indicator to environmentalists and a scapegoat to the timber industry the owl currently shapes the controversy into an either/or situation that only appears resolvable. The owl as a different ideograph for each group in synecdochal form, further reduces the controversy to either/or terms: life or death for the environmentalists; liberty or death for the timber industry. Yet the larger or real issue, which involves ecology and economy, is not an either/or dilemma, but a both/and contradiction. With the real issue, the owl as ideograph is not life or liberty, but life *and* liberty. We want our environment and our economy. This real issue is not resolvable in the either/or form of the owl conflict yet the contradictory desires of, "wanting our cake and eating it too," prolongs the dispute *in the owl's name*. To break gridlock, the environmentalists and the timber industry could rearrange the either/or dispute that creates a false dilemma of owls or jobs by "coaching," and then "extending" the synecdochic principle beyond immediate needs of the two groups.

By extending the synecdochic principle, the spotted owl can represent a *gerundive*. That is, when introduced in the conflict, the owl's nature is that of something *to be* either sacrificed or saved. In the same way that Burke (1969) describes the albatross in *The Ancient Mariner*, the owl "implicitly *contains* the future that is to become explicit" (p. 509, emphasis added). Also, the owl as the passive future is a consequence of the attitude about economics and the environment that brought this controversy into being ("neglect" over time). Environmentalists may like to think that the owl can save the forest, and loggers may want to believe that sacrificing the owl can save their jobs, but the owl can do neither. The owl is not a "savior," but it contains "salvation" and "sacrifice" to the extent that its future is in human hands.

The owl synecdoches essentially generate and maintain social conflict too vital to resolve. Even still, the lesson of the owl synecdoche is not that ecology and economy are incompatible, but that the longer it takes society as a whole to find the political courage to act on the problem, the harder it will be to procure a solution. As Burke prognosticated in 1937, "there is one little fellow named Ecology and in time we shall pay him more attention" (1984a, p. 150). Such a time has come. The owl synecdoches actually reveal that "the *total* economy of this planet cannot be guided by an efficient rationale alone," and "that the exploiting *part* must itself suffer if it too greatly disturbs the *balance* of the *whole*" (Burke, 1984a, p. 150, emphasis added). And how are the parts balanced? Driven by necessities of capitalism the timber industry amplifies the scope of bureaucratic resources, methods, and productive techniques. Driven by transformations of the environment, environmentalists stress the inevitability of a productive technique overemphasized by necessities of capitalism. Thus, the symbolic act of the two owls finally illustrates that the considerations of balance exceed any "single-tracked purpose" (Burke, 1984a, p. 150). This means taking distinctions back to their common ground of existence, so they may return in newer and better combinations. As long as the owl only offers a choice of life with the environment or liberty with the timber industry, it will prevent resolution and remain a problem in its own right.

Notes

1. This battle involves the protection of the northern spotted owl and diminishing old-growth forests in the Pacific Northwest. While focusing on the loss of timber jobs and the loss of ancient forests, it also represents the transformation of human *lifestyle* due to changes in the natural environment. In recent years, the timber crisis has involved Congress and the federal government. Less than 10% of the original forest remains undisturbed in the continental United States ("Environment's little big bird," 1990), yet Northwest timber harvests set record numbers during the 1980s. *The Oregonian*, Oregon's largest newspaper (published in Portland), reported that 70,000 acres of old-growth in Northwest national forests were cut each year during the 1980s (Durbin & Koberstein, 1990, p. A1). However, Oregon Senator Mark Hatfield predicted timber sale reductions due to the controversy could cost "Oregon and Washington 27,000 jobs, and as many as 54,000 jobs overall" (Hager, 1989, p. 2306).
2. The spotted owl is an impressive boreal species which leads a strictly nocturnal life in the middle and lower stories of tall old-growth forests where sunlight is noticeably dimmed throughout the daytime (Voous, 1989, pp. 235-236). They prefer to forage in old-growth conifer forests (at least two-hundred years old), use the younger forests much less, and rarely do they inhabit forests cleared or burned in the last twenty years. Research since 1979 suggests at least 400 hectares are needed to support one pair

of birds, but as the proportion of old-growth diminishes, the size of home ranges increases, (Forsman, Meslow, & Wright, 1984). Reasons for the owl's dependency on old-growth habitat include: nest-plat-form needs; broad temperature gradients; a need for roosting in multilayered canopy trees; prey-abundance/prey-availability variables (Carey, 1985). Forsman also observed that when areas harvested in an extensive forest reached roughly 80 hectares, owls "often disappeared," and clear-cut harvests "eliminated roosting, nesting and most foraging in the affected areas" (Forsman, 1976, p. 109). By 1980, he argued, since "clear-cutting reduced the quality" of its environment, "the best method of managing spotted owl populations . . . was to preserve the maximum amount of old-growth . . . and to avoid the creation of large cutover areas" (Forsman, 1980, p. 85).

3. McGee (1980a) states that ideographs are "material ideas" (p. 9), which as "a group of words and not a series of symbols" (p. 8-9), describe an "essentially social human condition" for a people (pp. 8-9). Also, ideographs constitute the "*conditions* of the society into which each of us is born" (1980a, p. 7). Thus, in a material sense, ideology exists "in and through the language which constitutes it" (McKerrow, 1989, p. 102; McGee, 1982). By suggesting an ideograph is not a symbol that represents an ideal, McGee's view of it as a "material idea" brings to mind a paradox of perfection that designates political commitments as real in a material sense while possessing both shared and ambiguous meaning (as a material, abstract, and "God" term). On the feminization of power, McGee (1980b) alludes to this paradox himself, saying that " 'liberty' is precisely a *spirit*, a feeling" and in "reification" of liberty we forget our "*primary duty*," which is "to materialize the thing itself" (p. 45, emphasis added). He also notes, there are times when "one swims in historically-material ideographs that have had the history (and hence the substance) sucked out of them" (McGee, 1983, p. 61). Can this mean that they are no longer ideographs as such, or does it mean that ideographs themselves can have both abstract and consensual meaning? With regard to public knowledge, McGee (1983) furthermore argues that ideographs such as economy, patriotism, and honor "*appear* to lack meaning *only* when applied to the alleged improprieties of the patronage system" (p. 61) yet if one begins with "the supposition that reality is hidden by appearance, truth by discourse" (McGee, 1990, p. 276), then the ideograph is limited in meaning because it is an idea nevertheless "realized" in and through discourse.

An important aspect about ideographs in public discourse and in McGee's conception of the term is the way in which they define people as products of "paradox" (material ideas). The "material" idea of "liberty" is still an idea, which suggests permeable and consensual meaning. As in Moore's (1988) study of ideographs in Mortimer Adler's concept of the "realizable ideal" in philosophic discourse, words like *liberty* seem to possess ambiguous and shared meaning that can also reveal particular motives of an ideologist, speaker, or group member (p. 88). Since ideographs can be seen as limited by particular interests as well as a defining term for society as a whole, this study proposes to extend McGee's notion, by showing how rhetorical tropes, particularly synecdoche, can function in social controversy to make ideographic meaning more tangible or concrete. Whereas an ideograph is an ultimate term for a society, an "ideograph in synecdochal form" can signify an "ultimate conflict" (economy versus ecology, preservation versus extinction), since differing representational forms may reflect divergent and perhaps incommensurable realities. Therefore, the notion of "representational" or "figurative ideograph" is useful because, unlike other terms that could be used to describe "the spotted owl" (e.g., significant symbol [Burke, 1968] or entitlement [Burke, 1966]), terms like the "spotted owl" function more as ideographs in synecdochal form. They define reality for each group, establish conditions of their "communities" and also "penalize us . . . as much as they protect us, for they prohibit our appreciation of *an alternative pattern of meaning. . . .*" (McGee, 1980a, p. 9, emphasis added).

4. There are other rhetorical studies that also illustrate the function of such ideographs as "life" and "liberty" to manage and express public discourse and social controversy (Condit, 1987; Condit & Lucaites, 1991; Moore, 1988; Railsback, 1984).

5. The attempts to protect owls that roost on BLM lands are important to the owl's survival, scientists argue, because they provide a bridge of old-growth between the Coast Range and the Oregon Cascades (Forsman, 1980; Thomas, 1990). The continued fragmentation in this region would, according to Thomas (1990), prevent owl dispersal through the forests of Western Oregon and lead to its extinction.

6. In addition to those who provide such specific scientific depictions, others lament over the inevitability of a sacred yet lost paradise. Religious practitioner Rip Lone Wolf described a low cloud formation below Enola Hill, a sacred ceremonial ground for the local Indian tribes, as a "veil being put on now because the spirits don't want us to see the desecration that's going on" (Durbin, 1991b, B1). By stressing "connectedness" between parts of the quality/quantity side in this equation, Native Americans feel Enola Hill is not an isolated ceremonial site, but part of a general area considered sacred. Some

who want to prevent logging around Enola Hill believe "the entire Cascade Range is sacred and nothing should occur there" (Durbin, 1991b, B1).

[7]As a way of paying tribute to the "norms" of society, Burke (1984a) notes that the adherence to "social obligations" not only justifies a group's existence, but justifies its freedom as well. Therefore, the issue is not one of either "individual freedom" *or* "social obligation," but rather it is "a weighing" of the various incidents where a freedom/social obligation ambivalence expresses itself (Burke, 1984a, p. 165).

Works Cited

Barnard, J. (1992, January 12). Jumble of efforts leads to chaos on the spotted owl. *The Oregonian*, p. C6.

Bella, R. (1991, May 25). Woodsmen chop up plans to bar logging. *The Oregonian*, pp. E1, E10

Blumenthal, L. (1991, October 17). Agency rescinds owl guidelines. *The Oregonian*, pp. B1, B8.

Broder, D. (1992, August 12). Stumping Quayle takes aim at Anita Hill, Hillary Clinton, spotted owl. *The Oregonian*, p. A11.

Burke, K. (1966). *Language as symbolic action: Essays on life, literature, and method*. Berkeley: University of California Press.

Burke, K. (1968). *Counter-statement*. Berkeley: University of California Press.

Burke, K. (1969). *A grammar of motives*. Berkeley: University of California Press.

Burke, K. (1970). *The rhetoric of religion: Studies in logology*. Berkeley: University of California Press.

Burke, K. (1984a). *Attitudes toward history* (3rd ed.). Berkeley: University of California Press.

Burke, K. (1984b). *Permanence and change: An anatomy of purpose* (3rd ed.). Berkeley: University of California Press.

Butterworth, B. (1991, December 22). New book tells the story of the West's rain forest. *The Oregonian*, p. L10.

Carey, A. (1985). A summary of the scientific basis for spotted owl management. In R.J. Gutierrez & A.B. Carey (Eds.), *Ecology and management of the spotted owl in the Pacific Northwest* (pp. 100-114). Portland, OR: U.S. Department of Agriculture, Forest Service, Gen. Tech. Report PNW-185.

Church, F. (1990, October 24). Mill owners struggling to survive. *The Oregonian*, pp. A1, A10-A12.

Condit, C. (1987). Crafting virtue: The rhetorical construction of public morality. *Quarterly Journal of Speech, 73*, 79-97.

Condit, C., & Lucaites, J. (1991). The rhetoric of equality and the expatriation of African Americans, 1776-1826. *Communication Studies, 42*, 1-21.

Congressional Record. (1991a, June 26), p. S 8701.

Congressional Record. (1991b, October 1), p. H 7126.

Davis, P. (1991a, September 14). BLM calls on "God Squad" to let its timber go. *Congressional Quarterly*, pp. 2611-2612.

Davis, P. (1991b, June 1). Ruling gives lawmakers a push to resolve spotted owl issue. *Congressional Quarterly*, pp. 1438-1439.

Durbin, K. (1990, September 20). Lou Gold. *The Oregonian*, p. A18.

Durbin, K. (1991a, December 24). Court backs timber sale ban. *The Oregonian*, pp. A1-A7.

Durbin, K. (1991b, February 4). Religious rights vs. land management. *The Oregonian*, p. B1.

Durbin, K. (1992a, January 28). Expert sees "precipitous" owl decline. *The Oregonian*, pp. B1, B8.

Durbin, K. (1992b, May 10). Interior Department tries to outflank owl. *The Oregonian*, pp. D1, D4.

Durbin, K. (1992c, January 31). Judge blocks timber sales. *The Oregonian*, pp. A1, A16.

Durbin, K. (1992d, February 19). Lujan pushes aside owl recovery plan. *The Oregonian*, pp. A1, A12.

Durbin, K. & Bella, R. (1992, January 9). Timber pickets haunt "God Squad." *The Oregonian*, pp. A1, A16.

Durbin, K. & Koberstein, P. (1990, September 20). Survival hinges on old-growth habitat. *The Oregonian*, pp. A1, A17-A18.

Dwyer, W. (1991, June 26). The owl and the law. *Congressional Record*, pp. S 8699-S 8700.

Environment's little big bird. (1990, April 16). *Time*, p. 21.

Forsman, E. (1976). *A preliminary investigation of the spotted owl in Oregon*. Unpublished Thesis, Oregon State University, Corvallis.

Forsman, E. (1980). *Habitat utilization by spotted owls in the West-Central Cascades of Oregon.* Unpublished doctoral dissertation, Oregon State University, Corvallis.

Forsman, E., Meslow, E., & Wright, H. (1984). Distribution and biology of the spotted owl in Oregon. *Wildlife Monographs, 87,* 1-64.

Gup, T. (1990, June 25). Owl vs. man. *Time,* pp. 56-63.

Hager, G. (1989, September 9). Small owl incites big battle over environment, jobs. *Congressional Quarterly,* pp. 2306-2309.

Hamburg, K. (1992, April 5). Douglas County reeling from the economic blues. *The Oregonian,* pp. R1, R5.

Koberstein, P. (1991, May 25). Northwest timber industry rips judge's decision to block sales. *The Oregonian,* p. E10.

La Follette, C. (1979). *Analysis of the Oregon interagency spotted owl management plan.* Eugene, OR: Cascade Holistic Economic Consultants.

Manzano, P. (1991, August 7). Economic woes blamed on owl, timber issue. *The Oregonian,* p. A11.

Mapes, J. (1992, August 20). NW activists rip Demos as environmental extremists. *The Oregonian,* p. A10.

Maser, C. (1988). *The redesigned forest.* San Pedro, CA: R. & E. Miles.

McCarthy, L. (1992, March 20). Foes stump to undercut timber sale. *The Oregonian,* pp. A1, A19.

McGee, M. (1980a). The "Ideograph": A link between rhetoric and ideology. *Quarterly Journal of Speech, 66,* 1-16.

McGee, M. (1980b). The origins of "Liberty": A feminization of power. *Communication Monographs, 47,* 23-45.

McGee, M. (1982). A materialist's conception of rhetoric. In R.E. McKerrow (Ed.), *Explorations in rhetoric* (pp. 23-48). Glenview, IL: Scott Foresman.

McGee, M. (1983). Public knowledge and ideological argumentation. *Communication Monographs, 50,* 47-65.

McGee, M. (1990). Text, context and the fragmentation of contemporary culture. *Western Journal of Speech Communication, 54,* 274-289.

McKerrow, R. (1989). Critical rhetoric: Theory and practice. *Communication Monographs, 56,* 91-111.

Meehan, B. (1990a, October 22). Factions tearing at the fabric of the forest. *The Oregonian,* pp. A1, A10-A13.

Meehan, B. (1990b, October 21). Lives in transition. *The Oregonian,* pp. A1, A22-A25.

Moore, M. (1988). The rhetoric of ideology: Confronting a critical dilemma. *Southern Communication Journal, 54,* 74-92.

Old-growth protection bill "open" to debate. (1991, March 12). *The Oregonian,* p. B10.

No peace for the owl. (1990, July 9). *Time,* p. 63.

Norse, E. (1990). *Ancient forests of the Pacific Northwest.* Washington, DC: Island.

Noss, R. (1991). From endangered species to biodiversity. In K.A. Kohm (Ed.), *Balancing on the brink of extinction: The endangered species act and lessons for the future* (pp. 227-246). Washington, DC: Island.

Painter, J., Jr. (1992, February 8). U.S. judge extends bar against logging BLM old growth. *The Oregonian,* p. B3.

Peterson, T. (1991). Telling the farmer's story: Competing responses to soil conservation rhetoric. *Quarterly Journal of Speech, 77,* 289-308.

Postrel, V. (1990). The environmental movement: A skeptical view. *Vital Speeches of the Day, 56,* pp. 729-732.

Pytte, A. (1990a, June 30). Bush hedges on spotted owl, forces Congress to choose. *Congressional Quarterly,* pp. 2043-2044.

Pytte, A. (1990b, September 29). Timber, spotted owl interests find middle ground elusive. *Congressional Quarterly,* pp. 3104-3107.

Railsback, C. (1984). The contemporary American abortion controversy: Stages in the argument. *Quarterly Journal of Speech, 70,* 410-424.

Robbins, W. (1990). *Hard times in paradise: Coos Bay, Oregon, 1850-1986.* Seattle: University of Washington Press.

Satchell, M. (1990, June 25). The endangered logger. *U.S. News & World Report,* pp. 27-29.

Sonner, S. (1991, August 12). Agency concurs, discounts owl factor. *The Oregonian,* pp. B1, B8.

Thomas, J. (1990). *A conservation strategy for the northern spotted owl.* Washington, DC: U.S. Government Printing Office.

Udall, S. & Olson, W. (1992, August 16). Jolly greed giant. *The Oregonian,* p. C7.

Ulrich, R. (1992a, March 25). Bush blamed for owl crisis. *The Oregonian*, pp. B1, B8.
Ulrich, R. (1992b, March 21). Lujan again delays decision on timber sales in Oregon. *The Oregonian*, p. B1, B4.
Voous, K. (1989). *Owls of the northern hemisphere*. Cambridge, MA: MIT Press.
Zuckerman, S. (1991). *Saving our ancient forests*. Los Angeles: Living Planet.

Rooted in the Soil:
How Understanding the Perspectives
of Landowners Can Enhance the
Management of Environmental Disputes
by Tarla Rai Peterson and Cristi Choat Horton

Disputes over management of dwindling natural resources, particularly habitats for endangered species, are provoking formidable hostilities throughout the United States. Lange (1993) and Moore (1993) detail one such dispute over preservation of ancient forests and northern spotted owl habitat in the Pacific Northwest. The natural resource conflict they examine centers around the economic impact of decisions regarding preservation of public land, primarily "ancient" forests administered by the U.S. National Forest Service. Environmentalists claim that large tracts of these forests should be preserved because they provide critical wildlife habitat and because "ancient" forest itself has become so rare that it is "endangered." Hostilities arising from this (still unresolved) environmental dispute have exacerbated local conflicts, indefinitely delayed reauthorization of the U.S. Endangered Species Act (ESA), and weakened the U.S. position in international environmental negotiations such as the 1992 United Nations Conference on Environment and Development.

Although disputes over preserving public land as habitat for endangered species have been fierce, attempts to preserve private property as habitat for endangered species further confound this already perplexing environmental conflict. While suspending the harvest of publicly owned timber in portions of the Pacific Northwest may bankrupt timber companies, school districts, and communities, it does not attack directly the almost inviolable notion of private property. In regions other than the Pacific and Rocky Mountains States, and Alaska, however, public ownership of land is rare. Although the endangered animals found in these regions belong to the public, their survival depends on preservation of habitat that largely belongs to individuals and for-profit corporations.

The 1990 listing of the golden-cheeked warbler (*Dendroica chrysoparia*) as an endangered species has fueled an already acrimonious debate among conservation agencies, environmental groups, and private landowners (mostly ranchers) in Texas (U.S. Department of Interior [USDI], 1991a, p. 6). Because the golden-cheeked warbler primarily inhabits private land, local property owners have interpreted the formal listing, as well as attempts to preserve habitat, as a direct threat to their property rights. Thirty-one counties, comprising approximately 41,871 square miles, define the geographic range of the species in Texas. The bird prefers cedar (*Juniperus ashei*) brakes with a mixture of mature cedar and oak woodlands as its habitat (USDI, 1990). Although cedar provides a home for the warbler, its dense canopy cover and litter of needles shade the ground, competing with grass for sunlight and water. Ranchers in the region attempt to control cedar to ensure sufficient grass to improve or maintain their rangeland's grazing capacity (Baccus, 1991). The U.S. Fish and Wildlife Service (USFWS), which has purchased some of the land needed to create a refuge for the warbler, states that "the primary land use [in the warbler's habitat] is ranching of commercial livestock, primarily goats and cattle. . . . In many instances, these ranching activities have helped to maintain habitats for the endangered birds." However, they add that in some cases "traditional vegetation clearing practices have resulted in fragmentation of forest areas and loss of nesting habitat" (USDI, 1991a, p. 9). This reduction and fragmentation of cedar stands poses a threat to the warbler's continued existence by degrading its habitat.

The conflict over golden-cheeked warbler habitat is replete with missed opportunities for identifying with landowners in ways that could enhance the constructive management of environmental disputes. Environmental activists and personnel representing natural resource agencies have articulated the need for golden-cheeked warbler habitat in both government documents and popular print media (for examples, see USDI, 1987, 1990, 1991a, 1991b; Collier, 1991). Their voices speak authoritatively from the pages of the official plan detailing how golden-cheeked warbler habitat will be preserved (USDI, 1991a). The voices of those whose land management decisions have preserved habitat appropriate for nesting by the golden-cheeked warbler are absent from these documents. Not surprisingly, these ranchers believe that their perspective has been ignored or ridiculed by environmental policy makers. These differing levels of involvement have important implications for environmental policy. By restricting opportunities to participate in the public sphere, the USFWS has assumed an adversarial position relative to an audience whose cooperation they desire. Further, without a vital and inclusive public sphere, democratic processes wither and die. Although property-owners' voices sometimes clash with those from conservation agencies and environmental groups, without them the discourse of environmental policy lacks vigor and depth.

Because environmental policy is public policy, its discourse should throb with the sometimes contentious sounds of public debate. Our analysis of voices that have been lost from this conflict demonstrates the need for practicing a communicatively rich theory of democratic government when designing and implementing environmental policy. We use mythic criticism of local landowners' discourse to illuminate their perspective. Mythemes[1] drawn from their discourse direct attention to the communicative implications of an environmental policy (endangered species management) that ignores individual communities. By focusing on these practices, our analysis uncovers an alternative mythic understanding of the American (U.S.) West that is grounded in the discourse of its central characters.

Huspek and Kendall (1991) point out that political voice "is a basic condition of freedom" (p. 1). Local property owners who are embroiled in this environmental conflict have chosen to withhold their voices from the political arena because they believe that the broader culture no longer accommodates their interests. Their choice to eschew the discursive struggle "to get their words and meanings accepted by others in an effort to secure limited material and symbolic resources" both reveals their disaffection and "amounts to a forfeiture of self-determination" on their part (Huspek & Kendall, p. 1). Without hope that discursive participation in mainstream politics offers them an authentic hearing, private land-owners such as these ranchers join other U.S. citizens who perceive that the public sphere is, at best, irrelevant to their lives.

One reason these landowners perceive themselves as political outsiders is that the rhetoric of endangered species management has assumed an elitist form that fails to ground itself in local cultural practices. Competition for natural resources produces a variety of complex and potentially conflicting situations wherein communication between opposing factions is essential. However, the USFWS, which is legally responsible for managing endangered species, has no programmatic means for involving the public in its decisions. Top-down decisions reached without the participation of those most directly impacted necessarily exacerbate these conflicts, whereas communication built on a foundation of mutual respect could encourage collaborative development of management policies. In this case, ranchers' apprehension regarding USFWS-sponsored "taking" of their property, combined with the USFWS's apprehension regarding rancher-sponsored degradation of warbler habitat, has prevented collaboration between the two groups. While we do not assume that collaborative decision-making will eliminate environmental conflicts, we think it will facilitate constructive dialogue that will enrich the environmental community.

Finally, ranchers' discourse offers a vision of the American West that is rooted in the life-world of its inhabitants. The mythemes Texas ranchers use to make sense of their world bear little resemblance to the frontier legends constructed and exploited by national culture centers.[2] Rather than viewing themselves as conquerors of the land, these "cowboys" have become one with it. Because they have learned to adapt to the ebb and flow of the land, water, plants, and animals that make up the landscape, they believe that they should be consulted when management decisions are made.

Although human interaction with the natural environment plays an increasingly central role in both local and global politics, few analyses of environmental conflicts appear in communication journals (Cantrill, 1993).[3] Communication analyses focusing on natural resource users such as fishers, ranchers, and loggers, whose economic livelihood directly depends on decisions regarding environmental policy, have been even more rare. Huspeck and Kendall's (1991) analysis of a discourse community formed by lumber workers, and Peterson's (1986b, 1991) examinations of U.S. farmers' historical ambivalence toward conservation are exceptions. Members of these groups are increasingly drawn into conflicts regarding natural resource management, however, creating both the need and the opportunity to include their perspective in environmental debates. As Burke (1969) explains, important social action occurs when we "put identification and division ambiguously together, so that [we] cannot know for certain just where one ends and the other begins, and [we] have the characteristic invitation to rhetoric" (p. 25). Although facilitating rhetorical exchanges between opposing groups cannot deny the presence of enmity regarding environmental policy, such exchanges are necessary for moving beyond factionalism to the potential for convergence across perspectives. If, as Burke argues, some level of consubstantiation is "necessary to any way of life," it certainly is an essential condition for moving endangered species policy from the realm of reactive motion into the realm of action (p. 21). Understanding the perspective of local landowners would provide agencies such as the USFWS with possibilities for transforming seemingly intransigent conflicts into public controversies. Although acting on such possibilities would destabilize many agencies, it seems appropriate for the public to participate in policy decisions regarding the environment within which they live.

Interviews with ranchers who inhabit the same region as the golden-cheeked warbler provide the primary texts for this analysis. Since the warbler's listing as an endangered species, our informants have been required either to sell part (or all) of their land to the U.S. government or to limit range management practices to those approved by the USFWS. We first place the conflict regarding golden-cheeked warbler habitat in its historical context by reviewing the development of the current ESA. Second, we explain the critical perspective guiding our collection of ranchers' discourse and outline our methods of analysis. Third, we explore the meaning system discovered through mythic criticism of ranchers' responses. Finally, we discuss the potential for convergence between perspectives toward the "natural" environment expressed by our informants' and by U.S. conservation agencies. This relationship clarifies both the challenges associated with maintaining a meaningful space for public discourse and the folly of relying on the cult of expertise when deciding how best to manage commonly held resources. If environmental policy discussions are reconceptualized as attempts to negotiate common ground based on points of consubstantiality, participants can infuse them with new life by exhibiting and legitimizing divergent approaches to the "natural" environment. Our goal is to show how communication that responds attentively to an audience's perspective can assist in retrieving potential points of affiliation among diverse groups.

Establishment of the Endangered Species Act

The conflict over management of golden-cheeked warbler habitat is an outgrowth of an array of environmental legislation that has emerged throughout the years. Its alleged purpose is to preserve and conserve a diversified biological system in the U.S. Originally, individual states had exclusive jurisdiction over wildlife conservation. However, in response to abuse by well-organized commercial interests, Congress intervened with the passage of the Lacey Act of 1900, which provided the first official indication that the loss of species was of national concern. In the 1960s Congress responded to public pressure to conserve species with the 1966 Endangered Species Preservation Act. In 1969 it revised the act to reflect concern for international wildlife conservation, to prohibit purchase or sale of species in violation of national, state, or foreign laws, and to designate specific ports for importing various species.

The currently enforced (1973) ESA was developed when it became apparent that the 1969 legislation did not provide adequate management tools to conserve vanishing species (Kohm, 1991). The new act was a response to an unacceptable rate of "fish, wildlife, and plants in the United States [being] rendered extinct as a consequence of economic growth and development untempered by adequate concern and conservation." Its purpose is to restore endangered species "to the point where they are again secure, self-sustaining members of their ecosystems" (USDI, 1987, p. 10). The 1973 act requires that criteria for deciding species' endangerment must be based on the best available scientific data and provides procedures for listing of endangered species. Section 9 ensures protection of endangered species' habitat and prohibits practices that destroy or degrade such habitat. Violators may be assessed criminal penalties up to $50,000 in fines, along with one year in prison, or civil damages up to $25,000 for each violation (USDI, 1973). The very existence of these provisions (to say nothing of their enforcement) has provoked hostility among property owners across the U.S.

Scheduled for reauthorization in 1992, the ESA's future remains unclear. On November 26, 1991, Rep. Gerry E. Studds of Massachusetts introduced the first formal reauthorization resolution, which would have increased funding and expanded the act to include "preventative" conservation of species before they are listed as "threatened" or "endangered" (H.R. 4045). Rep. William E. Dannemeyer of California and Rep. James V. Hansen of Utah countered with reauthorization bills that would have required the USDI to consider economic factors before deciding to list species as threatened or endangered (Satterfield, p. 10022). In 1992 Rep. Billy Tauzin of Louisiana and Rep. Jack Fields of Texas introduced a reauthorization bill that, while continuing to base listing decisions on scientific data, stipulated that species-recovery plans must include an assessment of economic impacts. The discovery of any "direct and indirect economic costs" to the private sector would enable the Secretary of the Interior to select a "no action" recovery plan, allowing the endangered species to continue its slide toward extinction.

Reauthorization bills for the ESA are directed to the Subcommittee on Fisheries and Wildlife Conservation and the Environment. In 1992 the Subcommittee chair announced that the committee would not proceed on ESA authorization until the Pacific Northwest crisis was resolved (Tauzin & Fields, 1992a; Bean, 1993; Isbel, 1993; quotations from Tauzin & Fields, 1992b). The current ESA remains in effect until further legislation is enacted, although possibilities for reauthorization are paralyzed by controversy. While the future of the ESA remains in limbo, local implementations, such as establishing a protected habitat for the golden-cheeked warbler, continue.

Despite the fact that all U.S. citizens are legal stakeholders in the golden-cheeked warbler conflict, the USFWS and local landowners (usually ranchers) have been most directly involved in the plan for the bird's recovery. The ESA gives the USFWS legal authority to ensure the preservation of golden-cheeked warbler habitat. Although its authority technically includes forced sales ("taking") of private land, its financial appropriation is insufficient to purchase adequate acreage. This funding gap, combined with a vague awareness of the U.S. tendency to equate private property rights with democracy, has led some wildlife managers to seek cooperation with private landowners. Private landowners, on the other hand, fear working with the USFWS, complaining that such relationships are marked by lack of due process. To date, the USFWS has been relatively unsuccessful in establishing cooperative agreements with private landowners.

The relative failure to establish cooperative agreements may be explained partially by a brief description of the public hearings held in Austin, Texas to discuss listing the golden-cheeked warbler as an endangered species.[4] The USFWS brought maps of the region on which they had marked ranches (or portions of ranches) they had selected·for a future wildlife refuge to the first public meeting. When ranchers questioned this procedure, they were assured that they would receive fair market value for their land. Those whose land was not identified for purchase by the USFWS voiced fears of losing the right to manage their private property. Several otherwise ordinary practices (i.e., cultivation, woody plant management, fencing, etc.) can be defined as "taking" warbler habitat and in violation of Section 9 of the ESA. Some landowners protested that the loss of these land-development activities should be considered confiscation of privately owned property without just compensation, and in violation of the Fifth Amendment. Others claimed that inability to manage cedar would hinder effective brush control practices, thereby reducing the value of their rangeland and limiting their rights as property holders (USDI, 1990; author's fieldnotes).

Following the hearings, plans to establish a means for preserving golden-cheeked warbler habitat proceeded oblivious to comments made at the hearings and continued hostility from local property owners. Groundbreaking ceremonies for the Balcones Canyonlands National Wildlife Refuge were held in October, 1992. The USFWS attempted to involve owners of prime warbler habitat in the preservation process by mailing them formal invitations to the ceremony. Not surprisingly, however, attendance consisted primarily of agency personnel and representatives from mainstream environmental groups (Collier, 1992; Singleton, 1992). A news photo of the gathering was captioned, "Political leaders take refuge" (McEntee, 1992). The refuge currently consists of 7,904 acres that the USFWS purchased from local landowners. The Nature Conservancy is negotiating the purchase of an additional 2,860 acres (which the USFWS will lease from them at a nominal fee). However, even with this addition, the refuge will contain less than half the acreage needed to provide adequate golden-cheeked warbler habitat, and local landowners have not shown eagerness to enter into formal cooperative agreements with their new neighbor (Personal Communication with Refuge Director D. Holle, Oct. 25, 1993). Two years after the refuge was established, personnel from other state and federal agencies charged with managing natural resources in warbler territory continued to distance themselves from the controversy by carefully informing their clients that they have no connection with the USFWS.[5]

Exploring the Ranchers' Perspectives

In an attempt to explain why local landowners exhibited continuing hostility toward USFWS efforts to conserve habitat for the golden-cheeked warbler, we examined mythological dimensions in ranchers' talk, then explored how that mythology drives ranchers' perceptions of their relationship to both the human and non-human environment. Understanding derived from this analysis suggests points of commonality from which to begin a dialogue between conflicting groups of natural resource users. While this dialogue is an important step in resolving the golden-cheeked warbler conflict, its significance extends far beyond the Texas hill country to include natural resource conflicts across the U.S. Additionally, it has implications regarding the relationship between public deliberation and democracy.

Informant-Directed Interviews

A growing number of communication scholars advocate the use of interpretive methods to uncover meaning systems within a community (Anderson, 1987). Lange (1990, 1993) demonstrates that by becoming a "participant observer" the researcher interacts within a particular culture, gaining insight about the meaning of social action from the perspective of its members. However, despite its value in studying cultural categories and themes, time scarcity and privacy issues sometimes combine to make participation-based ethnography impossible.

Lincoln and Guba (1985) argue that since each person constructs reality differently, a methodology that captures this uniqueness must drive the process of data collection. Because the face-to-face interview provides one of the most powerful methods for understanding how people order and assess their everyday world, Peterson et al. (1994) suggest qualitative interviewing as an appropriate method for research into cultural meaning systems. Higgins (1991) argues that the cultural differences between farmers and non-farmers lead them to divergent meaning systems. She advocates research relying on relatively unstructured interview protocols as a means for closing the intercultural gap that exists here. Similarly, ranchers and non-ranchers struggle with a communication gap. Although our analysis of ranchers' discourse does not go so far as to claim that ranchers form a culture completely distinct from non-ranchers, Higgins' identification of the need to conduct research that is cognizant of a communication gap between rhetor and audience is helpful. McCracken (1988) suggests a technique he refers to as the "long interview" as a means for stepping "into the mind of another person, to see and experience the world as they do themselves" (p. 9). This protocol relies on a few generalized questions related to the topic. Floating prompts that draw on terms introduced into the conversation by informants supplement the questions. The sequence in which the questions are asked is determined by the informant's responses. This relatively unstructured protocol avoids unnecessarily limiting the content or the form of an informant's discourse.

We cooperated with our informants in producing a text to help reveal their symbolic orientation. We used this text to unravel the orienting myth of a group that is directly impacted by the changes occurring in attitudes toward the environment and private property rights, thus disclosing possible points of identification from which to begin a dialogue. While we do not suffer from the delusion that such a text will resolve conflicts, it will encourage more meaningful participation in conversations needed to achieve that resolution.

As the self definition of a "rancher" is a socially constructed image of self in relation to land, the most appropriate way to gain insight was to ask our informants to talk about ordinary practices in which they and their neighbors participated. Interview questions were constructed to gain greater understanding of those aspects of our informants' meaning systems most directly related to their 1) self-image as ranchers, 2) image of the land they ranch, and 3) image of the appropriate relationship between rancher and land.[6] The interview transcripts provided us with texts from which we drew a qualitative assessment of how their discourse mediates the relationship between humans and natural resources.

Selection of Informants. The Federal Register identified 31 Texas counties as potential golden-cheeked warbler habitat (USDI, 1990). To determine where to conduct interviews, we asked representatives of the Agriculture Stabilization Conservation Service, Soil Conservation Service, and Texas Agriculture Extension Agency in each of the listed counties whether golden-cheeked warbler management was controversial in their counties. All agency personnel explained that controversy was more evident in the central and southern counties and that it peaked in Travis County.

We then obtained names of potential interviewees from the offices listed above. Appointments for personal interviews were obtained by telephone contact. If the contact was willing to participate, a convenient time and location for the interview was arranged. The names obtained from agency personnel were supplemented by "snowball" sampling (Rakow, 1986), with ranchers providing names of additional informants. Most ranchers were delighted to talk with us—on the condition that federal employees would not be able to identify remarks made by individuals.

We interviewed 28 ranchers from Burnet (2), Comal (1), Hamilton (5), Kendall (1), Kimble (9), Real (2), and Travis (8) counties. Sixty-eight percent of the participants were men while 32% were women. Participants' ages ranged from 25 to 70 years, with a median age of 49. Over 50% had a post high school education. Approximately 60% had been associated with agriculture since childhood (i.e., reared on a ranch, worked on a ranch, etc.). Eighty-two percent of the participants owned land; 18% leased, but did not own land; 25% both owned and leased land. Ranching provided primary income for 64% of the participants. Acreage owned and/or leased ranged from 400 to 7,500 acres.

Creating the Text for Analysis. All interviews were conducted by the authors. We traveled to the landowners' home counties, where we conducted interviews in locations ranging from private offices to coffee shops and pickup cabs. Interview length depended on the informant's interest, communication style, and competing time commitments, with the shortest interviews taking thirty minutes and the longest nearly two hours. All interviews were tape-recorded, then transcribed at a later date. After all interviews were conducted we provided each informant with a copy of her/his interview transcript.

Transcripts of the recorded interviews provided the primary text for a mythic analysis of the ranchers' meaning systems. Mythic criticism of the transcripts facilitated identification of peculiar patterns of meaning in our informants' world. We used fieldnotes taken during the interviews, letters to the editors of local newspapers, proceedings and notes from scientific symposia and public hearings, interviews with USFWS personnel, and newspaper and magazine articles to provide additional background for the controversy.

Mythic Criticism of Interview Transcripts

When analyzing our interview transcripts we adapted the five steps of interpretive analysis suggested in Peterson et al. (1994). First, we identified and developed individual themes in each transcript. Second, we determined which of these themes were most significant to our informants. Third, we examined the most significant themes for their mythic dimensions. Finally, we searched for relationships between the mythemes we had identified in step three. This method of analysis grows out of Ivie's (1987) procedure for identifying metaphor clusters and Peterson's (1990, 1991) analysis of mythic structures in farmers' discourse. Peterson incorporates interpretive interviews into rhetorical criticism to explain how farmers' relationship with their land influences interactions with outsiders, claiming that an understanding of the myths influencing farmers' interactions with governmental and private conservation agencies can enhance the quality of these interactions.

Our definition of myth is primarily functional; it follows from Slotkin's (1973) view that myth re-presents "the world vision and historical sense of a people or culture, reducing centuries of experience into a constellation of compelling metaphors" (pp. 6-7). Lincoln (1989) adds that myth gives history "a natural justification, making contingency appear eternal" (p. 5). It mediates between identification and division at two levels. First, by specifying the boundaries of correct behavior it helps people distinguish insiders from outsiders, and so order their own behaviors as to remain an insider. It also provides the mediation needed between the self and others, even those who share the same mythology, by allowing for individual variations within the sanctioned ways of being human.

We assume that myth is related, but not equivalent, to stories. Living myths must be transmitted among people, and stories and anecdotes often function as vehicles for that transmittal. Slotkin (1985, p. 23) claims that because "all of a culture's ideology is contained in myths," these myths become intrinsic to language. As well as serving as a coding device actors use to describe their world, myth is "a discursive act through which actors evoke the sentiments out of which society is actively constructed" (Lincoln, 1989, p. 25). Burke (1989) argues that the mythic dimension of discourse moves people "from the order of reason to the order of imagination," providing a "sense of oneness with the universe in which the individual's being is grounded" (p. 307). Basically myth provides a rhetorical structure within which people continually recreate themselves and their situations.

Our perspective toward mythic criticism thus rests on the assumption that simultaneous generalizability and applicability to specific instances in everyday life are the keys to a myth's living quality. These characteristics aid in the myth being widely appealing, universal within a given culture, and easily understood by its users. Myth provides flexibility by encompassing general perceptions with which participants identify. It sets up an image with a set of values, beliefs, and attitudes imprecise enough that members of a community can tap into them, identify with each other through them, and adequately interpret their situations. The "user of the myth accepts the myth, commits to it, identifies with it, uses it as a usual frame of reference" (Osborn, 1990, p. 122). The flexibility myth provides individuals is countered by the stability it provides communities. By offering a relatively secure set of categories for explaining existence, it enables its users to accept paradoxes without fully acknowledging their existence. However, with living myths that stability is not absolute, for each time a mytheme is shared, participants combine present perceptions with traditional patterns, forming a new version of the myth. The process continues as users confront new experiences, continually applying and modifying the myth with each use.

Mythic criticism of ranchers' discourse obtained through informant-directed interviews illuminates the particularities of this community's meaning system by unraveling intertwined values and drawing them apart for closer examination. Osborn (1990) describes mythic criticism as a means for discovering relationships between "culture-specific symbols that resonate important values" for a specific group and images that remind us of "what it means to be human" (p. 123). Doty (1986) adds that mythic criticism can facilitate exploration of social, psychological, literary, structural, and other interpretive questions. We are most interested in exploring how the mythemes we drew out of our informants' discourse function within Texas ranching culture. As a prelude to developing identification between ranchers and other participants in environmental disputes our analysis asks to what extent these mythemes justify social roles and hierarchies, convey values, and model experience.

Myth's ability to create an illusion of stability makes it especially enticing to people who fear they are at risk of extinction. In other words, as one's existence becomes more precarious, security becomes more salient. Rather than causing the myth of ranch life to evaporate, conflicts over environmental policy strengthen the need for mythic functions. As the world they have known slips away, their myths enable our informants to reinvent themselves as creatures that can inhabit the strange new world. Exploring the mythic dimensions of their discourse, then, draws attention to values that can sanction proposals and counterproposals.

Our analysis indicates that, although ranchers share the USFWS's interest in conservation of natural resources, their interest in conservation grows out of a unique meaning system that impedes their responses to USFWS methods. They define themselves as stewards, or protectors of the land, and identify the essential dimensions of stewardship as common sense, independence, and a unique human-land connection. Common sense is the *wisdom they have obtained from performing ranch activities*. Independence is the *freedom to make ethical judgements regarding specific ranching activities.* The human-land connection is an *attachment to the soil that assumes human health and soil health are interdependent.* According to their myth of stewardship, a good rancher uses common sense independently to preserve the human-land connection. In addition, the stewardship myth unifies otherwise disparate aspects of ranchers' self-definition. At the same time it authorizes an ethic of care for the land, it also justifies the paradoxical relationship between the three characteristics personified by "good" ranchers.

Characteristics of a Good Steward

Common sense, independence, and the human-land connection are interwoven with each other to create the good steward. Each makes the others plausible, and the loss of any would be felt throughout the ranchers' meaning system. Land is basic to ranchers' identity, providing both their "way of life" and their livelihood. Our informants told of how the land imputed meaning to their existence, while producing food for livestock and wildlife which, in turn, generated income (such as livestock sales, hunting leases). Interplay between the symbolic and material aspects of ranchers' relationship with the land guides them in everyday performance of ranch activities. Their self-image as stewards of the land is violated by forced implementation of land-use practices determined by outsiders to be essential for management of the warbler habitat. Because ranchers define themselves as stewards whose ethic is based on common sense, independence, and a human-land connection, they are threatened by USFWS discourse that ignores their experience, replaces personal choice with coercion, and trivializes their sense of connectedness with the land. From the rancher's perspective, formal authority provides USFWS employees with a tawdry substitute for knowledge.

Common Sense

Respect for "common sense" emerges throughout ranchers' discourse. This mytheme emphasizes that experience provides the most legitimate way of knowing the land. Experiences such as physical labor, mental uncertainty, and contests with nature provide a foundation for ranchers' decisions. Outsiders, including landowners who lack that experience, are unable to function as stewards should. The significance of this strand of stewardship is not that it is unique to ranchers. Rather, its significance lies in its use as justification for the remaining two dimensions (independence and connectedness with land), and in the epistemological foundation it provides. Ranchers' self-conscious expectation that experience produces knowledge leads them to define all knowledge (including that possessed by the USFWS) as limited to individual experience. Thus, knowledge is applicable in scenes similar to those where it was constructed, and its validity diminishes as one moves away from those scenes. This perspective provides ranchers with little motivation to privilege knowledge or "reality" proclaimed by "experts" who speak an alien tongue over knowledge developed from their own experiential base.

Common sense enables our informants to understand "far more about what it takes to take care of the land rather than abuse it" (C, R 17). They know "how many animals to put on an acre and . . . when the grass is so short that [they] need to move *all* the animals off of that acre" (C, R 17) because they have seen that "the wormiest cattle in the country are the ones that are on overgrazed land, because they got their mouth right on the dirt, picking them [worms] up" (B, R 22). In addition to personal experience, the "feel" for ranching is "culturally tied"—"more [of an] inheritable type of trait" (R, R 1) that comes from past generations' experiences working with the land. However, although the "trait" may be inherited from previous generations, it is a cultural rather than a genetic inheritance. The continuation of the knowledge is not ensured, but requires conscientious acceptance by the potential recipient.

Considering themselves equipped with proper insight to care for the land, ranchers have the knowledge to "do a better job" of caring for the land than those who lack experience. Part of that job is controlling "invaders," such as cedar, that out-compete the grass. One informant related the difficulty of past attempts to eradicate cedar: "I'll promise you that if you set out to clear every stick of cedar from the face of the earth . . . you'll never get it done. I don't care what you used. . . . We have cut the cedar two or three times on our place. We chained it once. We have had fire once, and we've cut it three or four times. We got more cedar now than we ever had" (H, R 9). After unsuccessfully trying several procedures, ranchers form definite opinions about cedar management. When discussing recurrent problems with cedar control, one commented:

> If we couldn't control cedar in this area . . . you couldn't ranch. That is just the bottom line. . . . I have about seven sections here on this place and about half or maybe 60% is cleared . . . and about every three to four years you have to go back over those same areas and clear them again. New growth cedar starts coming back in them, and if you don't get it, before long it is fifteen or twenty foot high, growing so thick that you can't grow grass or anything, and if you couldn't control the cedar . . . you can't ranch and it would be devastating on the wildlife too. (J, R 9)

A Burnet County rancher explained that despite techniques presented by experts, his experience led him to conclude, "I don't think man's ever going to whip cedar trees. I've only seen one cedar tree die in my lifetime, of natural causes. And that's because a mesquite tree grew up right beside it and the mesquite lived and the cedar died. And that's the only cedar tree I've ever seen die in my life" (P, R 72).

Whether the opposing opinion comes from a technical expert or city dweller, both are isolated from the experiential realities of ranching. The following justification for tranquilizing cattle illustrates how important personal experience is when making decisions:

> I put it to you that they [animal rights activists] have never seen a cow come out of a tranquilizer because half the time they die from it and the other half of the time . . . they come up crazy and if you go ahead and pin 'em down while they're young, they'll be over it in two days or one day and be done. When I was a kid, my Grandfather and I use to go from ranch to ranch and pick up wild old cows and gather them together, and we had to put them down with tranquilizers and things like that and sometimes

they do not come back out of it. And then sometimes when they do come out of it, they come up, and they come up mad, and they kill everybody that's in the pen that's big enough to die. [laughs] And, it's not safe, and it's not a smart practice. (B, R 16)

This rancher could reach back into his childhood to capitalize on a generational link with his grandfather when deciding whether to tranquilize cattle. By choosing to accept the inheritance offered by his ancestors, he magnified his own knowledge. His explanation also illustrates how the relationship between "culture-specific symbols [can] resonate important values" (Osborn, 1990, p. 123). In the telling, the rancher's boyhood experience with his grandfather becomes a parable for living amidst modern confusion.

This sort of experience qualifies a person for membership in a select group that neither owning land nor growing up on a ranch automatically ensures. Eagerness to encounter the trials, fight the battles, enjoy the pleasures, and learn from each experience is essential for membership. Wisdom acquired through experience enables ranchers to cope with challenges, problems, and uncertainties.

Independence

Common sense prepares ranchers for independence, the second mytheme within the stewardship myth. As with the first, its significance lies primarily in its contribution to the notion of stewardship, rather than in its uniqueness to ranchers. As one informant suggested, "I think that some of those things [decisions] should be left to the judgement of the individual who is taking care of the land" (C, R 17). Terms for independence reflected the importance of personal choice. "I don't know if you call ranching easy," a Burnet County rancher of 31 years stated, "but it's a great way of life. . . . I enjoy it." He added, "Even if I didn't make money and just could survive, I'd feel I'd been involved in it. I do it as a way of life. You know, I've spent 23 years down in the back porch of Austin in the construction business. Its pressures and things, you know. . . . It's just a good feeling to get out there where you don't have somebody telling you what to do and to make your own decisions" (P, R 28, 30). A Kimble County rancher declared, "People in the livestock business . . . they are so independent, and they have their own opinions" (R, R 1). "And each person has their own priorities and their own goals," another Burnet County rancher added (A, R 22). Part of independence, then, is autonomy—doing your own thing, being your own boss, making your own decisions, setting your own priorities and goals.

Although some people find such flexibility frustrating, a Hamilton County couple who chose to be interviewed in their living room thrived on that flexibility. "Actually you're your own boss. That's the easiest part," commented the woman (D, R 11). Nodding his head in assent, her partner added, "I just go ahead and do what I want to. . . . We may not be making any money, but we're never unemployed" (D, R 14). A Comal County rancher commented that "the easiest part is setting your own hours . . . the fact that you don't have someone else telling you what to do . . . because I worked for another guy for a while right after I graduated from college. I like it a lot better being my own boss" (O, R 13). The opportunity to make their own decisions eases their daily struggles. Even though their profession remains fraught with uncertainty, the stress accompanying that uncertainty is mitigated by the perception of personal freedom. Their sense of flexibility helps them to survive dramatic changes from the outside world.

When we asked our informants why they ranched, most were eager to respond but struggled to produce an answer they believed captured the essence of their purpose. Those who persisted, eventually turned to a story. During one conversation a Kimble county rancher attempted several times to explain why he continued to ranch. Finally, he told us the following story:

> What is the most independent lifestyle that you know of? If you had to pick one lifestyle that independence is its hallmark what is that? . . . Our history, our romance. The part makes it such a wonderful lifestyle is . . . if you get five ranchers in the same room and ask them, "Ok at lamb marking time, how do you round your lambs up?" [First rancher's reply:] "Well, we still do it the old way. We are at the back of the pasture by sun-up; we round our sheep up before it gets hot, so they won't lay down in the bushes. . . . We get them in and cut the lambs off the ewes, and I still use the old all-in-one castrator. I think that is the best way; that way you pull the cord out . . . then I doctor them with the docking fluid, and then we'll hold them all up in the trap [small pasture] for a day or so until the lambs all find their mamas and they get back over the shock." "Nah," second [rancher] will say. "We use a four-wheeler because we don't like to keep the horses up and feed them. We feel that it is a whole lot cheaper to do that, and we use rubberbands on ours [lambs] because we find that the trauma and the stress isn't as bad." And the third [rancher] says, "Shoot, I honk my stuff up [the rancher is using his pick-up truck horn to call in his livestock]. I got a cleared trap [small pasture] out there that is three hundred acres. I can honk every ewe and her lamb in. I pour my cowboys out of a sack [the rancher is using feed to lure the stock]. I don't have to keep a horse or a four-wheeler. I can get all of my stuff up . . . and we use a burdizzo, and we'll earmark 'em; we'll swallow fork [cutting a niche in the lamb's ear for identification] the older ewe lambs one way, the buck lambs the other way." . . . So, [our informant concluded] by its very nature no one does the same thing. (H, R 16)

This informant was trying to paint for us a picture of how the rancher uses wisdom gained from personal experience to make decisions for the benefit of domestic animals raised on the land. In his story, independence enables ranchers to use their experience to care properly for their animals' health. Our informants insisted that their "very nature" required ranchers "to do their own thing." They could not function without independence because the freedom to decide how best to manage their land and livestock was vital to their ability to implement practices that their common sense told them would nurture the life on their ranch.

Human-Land Connection

Common sense combined with independent action culminates in ranchers' awareness of the human-land connection. One rancher portrayed the depth to which his identification with the land extended when he told us, "I feel like I have roots growing right out of my feet right into this land out here, and if you think I'm going to do something to it that is going to be environmentally catastrophic to it, that's a joke, and I would defend it [the land] against anything" (R, R 18). This awareness of the human-land connection contributes to a holistic attitude towards the ecological system in which they participate. Our informant described his belief that the struggle to take care of the land led ranchers to develop a sense of stewardship. He explained that "most people that own country . . . they kind of have their own environmental attitude, and the majority of the people that came by the country the hard way, they are going to take care of it" (R, R 3). Experience with the land forms the basis for an environmental ethic that requires fierce commitment to sustain and protect the biotic web.

Experience unites ranchers with land, which enables them to operationalize important symbolic values. For example, working hard to acquire, care for, and maintain the land is a value evident in our informants' discourse. They gain a sense of pride in their accomplishments when they combine knowledge of the land with their work ethic. One rancher proudly explained that "I came into this world without any land. . . . My family didn't own any land. But over a period of time, my family would buy at high prices about 400 acres of land and pay for it. . . . And that's a fairly good accomplishment, you know, in these days" (P, R 100).

Descriptions of ranching as a way of life reveal an emotional connection to the land, and also illustrate how symbolic and material aspects of this meaning system are intertwined. A Kimble County rancher's description of sharing a "common sense of stewardship and pride in our family land" (H, R 1) reflected her symbolic identification with land. Another informant emphasized the strength of his bond to the land by explaining that the land had enriched his experience as a parent. He stated, "If you don't like to ranch, don't ranch . . . but if you enjoy doing it, do it. I raised my two children here on this place and I'm very proud of them. They both turned out real good. They have some common sense and a fairly good education, and they turned out to be good people, and I think raising them like this had a lot to do with it" (J, R 2). This interpretation of the land's positive influence on their children galvanizes the bond between ranchers and their land. A Burnet County landowner captured the reciprocal nature of the relationship between human and land when he told us that "any kind of agriculture is rewarding. You go through the seasons, and you plant, and you harvest, and suffer all the grief that is in between. But you have a beginning and you have an end" (A, R 62). The seasonal nature of their work experience regularly reminds ranchers of their interdependency with the biotic web.

Our informants described themselves as inextricably connected elements in this diversified system. A Hamilton County man indicated his reluctance to exterminate any species, reserving that task for God: "I don't think any animal ought to be wiped off the face of the this earth because I think that its all a link and chain the good Lord put here. And, we are not the ones who are left to determine whether it needs to leave or not. He put it here for some reason" (B, R 15). However, a Burnet County rancher indicated that, while all species are important, environmental ethics that ignore the needs of humans are inappropriate. He explained, "A preservation attitude will not—or concept—will not help the species. It has to be a conservation attitude. If they want to eliminate mankind from the system and his activities—Umm—I don't think you can do that. Yeah, they have to be considered. We are part of the system" (A, R 91). The human-land connection mytheme thus extends to the interdependence of all life forms (including humans), because all depend on the land for their survival.

Common sense leads ranchers to appreciate diversity and to recognize that nature includes more than the beautiful. They have learned that nature's only constant is change, and that change often is violent. They regularly experience disease, predation, birth, and death, all of which exemplify violent aspects of the natural world. One man discussed his lambing operation with us: "Right now sheep are lambing, and you can go down there and see baby lambs that are not an hour old—and that sort of thing is an enjoyable part of it." Both his eye contact and his voice broke as he continued, "Of course dragging out the dead ones, that's not all that great" (D, R 19). A Hamilton County rancher expanded on this idea:

> We have a lot of city people who come out here, and they just think that oh, this is the easiest thing in the world. They don't see the underlying things that go on, the tragedies. There's little daily tragedies. . . . When you're from the country, you understand the normal things that happen through life, but people in the cities don't see those things, and when they see . . . animals that are sick or dying or dead, they become very overly emotional. They don't see it in its natural light. (D, R 16)

These experiences present both birth and death as integral to life, rather than presenting life and death as opposites. According to our informants, outsiders' delicate sensibilities regarding death and suffering indicate failure to understand biotic "reality."

People who have developed considerable sensitivity to the fundamental organization of the biota are offended by claims that their struggle to coexist with the "natural" world cannot be compatible with wildlife. One informant explained:

> I don't want to see any animal gone, but if I have to choose between the warbler and my little one, the warbler will lose every time. . . . But you know, I don't think that we have to make that choice. I think that I can still take out my underbrush and still leave them some nests. We have a lot of big, big, old cedar trees here, and there's the main thing. From what I understand, the big ones are the main things that we can't take out. If that's true then that doesn't hurt me at all because I don't need to take the big ones out. I only get the ones that are two feet tall, and when they get thicker, I may have to take a few out because we run a cross fence so we can keep a more ecological state on the ranch. But we're talking about a strip, wide enough to run a fence through, you know. (B, R 24)

Another echoed this sentiment, "I don't think that ranching is necessarily detrimental to the golden-cheeked warbler. I think they're compatible" (P, R 21). Rather than attempting to exterminate wildlife, they have attempted to sustain the biotic web by incorporating diversity into their range-management practices.

These symbolic connections to the land rest firmly in materiality, for land provides the economic resources needed to maintain their lifestyle. It produces cash crops for sale, grass for livestock production, and habitat for wildlife (which generates income from hunting leases). Most of our informants, however, described money as a necessary evil required to maintain a way of life that allowed them to operationalize their values. One Kimble County man chuckled as he explained, "I grew up on a ranch when I was young and ranched all of my life and liked to ranch. That's the reason that I ranch is because I like to do it. I just love to do it. It is the best life in the world and the poorest living there is" (J, R 1). Ranchers see themselves as enmeshed in a complex web of life, along with their land, other domestic plants and animals, and wildlife. They contribute to the rich texture of this web by making independent judgments based on their common sense.

Ranchers' Distinctive Twist on Stewardship

Practices emerging from common sense, independence, and the human-land connection merge to create a distinctive tale of stewardship that relates to other mythic tales basic to U.S. culture. We will now explore present and potential connections between stewardship (as articulated by our informants), frontier myths, and agrarian myths.

Stewards Are Not Frontier Heroes

Slotkin (1985, p. 15) argues that "the frontier myth is arguably the longest-lived of American myths with origins in the colonial period and a powerful continuing presence in contemporary culture." The basic tenets of the frontier myth in the United States are derived from a Western European world view. European explorers and settlers saw the New World as wilderness and perceived a challenge to subdue it. The appearance of unlimited resources invited exploitation, and the vast empty spaces provided a place for unwanted or unneeded people (Peterson, 1990). The Turner Thesis (1947) both popularized and legitimized the frontier myth as an appropriate explanation for U.S. patterns of thought and action. For example, Short (1987, pp. 4, 5) claims that "the [U.S.] frontier experience help[ed] shape a unique civilization." Through their experiences on the frontier, "Americans shed their old-world cultural baggage and assumed traits that set them apart from their forefathers: traits being primarily individualism, democracy, nationalism, and mobility." Frontier heroes, then, venture where others dare not go. They are gamblers who can win and lose a fortune overnight. Although they prepare the path for civilization, they are forever exiled from its comforts. Hundreds of popular culture products ranging from movies to books to clothing have further reified this image of the American West and its human inhabitants.

Peterson (1991) argues that U.S. farmers are motivated by values emanating from the frontier myth. However, our informants did not describe themselves as frontier heroes, at least not in a stereotypical sense. While they did not reject the frontier myth, they did not see it as central to their roles as land stewards. In fact, they attributed values normally associated with the frontier myth to those ranchers who are characterized as "bad stewards." Our informants were proud of their willingness to exercise voluntary restraint when working the land. Rather than glorifying the frontier notion of "conquering" the land, they ascribed to Leopold's (1966) claim that "there is value in any experience that exercises those ethical restraints collectively called 'sportsmanship'" (p. 178). Some people might claim that Leopold's "sportsmanship" ethic is inappropriate for this context because the sportsperson loses game by behaving with restraint, while the rancher gains long-term income by behaving with restraint. However, we consider the application especially relevant to conflicts over endangered species habitat because it is unlikely that any individual will reap economic benefits in her/his lifetime by exercising restraint. The common practice of leaving "wild" areas for non-game wild animals such as songbirds, rather than using all available land for grazing, is not designed to produce economic benefits for anyone on *any* time scale.

Additionally, independence, a value primarily cited as an end (purpose) in the frontier myth, is described primarily as a means (agency) by our informants. It enables ranchers to prove themselves worthy of a place in both their cultural and biotic communities. Independence is required because stewardship decisions must be "dictated by [their] own conscience, rather than by a mob of onlookers" (Leopold, 1966, p. 178). Contrary to popular opinion, overgrazed land is not easily identified by visual inspection. What may appear to an uneducated observer to be "overgrazed," may be extremely nutritious native plants that have adapted to the extremes of a particular locale. On the other hand, the lush, emerald-colored vegetation so appreciated by tourists may be a shallow-rooted regrowth (i.e., "broomweed," which grows in areas that have been severely overgrazed) that fails to support life and contributes to erosion. In the golden-cheeked warbler case, as in an increasing number of endangered species conflicts, the primary habitat needed by the targeted wildlife species is privately owned. Onlookers undermine the necessary cooperation between ranchers and the environmentally oriented public when they devalue the ranchers' ethical code by categorizing it as a variant of the stereotypical frontier myth.

Increasingly confining regulations imply that ranchers' common sense is irrelevant to proper environmental management. These regulations also devalue ranchers' sense of connectedness with the larger landscape. Insensitivity to an experimental mode of knowing and to the sense of connection with the biota may unnecessarily exacerbate conflict between ranchers and endangered-species habitat managers, as well as sharpen political hostilities between those who would secure the public good by conserving natural resources and those who would secure it by maintaining private property rights.

Stewards Are Agrarians

While our informants' tales either challenged or ignored the frontier myth, they echoed sentiments celebrated in the agrarian myth. Jeffersonian agrarianism emphasizes the yeoman farmer's status as a privileged stakeholder in democratic society. "For Jefferson, the agrarian enterprise had a special character because of its association with nature" (Peterson, 1991, p. 293). God had created land and had beckoned the yeoman farmer to cultivate the soil. The farmer's well-being was "not merely physical, it was moral; it was not merely secular but religious." Rural life instilled special values of independence, wholesomeness, happiness, healthiness, and integrity. These distinctive characteristics enabled the farmer to become the "best and most reliable sort of citizen," deserving of society's protection (Braden, 1975, p. 117). Because farmers lived on their own land and were self-sufficient, their way of life was uniquely productive, and the continuing presence of an agrarian landscape enabled modern society to reconcile the contradictions of urbanization and industrialization (Peterson, 1991). Our informants' discourse reflected the Jeffersonian emphasis on living and working on one's own land. It was inconceivable to them that the USFWS could serve the public interest while attempting to restrict private property rights.

A Kendall County rancher explained the importance of the agrarian ideal to his life: "Living in the country—it's more peaceful and it's quieter and it's more restful. If you get far enough away from a large city and the lights, you can see the Milky Way, see the stars. So country living is just simply a very pleasurable type of living" (K, R 3). More than anything else, this individual ranched because he preferred the rural over the urban atmosphere. One Hamilton County rancher expressed her agrarian values in her self-definition: "To be a rancher—they actually have to live close to the earth. . . . If you do not take care of what you own, you will lose altogether. So, therefore, almost all ranchers tend to their soil, and . . . they actually have to be husband of their country" (D, R 6). As our informants described the romantic agrarian idyll they enjoyed, a sense of contentment radiated from the faces that had contorted when describing recent struggles to protect their land from drought or government regulations. Although none had heard of Wendell Berry, they shared his belief that the most lasting bonds between themselves and their land "were not merely those of economics and property, but those, at once more feeling and more practical, that come from the investment in a place and a community of work, devotion, knowledge, memory, and association" (1986, pp. 143-144). The influence of agrarian thought on our informants' concept of stewardship was evident throughout their interviews.

How Stewardship Holds the Ranchers' World Together

Our informants described a rancher as one who resides on or near her/his land. Most described their life as a 24-hour a day, seven days a week, 365 days of the year job. They talked constantly of "making the rounds," which entailed taking a general inventory of their operation. Economic considerations were important because failure meant they would have to leave the ranch. For them, proximity to the land was much more important than whether they owned or leased an acreage.

Common sense contributed to our informants' self-images because only experience could teach ranchers how to be stewards. Although growing up on a ranch introduced them to the land, knowledge was not automatic. Only those who worked with nature, battling both natural and artificial intruders, achieved such knowledge. Common sense emerged from their sustained struggle in behalf of their land. Such knowledge instructed ranchers to exert constant vigilance over the land. Experience with range management practices, seasonal changes, weather and market fluctuations, and industry politics all influenced operations. Tangible results of their physical labor influenced decisions about livestock and range management. They gleaned knowledge from both their ancestors and personal experience to reduce uncertainty and guide them in interpreting new situations.

Within this scenario, ranchers who continually battled with encroaching cedar "knew" it was impossible to eradicate cedar or other invading species (prickly pear, mesquite, thistles, horehound, etc.). They experienced the frustration of spending untold hours and dollars attempting to manage cedar by burning, chaining, spraying, dozing, etc., only to see new growth cedar emerge within what seemed like moments. Given this experiential base, USFWS attempts to preserve cedar seem not only unnecessary, but even somewhat perverse.

Ranchers also described independence, or freedom to make ethical judgments regarding specific ranching activities, as vital for them to function as good stewards. The story describing how three ranchers used three different means to gather their sheep, castrate their buck lambs, and prevent infection emphasizes that they each made different decisions, based on common sense, to accomplish the same thing: care for lambs as efficiently and humanely as possible. The storyteller evidenced pure delight in the diversity illustrated by his tale. It functioned not only to convey important information about stewardship to us but also provided him an opportunity to re-experience his affinity with other members of his group. However, while our informants took pride in the independence that allowed them to set their own hours, be their own bosses, and establish their own priorities, the continuation of these pleasures did not provide primary justification for independence. Instead, independence was a means of providing proper care for the land.

Independence was important because it was the primary means of proving willingness to exercise voluntary restraint when managing land. Ranchers are not unique among U.S. groups in valuing independence. The significance of this mytheme lies more in the way it relates to their sense of stewardship. First, our informants argued that, by usurping the decisions regarding how best to care for land, government officials discredit ranchers' experiential base. Independence provides the only means whereby they can prove their worthiness as good stewards. Only if they are free to use their common sense to care for the land can they both display and re-create their sense of connectedness within the biotic community. Independence compels ranchers to be accountable for their actions towards the land.

The essence of stewardship is rooted in the connection between human and land. Our informants, who saw themselves enmeshed with their land in a biotic web, felt responsible for protecting the biological diversity on their land. Thus, as good stewards they assumed responsibility for managing the land in ways that encourage sustenance of a multi-species system. They perceived that living and working with land enriched the aesthetic quality of their lives, instilled common sense, and developed an appreciation for nature. Their understanding of humans' role in the biota led to an appreciation for diversified habitats on their ranches. Many proudly described the techniques they used to protect habitat for "their" turkey, deer, quail, dove, and various songbirds. However, because ranchers defined themselves almost exclusively in terms of their relationship to land, they insisted that humans were an appropriate part of the system. Because they assumed complete interconnection with their land, it became more than an object, or a means of "making a living." Land became life: their symbol for personal identity, livelihood, and cultural survival.

The belief that *human survival depends on healthy soil* served as a focal point for decisions based in "common sense." Over the years, the land had provided the scene wherein ranchers operationalized their strong work ethic. Our informants demonstrated a deep sense of pride in labor spent acquiring and "improving" the land, sharing tales about how their grandparents and parents had struggled to purchase the land, pay off mortgages, and pay property and inheritance taxes, etc. Their detailed descriptions of how they had improved the land by applying conservation practices recommended by the Soil Conservation Service indicate that they are not uniformly hostile to participation in government sponsored projects. Finally, they ascribed much more than physical survival to the opportunity of working closely with the land. In fact, most interviewees attributed their children's successful lives to growing up on a working ranch.

Economic rationality, while not the primary motivator, also connected people to the land, for land provided "a living." As one reasoned, "We're anxious to do what is good for the land, of course, because we make our living on the land" (C, R 10). The ranching operation provided the primary source of income for most of our informants, and many claimed that netting a profit was difficult. Although they shared the (perhaps naive) belief that other businesses would provide much easier ways to make a living, they still preferred to ranch. Most had tried other occupations such as the military, construction, or real estate, but had returned to ranching.

The stewardship myth drawn out of these three mythemes defined the appropriate relationship between humans and land. Common sense first enabled them to manage their land independently. Secondly, it increased their awareness of interconnections between themselves and their land. This awareness translated into an environmental ethic that featured the value of biological diversity.

Preserving Stability by Obscuring Oppositions

The ranchers' tale, however, fails to respond to at least three crucial issues. Our informants acknowledged that, although stewardship was the ideal, some ranchers failed to measure up. In order for a myth to function as a cultural guide, it must provide means for redeeming, or expelling, those who violate cultural taboos. The stewardship myth is silent on this question. Most wildlife indigenous to the U.S. belongs to the citizenry at large, and designated state and federal agencies are charged with managing these common resources for the benefit of the general public. The golden-cheeked warbler is, therefore, public property. The citizenry has chosen (indirectly) to insure the bird's existence, which is dependent on management decisions regarding private property. Current renditions of the stewardship myth provide no patterns for resolving conflicts with landowners who lack the experiential base to sense their connectedness with their land. In fact, its reliance on the sanctity of private property forbids any group or individual to interfere with an owner's property management choices.

Second, as is the case in all worldviews, elements of the stewardship myth contradict each other. The most obvious potential for conflict arises between the values of interconnection and independence. The biotic web described by ranchers includes not only themselves, and their land, but also other humans. They repeatedly insist that humans must be considered as part of the biota. Ranchers' potential interdependence within that web, however, is severely limited by their concurrent need for independence from other members of their own species.

Other contradictions emerge at the level of practice. For example, ranchers' profound connection with their land sometimes leads to assumptions that conflict with those their knowledge would encourage. Seemingly direct connections with reality, such as those experienced through the senses, help create an illusion of stability in an unpredictable world. Although common sense, which is derived from experience, tells them that visual signs are notoriously inaccurate in determining the health of a pasture, they find comfort in the sensual connection produced by visual images. Hanselka, et al. (1990) illustrate this tendency when pointing out that despite their awareness of its inaccuracy, ranchers rely primarily on "visual inspection of pastures" to monitor the effect of stocking on range conditions (p. 8). In a world where little can be trusted, visual images provide a physical connection between human and land. The problem, in this case, is that ranchers achieve a sense of connectedness with the land at the expense of their common sense.

We are not advocating replacing the stewardship myth with another. In the first place, myths grow up with their cultures and display incredible resiliency against the tinkering of outsiders (Peterson, 1991). As Doty (1986) declares, "Myth expresses what is absolutely real to people" (64). Second, Ivie (1987) cautions against judging any metaphorical construct too harshly, explaining that "regardless of how compelling any metaphor may be . . . its limitations eventually are encountered in its application" (p. 179). Realistic awareness of shortcomings within the stewardship myth need not translate into deterministic acceptance of the present condition. Peterson (1991) argues that "by making mythic images more explicit, we create opportunities to consider breaching old boundaries" (p. 305). The point of this critique is to clarify dimensions of stewardship that create fundamentally dysfunctional perspectives by impeding cooperation between landowners such as our informants and other communities within U.S. culture. That clarification opens the way for re-visioning what it means to own property that, because of its semi-natural condition, provides vital habitat for wildlife.

Premises Shared by Ranchers and Conservation Agencies

In a living myth, otherwise distinct mythemes interweave to support a complex web of beliefs and actions. Stewardship provides our informants with the primary image for what it means to be human. The values of common sense, independence, and human-land connection are specific individuations of this image. Ranchers judge not only themselves, but also others associated with land management, by how completely they incorporate these values into their conduct. The stewardship ethic they articulate protects their values, their income, and their identity. The concept of human stewardship over non-human life forms can complement most conservation orientations (with the possible exception of deep ecology and ecofeminism). Thus, it would be in the interests of both professional and nonprofessional environmentalists to validate, rather than discredit, this perspective when communicating with or about those private landowners upon whom they rely to provide wildlife habitat.

U.S. agencies charged with management of natural resources (including endangered species) subscribe to some version of Aldo Leopold's (1966) land ethic, as do the ranchers we interviewed. The primary difference is that members of the first group probably read Leopold's work as a part of their formal education in "applied ecology," while members of the second group may not have heard his name. Although Leopold's professional writing focused more on wilderness management than on traditional agriculture, he repeatedly argued that a successful land ethic must develop from within the community of private landholders, rather than being established by outside experts.[7] His effort to restore the vitality of the worn-out river-bottom farm he purchased in Wisconsin provided him with an opportunity to live the practices he advocated. Leopold came to believe that a close relationship, based on responsible human action, exists between humans and land. In the final section of *A Sand County Almanac and Sketches Here and There* (where he sets forth his land ethic), he advocates that modern culture is improved by experiences that renew contact between humans and wild nature. He describes the three characteristics that develop as a result of this contact as "split-rail" values, "man-earth experiences," and "sportsmanship" (pp. 177, 178). The "split-rail" value refers to physical experiences that remind people of their "distinctive national origin, increasing their awareness of history" (p. 177). "Man-earth experiences" remind humans of their dependency on other life forms. "Sportsmanship" is found in any experience that encourages the individual to exercise ethical restraints.

The dimensions of stewardship identified by our informants have an uncanny resemblance to the three values articulated by Leopold. Ranching is the experience that puts humans into everyday contact with nature. Leopold's definition of the "split-rail" value fits with the common-sense knowledge that ranchers respect. They work hard, not because the law requires it of them, but because they are loyal to the land and to their ancestors. Much like Leopold's "sportsmanship" value, our informants' peculiar notion of independence as a means of assuring one's place within the community emphasizes the principle of ethical restraint. Ranchers use common sense to guide their judgments about appropriate actions towards the land. Voluntary adherence to their environmental code encourages them to practice responsible stewardship, which includes leaving habitat expressly designated for wildlife. The final characteristic, the "man-earth experience," parallels ranchers' human-land connection. Ranchers' experiences provide them with a knowledge that develops only from living for a sustained amount of time with the land and heightens their awareness of humanity's existence as part of the biotic web. Their experiences shape an environmental attitude that, in turn, strengthens their connection with nature. They express a strong belief that their own existence (both aesthetic and economic) is inextricably bound to the land. As stewards, they view themselves as caught up in a struggle to preserve the integrity of the biotic web on and around their land, while providing food and fiber for human civilization.

Because environmental conflict such as that over golden-cheeked warbler habitat will continue to proliferate, it seems counterproductive for environmental professionals to ignore the similarities between these two ethical perspectives. Acknowledgement and legitimization of ranchers' chosen role as land stewards does not necessarily entail endorsement of specific practices, for all roles are subject to multiple performances. It does, however, provide the opportunity for dialogue among all people who share an interest in natural environments. Rather than violating the landowners' self-image, this more profitable approach would stress common values and interests shared by ranchers and USFWS personnel. De-valuing ranchers' common sense breaks down the human-land connection and with it the potential for constructing a partnership for managing natural resources. Given the need to preserve habitat that is privately owned, disregarding landowners' perspectives eliminates an important voice from the debate over management of endangered species.

Opportunities to Enrich the Public Voice

Despite the possibilities for developing partnerships within the golden-cheeked warbler controversy, only shrinking, isolated pockets of people work *directly* with nature on a daily basis. Given that decision-making regarding environmental policy actually may become less efficient upon the retrieval of their voices, some may prefer to leave them silent. There are, after all, fundamental differences between the goals of the USFWS and those of our informants. Perhaps their disenchantment with public discourse is all to the good. Justice Harlan cautions against this tendency however, when he observes that democratic dialogue "may often appear to be only verbal tumult, discord, and even offensive utterance." He adds, however, that this "verbal cacophony" is a "necessary side effect" of the demands on a public discourse that must enable divergent versions of collective identity to emerge (Post, 1993, p. 663). Public discourse, then, is the process whereby the public is "constituted through the reconciliation of individual and collective autonomy" (p. 671). This means that all versions of reality, all legislative enactments, remain open to inquiry. A lively public discourse requires that the collective identities and power relationships among "environmentalists," "ranchers," and "government bureaucrats" always remain open-ended.

Post points out that "democracy attempts to reconcile individual autonomy with collective self-determination by subordinating governmental decision making to communicative processes sufficient to instill in citizens a sense of participation, legitimacy, identification" (p. 660). When the public sphere is healthy, even citizens who disagree with legislative enactments or their means of implementation remain participants in the political community because of their engagement in these communicative processes. In contrast, people who owned golden-cheeked warbler habitat learned of the decision that would profoundly affect their lives only at the implementation stage. They did not hear about the proposed Balcones Canyonlands National Wildlife Refuge until the USFWS informed them that, as a part of the recovery plan for the golden-cheeked warbler, the U.S. Government had decided to convert some of their land into a refuge. The plan required some owners to sell their property and required others to obtain USFWS authorization for future land management practices.

The significance of public participation in political dialogue has been questioned by scholars from a variety of disciplines in both the social and physical sciences. They have pointed out that because human beings are subject to natural laws (such as gravity), to institutional structures (such as bureaucracy), and cultural rules (such as racism), freedom is merely an illusion. While this denial of freedom presents an important critique of modern society, it can limit us to viewing humans as objects of regulation, simply subject to the laws of cause and effect. However, as Burke (1984) argues, while the human experience is grounded in material existence, materiality is insufficient to explain human motivation. Rather, more complete explanation can be achieved by exploring symbolic action, or the creative means of provoking cooperation. There is no question that the quality of our public discourse is problematic, and that the ideals of self-determination differ from the realities of U.S. politics. However, democratic self-governance would be all but impossible in the absence of that public discourse. Goodnight (1992) argues that an emphasis on expanding the possibilities for participation in public discourse need not preclude critique, and may aid in the needed "recovery of the public sphere" as a locus for resolving disputes (p. 254).

Conflicts over management of habitat for endangered species offer an especially rich context for exploring the problems associated with the elitism that threatens to further erode the public sphere. A USFWS refuge manager illustrated this elitism when he explained, "We got real good reasons and we got real good laws that tell us how we will operate the refuge system. And it's not a democracy" (L, R 44). He was not interested in the input of people who were not "cosmopolitan." Instead, he worried that it "is kind of scary in today's world when you think about making your decisions based on what you've seen within 15 miles of your home for all your life" (L, R 46). However, managing privately owned land for a publicly owned resource complicates this approach. The USFWS needs the cooperation of private land-owners to provide habitat for those animals and plants it has listed as threatened or endangered (much less the hundreds on its waiting lists).[8] Landowners are aware that the "habitat" they manage is attractive because it remains capable of sustaining the targeted endangered species, while surrounding habitat has been degraded. Yet, rather than including the people who have maintained and enhanced these habitats in the decision making process, the USFWS has presented landowners with finished plans for habitat management.

Attempts to negotiate the intricate channel between managing habitat for endangered species and the venerated institution of private property illuminate the legal labyrinth regarding private property rights that environmental regulations have revealed. The Anglo-American common law tradition treats private property and liberty of contract as fundamental institutions that should be limited as little as possible (Epstein, 1985). Although it is impossible to say precisely how much unilateral control one must retain over a piece of land for that land to count as one's private property, as a general rule the concept of land as private property weakens as the law wrests unilateral control from the hands of a landowner. At some point, the individual retains so little control over land as to make the appellation *private* property meaningless (Varner, 1994).

Our informants, along with the larger U.S. culture, place a premium on the protection of property rights. However, they have learned that if an endangered species is discovered to inhabit their land (or geographically similar land that is near their land), they may be required to sell the property or to alter their management practices. If someone, even someone who lacks experiential knowledge, determines that certain practices may damage the endangered species' habitat, the person who has held stewardship over that land loses decision-making power. Most current environmental regulations (i.e., clean air and clean water) can be justified because they prevent harm to other persons. However, endangered species management policies treat land as a public resource which is owned in common and which individuals only hold in a stewardship capacity (Varner, 1994). Although our informants did not elaborate on how the stewardship myth transforms the concept of private property, some modification seems possible within the notion of owner as steward or trustee. Perhaps further discussion of the stewardship myth could help specify to what extent, and in which directions, the current growth in environmental regulation is compatible with land as private property. However, by delegitimizing the ranchers' culture, USFWS rhetoric precludes discussion.

Dialogue holds great potential for U.S. environmentalism, for our informants told of an American West where one's independence primarily functioned to foster inclusion in both the cultural and biotic communities. Our informants created an idealized scenario wherein they became consubstantial with the land. Although the theme of struggle which is so fundamental to the frontier myth remains important in their story, theirs is a struggle to protect, rather than to subdue, the land. By their own admission, the degree to which each landowner achieves that state varies widely across time and space. However, the myth of stewardship provides a way for them to connect the particularities of their own situations with the broader community of those who work directly with nature. Through it, they make sense of the contradictions within their lives, without negating them. Whether stewardship creates a more or less "accurate" picture of ranch life than the traditional frontier myth, is a matter of less importance than its value as a vehicle for explaining the lives of landowners (both to themselves and to others). It conveys the essence of their individual struggles, while its ideas are general enough to apply in each person's situation. Burke (1989) suggests that an appropriate myth for contemporary society must offer "a vision that transcend[s] the political, yet that ha[s] political attitudes interwoven with it" (p. 310). A revised concept of stewardship may offer such a vision, while encouraging the retrieval of lost voices and easing their way back into the public sphere. Although each new voice adds to the discordance of an already boisterous debate, U.S. environmentalism rings hollow if it silences the rancher who is rooted in the land.

Notes

1. Doty (1986) uses the term "mytheme" to identify individual mythic themes that emerge from a text. Taken together, these mythemes constitute a "mythological network" that defines the world and the place of humans within that world (pp. 10-29).
2. There are several popular renditions of the frontier myth. The 20th-century frontier has been identified with increasingly diverse scenes, such as the "old west," outer space, the inner city, the subconscious, and darkness. For a summary of frontier images associated with European settlement of North America, as well as those commonly found in contemporary U.S. culture, see Peterson (1986a), pp. 17-32. Although there are many variants of the U.S. frontier myth, all emphasize human control over nature. For a thorough discussion of this myth see Slotkin (1985).
3. Oravec (1981) provided one of the earliest analyses of environmental discourse with her rhetorical criticism of John Muir's rhetoric of preservationism. Environmental crises that directly threaten human health have provoked the majority of communication analyses. Farrell and Goodnight (1981) explored the inadequacy of language used to respond to the partial meltdown at the Three Mile Island nuclear power-generating plant, and Luke (1987) examined the rhetorical strategies used by the media to portray the Chernobyl disaster. Waddell (1990) analyzed the role of *pathos* in a policy-making process surrounding potentially hazardous recombinant DNA experiments. Krendal, Olson, & Burke (1992) and Renz (1992) examined responses to health risks associated with incineration effects and recycling behavior.
Others have studied communicative dimensions of environmental organizations. Lange (1990) and Short (1991) presented (respectively) a cultural analysis and a rhetorical analysis of Earth First!'s radicalism. Bullis and Thompkins (1989) examined organizational change in the U.S. National Forest Service. Additional work has focused on the rhetoric of environmental disputes. Cox (1982) critiqued the rhetorical strategy of representing an opponent's decisions as irreversibly damaging to nature. Oravec (1984) analyzed differential constructions of the "public good" in the Hetch Hetchy controversy, and Peterson (1988) explored the construction of authority in a hearing on wilderness designation. Williams and Treadaway (1992) critiqued Exxon's response to the Valdez oil tanker spill. Lange (1993) provided a broad cultural analysis of the forest management conflict in the Pacific Northwest, and Moore (1993) analyzed the public argument surrounding management of habitat for the northern spotted owl.
4. The existence of public hearings does not ensure public participation in policy formation. Davies (1984) argues that public hearings tend to be occasions for examination and justification of decisions already made rather than occasions for public participation in decision making. Caldwell (1988) indicates that public participation in Environmental Impact Analysis is accepted by government officials as "inevitable," but not useful (p. 80). Goodnight (1982) argues that although such forums "are festooned with the trappings of deliberation . . . they are designed to succeed by means inimical to . . . active participation" (p. 215).
5. Personnel from Texas Agricultural Extension Agency, the U.S. Soil Conservation Service, and Texas Parks and Wildlife Department also have corroborated this information in personal interviews with both authors.
6. The following questions were used as a general guide for interviews:
    1. Do you ranch?
    2. What type of operation do you run?
    3. How has ranching changed since you began?
    4. What do you think are the easiest aspects of ranching now?
    5. What do you think are the most difficult aspects of ranching now?
    6. Do you participate in government programs?
    7. Do you feel the benefits of the programs outweigh the costs?
    8. How much effect does the overall economy have on the way you ranch?
    9. In general, how do you feel about the Endangered Species Act?
    10. What have you heard about the golden-cheeked warbler and the juniper issue?
    11. To what extent do you feel the Endangered Species Act has affected you?
    12. How do you feel about the status of your land?
    13. Do you feel you were informed about the public meetings on the listing of the golden-cheeked warbler?
        Quotations from interview transcripts are identified with two letters and a number. The letters identify the speaker, and the number identifies the utterance within that speaker's transcript.

7. For a complete bibliography of Aldo Leopold's publications see Leopold (1991) pp. 349-370.

8. This is even more critical when considering endangered plants, the continued existence of which probably has more direct repercussions for human survival than does the survival of any endangered animal. Unlike animals, wild plants belong to the property owner, who can destroy them if their existence presents management difficulties.

Works Cited

Anderson, J. A. (1987). *Communication research: Issues and methods.* New York: McGraw-Hill.

Baccus, J. T. (1991, September). Juniper management for the golden-cheeked warbler. In *Managing rangelands and endangered species: Compassion, compatibility, and compromise.* Symposium conducted at the meeting of the Texas Section, Society for Range Management, Austin, TX.

Bean, M. J. (1993, May/June). Fortify the act. *National Parks.* pp. 22-23.

Berry, W. (1986). *The unsettling of America: Culture & agriculture.* New York: Avon.

Braden, W. (1975). Myths in a rhetorical context. *The Southern Speech Communication Journal, 40,* 113-126.

Bullis, C., & Tompkins, P. K. (1989). The forest ranger revisited: A study of control practices and identification. *Communication Monographs, 56,* 287-306.

Burke, K. (1969). *A Rhetoric of motives.* Berkeley, CA: University of California Press.

Burke, K. (1984). *Permanence and change* (3rd ed.). Berkeley, CA: University of California Press.

Burke, K. (1989). Ideology and myth. In J. R. Gusfield (Ed.), *Kenneth Burke on symbols and society* (pp. 303-315). Chicago: University of Chicago Press. (Original work published 1947.)

Caldwell, L. K. (1988). Environmental Impact Analysis (EIA): Origins, evolution, and future directions. *Policy Studies Review, 8,* 75-83.

Cantrill, J. G. (1993). Communication and our environment: Categorizing research in environmental advocacy. *Journal of Applied Communication Research, 21,* 66-95.

Collier, B. (1991, August). Balcones Canyonlands conservation plan. *Texas Parks & Wildlife,* pp. 4-12.

Collier, B. (1992, October 17). Dignitaries celebrate opening of refuge. *Austin American Statesman,* p. B5.

Cox, J. R. (1982). The die is cast: Topical and ontological dimensions of the *locus* of the irreparable. *Quarterly Journal of Speech, 68,* 227-239.

Davies, R. (1984). The Sizewell B Nuclear Inquiry: An analysis of public participation in decisionmaking about nuclear power. *Science, Technology, & Human Values, 9,* 21-32.

Doty, W. G. (1986). *Mythography: The study of myths and rituals.* Tuscaloosa, AL: The University of Alabama Press.

Epstein, R. (1985). *Takings: Private property and the power of eminent domain.* Cambridge, MA: Polity Press.

Farrell, T. B. & Goodnight, G. T. (1981). Accidental rhetoric: The root metaphors of Three Mile Island. *Communication Monographs, 48,* 272-300.

Goodnight, G. T. (1982). The personal, technical, and public spheres of argument: A speculative inquiry into the art of public deliberation. *Journal of the American Forensic Association, 18,* 214-227.

Goodnight, G. T. (1992). Habermas, the public sphere, and controversy. *International Journal of Public Opinion Research, 4,* 243-255.

Hanselka, C. W., McGinty, A., Rector, B. S., Rowan, R. C., & White, L. D. (1990, September). *Grazing and brush management on Texas rangelands: An analysis of management decisions.* Texas Agricultural Extension Service, The Texas A&M University System, College Station, TX.

Higgins, M. A. (1991). Bridging the communication gap between farmers and nonfarmers. *Journal of Applied Communication Research, 19,* 217-222.

Holle, D. (October 1993). Personal communication with author.

Huspek, M. & Kendall, K. E. (1991). On withholding political voice: An analysis of the political vocabulary of a 'non-political' speech community. *Quarterly Journal of Speech, 77,* 1-19.

Isbel, C. M. (1993, March-April). Endangered species update. *Audubon,* 111-113.

Ivie, R. L. (1987). Metaphor and the rhetorical invention of cold war "idealists." *Communication Monographs, 54,* 165-182.

Kohm, K. A. (1991). The act's history and framework. In K. A. Kohm (Ed.), *Balancing on the brink of extinction: The Endangered Species Act and lessons for the future* (pp. 10-22). Washington, DC: Island Press.

Krendal, D. A., Olson, B., & Burke, R. (1992). Preparing for the environmental decade: A field experiment on recycling behavior. *Journal of Applied Communication Research, 20*, 19-36.

Lange, J. (1990). Refusal to compromise: The case of Earth First! *Western Journal of Speech Communication, 54*, 473-494.

Lange, J. (1993). The logic of competing information campaigns: Conflict over old growth and the spotted owl. *Communication Monographs, 60*, 239-257.

Leopold, A. (1966). *A Sand County almanac, and Sketches here and there.* New York: Oxford University Press.

Leopold, A. (1991). *The river of the mother of god and other essays by Aldo Leopold.* S. L. Flader and J. B. Callicott (Eds.). Madison, WI: University of Wisconsin Press.

Lincoln, B. (1989). *Discourse and the construction of society: Comparitive studies of myth, ritual and classification.* New York: Oxford University Press.

Lincoln, Y. & Guba, E. (1985) *Naturalistic inquiry.* Beverly Hills, CA: Sage.

Luke, T. W. (1987). Chernobyl: The packaging of transnational ecological disaster. *Critical Studies in Mass Communication, 4*, 351-375.

McCracken, G. (1988). *The long interview.* Newbury Park, CA: Sage.

McEntee, R. (1992, October 17). Political leaders take refuge (photo caption). *Austin American Statesman,* p. B5.

Moore, M. P. (1993). Constructing irreconcilable conflict: The function of synecdoche in the spotted owl controversy. *Communication Monographs, 60*, 258-274.

Oravec, C. (1981). John Muir, Yosemite, and the sublime response: A study in the rhetoric of preservationism. *Quarterly Journal of Speech, 67*, 245-258

Oravec, C. (1984). Conservation vs. preservation: The public interest in the Hetch-Hetchy controversy. *Quarterly Journal of Speech, 70*, 444-458.

Osborn, M. (1990). In defense of broad mythic criticism. A reply to Rowland. *Communication Studies, 41*, 121-127.

Peterson, T. R. (1986a). *Conceptual metaphor in soil conservation service rhetoric and farmers' responses.* Unpublished doctoral dissertation, Washington State University.

Peterson, T. R. (1986b). The will to conservation: A Burkeian analysis of dust bowl rhetoric and American farming motives. *Southern Speech Communication Journal, 52*, 1-21.

Peterson, T. R. (1988). The rhetorical construction of institutional authority in a senate subcommittee hearing on wilderness legislation. *Western Journal of Speech Communication, 52*, 259-276.

Peterson, T. R. (1990). Jefferson's yeoman farmer as frontier hero: A self-defeating mythic structure. *Agriculture and Human Values, 7*, 9-19.

Peterson, T. R. (1991). Telling the farmers' story: Competing responses to soil conservation rhetoric. *Quarterly Journal of Speech, 77*, 289-308.

Peterson, T. R., Witte, K., Enkerlin-Hoefflich, E., Espericueta, L., Flora, J. T., Florey, N., Loughran, T., & Stuart, R. (1994). Using informant directed interviews to discover risk orientation: How formative evaluations based in interpretive analysis can improve persuasive safety campaigns. *Journal of Applied Communication Research, 22*, 199-215.

Post, R. (1993). Managing deliberation: The quandary of democratic dialogue. *Ethics, 103*, 654-678.

Rakow, L. (1986). Rethinking gender research in communication. *Journal of Communication, 36*, 11-26.

Renz, M. A. (1992). Communicating about environmental risk: An examination of a Minnesota county's communication on incineration. *Journal of Applied Communication Research, 20*, 1-18.

Satterfield, J. E. (1993). A tale of sound and fury: The environmental record of the 102nd Congress. *Environmental Law Reporter, 23*, 10015-10025.

Short, B. (1987, November). *The plundered province: Rhetorical form and the history of the American west.* Paper presented at the meeting of the Speech Communication Association, Boston, MA.

Short, B. (1991). Earth First! and the rhetoric of moral confrontation. *Communication Studies, 42*, 172-188.

Singleton, J. (1992, October 22). Birds go south; dignitaries gather at wildlife refuge. *North Lake Travis Log.*

Slotkin, R. (1973). *Regeneration through violence: The mythology of the American frontier, 1600-1860.* Middletown, CN: Wesleyan University Press.

Slotkin, R. (1985). *The fatal environment: The myth of the frontier in the age of industrialization, 1800-1890.* New York: Athenaeum Press.

Tauzin, B. and Fields, J. (Aug. 5, 1992a). Letter to colleagues.

Tauzin, B. and Fields, J. (Aug. 5, 1992b). *ESA Reform Bill: Summary of Major Concepts.*

Turner, F. J. (1947). *The frontier in American history.* New York: Henry Holt.

U.S. Department of Interior. (1973, December 28). *Endangered Species Act of 1973* (Pub. L. 93-205,81 Stat. 884; current version at 16 U.S.C. (1531-1543)).

U.S. Department of Interior, U.S. Fish and Wildlife Service. (1987). Two animals proposed for listing. *Endangered Species Technical Bulletin,* 11, 8-14.

U.S. Department of Interior, U.S. Fish and Wildlife Service. (1990). *Endangered and threatened wildlife and plants: Final rule to list the golden-cheeked warbler as endangered* (Federal Register, Vol. 55, No. 249, 53153-53160). Washington, DC: U.S. Government Printing Office.

U.S. Department of Interior, U.S. Fish and Wildlife Service. (1991a). *Land protection plant for Balcones Canyonlands National Wildlife Refuge: Travis, Burnet, and Williamson Counties, Texas.* Austin, TX.

U.S. Department of Interior, U.S. Fish and Wildlife Service. (1991b). *Proposed Balcones, Canyonlands National Wildlife Refuge: Draft environmental assessment.* Austin, TX.

Waddell, C. (1990). The role of *pathos* in the decision-making process: A study in the rhetoric of science policy. *Quarterly Journal of Speech,* 76, 381-401.

Williams, D. E. & Treadaway, G. (1992). Exxon and the Valdez accident: A failure in crisis communication. *Communication Studies,* 43, 56-64.

Varner, G. E. (1994). Environmental law and the eclipse of land as private property. In F. Ferre & P. Hartel (Eds.), *Ethics and environmental policy: Theory meets practice* (pp. 142-160). Athens, GA: University of Georgia Press.

Determined Opposition:
The Wise Use Movement
Challenges Environmentalism
by Phil Brick

Until recently, the idea of a broadly based anti-environmental movement was virtually unthinkable. Since the first Earth Day in 1970, the U.S. environmental movement has enjoyed high levels of public support, fighting for tougher laws to protect the nation's air, water, and natural resources. Now, a well-organized coalition, known as the "Wise Use movement," has emerged to fight these laws and seems to be gaining momentum and political clout in Congress and many state legislatures. Whether the issue is endangered species, wetlands, clean air, or safe drinking water, the environmental movement seems everywhere to be on the defensive against Wise Use assaults that cleverly combine populist rhetoric with corporate-backed political organizing.

Although the environmental movement first dismissed them as extremists or "puppets of industry," the dramatic rise of Wise Use groups coincides with a remarkable reversal of fortune for environmental organizations. To appreciate this reversal, it is useful to recall the high tide of support the environmental movement enjoyed just five years ago. By 1990, polls showed that nearly 8 in 10 U.S. citizens considered themselves to be "environmentalists," and membership in environmental organizations reached record levels following the "greenhouse summer" of 1988 and the wreck of the Exxon Valdez in 1989.[1] However, after steady increases in membership and revenue in the 1980s, some groups, including Greenpeace and the Wilderness Society, have lost a third of their members since 1990.[2]

Environmentalists have also had difficulty securing strong commitments from U.S. presidents. George Bush seemed to renege on his promise to be an "environmental president,"[3] but the environmental movement took heart in the election of Bill Clinton and his running mate, committed environmentalist Al Gore. The

Clinton administration appointed prominent environmentalists to top cabinet-level positions, including Bruce Babbitt (president of the League of Conservation Voters) to the Department of Interior and Carol Browner (a prominent public policy environmentalist) to lead the Environmental Protection Agency (EPA). Yet two years later, the Clinton administration seemed to have abandoned most of its environmental initiatives, including cabinet-level status for EPA, strengthening the Clean Water Act, reauthorization of the Endangered Species Act, and mining and range reform on the nation's public lands.[4]

Green hopes finally faded as Republicans swept both houses of Congress in November 1994. Although eviscerating environmental laws was not an explicit provision in the Republican "Contract With America," it took fewer than 100 days for environmental groups to realize that key provisions of the contract were dangerous. The emphasis on regulatory reform, eliminating unfunded mandates, and expanding private property rights aims at the heart of key environmental laws, including the Clean Water Act, the Clean Air Act, and the Endangered Species Act.[5] Environmental lobbyists, long used to having liberal access to legislators, now complain of being left out of the loop as legislators turn to industry to help them rewrite laws.[6]

Indeed, in the midst of a hostile era, an outspoken opposition has gained a foothold in both industry and government. Senator Slade Gorton's (R-Wash.) proposed revisions of the Endangered Species Act, for example, were written by Wise Use groups, including the Endangered Species Reform Coalition and the Endangered Species Coordinating Council.[7] How environmentalists react to, and fight, Wise Use groups may shape environmental politics in the United States for many years to come.

Explaining Environmental Woes

What accounts for the environmental movement's apparent reversal of political fortune? This question is particularly perplexing because opinion polls consistently indicate that environmental goals continue to enjoy high levels of public support. For example, in a poll of registered voters conducted a month after the 1994 elections, voters were more than twice as likely to say current laws and regulations protecting the environment don't go far enough (41 percent) as they were to say the laws go too far (18 percent).[8] Somehow, the environmental movement's ability to translate broad public support for a cleaner environment into effective public policy is slipping.

Part of the problem can be explained by the movement's own success and the changing nature of environmental problems. First, U.S. rivers, lakes, and air are cleaner today than on the first Earth Day in 1970, the direct result of tough regulations long sought by environmental groups. But a cleaner environment also makes it harder to convince the public that continued vigilance is necessary. This is perhaps reflected in polls showing that fewer than five percent of the U.S. public views the environment as one of the nation's most pressing problems.[9] Second, much of the "easy work" has already been done. For example, it is relatively simple, from a regulatory point of view, to clean up point source pollution (i.e., effluent from factories). Point source pollution typically occurs in high quantities, making it a good target for regulation that benefits many and burdens only a few. But now the cleanup work remaining most often involves non-point source problems (i.e., runoff from farms) and mobile sources (i.e., auto emissions). These sources are harder to regulate because they place burdens on the many instead of the few—for example, annual emission tests for car owners. EPA regulations requiring testing of private automobile emissions under 1990 amendments to the Clean Air Act produced a popular revolt in several states, including Maine, Texas, Delaware, and Louisiana.[10] Similarly, many property owners are unhappy with regulations, especially those protecting wetlands, that prohibit them from developing their property.

There is also growing anxiety about the costs of environmental regulations and their effect on the economy. Facing stiff competition in an increasingly global marketplace, industry is anxious to cut costs by reducing environmental regulations. The United States spent $140 billion in 1994 to comply with EPA regulations, about 2.2 percent of gross domestic product and roughly equivalent to what the federal government spent on Medicare. But the federal government pays only 15 percent of these costs, leaving private businesses to pick up 60 percent of the tab.[11] The U.S. public wants a healthy environment, but in an era of budget cuts, antigovernment sentiments, and industry belt-tightening, it is less clear how much they are willing to sacrifice for it.

Finally, the environmental movement's woes are exacerbated by an acute identity crisis. National organizations and more radical regional groups disagree on how far the movement should go in expanding its claims and broadening its constituency.[12] As Brock Evans of the National Audubon Society lamented, national groups "are being savaged from the left and the right—the Wide Abuse people [as he calls them] are attacking us for being too tough, and our own people on the left are attacking us for not being tough enough. And the center cannot hold."[13]

The Wise Use Movement

Explaining recent troubles only in terms of dynamics within the movement would miss the single most important change in U.S. environmental politics since the first Earth Day: For the first time, the environmental movement faces an opposition that has political and ideological coherence and is capable of organizing on a broad scale. This opposition, the Wise Use movement, is a coalition of industrial, agricultural, and conservative political interest groups organized to capitalize on a relatively narrow, but committed, support base in a way that environmental groups seem to have lost.[14] Wise Use groups, both local and national, now resist every new environmental initiative and are attempting to roll back existing environmental laws in the name of protecting free enterprise and private property from excessive regulations. Many environmentalists see the movement as little more than a collection of phony citizen groups organized by big business to do its bidding. As Jay Hair, president of the National Wildlife Federation, put it, "the self-proclaimed 'Wise Use Agenda' is merely a wise disguise for a well-financed, industry-backed campaign that preys upon the economic woes and fears of U.S. citizens."[15]

But the Wise Use movement is much more than a collection of front groups for industry. Instead, it reflects the growing sophistication of right-wing political organizing in the United States, which is becoming increasingly adept at combining ideological guidance (developed at think tanks such as the Heritage Foundation or the Cato Institute), legal advocacy (developed by conservative public interest law firms such as the Pacific Legal Foundation or the Mountain States Legal Foundation), and grassroots political organizing through industry trade associations and local nonprofit organizations.[16]

The Wise Use movement is organized along similar lines. It has national umbrella groups, such as the Center for the Defense of Free Enterprise in Bellevue, Washington, which publishes anti-environmental literature from its own publishing house and has its own legal defense fund. Through these groups, ideas are spread to a network of grassroots organizations, whose members in turn write letters to legislators and local print media. Wise Use organizers boast that they can inundate legislators with thousands of letters against pending environmental legislation in just hours via a nationwide fax network.[17] Underwriting the Wise Use network, of course, is money from industry, mostly from the timber, mining, agriculture, real estate, chemical, oil and gas, and off-road vehicle manufacturing industries.[18]

Apart from the direct challenge to environmental groups' political power, the rise of a coherent opposition has other, more subtle effects. The coalition's populist overtones make the environmental movement's claim to represent the larger public interest—largely unchallenged for 25 years—politically insecure. As forest activist Jeffrey St. Clair put it, "once feared as the most powerful public interest group in America, the environmental movement is now accurately perceived as a special interest group."[19] Shorn of its public interest status, the environmental movement now finds its access to legislators and the media more problematic. In covering environmental topics, for example, the media balances its coverage by airing the views of both sides. And the environmental movement faces an organized and outspoken other side, which changes and redefines the dynamics of the debate.[20] For example, in 1993, a backlash against environmental programs to reduce ozone depletion and prevent global warming received widespread media attention after conservative commentators such as George Will and Rush Limbaugh dismissed all warnings of environmental doom as "scaremongering" and "hoaxes."[21]

The Rise of Anti-Environmentalism

Anti-environmentalism in the United States is not new, with traditional strongholds in agriculture, labor, and industry that have consistently resisted the costs imposed by environmental regulations.[22] Responding to this discontent, Ronald Reagan was the first U.S. president to make a concerted effort to reverse the tide of environmental regulation, which he believed hurt private enterprise and facilitated undesirable expansion of bureaucratic power. But the soldiers he enlisted in his cause, James Watt and Anne Gorsuch Burford, proved to be easy political targets. Neither Watt nor Burford developed the necessary political cover to support their assault on popular environmental laws, and they underestimated environmentalism's depth and power as a broader social movement.[23] Environmentalists successfully demonstrated that the Reagan appointees were too close to the industries they were supposed to be regulating and too willing to give away public resources to private developers.[24] Within three years, both Watt and Burford had been replaced. Reagan continued to resist attempts to strengthen environmental laws during the rest of his tenure but often found bipartisan opposition in Congress.

At the same time, however, the seeds of a more sophisticated anti-environmental movement were being sown. In an obscure 1980 timber industry trade magazine, timber consultant (and future Wise Use organizer) Ron Arnold bitterly criticized industry's clumsy attempts to fight environmentalists and offered prescriptions for a more coherent anti-environmental movement that would come to fruition 10 years later.[25] Arnold argued that using their current tactics, industry would always lose in battles with environmentalists because industry arguments would appear parochial and tainted with self-interest compared with environmental appeals. Arnold suggested that industry instead should replicate citizen action groups common in the environmental movement to give their message the appearance of a broad, public-spirited movement. As Arnold concluded, "Long experience has shown that it is the plain, unvarnished truth spoken by plain, unvarnished citizens, not statements by full-time lobbyists or public communicators, that is most persuasive in shaping public opinion."[26]

Arnold understood that in a pluralist system of competing interest groups, those groups with the coherence and energy of a grassroots support base are most effective. Such groups are especially successful in attracting the attention of politicians looking for reliable voting blocs, favorable media opportunities, and of course, money.[27]

In 1988, Arnold began assembling an eclectic array of interest groups, including traditional opponents of environmental regulation such as natural resource industry trade groups, chemical and pesticide manufacturers, fishermen, real estate developers, off-road vehicle enthusiasts, private property rights advocates, and conservative ideological groups. This was the first attempt to combine interests that previously saw little in common with each other.[28] The coalition is held together by a common disdain for environmentalism, which it sees as the principal threat to either their livelihoods or their way of life. Since 1988, Wise Use groups with names such as People for the West! (which lobbies against mining reform) and the Alliance for America (a coalition of land and property rights groups) have flourished, some with direct industry funding, but others more spontaneously, especially around property rights and public lands issues.[29] Movement leaders report growth from 200 organizations in 1988 to as many as 1,500 groups nationwide in 1995.[30] According to Ron Arnold, "[Wise Use] mailing lists reach more than three million people. Of those, one million actively participate in meetings and write occasional letters to legislators, and 250,000 are 'hard core' activists who are active in their communities and will respond quickly to fax alerts."[31]

Tactics

Two factors account for the determination and growth of Wise Use groups. First, their members are highly motivated ideologically, identifying environmental laws with all the ills they see in the liberal establishment.[32] Second, activists are convinced that environmental regulations threaten jobs, especially for rural U.S. residents. Wise Use groups are generally angrier and hungrier than their environmental counterparts, organizing intensively at the local level, especially in rural areas.[33] Despite their largely anti-environmental agenda, nearly all Wise Use groups cloak themselves in green clothing, claiming to represent the "middle ground between extreme environmentalism and extreme industrialism."[34] Their rhetoric often accuses environmentalists of "putting rats ahead of family wage jobs," impeding economic progress, and "drowning individual rights with big government rules and regulations."[35] Indeed, these sentiments capture the key political issues anti-environmentalists have promoted in recent years: the problems with big government, threats to private property rights, and the loss of jobs due to environmental regulations.

The Watermelon Theme

First, the Wise Use movement depicts environmentalists as predisposed to big government solutions and intrusive regulations. One of their common metaphors describes environmentalism as a watermelon: green on the outside but red on the inside—a joke often repeated on conservative talk radio shows and in Wise Use publications. This tactic has been particularly effective because the U.S. public is increasingly skeptical about the government's ability to solve complex social problems. Polls show that concerns about the role of government, not the state of the economy, most strongly influenced the 1994 election results. Further, those expressing concern about taxes and the size of government as most important in determining their vote outnumbered those identifying environmental issues by more than three to one.[36]

Strong anti-government sentiments help explain the 104th Congress's assault on environmental laws. Although the word "environment" did not appear in the Republicans' Contract with America, House leaders were able to push through regulatory reform measures that would weaken environmental laws such as the Clean Air and Clean Water Acts. Thus, anti-environmental forces are using public disenchantment with government to launch a serious, though indirect, assault on environmental regulations.[37] The strategy puts environmentalists in the uncomfortable position of defending federal regulations at a time when it is politically inexpedient to do so. As Debbie Sease, the Sierra Club's legislative director, lamented, "We have a tremendous problem. We have to go out, reach the public, and get them to understand that they don't want to throw out good environmental legislation with government itself."[38]

After the April 1995 bombing of a federal building in Oklahoma City, which was linked to radical anti-government militia groups, Wise Use leaders have begun to distance themselves from the strong anti-government rhetoric that characterized past campaigns.[39] For some Wise Use groups, this will be difficult, as they have either explicitly endorsed the militia movement or have made virulent anti-government rhetoric an integral part of their organizational appeal.[40]

Private Property Rights

Closely related to their anti-government tactic, but worthy of separate discussion, is the Wise Use movement's focus on private property rights. It is perhaps their most powerful tactic. By portraying government regulations as a threat to private property rights, they touch on deeply held American values of rugged individualism and self-determination—the issue is both eloquently framed and politically charismatic. The argument boils down to this: The Fifth Amendment to the U.S. Constitution guarantees compensation for property taken by eminent domain. Property rights advocates want compensation extended to property "taken" by government regulations, even if the "taking" is only partial.[41] They argue, for example, that because regulations prohibiting the filling of wetlands may make development difficult or impossible and therefore decrease the land's value, the government should compensate landowners, thus paying the true cost of regulation.[42] Several recent Supreme Court rulings, including *Lucas v South Carolina Coastal Commission* (1992) and *Dolan v City of Tigard*, have emboldened property rights advocates, though the legal future of "regulatory takings" is far from clear, and the issue continues to be debated.[43] "Takings" bills have been introduced in dozens of states and are a key provision in the Republican Contract with America.

Environmentalists argue that paying property owners to obey existing laws is not only bad public policy, but it would make most environmental regulations too expensive to implement.[44] However, they recognize that they are treading on sacred ground. Tarso Ramos, a researcher at the Western States Center in Portland, Oregon, describes the Wise Use movement's use of takings as an organizing strategy as a kind of "deviant genius": "It automatically puts environmentalists in the position of defending the federal government, and appeals to anyone who has ever had any kind of negative experience with the federal government, which is a hell of a lot of people."[45]

Wise Use organizers have effectively capitalized on this anger with a highly effective strategy of "politics by anecdote": Small landowners who have suffered financially as the result of wetland regulations or endangered species restrictions are paraded before the media and congressional committees.[46]

The "Jobs versus Environment" Theme

Despite the strength of the first two tactics, many environmentalists concede that the Wise Use movement's greatest success has been to frame key environmental disputes in terms of "jobs versus the environment."[47] This issue taps voter anxiety about the economy, suggesting that environmental protection costs jobs. Although studies have shown the opposite—that overall job growth is strongly correlated with laws protecting the environment—such arguments do not have the political appeal of unemployed loggers demonstrating against spotted owl restrictions on the evening news (nor are they much comfort to the loggers themselves).[48] These images resonate with many U.S. citizens anxious about job security: Family wage jobs for unskilled workers are dwindling, corporations are downsizing, and real wages have been stagnant since 1990.[49] Analysts point out that the U.S. public is less likely to blame corporations for stagnation in labor markets, turning instead to government and other scapegoats who might be seen as taking jobs, including immigrants and environmentalists.[50] One poll found more than half of all respondents agreeing that "environmentalists care more about animals and habitats than about people's jobs."[51]

New Solutions

It is easy for environmentalists to find solace in polls indicating high levels of support for environmental laws promoting public health, conservation of natural resources, and endangered species. It is much harder to convert that support into effective public policy, especially when an increasingly divided environmental movement must face a well-organized and ideologically energized countermovement. It remains to be seen whether or not environmentalism can recapture the public's imagination and renew a sense of commitment to its causes, especially when other social issues such as welfare, health care, and crime currently loom larger in voters' minds.[52] Thus far, the environmental movement has had difficulty adapting to its new political predicament. Its primary response seems to be an attempt to rally traditional supporters to convince legislators to leave environmental laws, and the bureaucracies that implement them, intact. Environmental catastrophe is predicted if this effort fails.[53] At the same time, environmentalists have sought to discredit their opposition by highlighting its connections to industry and its "astroturf" (phony grassroots) nature.[54] This basic strategy has served environmental groups well for decades: Focus attention on an environmental problem about to take us over the precipice, identify an evil culprit, and then rally the troops. But this "doom and gloom" strategy may not be well-suited to today's political setting. Environmentalists are confronting a well-organized opposition, which constantly refutes environmental claims, produces media images of ordinary people who say they will be harmed by environmental restrictions, and points to the growth and rigidity of environmental bureaucracies in federal and state governments.

To succeed, the environmental movement must begin to rethink old strategies and reinvent itself. Environmental problems today are more complex than they were 25 years ago and will require a more creative and diverse set of policy prescriptions than the prohibitive regulations that have characterized the last two decades. Although the U.S. environment has improved due to these regulations, it is also clear that some of them do not work as well as they should. In addition, many generate intense opposition without generating an equally committed constituency.

The Endangered Species Act is perhaps a good example. As Wilderness Society president Jon Roush argues, policies protecting endangered species violate all the prescriptions for popular support:

> They demand that people change deep habits of environmental behavior. They restrict access to resources and limit their use. They demand that people not use available technologies and materials. They claim benefits that are obscure and hard to prove. They ask us to forego benefits today for theoretical ones in the indeterminate future.[55]

And, as Wise Use groups have demonstrated, it creates a committed opposition among people skeptical of government and insecure about their economic futures. The political incompetence of the endangered species legislation, however well intentioned, is summed up by the Wise Use question, "Which would you rather have, a family wage job or a kangaroo rat?" Amid strong anti-regulatory sentiments and a media that favors catchy sound bites over close analysis, rational arguments suggesting that this question is based on a false dichotomy will fall on deaf ears.[56]

New approaches to environmental problems are needed, and, given the current climate of disillusionment with government, they will have to rely less on regulatory coercion and more on market-based programs and local initiatives. If environmentalists vote with their feet and with their pocketbooks, the shift toward such approaches has already begun. While well-known national groups, including the Sierra Club, Greenpeace, the Wilderness Society, and Audubon, have all lost members and revenue since 1990, two groups, the Environmental Defense Fund (EDF) and the Nature Conservancy (TNC), have thrived.[57] EDF membership grew from 100,000 in 1990 to 250,000 in 1994, with budget increases of more than 30 percent.[58] TNC also did well during this period, gaining more than 100,000 new members and increasing its revenues from approximately $138 million in 1990 to $308 million in 1994.[59] Both groups use approaches that differ substantially from the big "beltway" environmental groups.

EDF emphasizes market-based solutions to environmental problems. It is best known for helping draft provisions of the 1990 Clean Air Act that allow firms to sell pollution credits to less efficient firms, thereby rewarding innovative companies who meet or exceed clean air standards and providing incentives for others to follow. EDF is also working on a plan to offer financial incentives to land owners who set aside land for endangered species and is involved in negotiating solutions to simmering land and water use conflicts that have been tied up in the courts for years.[60]

Many in the Wise Use movement have identified TNC as enemy number one. TNC is not only the wealthiest environmental group, it also works with the federal government, often selling back land with strict conservation easements preventing future development.[61] TNC focuses on acquiring habitat critical to threatened and endangered species. It has recently shifted its strategy to work more closely with local communities in an effort to balance economic and conservation goals. For example, TNC worked with the California Rice Industry Association and local rice farmers to make arrangements for seasonal wetlands in California's Sacramento Valley. The changes benefited migratory waterfowl whose numbers had dwindled from 12 million in the late 1970s to 3 million in 1993 because of habitat degradation.[62]

Also, the environmental movement may already be shifting its focus toward membership in more local and regional groups. Many believe that these grassroots groups represent the future of U.S. environmentalism, with attention on local concerns and not on problems in other parts of the country or even overseas.[63] Often more strident in their claims, local and regional groups also tend to have more active members than the checkbook activists who send $25 or $35 to a national environmental organization every year.

The Road Ahead

Ultimately, defending the progress in environmental protection made since 1970 and defining new goals will depend on the attitudes of the U.S. public and the ability of the environmental movement to create and capture those attitudes and translate them into effective public policy. At the moment, the movement seems to be between visions. At the same time, a new opposition movement is articulating a vision of its own, emphasizing freedom from burdensome regulations and promising economic renewal. But with the exception of a few empty platitudes about close connections between private property ownership and stewardship of natural resources, Wise Use groups have no positive program to work toward the clean air, water, and protection of public lands that the public will continue to demand.[64] For this reason, the Wise Use appeal will be limited in the long run, especially if the environmental movement can articulate a vision for the next century that is both ecologically sound and politically savvy.

Notes

1. G. Huber, "Americans Report High Levels of Environmental Concern, Activity," *The Gallup Poll Monthly,* April 1991, 6-12. For an analysis of the surge in public support for environmental issues in the late 1980s, see R. E. Dunlap, "Trends in Public Opinion Toward Environmental Issues: 1965-1990," in R. E. Dunlap and A. G. Mertig, eds., *American Environmentalism: The U.S. Environmental Movement, 1970-1990* (Washington, D.C.: Taylor and Francis, 1992), 89-116; and R. E. Dunlap, "Public Opinion in the 1980s: Clear Consensus, Ambiguous Commitment," *Environment,* December 1991, 10. Also useful is C. J. Bosso, "After the Movement: Environmental Activism in the 1990s," in N. J. Vig and M. E. Kraft, eds., *Environmental Policy in the 1990s: Toward a New Agenda* (Washington, D.C.: Congressional Quarterly Press, 1994), 31-50.
2. For an analysis of the growth of national environmental organizations, see R. C. Mitchell, A. G. Mertig, and R. E. Dunlap, "Twenty Years of Environmental Mobilization: Trends Among National Environmental Organizations," in Dunlap and Mertig, note 1 above, 11-26. On the recent troubles of environmental groups, see F. Clifford, "Environmental Movement Struggling as Clout Fades," *Los Angeles Times,* 21 September 1991, A1; and K. Schneider, "Big Environment Hits a Recession," *New York Times,* 1 January 1995, F4. It is interesting to note that Canadian groups are suffering similar woes. See M. Nichols, "The Greying of the Greens," *Maclean's,* 25 April 1994, 54-55.
3. On the Bush administration's environmental record, see K. Schneider, "Environmental Policy: It's a Jungle in There," *New York Times,* 7 June 1992, D1.
4. See M. Dowie, "A Lighter Shade of Green," *Utne Reader,* July/August 1994, 73-80.
5. See P. Portney, "Beware of Killer Clauses Inside the GOP's 'Contract'," *Washington Post Weekly Edition,* 23-29 January 1995, 21.

6. T. Egan, "Industry Reshapes Endangered Species Act," *New York Times,* 13 April 1995, A9; J. H. Cushman Jr., "House and Science Panels Clash on Wetlands' Fate," *New York Times,* 7 April 1995, A8.

7. K. Kilmer, "Industry Re-writes ESA," *New Voices* 4, no. 4 (1995): 5. Members of the Endangered Species Reform Coalition include the Boise Cascade Political Fund (timber industry) and the Newmont Mining Corporation Political Action Committee.

8. Poll conducted for the National Wildlife Federation by Peter D. Hart Research Associates, 1-4 December 1994.

9. Clifford, note 2 above, page A22.

10. S. H. Verhovek, "Texas Joins Parade of States Colliding with Clean Air Act," *New York Times,* 14 February 1995, A1.

11. Portney, note 5 above, page 21. See also K. Schneider, "As Earth Day Turns 25, Life Gets Complicated," *New York Times,* 16 April 1995, E6. State and local governments account for the remaining 25%.

12. A recent review of tensions in the environmental movement is R. Braile, "What the Hell Are We Fighting For?" *Garbage,* Fall 1994, 28-35. For a larger overview, see R. Gottlieb, *Forcing the Spring: The Transformation of the American Environmental Movement* (Washington, D.C.: Island Press, 1993). A good example of the debate concerning radical environmentalism is M. L. Lewis, *Green Delusions: An Environmentalist Critique of Radical Environmentalism* (Durham, N.C.: Duke University Press, 1992). For an exploration of tensions between local and national groups, see G. Machlis, "The Tension between Local and National Conservation Groups in the Democratic Regime," *Society and Natural Resources* 3, no. 3 (1990): 267-79; and T. Arrandale, "The Mid-Life Crisis of the Environmental Lobby," *Governing,* April 1992, 32-36.

13. Cited in Braile, note 12 above, page 34.

14. For a summary of the Wise Use movement, see J. Krakauer, "Brownfellas," *Outside Magazine,* December 1991, 69-72, 114-16. Other interpretations from environmental publications include W. Poole, "Neither Wise Nor Well," *Sierra,* November/December 1992, 58-61; C. Berlet and W. K. Burke, "Corporate Fronts: Inside the Anti-Environmental Movement," *Greenpeace,* January/February/March 1991, 8-12; and a series by R. Stapleton, "Greed vs. Green," *National Parks,* November/December 1992, 32-37; R. Stapleton, "On the Western Front," *National Parks,* January/February 1993, 32-36; and R. Stapleton, "A Call to Action," *National Parks,* March/April 1993, 37-40.

15. Jay Hair, cited in T. Lewis, "Cloaked in a Wise Disguise," in J. Echeverria and R. Eby, *Let the People Judge: Wise Use and the Private Property Rights Movement* (Washington, D.C.: Island Press, 1995), 13-20. An insightful window into the environmental movement's response to Wise Use is a study commissioned by the Wilderness Society, researched and written by the consulting firm of MacWilliams Cosgrove Snider, *The Wise Use Movement: Strategic Analysis and Fifty State Review,* January 1993. It is available from the Clearinghouse on Environmental Advocacy and Research in Washington, D.C.

16. For analysis of the growing influence of right-wing think tanks, see B. Ruben, "Getting the Wrong Idea," *Environmental Action,* Spring 1995, 21-26. The Heritage Foundation, for example, claims it gets 200 or more stories in newspapers around the country from almost every position paper it sends out. The combined annual budgets of Heritage, Cato, and the American Enterprise Institute are more than $40 million, with large corporate backers, including Coors, Amoco, and Philip Morris.

17. See M. L. Knox, "The World According to Cushman," *Wilderness,* Spring 1993, 28-31.

18. A readily available resource on the Wise Use movement, including sources of funding and short summaries of Wise Use groups, is C. Deal, *The Greenpeace Guide to Anti-Environmental Organizations* (Berkeley, Calif.: Odonian Press, 1993).

19. Cited in P. Mazza, "Ecoactivists Call for Grassroots Rebellion," *Portland Alliance* 15, no. 2 (1995): 6.

20. For a discussion of Wise Use and the media, see Society of Environmental Journalists, "Working Journalists Speak Out on Wise Use," in Echeverria and Eby, note 15 above, pages 348-54.

21. S. Begley, "Is the Ozone Hole in Our Heads?" *Newsweek,* 11 October 1993, 71; S. Budiansky, "The Doomsday Myths," *U.S. News and World Report,* 13 December 1993, 81-91; and J. Olstead, "Global Warming on the Dock," *Geographical,* September 1993, 12-16. Sources suggesting ozone and global warming issues are hoaxes include D. L. Ray and L. Guzzo, *Environmental Overkill* (Washington, D.C.: Regnery Gateway, 1993); and R. A. Maduro and R. Schauerhammer, *The Holes in the Ozone Scare* (Washington, D.C.: 21st Century Associates, 1992). For an analysis of the ozone debate and the politics of science, see F. S. Rowland, "President's Lecture: The Need for Scientific Communication with the Public," *Science* 260 (11 June 1993), 1571-76. A point-by-point refutation of Rush Limbaugh on the environment is in L. Haimson, M. Oppenheimer, and D. Wilcove, *The Way Things Really Are: Debunking Rush Limbaugh on the Environment,* (Washington, D.C.: Environmental Defense Fund, 1995).

22. S. P. Hays, *Beauty, Health, and Permanence: Environmental Politics in the United States, 1955-85* (Cambridge, U.K.: Cambridge University Press, 1987).

23. See discussion in P. Shabecoff, *A Fierce Green Fire* (New York: Hill and Wang, 1993), 203-30; and M. Sagoff, "The Great Environmental Awakening," *The American Prospect,* Spring 1992, 39-47. Although resistance to environmental regulation was strong in the early 1980s, it lacked coherence as a larger social movement. For an articulation of an early challenge to environmentalism from academia, see J. Simon, *The Ultimate Resource* (Princeton, N.J.: Princeton University Press, 1981); and W. Tucker, *Progress and Privilege: America and the Age of Environmentalism* (Garden City, N.Y.: Anchor Press/Doubleday, 1982).

24. On the controversy over public resources, see R. McGreggor Cawley, *Federal Land, Western Anger: The Sagebrush Rebellion and Environmental Politics* (Lawrence, Kan.: University of Kansas Press, 1993).

25. R. Arnold, "The Environmental Battle," a series of eight articles appearing in *Logging Management,* March 1979-May 1980. Much of this material appears in R. Arnold, *Ecology Wars: Environmentalism as if People Mattered* (Bellevue, Wash.: Free Enterprise Press, 1993), chapters 7 and 8.

26. Ibid., pages 60-61.

27. A classic critique of interest group pluralism is T. Lowi, *The End of Liberalism,* 2nd ed., (New York: W. W. Norton, 1979).

28. Miners and ranchers, for example, have long viewed each other with mutual suspicion. The same could be said for fishermen and the timber industry in anadromous fishery areas such as the Pacific Northwest. For a discussion of tensions within the Wise Use movement, see C. Safina and S. Iudicello, "Wise Use Below High Tide Line: Threats and Opportunities," in Echeverria and Eby, note 15 above, pages 119-29; and J. Ellis, "Taking on the Anti-Environmentalists," ibid., pages 295-303.

29. For a state-by-state review of the growth of Wise Use groups across the nation, see MacWilliams Cosgrove Snider, note 15 above, pages 57-272. Many groups have names that obfuscate their intentions. For example, The National Wetlands Coalition, with a duck flying over cattails as a logo, is a leading opponent of attempts to preserve wetlands. It is sponsored by oil and gas companies and real estate developers. See T. Lewis, "Cloaked in a Wise Disguise," in Echeverria and Eby, note 15 above, pages 13-20.

30. Measuring the growth of Wise Use groups is difficult, but one way to gauge their growth is to simply count the groups that umbrella groups say are affiliated with the movement. See R. Arnold and A. Gottlieb, *The Wise Use Agenda* (Bellevue, Wash.: Free Enterprise Press, 1988), 157-66, which lists 224 groups in 1988; and W. P. Pendley, *It Takes a Hero* (Bellevue, Wash.: Free Enterprise Press, 1994), which lists more than 1,000 groups in 1994. Ron Arnold estimates the movement to include "somewhere between 1,100 and 1,500 groups."

31. Ron Arnold, Center for the Defense of Free Enterprise, personal communication with the author, 12 June 1995.

32. Gregg Easterbrook describes environmentalism as the most enduring and successful liberal movement of the 20th century, so it only makes sense that conservatives find it an attractive target. See G. Easterbrook, *A Moment on the Earth* (New York: Viking, 1995).

33. Known among activists as "Wise Use horror stories," there are numerous examples of Wise Use organizers getting hundreds of angry activists out to public meetings where environmental plans are to be discussed. The most famous is the debacle over the Greater Yellowstone Vision Document in 1990-91. See R. Ekey, "Wise Use and the Greater Yellowstone Vision Document: Lessons Learned," in Echeverria and Eby, note 15 above, pages 339-47.

34. For articulation of this theme, see Arnold, note 25 above, chapter 1.

35. Ibid.

36. National Wildlife Federation poll, note 8 above, page 2. See also D. W. Moore, "Role of Government, Not the Economy, Generated Voter Turnout," *Gallup Poll Monthly,* November 1994, 13-15.

37. J. H. Cushman Jr., "Republicans Clear-Cut Regulatory Timberland," *New York Times,* 5 March 1995, E16.

38. Cited in Braile, note 12 above, page 32.

39. Environmentalists have been making much of the connections between Wise Use groups and the militia movement. See, for example, D. Helvarg, "The Anti-Enviro Connection," *The Nation,* 22 May 1995, 722-24.

40. For example, the National Federal Lands Conference (a Utah-based Wise Use group advocating private rights on public lands and a wellspring for the county supremacy movement) explicitly endorsed the militia movement in their newsletters in the fall of 1994. See J. Faulkner, "Why There is a Need for the Militia in America," *Federal Lands Update,* October 1994, 1-6.

41. For a statement of the legal theory behind "takings," see R. Epstein, *Takings, Private Property, and the Power of Eminent Domain* (Cambridge, Mass.: Harvard University Press, 1985). A recent political interpretation is C. V. Conda and M. D. LaRochelle, "The New Populism: The Rise of the Property Rights Movement," *Commonsense* 1, no. 4 (Fall 1994): 79-98. See also B. Moulton, "Law—Takings Legislation: Protection of Property Rights or Threat to the Public Interest?" *Environment*, March 1995, 44.

42. The logic of the argument is similar to another cause championed by Wise Use, the battle to eliminate "unfunded mandates" passed by Congress and "foisted upon state and local governments." By requiring the federal government to pay for any regulations it imposes, unfunded mandate activists, like their private property rights counterparts, hope to dramatically reduce the power of the federal government to regulate by making such regulations prohibitively expensive.

43. For a summary and review of *Lucas*, see L. Halper, "A New View of Regulatory Takings?" *Environment*, January/February 1994 and R. H. Platt, "Law—Parsing *Dolan*," *Environment*, October 1994, 4. A summary and debate of the *Dolan* decision is in W. Funk, "Reading Dolan v. City of Tigard," and L. Watters, "Dolan v. City of Tigard: Another Step in the Restoration of the Takings Clause," both in *NRLI News* 5, no. 1 (1994): 7-9.

44. C. J. Duerksen and R. J. Roddewig, *Takings Law in Plain English* (Washington, D.C.: American Resources Information Network, 1994); K. Zimmerman and D. Abelson, *Takings Law: A Guide to Government, Property, and the Constitution* (Boulder, Colo.: Land and Water Fund of the Rockies, 1993); J. T. Mathews, "Takings Exception," *Washington Post*, 14 February 1994, A15; and A. Diamant, "Government Takings? What About Givings?" *Christian Science Monitor*, 24 February 1995. See also discussion in Echeverria and Eby, note 15 above, pages 141-88.

45. Cited in W. K. Burke, "The Wise Use Movement: Right Wing Anti-Environmentalism," *The Public Eye*, June 1993, 5. For a primer on property rights issues, see Echeverria and Eby, note 15 above, pages 141-88; and B. Yandle, ed., *Land Rights: The 1990s Property Rights Rebellion* (Lanham, Md.: Rowman and Littlefield, 1995).

46. The most recent anecdote to make the rounds is the story of a farmer in Fresno, California, who ran into difficulties with endangered kangaroo rats on his property, attracting the attention of the Wise Use network. The farmer's cause was championed on the House floor by Rep. Richard Pombo. See T. Platt, "Kill a Rat, Go to Prison?" *Land Rights Letter* 9, no. 10 (1994). See also M. Arax, "U.S. Dismisses Charges that Farmer Killed Rare Rats," *Los Angeles Times*, 18 January 1995.

47. Jim Norton of the Wilderness Society explained how the timber industry exploits this issue: "They can close down an old, inefficient mill, start shipping all the wood over to their new mill, and blame environmentalists for the loss of jobs." Cited in K. O'Callahan, "Whose Agenda for America?" *Audubon*, September/October 1992, 82-91.

48. For discussion, see R. H. Bezdek, "Environment and Economy: What's the Bottom Line?" *Environment*, September 1993, 6. Still, studies show that mill modernization and changes in market conditions go much farther to explain the loss of jobs in the timber industry than the spotted owl. See A. K. Cook, "Increasing Poverty in Timber-Dependent Areas in Western Washington," *Society and Natural Resources* 8 (1995): 97-109; and H. M. Anderson and J. T. Olson, *Federal Forests and the Economic Base of the Pacific Northwest* (Washington, D.C.: The Wilderness Society, 1991).

49. L. Uchitelle, "Recovery? Not in Your Paycheck," *New York Times*, 8 January 1995, E6.

50. Labor Secretary Robert B. Reich points to what he calls the "anxious class," which is concerned about job security but no longer mobilized by organized labor to blame business. L. Uchitelle, "The Rise of the Losing Class," *New York Times*, 20 November 1994, E1. An example of blaming environmentalists for economic woes is B. Currie, "A Very Green Recession," *Ecologic*, March 1992, 7.

51. Poll conducted for the American Resources Information Network by Peter D. Hart Research Associates, 8-12 June 1993.

52. National Wildlife Federation poll, note 8 above, page 2.

53. See printed flyer produced jointly by 15 national environmental organizations, from Audubon to the Wilderness Society, "How to Defend Our Environmental Laws: A Citizen Action Guide," 1994.

54. "Astroturf" lobbying has grown tremendously in recent years. Organizers use automated fax machines to generate thousands of letters to Congress, giving legislators the impression of strong grassroots concern where there may be none. See J. Fritsch, "The Grassroots, Just a Free Phone Call Away," *New York Times*, 23 June 1995, A1. See also E. Kolbert, "When a Grassroots Drive Actually Isn't," *New York Times*, 26 March 1995, A1.

55. J. Roush, "Freedom and Responsibility: What We Can Learn from the Wise Use Movement," in Echeverria and Eby, note 15 above, page 8. For a further discussion of the problems with the Endangered Species Act, see G. Easterbrook, "The Birds," *The New Republic*, 28 March 1994, 22-29.

56. An excellent analysis of how environmental and Wise Use groups manipulate media symbols is J. Lange, "The Logic of Competing Information Campaigns: Conflict Over Old Growth and the Spotted Owl," *Communication Monographs* 60 (1993), 239-57.

57. For a summary of environmental groups, see N. Martel and B. Holman, "Inside the Environmental Movement 1994," *Outside*, March 1994, 65-73.

58. See Clifford, note 2 above, page A24.

59. Financial summaries in *Nature Conservancy*, November/December 1990, page 43 and January/February 1995, page 35.

60. Clifford, note 2 above, page A22.

61. TNC is labeled "economy trasher #1" in R. Arnold and A. Gottlieb, *Trashing the Economy* (Bellevue, Wash.: Free Enterprise Press, 1994).

62. J. Emory, "Just Add Water," *Nature Conservancy*, November/December 1994, 11-15. The Nature Conservancy's shift toward community-based conservation is outlined in D. Williamson and M. Cheater, "Winning the West," *Nature Conservancy*, January/February 1993, 18-25.

63. See Braile, note 12 above, and K. Yablon, "Meanwhile, Closer to the Ground," *Outside*, March 1994, 73.

64. Some conservative commentators have come to a similar conclusion. As Alston Chase writes, "Guided by economic theory and political principles, [Republicans] have limited their critiques to complaining (rightly) that efforts to 'save the earth' cost jobs and threaten liberty. And while their allies in the 'Wise Use' movement advocate sagacious stewardship, these proponents have not spelled out a clear agenda for doing so." A. Chase, "GOP Must Define True Environmental Policy," *Blue Ribbon Magazine*, January 1995, 18.

Rhetoric, Environmentalism, and Environmental Ethics

by Michael Bruner and Max Oelschlaeger

I. Introduction

An examination of ordinary language confirms that rhetoric has a bad reputation in the United States. "Rhetoric" for some is equivalent to "hot air," something that unethical politicians produce. Others define rhetoric as manipulation, something that unethical salespeople do. According to the most favorable view, it is "eloquent speaking," something attributed to Jesse Jackson or Barbara Jordan.[1]

The prejudice against rhetoric is not new. In Plato's dialogue *Gorgias,* Socrates opposes the unethical teachers of oratory, who, for a price, teach a student with little knowledge of some subject matter how to sway an audience.[2] Other philosophers developed and sustained the anti-rhetoric tradition by proclaiming that philosophy was devoted to discovering truth, while rhetoric was concerned with swaying opinion, with little respect for truth. The legacy is that too often rhetoric, at its best, is seen as technique and, at its worst, as deception. Many persons inside and outside of the environmental movement have little appreciation for the tradition of "noble rhetoric."

What, then, is rhetoric, and how does rhetoric differ from other disciplines, such as philosophy or ethics? Aristotle notes "that rhetoric is not bound up with a single definite class of subjects, but is as universal as dialectic. . . ." He goes on to observe that "It thus appears that rhetoric is an offshoot of dialectic and also of ethical studies. Ethical studies may fairly be called political; and for this reason rhetoric masquerades as political science. . . ."[3] Wayne Booth also explores the issue of rhetoric's identity:

> I would expect some readers to be puzzled about where in the intellectual landscape . . . rhetorical study lies. . . . I start out, then, like theologians these days, knowing that many readers will think I have no subject matter, and that those who grant me a subject may consider my way of working in it disreputable as compared with their own.[4]

Drawing upon the insights of Aristotle and Booth, we suggest that although rhetoric may be treated systematically, it is easier to conceptualize it as a transdisciplinary endeavor involving "the art of discovering warrantable beliefs and improving those beliefs in shared discourse."[5] Richard Rorty argues that philosophers are well-advised to give up the metaphysical comforts inherent in their tradition, that is, "the conception of a discipline that unites the argumentative rigor made possible by an appeal to commonly shared criteria with the ability to decide issues of ultimate significance for our lives."[6] In its place Rorty argues for what we call a rhetorical philosophy, in which philosophers abandon the quest for foundational arguments and knockdown arguments and replace it with the effort to promote solidarity in a community. So construed, ecophilosophers might "see the gap between truth and justification not as something to be bridged by isolating a natural and transcultural sort of rationality which can be used to criticize certain cultures and praise others, but simply as the gap between the actual good and the possible better."[7]

The prejudice against rhetoric arguably does not serve either the environmental movement or environmental ethics well. One is reminded of Karl Marx's notion that philosophers have long speculated about the world, but they have not often changed it. Polls indicate that Americans have been "green" throughout the 1970s and 1980s.[8] Yet by most indices, such as population growth, extinction of species, increase in atmospheric CO_2 levels, ozone depletion, and acid rain, the environmental crisis is worse today than it was on the occasion of the first Earth Day (22 April 1970).[9] One reason, as Samuel P. Hays points out, is that the 1980s witnessed an anti-environmental revolution that "set out to undo the environmental work of the preceding two decades of Republican and Democratic leadership."[10] Hays argues that the Reagan administration systematically excluded even environmental moderates from its own ranks, worked through the Office of Management and Budget to avoid public debate over its anti-environmental agenda, implemented policies to limit enforcement of environmental statutes, and attempted to privatize the lands and waters held in public trust.

Anti-environmental politicians have been effective in accomplishing their objectives at least in part because of their ability to articulate persuasive rationales through slogans, myths, and narratives. For example, former President Ronald Reagan, identified by a *Time* magazine cover as "The Great Communicator," once remarked that he didn't trust air he couldn't see. Reagan's knack for an apt phrase, an appropriate anecdote, use of humor, and ability to draw upon metaphor to express a vision (e.g., "Evil Empire") contributed to his rhetorical effectiveness. Further, his reassuring, even grandfatherly, demeanor helped recontextualize environmentalism as an invention of radicals—fringe groups, special interest groups, the liberal media, tree huggers, and people haters—who opposed the dominant myth of the "American way of life."[11] By rallying support for an anti-environmental agenda, Hays argues, Reagan was promoting business as usual—that is, the short-run economic benefits of letting corporations and consumers avoid change. Voters elected Reagan at least in part because they believed that environmentalism would raise taxes, depress economic activity, and cost some people their jobs.[12] Simultaneously, they discounted the long-term costs of anti-environmentalism (reduction of biodiversity, allergies caused by airborne pollutants, and so on).

While former President Bush was not as effective a communicator as Reagan, by repeatedly proclaiming himself to be "the environmental president," on occasions replete with scenic "photo opp's," Bush posed as a leader genuinely concerned about conservation. This image was sometimes undercut by other, less successful, rhetorical ploys, such as the attempt to redefine "wetlands"—a misguided, ecologically illiterate attempt to promote business interests at the expense of endangered species. The Orwellian overtones of Bush's rhetoric led such mainline environmental groups as the Sierra Club to characterize the Bush administration as an "ongoing environmental disaster" and the President as an environmental poseur, an "imposter," during the 1992 presidential campaign.[13]

In the 1992 campaign Bush attempted to blur inconsistencies in his record by extolling "his" achievements, on the one hand, such as the Clean Air Act, while, on the other hand, pointing out that his environmental policy was predicated on "wise use." Wise use meant, for example, that he would never choose to protect endangered species, such as the spotted owl, over the interests of working Americans. "Wise use conservation" is another rhetorical ploy, a new name for an anthropocentric, ecologically uninformed conservation philosophy formulated by Gifford Pinchot and President Theodore Roosevelt at the turn of the century. Bush's casting of arguments over endangered species as "owls versus people" is essentially manipulative, diverting the democratic debate from more fundamental issues, such as sustainable forestry that provides jobs for people *and* habitat for creatures, the formulas through which the National Forest Service is funded, the long-term ecological role of old-growth forests, especially as this role involves biodiversity, and the question of what public interests are served by the logging of old-growth forests.

The anti-environmental movement's use of rhetorical strategies has affected environmentalism in several ways. First, environmentalism continues to be *misconstrued* along conservative-liberal or left-right lines. No doubt, environmentalism entails politics. Nevertheless, recent analyses, such as Robert Paehlke's, show that the politics of environmentalism cannot be adequately characterized as a left-right issue. "Left and right are still relevant," Paehlke argues, "but they are no longer sufficient."[14] As a minimum he proposes that we also incorporate "environmentalism" and "anti-environmentalism" as an ideological continuum to help us in our analyses.[15] As Paehlke notes, many conservatives are in fact environmentalists.

Thomas Fleming, the editor of the conservative journal, *The Chronicles,* argues that *true* conservatives are compelled by scientific evidence to take environmental problems seriously because they threaten the future of a market society.[6] Still, anti-environmental conservatives have managed to cast the environmental movement as pessimistic and alarmist. Even worse, environmentalism has been linked to a loss of jobs, to a decrease in the quality of life, and to a restrictive life style characterized by sacrifice and suffering. The rhetorical strategy of the *anti-environmental right* to name environmentalism as a liberal ploy obscures at least three fundamental issues. First, environmentalism is not categorically in opposition to the basic premises of a market society, though it rejects the premise that public policy involving ecological issues can be reduced to economic decision making. As Mark Sagoff argues, environmentalism is not a function of our individual preferences for big government or limited government, for a welfare state or a military-industrial state. Rather environmental laws reflect "what we believe, what we are, what we stand for as a nation, not simply what we wish to buy as individuals. Social regulation reflects public values we choose collectively, and these may conflict with wants and interests we pursue individually."[17] Even though Americans might, for example, choose to restrict logging in old-growth forests, such a policy, democratically determined, does not entail abandoning the basic structures of the market.

Second, environmentalism has been mislabelled as a contest between people and nature; this is a false opposition, since the fate of the biophysical world is in large measure our own. The second scientific revolution, engendered by Darwin and Clausius, forces the conclusion that humankind, whatever its illusions, is inextricably tied to biophysical processes.[18] Accordingly, to conceptualize the issues involved in preserving biodiversity as a choice between either jobs for people or habitat for endangered species is a *false dichotomy.* As Stephen Meyer's research makes clear, anti-environmentalists have used specious arguments to make such claims.[19]

Third, the *potential power* of environmentalism as a social movement has been co-opted. Lance deHaven-Smith argues that what began as a challenge to the industrial growth paradigm, "rejecting consumption, unrestricted economic growth, and exploitation of the natural environment," has been preempted by the power structure through "marginal adjustments to economic activity. The capitalist imperative of unlimited economic growth was maintained, even though many of the relatively innocuous demands of the environmental movement were met."[20]

The failure of the environmental movement to promote consequential discussion of economic goals, especially the goal of unrestricted economic growth regardless of ecological effects (so-called economic externalities), does not encourage optimism about the future.[21] The magnitude and gravity of ecocrisis is now so obvious that even inherently conservative scientific institutions are calling for immediate action. For example, the Royal Society of London and the National Academy of Science recently issued a joint communique, warning that science and technology may soon be incapable of helping humankind address the issues unless *meaningful actions* are initiated immediately. Nevertheless, to listen to the leaders of the anti-environmental movement, as Paul Ekins notes, "one would be forgiven for not noticing that there was ... [an environmental] crisis."[22] It was not without reason that George Bush was named by journalists as the "Grinch of Rio" on the occasion of the Earth Summit.[23] The status quo rules.

II. Environmental Ethics: Into the Breech

The years between then—that is, Earth Day One—and now not only bear testimony to the anti-environmental revolution, but also have witnessed the emergence of environmental ethics as a specialty, replete with its own journals, such as *Environmental Ethics,* the first and most prominent. Clearly, environmental ethics has much to offer a culture that flirts with ecocatastrophe. Its debates have sharpened our grasp of many issues and problems. Just as clearly, however, given the continued increase of indices measuring ecological degradation, ecophilosophy has not to this date effected consequential societal changes.

One reason may be that environmental ethics, whatever else, is a specialized form of discourse that less and less resembles the prose found in Leopold's *Sand County Almanac,* and more and more revolves around either arcane discussions of such issues as ethical monism, moral considerability, intrinsic value, and the like, or disputes among contending factions in ecophilosophy (ecofeminism, deep ecology, social ecology, and so on). However, in order for discourse to promote social change, it must achieve a hearing before a large audience.[24] By this criterion, environmental ethics has not been effective discourse.

The failure of environmental ethics is also explained by the fact that the new and the tentative have to compete with the old and the established, that is, the established ideological framework (the dominant myth) that governs society. Little wonder, then, that the anti-environmental agenda has triumphed over the advocates of Leopoldian land ethics, deep ecology, ecofeminism, or any other environmental ethic. Anti-environmentalists play to the established cultural narrative: that "Man" is over nature, that nature is nothing more than an ecomachine which we technologically manipulate, and that a good society is one which totally fulfills itself through market preferences.

Furthermore there simply is no ecophilosophical position in general, no one ecofeminist paradigm, no one deep ecological platform, no moral monism, to which ecophilosophers can appeal. The scandal of philosophy, since the beginning, has been that no two philosophers ever agree about anything—an overstatement, to be sure, yet close to the mark in environmental ethics. Even worse, perhaps, is Alasdair MacIntrye's argument that post-Enlightenment ethical discourse is a failed project.[25] Environmental ethics seems to mirror his description of ethics: "The most striking feature of contemporary moral utterances is that so much of it is used to express disagreements; and the most striking feature of the debates in which these disagreements are expressed is their interminable character."[26]

How can lay publics place faith in environmental ethics when ecophilosophers have no faith in one another—when they produce an endless string of arguments demonstrating that so and so is wrong, dazed, bemused, or even crazed? Most recent issues of *Environmental Ethics* contain at least one essay, written by someone representing one particular kind of ecophilosophy, showing how some other kind of philosophy offers an inadequate foundation for or account of environmental ethics because of conceptual confusions, blunders of logic, mysticism, mean spiritedness and so on. The essays often dwell on personality, and who said what first, or last, or published what and when, or misinterpreted what someone said sometime that they can't remember. One must wonder, ultimately, just what it is that is at stake: academic reputations, promotions, power, or actually effecting changes in human behavior that lead toward sustainability?

To sum up, since ecophilosophical discourse generally flies in the face of the prevailing social paradigm, and offers its ethical insights and ecological panaceas in a language that is not accessible to lay publics, it appears to be null and void from the beginning. In other words, environmental ethics appears to be incapable of moving a democratic majority to support policies leading toward sustainability. From a traditional philosophical point of view, this situation is not a philosophical problem, since emphasis is placed primarily on identifying basic principles and providing supporting arguments. From a rhetorical point of view, however, it is, since effective philosophical discourse necessarily promotes societal transformation. K. M. Sayre, for example, recently tweaked the beard of the lion in its own den, noting that "If norms encouraging conservation and proscribing pollution were actually in force in industrial society, it would not be the result of ethical theory; and the fact that currently they are not in force is not alleviated by any amount of adroit ethical reasoning."[27]

Moreover, empirical studies of public opinion and voting behavior reveal an apparent *paradox:* more than two-thirds of adult Americans consider themselves environmentalists even while the noose of ecocrisis continues to tighten around their collective necks. This paradox disappears, however, deHaven-Smith argues, once we realize that there is no empirical data to support the hypothesis that the environmental movement involves any general "philosophical reorientation of public opinion. . . ."[28] On the contrary, he continues, people become environmentalists not because of "environmental philosophy," but rather because of local issues adversely affecting or threatening to affect the quality of their own lives (water quality, siting of a nuclear power plant, waste, and so on). The environmental movement, on this argument, is better conceptualized not as a mass public inspired by environmental ethics, but as a number of so-called local-issue publics addressing ecological dysfunctions.

III. Ecophilosophy and the Rhetorical Turn

Perhaps it is more important for ecophilosophers to be useful, that is, help society move itself toward sustainability, than anything else. Historically, philosophers have most often wanted to be right: namely, produce knockdown arguments on epistemology, metaphysics, or ethics, think ideas of Cartesian clarity and distinctness, and pen master narratives (like the Greeks or the Enlightenment philosophers) that found new ages. Contemporary environmental philosophy has more than a passing similarity to this project. For example, a recent essay by J. Baird Callicott implies that environmental ethics is a failure because of its pluralism, and that a moral monism—that is, a master narrative—is what ecophilosophy needs to turn the tide.[29]

Since the so-called linguistic turn in philosophy, dated for convenience from the later Wittgenstein, something has happened within a part of the community of philosophers that suggests an alternative project.[30] While no extended discussion of the linguistic turn is possible here, we can quickly recapitulate that project by considering Rorty's work. He argues that epistemology (as traditionally conceived) is no longer useful; rather it is better to think of *conversation as the context in which knowledge is defined.*[31] For philosophers who have taken the linguistic turn, the notions that philosophy is one thing and rhetoric something else, or that philosophy deals with timeless truths and rhetoric merely with ephemeral means of persuasion, are not cogent. Twentieth-century philosophy and rhetoric are now thought by affirmative postmodernists to have merged into an interdisciplinary theory of language. More pointedly, the conception of rhetoric

> has grown to encompass a theory of language as a form of social behavior, of intention and interpretation as the determinants of meaning, in the way that knowledge is created by argument, and in the way that ideology and power are extended through discourse. In short, rhetoric has become a comprehensive theory of language as *effective discourse.*[32]

So pervasive are the implications of the linguistic turn that, as Stephen Toulmin argues, even the very *forms of argument* are now comprehended as linguistically and temporally dependent. While analytic philosophy has hoped for *field invariant criteria* by which to judge arguments (that is, "a single, universal set of criteria applicable in all fields of argument alike"), including those of environmental ethics, that hope has not been fulfilled.[33] Perhaps some ecophilosophers and rhetoricians have come full circle back to one of Aristotle's definitions of rhetoric: "Rhetoric is the counterpart of Dialectic."[34] Of course, Aristotle's logic does not reflect the linguistic turn, since he envisioned logic as permanently constrained by the three "laws" of thought. Today, as Toulmin points out, any credible account of argument is necessarily historical. "To think up new and better methods of arguing in any field is to make a major advance, not just in logic, but in the substantive field itself: great logical innovations are part and parcel of great scientific, moral, political, or legal innovations."[35]

From a contemporary rhetorical standpoint, if the ecophilosophical project is to be successful in a democratic context, that is, actually help transform the industrial growth society into a sustainable society, then it must meet at least three criteria. (1) Its discourse must be cognitively plausible. Here environmental ethics gets high marks, since its arguments are ingenious, carefully crafted, and supported by an avalanche of ecological data. (2) It must evoke sentiment. For a democratic society to move in a new direction, even if *good reasons* exist, a strong majority must *feel* a compelling need to do so. Here, in contrast to its cognitive plausibility, environmental ethics gets a lower mark. Most ecophilosophers do not attempt to move their audiences emotionally, even though (in most cases) they themselves have been motivated by the strong feelings they have for the natural world.[36] (3) To be efficacious, ecophilosophical discourse must reach a majority of the people, that is, gain a wide audience and hearing. Here environmental ethics gets its lowest marks.[37] Insofar as environmental philosophy aspires to be *effective discourse,* then it needs to reconsider its pretense of producing knockdown arguments, philosophical foundations, and master narratives, and begin attending to the resources that rhetoric offers. These resources are considerable, and no exhaustive discussion can here be offered. However, a few current perspectives might help explain the value of rhetoric to environmental ethics.

One thing that rhetoric teaches its practitioners is the importance of identifying the audience. Ecophilosophical discourse, we have suggested above, generally tends to aim at a social elite: namely, other ecophilosophers. How else are we to explain that "byzantine artifact," as Gary Snyder so hilariously names it, called the academic paper.[38] Insofar as ecophilosophical discourse is oriented toward experts, the potential of its language to engage issue publics in conversation and ultimately to influence their behavior is limited if not eliminated. The consequence is that the bureaucratic-political elite that manages the industrial growth society maintains political dominance, providing almost unchallenged cognitive and perceptual filters (ideological frames) through which diverse publics perceive environmental issues and policies. The success of the Reagan-Bush anti-environmental revolution arguably confirms this judgment. The point is not that ecophilosophical discourse is unimportant or irrelevant to the political process. *It is very important if society is to evolve within any reasonable time frame toward sustainability.* Nevertheless, the failure of the environmental movement implies that it has been co-opted and that ecophilosophy has not met either criterion (2) or (3) above.

In addition, rhetoric teaches that *all* language is persuasive, the primary means by which we come to know and then to share what we know about the world. In this deep sense, rhetoric constructs social realities and our perspectives on them. Meaning and knowledge—what is accepted as important and true—are rhetorical through and through.[39] Philosophers who have taken the linguistic turn, such as Rorty and Toulmin, have helped to advance this case, that is, the rhetorical nature of social reality. Rorty argues, for example, that metaphor is the essential element of moral and intellectual progress.[40] Toulmin argues persuasively, as already noted, for the evolutionary nature of successful, that is, persuasive argument.[41] Scholars sometimes use the phrase "epistemic rhetoric" when referring to this perspective.[42]

An extended discussion of postmodern philosophy and epistemic rhetoric, however, lies beyond the scope of the present essay. Premised on the notion that language *per se* is rhetorical, we need to consider three other dimensions of rhetoric—namely, its critical, persuasive, and architectonic aspects—in relation to ecophilosophical discourse and its efficacy.[43]

IV. Critical Rhetoric

Above all else, critical rhetoric reveals the *discourse of power* that overdetermines discussion of the environmental agenda, that is, contextualizes the issues in ways which lead to narrowly defined debates over policy that inevitably lead to pre-established ends that are themselves never discussed. Neil Evernden, for example, suggests that ecologically informed narrative has not, to this day, done anything more than patch and bandage the wounds caused by the industrial growth paradigm.[44] Its potential to facilitate a cultural conversation among diverse issue publics about sustainability is subverted by the prevailing "resource conservation paradigm," carefully nurtured and maintained by an expert establishment that plies technological fixes to environmental dysfunctions. By ignoring the discourse of power, the ecophilosophical community is defeated before it starts, since it is the very ends of society that environmental ethics wants to call into question.

Raymie McKerrow argues that "the task of a critical rhetoric is to undermine and expose the discourse of power in order to thwart its effects in a social relation.

. . ."[45] In this context, it is useful, as R. J. Johnston suggests, to describe environmentalism as a contest between two elites, one "technocratic," including economists, environmental engineers, and perhaps the majority of environmental scientists, and the other "humanistic," including environmental historians, ethicists, and others in the "radical amateur tradition" (as Stephen Fox terms them).[46] The technocratic elite at present rules, in part, because the dominant myth overdetermines the perceptions of lay publics, and, in part, as we contend, because ecophilosophers have not communicated effectively: "Thus the struggle continues, between the momentum of the dominant mode of production on the one hand [and its defenders, the technocratic elite] and the claims [by environmental ethicists] that it is destroying the earth on the other."[47]

So conceptualized, critical rhetoric could prove instrumental in helping environmental ethicists gain a hearing by revealing the discourse of power that precludes cultural conversation about sustainability. In part, critical rhetoric can do so simply by focusing attention on the power of words. For example, consider that Arthur Tansley's subtle but overwhelming influence on mainstream ecology turned virtually on a single word: *ecosystem*. Joel Kingsolver and Robert Paine note that Tansley's "The Use and Abuse of Vegetational Concepts and Terms" systematically dismantled the idea of "the ecological *community* as a complex organism."[48] As a result, the practitioners of academic ecology now refer to and conceptualize the natural world as an *ecosystem* rather than as a biotic community. Donald Worster points out that Tansley "wanted to strike the word 'community' from his science's vocabulary because of connotations that he considered misleading and anthropomorphic. . . ." By substituting the word *ecosystem* in its place, Tansley divorced himself as a person from the natural community of life and attempted to confine nature study to "the purely material exchange of energy and of such chemical substances as water, phosphorus, nitrogen, and other nutrients. . . ."[49]

In this way, mainstream ecology perpetuates the paradigm of classical physics, especially in its denial of any connection between knowing subjects and known objects (since to claim any connection, as does deep ecology, is mysticism) and in its emphasis on "scientific" measurement of ecosystem energetics. The result, Evernden argues, is that ecologically inspired ethical discourse cannot in principle add its voice to or participate in any cultural conversation about sustainability; rather, the voice of ecology is functionally constrained to serve the ends of the industrial state. Whatever the appeal to ecophilosophers of Leopoldian land ethics, his position is far from dominant among professional ecologists. As Robert P. McIntosh points out, Leopoldian land ethics, revolving around the concept of the biotic community of which humankind is a part, "transformed ecological concerns into problems of ethics, morality and aesthetics as well as science." Yet, under Tansley's influence (and others who trailed in his wake), ecological insights have not been successfully integrated into the cultural conversation about the basic goals and directions of industrial society. For the most part, ecology has dealt only with functionally defined and circumscribed aspects of environmental problems.[50]

Critical rhetoric might also help recontextualize the debate on an environmental agenda—local, national, or global—in ways that incorporate environmental ethics, bringing to light issues such as the legitimacy of the industrial growth paradigm itself and the bureaucratic experts who manage it.[51] In this regard, Donald McCloskey's *The Rhetoric of Economics* is useful because it shows how contemporary economic discourse is built upon a philosophical foundation (namely, classical physics and logical positivism) that has crumbled. By claiming predictive utility (and causal control), McIntosh wryly observes, economists have had great success "in persuading governments that their advice is sound" while ecologists have remained largely outside the corridors of power.[52] The mindless pursuit of economic growth in general, premised on the assumption that any and all growth is good, and the dominance of the 1992 presidential campaign by economic issues show the overwhelming power of economic discourse. Yet, even the claim that the defining feature of science is prediction is dubious, let alone the claim that economic science possesses it.[53]

Nonetheless, economists and econometricians remain the heavy hitters in Washington, D.C.[54] and anti-environmentalists are still able to recast environmental issues, such as arguments about old-growth forest, in terms of an "economy versus ecology" dichotomy. Our point is simple: *whoever defines the terms of the public debate determines its outcomes.* If environmental issues are conceptualized, for example, in terms of "owls versus people," then the owls (and the habitat that sustains them) do not have much of a future.[55] A critical rhetoric, such as McCloskey's, exposes the poverty of imagination inherent in reducing environmental issues to economic questions and reinforces such arguments as those advanced by Mark Sagoff in *The Economy of the Earth:* the reduction of environmental issues to economic questions is an inherently specious strategy. Unless we, as an expert community, can show why casting the debate in terms of jobs for people versus protection for owls is a false dichotomy, and more generally drive home the point of Sagoff's argument, then lay publics will perceive environmental issues in that way.[56]

V. Rhetoric as Architectonic

Richard McKeon suggests that rhetoric also functions architectonically.[57] In part, an *architectonic rhetoric* entails rejoining eloquence and wisdom in ways that are persuasive and critical. However, rhetoric as architectonic is also transformative—that is, productive of a new cultural order. The IE root is *tekhs,* as in "weaving" or "building," and the Latin *textere,* "to compose," as in a *text.*[58] "If rhetoric is to be used to contribute to the formation of the culture of the modern [better: postmodern] world," McKeon argues, "it should function productively in the resolution of new problems and architectonically in the formation of new inclusive communities."[59]

It is just such inclusive communities that such individuals as Aldo Leopold and, more recently, Susan Griffin and Gary Snyder, imaginatively describe in their *texts*. Viewed architectonically, Leopold's land ethic envisions a new living space in which humankind is bound up with the land community, not as its conqueror, but as plain citizen. Griffin's *Woman and Nature* articulates a cognitively persuasive and affectively powerful vision of humankind reconnected with the continuum of life. "We are nature seeing nature," she writes. "We are nature with a concept of nature. . . . Nature speaking of nature to nature."[60] Snyder's Pulitzer prize-winning *Turtle Island* aspires to function as effective discourse reconnecting humankind with the Earth through myth (the turtle's back upon which humans live). In "Tomorrow's Song" Snyder envisions a sustainable, inclusive society where we humans are "At work and in our place: / *in the service / of the wilderness / of life / of death / of the Mother's breasts.*"[61] More recently Snyder argues that we need to open a dialogue "among all beings" and to explore "a rhetoric of ecological relationships."[62]

In a similar fashion, such environmental historians as Donald Worster and Carolyn Merchant have grasped the architectonic potential of ecological discourse, introducing such terms as "the age of ecology" and "the global ecological revolution" in their work.[63] In present context, although neither a definitive nor an exhaustive account of an architectonic rhetoric is feasible, the basic notion can be grasped through an *argument from analogy:* namely, just as the language of classical physics transformed the medieval world, so a *rhetoric of ecology* (alternatively, evolutionary science) might transform the modern world.

A number of scholars, including not only Worster and Merchant, but also Leo Marx, Ernst Mayr, and Ilya Prigogine, have helped us recognize the influence of classical science on the modern world.[64] Consider, for example, the influence of a Newtonian paradigm on politics, epitomized by Hobbes and Locke, on economics, epitomized by Adam Smith's *Wealth of Nations,* and on psychology, epitomized by Hume and behaviorism. Collectively considered, these developments set the modern world on its primary project: the domination of nature. René Descartes perhaps caught the fundamental idea in his statement that through physics humankind would render itself "the master and possessor of nature."[65]

Just as the first scientific revolution engendered by physics influenced humankind's conceptualization of the world, the things in the world, and the relations among the things in the world, so a second scientific revolution, engendered largely by evolutionary biology, is presently swaying us. A rhetoric of ecology might systematically explore the architectonic implications of this paradigm—the new symbols, myths, and metaphors that it enables.[66] Moreover, if the analogy holds between the first and second scientific revolutions, then significant sociocultural transformations will likely occur in the next century. Through the work of Snyder, Griffin, and Leopold, for example, we can glimpse the changes in economics, politics, psychology, and philosophy portended by ecological discourse. Alternatively stated, ecological narrative can influence the legitimating narrative of the West.

VI. Persuasive Rhetoric

Aristotle appreciated the two sides of what we are calling "persuasive rhetoric." On the one hand, he wrote an ordinary language definition of rhetoric: "Rhetorical study is concerned with the modes of persuasion." Of the modes of persuasion, the credibility of the speaker is the most important: "This is true generally whatever the question is, and absolutely true where exact certainty is impossible and opinions are divided." On the other hand, Aristotle understood that persuasion is based on insight and empathy: "Rhetoric may be defined as the faculty of observing in any given case the available means of persuasion."[67]

The challenge for environmentalists is to identify available means of persuasion, situation by situation, and then to find credible images and spokespeople to interact with audiences. While traditional conceptions of rhetoric are relevant, there is a need to break from linear (Aristotelian) models of persuasion. The linear model, formalized in David Berlo's source-message-channel-receiver model (SMCR),[68] has the defect of reducing persuasion to a "silver bullet"-like message that hits receivers and has effects. Our view of persuasion is that the so-called "receiver," for want of a better term, actually persuades himself or herself. A more interactive view of persuasion, sensitive to context, has the advantage of preserving freedom of choice and accountability, emphases that are appropriate for environmental ethics, bioregionalism, and citizen democracy. It is also consistent with deHaven-Smith's observation that environmentalism begins at a local level with issue publics rather than at a general philosophical level.[69]

Such theorists as Jurgen Habermas seem to be moving in this direction in writing about "moral consciousness and communicative action."[70] One of his principles of discourse ethics is that at the highest level of moral argument parties engage in ideal role taking and orient themselves toward procedures for justifying norms.[71] While this move appears to be at an abstract level of cognition, Habermas affirms that ideal perspective taking means respect for the other person's argument and an orientation toward mutual understanding and social action.

VII. Conclusion

Our thesis has been that rhetoric offers resources to the ecophilosophical community that increase its potential to effect change in society. In part, our argument complements Sayre's claim that *empirical information about human values and norms* might help us help our culture move toward sustainability. He asserts that "an understanding of *how* moral norms become instituted, in the sense of the social forces by which such norms are set in place" might help the ethical theorist "contribute substantially toward the establishment of norms that [actually] protect the environment."[72] We contend that ecophilosophers might employ critical, architectonic, and persuasive rhetorical tools not only to grasp how moral norms are established and maintained, but also to change them. The techniques of *critical rhetoric* might help to open conversations that are closed, so that the ends discussed by environmental ethicists might actually be considered. *Persuasive rhetoric* might assist ecophilosophy in getting its message heard, at least in part by evoking the sentiments that are essential to social transformation.[73] Moreover, *architectonic rhetoric* facilitates the use of ecological narrative in environmental ethics.

We hope that it is clear that our project is not only the reclamation of rhetoric, but also a call for environmentalists to enter into conversations and arguments with anti-environmental factions and with the inattentive public. At one level, we envision that these interactions will be convincing in a traditional sense of persuasive rhetoric; ecophilosophers often possess both eloquence and wisdom, and they need not shy away from using these skills in combination. At another level, we believe that philosophical criticism functions rhetorically to open closed conversations and expose the discourse of power that has contributed to the failure of environmentalism. At the third level, we seek with others to develop and articulate slogans, myths, and narratives that will be influential in a deep or architectonic sense.

One of the pressing needs in the environmental movement today is for a metaphor or an alternative discourse paradigm that resonates with the lived experiences of non-elite publics. At its most basic level, architectonic rhetoric begins with a symbol (or even an image). The most pervasive cultural symbol of the modern age, as Leo Marx argues, is *the machine*.[74] Perhaps the need is to replace the "machine" metaphor. Perhaps the need is to develop a narrative other than the "Global Village" or "Spaceship Earth." Cheney's notion of bioregional narrative is one possibility. Certainly, neither gloom and doom rhetoric nor the rhetoric of sacrifice appear to resonate with audiences in the United States. A way must be found to escape the horns of the jobs-or-environment dilemma heard in public discourse today if the environmental movement is to facilitate transition to sustainability.

Common sense recoils from the notion that inattentive publics or interest groups can be persuaded by appeals that condemn an entire way of life. More specifically, it is unlikely that the simplest solution—jobs *and* the environment—has sufficient appeal in a time of polarized viewpoints and economic hardship. Common sense also suggests that diverse publics in the United States may not understand or respond to talk about changing from a modern to a postmodern paradigm. Where and how can one achieve a "paradigm shift"? Thomas Kuhn argues that paradigm shifts are impossible for most persons working within the old paradigm.[75] So framed, environmentalists might spend more time in conversations with children and young adults. We suggest, for example, that evocative drawings and videos may be especially suited for children and young adults in this visual age.[76] The natural world, fortunately, is an almost ideal visual subject. It is not beyond the pale to imagine an eco-*Sesame Street* or an eco-*Boyz 'N the Hood*[77] if the environmental movement is to transform its highly specialized form of discourse into an evocative rhetoric.[78] We also suggest that environmentalism must grow out of a life world. (Pepsico and McDonald's do not sell soft drinks or hamburgers as much as they sell images of a life world.) To this end, individuals must experience grass, rain, and mountains. A holistic life world and a visual architectonic rhetoric, then, may be some of the basic elements for correcting mistaken impressions of the environmental movement and for regaining its co-opted power.

Notes

1. This view of rhetoric confirms the influence of alphabetization, and the concomitant shift from orality to literacy, on the course of Western culture. Cicero (106-43 b.c.e.), according to Marshall McLuhan, questioned the breech created by professional philosophers "between eloquence and wisdom, between practical knowledge and knowledge which these men professed to follow for its own sake. Before Socrates learning had been the preceptress of living rightly and speaking well. But with Socrates came

the division between the tongue and the heart." Marshall McLuhan, *The Gutenberg Galaxy: The Making of Typographic Man* (Toronto: University of Toronto Press, 1962), p. 24.

2. See Eric A. Havelock, *Preface to Plato* (Cambridge: Harvard University Press, 1963), for discussion of the turn from orality to literacy and how this turn influenced Plato's attitudes. Also see Walter J. Ong, *Orality and Literacy: The Technologizing of the Word* (New York: Routledge, 1982). Ong argues that philosophy is an artifact of literate cultures. Therein lies the philosophical bias against rhetoric. Literate cultures think of orality as "overvaluing and overpracticing rhetoric." However, Ong continues, "In primary oral cultures, even business is not business: it is fundamentally rhetoric." For an insightful account by a contemporary philosopher of the importance of rhetoric, see Richard McKeon, *Rhetoric: Essays in Invention and Discovery* (Woodbridge, Conn.: Ox Bow Press, 1987).

3. Aristotle, *Rhetoric,* bk. 1, chap. 1.

4. Wayne Booth, *Modern Dogma and the Rhetoric of Assent* (Chicago: University of Chicago Press, 1974), p. xii.

5. Booth, *Modern Dogma,* p. xiii.

6. Richard Rorty, *Objectivity, Relativism, and Truth: Philosophical Papers,* (Cambridge: Cambridge University Press, 1991), vol. 1, p. 75.

7. Booth, *Modern Dogma,* pp. 22-23.

8. Cf. William D. Ruckelshaus, "Toward a Sustainable World," *Scientific American* 261 (September 1989): 166-74.

9. See Lester R. Brown, Hal Kane, and Ed Ayres, *Vital Signs 1993* (Washington, DC: Worldwatch Institute, 1993).

10. Samuel P. Hays, *Beauty, Health, and Permanence: Environmental Politics in the United States, 1955-1985* (Cambridge: Cambridge University Press, 1987), p. 491.

11. See W. Charles Redding and Edward D. Steele, "The American Value System: Premises for Persuasion," *Western Journal of Speech Communication* 26 (Spring 1962): 83-91.

12. See Stephen M. Meyer, *Environmentalism and Economic Prosperity: Testing the Environmental Impact Hypothesis* (Cambridge: MIT Project on Environmental Politics and Policy, 1992). Meyer argues that "states can pursue environmental quality without fear of impeding economic prosperity. For those who continue to argue that environmentalism hurts economic growth and prosperity the burden of proof now falls clearly on their shoulders" (p. 43). Also see Stephen M. Meyer, "Environmentalism and Economic Prosperity: An Update" (Cambridge: MIT Project on Environmental Politics and Policy, 1993).

13. *Sierra* 77 (September-October 1992): 46.

14. Robert C. Paehlke, *Environmentalism and the Future of Progressive Politics* (New Haven: Yale University Press, 1989), p. 189.

15. Is environmentalism an ideology? Alvin Gouldner argues that "the ecological movement leads science toward politicalization and political programs, and toward a more unified, autonomous ideology of its own." Alvin Ward Gouldner, *The Dialectic of Ideology and Technology* (New York: Oxford University Press, 1976), p. 273. We agree with Gouldner that an ideological analysis of environmentalism, especially in relationship to capitalism, science, and technology, is a potentially illuminating inquiry. However, in this essay we steer away from the concept for two reasons: first, because our discussion of rhetoric encompasses Gouldner's view that ideology is language that reconstitutes community, and second, because Gouldner's concept of ideology carries the baggage of European intellectual history—from Marx to Habermas.

16. Thomas Fleming, *Chronicles* (August 1990): 7.

17. Mark Sagoff, *The Economy of the Earth* (Cambridge: Cambridge University Press, 1988), pp. 16-17.

18. Among many, see Nicholas Georgescu-Roegen, *The Entropy Law and the Economic Process* (Cambridge: Harvard University Press, 1971), and Ilya Prigogine and Isabelle Stengers, *Order Out of Chaos: Man's New Dialogue with Nature* (New York: Bantam Books, 1984).

19. Meyer, *Environmentalism and Economic Prosperity.*

20. Lance deHaven-Smith, *Environmental Concern in Florida and the Nation* (Gainesville: University of Florida Press, 1991), p. 4.

21. An excellent discussion of economic growth in ecological context can be found in Herman E. Daly and John B. Cobb, Jr., *For the Common Good: Redirecting the Economy toward Community, the Environment, and a Sustainable Future* (Boston: Beacon Press, 1989). See also various articles in the *Journal of Ecological Economics.*

22. Paul Ekins, *The Gaia Atlas of Green Economics* (New York: Anchor Books, 1992), p. 9.

23. Sharon Begley, "The Grinch of Rio," *Newsweek* 119 (15 June 1992): 30-32. See also *International Society for Environmental Ethics Newsletter* 3 (Summer 1992): 4-19, for a useful report on the Earth Summit.

24. *Environmental Ethics* presently has fewer than 2000 subscribers, of which approximately 1200 are institutions.

25. Alasdair MacIntyre, *After Virtue: A Study in Moral Theory,* 2d ed. (Notre Dame: University of Notre Dame Press, 1984), pp. 1-5 and passim. MacIntrye also envisions a way around this problem (p. 258), one largely consistent with but beyond the scope of this essay. That is, the rhetorical tradition offers a plausible solution to the failure of ethical philosophical discourse, since conversation is the primary means by which a community can work toward a good society (which is minimally a sustainable society, since *an unsustainable society is self-defeating*).

26. MacIntyre, *After Virtue,* p. 6. Eugene C. Hargrove's arguments in some ways parallel MacIntyre's, though his derivation is different. Hargrove argues that "the rise of emotivism out of logical positivism" has tended to undercut environmental ethics, not only because of the diversity in environmental ethics, but because economic judgments of environmental value have, in comparison to those of environmental ethics, appeared to be objective. Eugene C. Hargrove, *Foundations of Environmental Ethics* (New York: Prentice Hall, 1989), p. 210.

27. Kenneth M. Sayre, "An Alternative View of Environmental Ethics," *Environmental Ethics* 13 (1991): 200.

28. deHaven-Smith, *Environmental Concern,* pp. 5-15.

29. J. Baird Callicott, "The Case Against Moral Pluralism," *Environmental Ethics* 12 (1990): 99-124. However, other philosophers, such as Hargrove, argue that environmental ethics is rooted in a number of different traditions. In his opinion, environmental ethics neither has had nor does it need a single foundation.

30. See Ludwig Wittgenstein, *Philosophical Investigations* (New York: Macmillan Company, 1953); see also Avner Cohen and Marcelo Dascal, eds., *The Institution of Philosophy: A Discipline in Crisis?* (LaSalle: Open Court, 1989), for a variety of papers concerning philosophy after the linguistic turn, as well as Robert C. Solomon, "Beyond Reason: The Importance of Emotion in Philosophy," in James Olgivy, ed., *Revisioning Philosophy* (Albany: State University of New York Press, 1992).

31. See Richard Rorty, *Philosophy and the Mirror of Nature* (Princeton: Princeton University Press, 1979), p. 389. Jim Cheney raises objections to the linguistic turn generally, and to Rorty more specifically, in "Postmodern Environmental Ethics: Ethics as Bioregional Narrative," *Environmental Ethics* 11 (1989): 117-34. Cheney's objections to the linguistic turn are arguably met, however, in John S. Dryzek, "Green Reason: Communicative Ethics for the Biosphere," *Environmental Ethics* 12 (1990): 195-210, and David Abram, "Merleau-Ponty and the Voice of the Earth," *Environmental Ethics* 10 (1988): 101-20. To accept the premise that language overdetermines human behavior does not also entail the conclusion that, as Cheney argues, "it's language all the way down." Environmental ethics as conversation does not reduce the biophysical world to language but rather aims, as for example Leopold's land ethic does, to incorporate the natural world into human discourse. The dominant conversation, as most environmental ethicists agree, marginalizes the biophysical world.

32. Patricia Bizzell and Bruce Herzberg, eds., *The Rhetorical Tradition: Readings from Classical Times to the Present* (Boston: Bedford Books of St. Martin's Press, 1990), p. 899 (emphasis added).

33. Stephen Edelston Toulmin, *The Uses of Argument* (Cambridge: Cambridge University Press, 1958), p. 39. Also see MacIntyre, *After Virtue,* esp. chap. 5, "Why the Enlightenment Project of Justifying Morality Had to Fail." The fateful fall, in MacIntyre's opinion, occurred when moral philosophy excluded functional concepts from its arguments. It is precisely such functional concepts, we argue, that an architectonic rhetoric might reincorporate into cultural conversation on environmental ethics. Leopold's land ethic (that is, his prescriptive statements about good behavior) is itself based on the functional concept of the biotic community (itself derived from the descriptive statements of ecological science). See below, sec. 5.

34. Aristotle, *Rhetoric,* bk. 1, chap. 1. Several issues arise at this juncture going beyond our scope. Are we, for example, to translate *antistrophos* as "counterpart," as here, or "correlative," "coordinate," or "converse." See George A. Kennedy, ed. and trans., *Aristotle on Rhetoric: A Theory of Civic Discourse* (New York: Oxford University Press, 1991), and Lawrence D. Green, "Aristotelian Rhetoric, Dialectic, and the Traditions of *Antistrophos*," *Rhetorica* 8 (1990): 5-27. A comprehensive study of the rhetoric of environmentalism necessarily deals with such issues.

35. Toulmin, *The Uses of Argument,* p. 256.

36. See, for example, Edward O. Wilson, *Biophilia* (Cambridge: Harvard University Press, 1984). Wilson makes clear that his environmental ethic grows out of his love of life (biophilia). "The goal is to join emotion with the rational analysis of emotion in order to create a deeper and more enduring conservation ethic" (p. 130). Many if not most ecophilosophers have themselves experienced nature

emotionally, and also recognize the influence of feeling in the work of such consequential authors as Susan Griffin (e.g., *Woman and Nature*) and John Muir (e.g., *My First Summer*).

37. These criteria are developed in Bruce Lincoln, *Discourse and the Transformation of Society: Comparative Studies of Myth, Ritual, and Classification* (New York: Oxford University Press, 1989). Support for the first criterion is not required for a philosophical readership. Support for the second criterion comes from a variety of sources, including (in addition to Plato) cognitive science and sociobiology. See especially E. O. Wilson, *Sociobiology: The Abridged Edition* (Cambridge: Harvard University Press, 1980), esp. pp. 3-4, and *Biophilia*. Support for the third criterion comes from political science. See Robert A. Dahl, *Democracy and Its Critics* (New Haven: Yale University Press, 1989), and R. J. Johnston, *Environmental Problems: Nature, Economy and State* (London: Belhaven Press, 1989).

38. Gary Snyder, *Practice of the Wild: Essays by Gary Snyder* (San Francisco: North Point Press, 1990), p. 17.

39. See, for example, Peter Berger and Thomas Luckmann, *The Social Construction of Reality* (New York: Doubleday/Anchor Books, 1967).

40. See Rorty, *Objectivity, Relativism, and Truth.*

41. See Toulmin, *The Uses of Argument.*

42. See Robert Scott, "On Viewing Rhetoric as Epistemic: Ten Years Later," *Central States Speech Journal* 27 (1976): 258-66.

43. Present context precludes developing these terms in detail. Readers interested in doing so might consult R. McKeon, *Rhetoric,* Michael Calvin McGee, "Text, Context, and the Fragmentation of Contemporary Culture," *Western Journal of Speech Communication* 54 (1990): 274-89, Raymie McKerrow, "Critical Rhetoric: Theory and Praxis," *Communication Monographs* 56 (June 1989): 91-111, and J. Michael Sproule, "The New Managerial Rhetoric and the Old Criticism," *Quarterly Journal of Speech* 74 (1988): 468-86.

44. Neil Evernden, "Ecology in Conservation and Conversation," in Max Oelschlaeger, ed., *After Earth Day: Continuing the Conservation Effort* (Denton: University of North Texas Press, 1992), pp. 73-82.

45. McKerrow, "Critical Rhetoric," p. 98.

46. Stephen Fox, *The American Conservation Movement: John Muir and His Legacy* (Madison: University of Wisconsin Press, 1985), esp. pp. 333-57. Johnston, *Environmental Problems,* uses the term *humanistic* without anthropocentric implications.

47. Johnston, *Environmental Problems,* p. 186.

48. Joel G. Kingsolver and Robert T. Paine, "Conversational Biology and Ecological Debate," in Leslie A. Real and James H. Brown, eds., *Foundations of Ecology: Classic Papers with Commentaries* (Chicago: University of Chicago Press, 1991), p. 310.

49. Donald Worster, *Nature's Economy: A History of Ecological Ideas* (Cambridge: Cambridge University Press, 1985), pp. 301-02. See Kingsolver and Paine, *Foundations of Ecology,* for a number of other papers, such Raymond L. Lindeman's "The Trophic-Dynamic Aspect of Ecology" (1942), that pushed mainstream ecology in the narrowly functional direction envisioned by Tansley. More generally, critical rhetoric is essential to what Ernst Mayr calls "a science of science, a discipline that "would combine the sociology of science, the history of science, the philosophy of science, and the psychology of science with whatever generalizations one can make about the activities of scientists and about the development and methodology of science." Ernest Mayr, *The Growth of Biological Thought: Diversity, Evolution, and Inheritance* (Cambridge: Harvard University Press, 1982), p. 829. Our remarks here are merely indicative of the direction that ecophilosophical inquiry, informed by critical rhetoric, might move rather than an exhaustive account.

50. Robert P. McIntosh, *The Background of Ecology: Concept and Theory* (Cambridge: Cambridge University Press, 1985), p. 168. For further discussion see McIntosh, chap. 8, "Ecology and Environment," and Neil Evernden, *The Social Creation of Nature* (Baltimore: Johns Hopkins University Press, 1992), passim.

51. MacIntyre's discussion of the inherently amoral character of bureaucratic experts is unexcelled. See *After Virtue,* esp. chap. 6. Also see Evernden, "Ecology in Conversation or Conservation," where he argues that the Brundtland report is a product of the bureaucratic mentality.

52. McIntosh, *Background of Ecology,* p. 303.

53. Donald N. McCloskey, *The Rhetoric of Economics* (Madison: University of Wisconsin Press, 1985), pp. 15.

54. See McIntosh, *Background of Ecology,* p. 303.

55. See also Tom Birch, "The Incarceration of Wildness: Wilderness Areas as Prisons," *Environmental Ethics* 12 (1990): 3-26.

56. The reduction of environmental questions to the single question, that is, "How much are you willing to pay?" is a variant on this theme, but outside our scope.

57. See especially "The Use of Rhetoric in a Technological Age: Architectonic Productive Arts," in *Rhetoric*, pp. 1-24.

58. The root is identifiable in a number of words, such as architecture, technology, technique, text, context, and textuality. Browning writes (in *Red Cotton Night-Cap Country*) of "That far land we dream about, Where every man is his own architect."

59. McKeon, *Rhetoric*, p. 2.

60. Susan Griffin, *Woman and Nature: The Roaring Inside Her* (New York: Harper and Row, Publishers, 1978), p. 226.

61. Gary Snyder, *Turtle Island* (New York: New Directions, 1974), p. 77.

62. Snyder, *Practice of the Wild*, p. 68.

63. Worster, *Nature's Economy*, and Carolyn Merchant, *Ecological Revolutions: Nature, Gender, and Science in New England* (Chapel Hill: University of North Carolina Press, 1989).

64. See Leo Marx, *The Machine in the Garden: Technology and the Pastoral Ideal in America* (New York: Oxford University Press, 1964); Mayr, *Growth of Biological Thought;* and Prigogine and Stengers, *Order Out of Chaos.*

65. René Descartes, *Rules for the Direction of Mind, Discourse on the Method, Meditations on First Philosophy, Objections against the Meditations and Replies, The Geometry,* in Robert Maynard Hutchins, ed., *Great Books of the Western World* (Chicago: Encyclopedia Britannica, 1952), vol. 31, p. 61 (emphasis added).

66. Compare Daniel Botkin, *Discordant Harmonics: A New Ecology for the Twenty-first Century* (New York: Oxford University Press, 1990), who writes that our failure to deal with the environmental crisis requires in part "a change in metaphor, myth, and assumption" (p. vii).

67. *Rhetoric*, bk. 1, chap. 2.

68. David K. Berlo, *The Process of Communication* (New York: Holt, Rinehart, and Winston, 1960).

69. The importance of people living in place has not gone unnoticed in the ecophilosophical literature. See, for example, Snyder, *Turtle Island,* p. 101; Jim Cheney, "Bioregional Narrative"; and Dolores LaChapelle, *Earth Wisdom* (Silverton, Colo.: Finn Hill Arts, 1978). Also consider that Leopold scholars generally believe his turn in the direction of the land ethic was precipitated by his experiences at "The Shack," where he became personally involved in restoration ecology.

70. Jurgen Habermas, *Moral Consciousness and Communicative Action* (Cambridge: MIT Press, 1991).

71. Ibid., pp. 166-67.

72. Sayre, "Alternative View of Environmental Ethics," p. 207.

73. Lincoln argues in *Discourse and the Construction of Society* that sentiment "either holds society together or takes it apart" and that discourse is "the chief instrument with which such sentiment may be aroused, manipulated, and rendered dormant . . . " (p. 11).

74. Marx, *The Machine in the Garden.*

75. See Thomas S. Kuhn, *The Structure of Scientific Revolutions,* 2d ed. (Chicago: University of Chicago Press, 1970).

76. Some communication theorists object to the use of electronic media by environmentalists, especially on the grounds that such media are teleproxemic, creating the illusion of nearness to nature when in fact the viewer remains disconnected. See Stephen Duplantier, "Archetypal Communication: Ecology, Psyche and Utopia in a Teleproxemic World" (Ph.D. diss., University of Southern Mississippi, 1992). While Duplantier's thesis has merit, his argument does not support the conclusion that environmentalists should not employ electronic media in persuasion. McLuhan's arguments that the electronic media have an intrinsically organic character are more persuasive. He argues that the electronic media put "the mythic or collective dimension of human experience fully into the conscious wake-a-day world" in addition to expanding our sense-ratios beyond the confines of literacy (*The Gutenberg Galaxy*, p. 278).

77. The environmental movement has too often allowed itself to be portrayed as a "luxury" item for suburban residents who have time and money to waste.

78. "This Island Earth," an ecologically oriented video featuring Kenny Loggins and Gloria Estefan, aired nationally on the Disney Channel (27 October 1992). Written by Victoria Costello, "This Island Earth" is part one of a six-hour series sponsored by the National Audubon Society and the Arm and Hammer Division of Church and Dwight Company. The video effectively presents, in a compelling musical and stunning visual way, a pro-conservation message for adolescent through early-teenage groups.

Index

A

Abbey, Edward 112–113, 117
  Ecodefense: A Field Guide to Monkeywrenching 112–113, 114, 115
  Monkey Wrench Gang, The 112–113
  see also: Earth First!; monkeywrenching
accidental public 97–98
accidental rhetoric, see: Three Mile Island
Acquired Immunodeficiency Syndrome, see: AIDS
agitative rhetoric, see: confrontational rhetoric
agrarianism 182–183
AIDS 63
alarming statements 91
Alaskan Lands Act 9
Alexander, A.
  and Pearce and Littlejohn 127
American Association for the Advancement of Science 56
American Civic Association 27
American Forest Council 138
ancient forests, see: old growth forests
Anderson, J. A. 171
Andrews, J. 108–109
Antczak, Frederick 58, 62
  quoted 64, 68
anthropocentric ethics, see: homocentric ethics
anthropomorphism, in *Silent Spring* 47, 48
anti-environmental rhetoric xviii, 210–211, 213
  advocacy of 125, 126
  strategies 211–212
  see also: hysteria; Wise Use movement
anti-government rhetoric 200–201
antithetical frame, see: reframe
apocalyptic rhetoric 45–46
appeals
  dissonant 60–61, 68
  Ehrlich's 57–61, 63–64
  Merchant's categories of 63–64
architectonic rhetoric 218–219, 220, 221
Aristotle 4–5
  definition of rhetoric 215
  persuasive rhetoric 219–220
  quoted xi, 57, 209
  realm of rhetoric 65
  Topics III 2, 3
Arnold, Ron 199
artificial public 26–27
atomic energy 81

Atomic Energy Commission 81, 99
audiences
  alienating 58, 59
  construction of 57–58, 59
  ecophilosophical 215–216
  engaging 62
  environmental ethics 215–216
  inexorable 55–56
  Population Bomb, The, see: *Population Bomb, The*
  reconstituting 62, 64, 65, 66–68
  see also: appeals
Audubon, loss of members 203

B

Bageus, J. T. 166
Bailey, H. Jr. xv
  quoted 108
Bailey, Ronald 36
Balcones Canyonlands National Wildlife Refuge 170, 189
Bantz, C. R. 140
Barnard, J. 145
Barol, B. 118
Barrett, William
  quoted 6, 80–81
Barthes, Roland 92
Bascue, L. O.
  and Lawrence 14
Baum, B. 136
Baumgartner, M.
  quoted 112
Bean, M. J. 169
Beard, Charles
  quoted 78–79
Being and Time (Heidegger) 6
Bella, R. 152
  and Durbin 152
Bennett, W. L. 140
Berger, C. R. 126
Berger, J. 118
Berlo, David 220
Berry, Wendell 47, 183
bio-evolutionary reductionism 61
"Biodiversity Studies: Science and Policy" 63, 64
bioregional narrative 221
biotic community, see: ecosystem
birth control 11–12, 14
  compulsory 60–61, 62